The Role of Theoretical Debate in the Evolution of National and International Patent Protection

Legal History Library

VOLUME 52

Studies in the History of International Law

VOLUME 20

The titles published in this series are listed at *brill.com/shil*

The Role of Theoretical Debate in the Evolution of National and International Patent Protection

From the French Revolution to the Paris Convention of 1883

By

Louise J. Duncan

BRILL
NIJHOFF

LEIDEN | BOSTON

Cover illustration: Zhu Jiamin, Pixabay.com

The Library of Congress Cataloging-in-Publication Data is available online at https://catalog.loc.gov
LC record available at https://lccn.loc.gov/2021035695

Typeface for the Latin, Greek, and Cyrillic scripts: "Brill". See and download: brill.com/brill-typeface.

ISSN 1874-1793
ISBN 978-90-04-46976-1 (hardback)
ISBN 978-90-04-47012-5 (e-book)

Contents

Preface

This book originally began its existence as a PhD thesis "From Privileges to the Paris Convention: The Role of Theoretical Debate in the Evolution of National and International Patent Protection" which I studied and completed at Monash University during the 1990s, under the supervision of Professor Sam Ricketson. The PhD degree was awarded to me in 1998.

In the early 1990s I became interested in the study of the history of the patent system when I was employed at both the University of Melbourne and Monash University as Research Fellow to Professor Ricketson to assist him with the analysis of primary and secondary sources relating to his proposed work on the Paris Convention for the Protection of Industrial Property. Some years later, in 2015, Professor Ricketson's commentary on the Paris Convention was published by Oxford University Press.

I am indebted to Professor Ricketson for the opportunity to work on his project relating to the history of the Paris Convention during the early 1990s. This opportunity resulted in my development of a keen interest in the history of the patent system, particularly in the United Kingdom and Europe, with my enthusiasm for the subject resulting in my decision to undertake PhD studies. In particular, I was very interested to pursue the question of the role of theoretical debates in the evolution of national and international patent protection.

At the time when I completed my PhD studies more than twenty years ago, there was unfortunately limited interest in commentaries on patent history, and specifically on theoretical matters related to this topic. Consequently, the thesis was unpublished at the time. However, beginning in the 2000s, there has been a gradual increase in interest in the history of patent law, and the theories underpinning the patent system. Consequently, as a result of multiple requests received, it has been decided to finally publish the thesis in the form of this book, suitably amended and updated for a wider readership. As noted in the Postscript, theoretical debates in relation to the utility of the patent system continue today, and it is important to understand that these debates are not new, and that such debates have shaped the national and international patent systems that we see today.

Introduction

On Thursday, 4 November 1880, the first session of the International Conference for the Protection of Industrial Property took place in Paris in the elegant surroundings of the French Ministry of Foreign Affairs. The distinguished representatives of sixteen nations[1] were formally welcomed to the Conference by M. Barthélemy Saint-Hilaire, French Minister of Foreign Affairs and M. Tirard, French Minister of Agriculture and Commerce. In the course of his welcoming address, M. Tirard made the following statement:

> La recherche des moyens propres á garantir la propriété du travail sous toutes ses formes, sans nuire á la diffusion des progrés scientifiques, industriels et artistiques, est depuis longtemps un object d'études approfondies de la part des législateurs de tous les pays.
>
> Aussi la question a-t-elle déjá fait un grand pas. Tout le monde reconnaît aujourd'hui que, bien loin de nuire á l'avancement des sciences et des arts, la protection accordée á la propriété individuelle dans toutes les branches du travail, est le moyen le plus sûr d'ajouter des progrés nouveaux aux progrés déjá réalisés.
>
> C'est ainsi que depuis cinquante ans la plupart des Etats, sous des formes diverses, et pour ne parler que des choses qui nous occupent en ce moment, ont fait une legislation spéciale sur les brevets d'invention, les dessins et modéles industriels, les marques de fabrique, et les noms et raisons de commerce.
>
> … Ils ont pensé qu'il était necessaire de mettre en harmonie les progrés de la civilisation avec les conquêtes de la science, et qu'il était temps, comme corollaire de la rapidité et de la facilité des échanges, de protéger partout la propriété du travail contre les entreprises audacieuses et criminelles des plagiaires, des contrefacteurs et des usurpateurs de noms et marques de fabrique.
>
> Ils ont pensé, en un mot, que la protection de la propriété Industrielle, commerciale, artistique et littéraire ne devait pas être circonscrite au seul

1 Austria, Hungary, Belgium, Brazil, United States of America, France, Great Britain, Italy, Netherlands, Portugal, Russia, Sweden, Norway, Switzerland, Uruguay and Venezuela. Note that 20 nations had sent delegates to the 1880 Paris Conference, but the delegates from Guatemala, Luxembourg, Salvador and Turkey did not attend the opening session. France, Ministére des Affaires étrangéres, *Conférence Internationale pour la protection de la propriété Industrielle* (Paris 1880), 14–15.

 | DOI:10.1163/9789004470125_002

> pays oú cette propriété a pris naissance, mais qu'il fallait l'étendre par delá les frontiéres.[2]

In his speech, Tirard described an international movement in favour of comprehensive protection of industrial property rights, and suggested that the convening of the 1880 Diplomatic Conference was a natural progression from the laws and philosophies concerning industrial property which had developed in many countries in the previous fifty years. Although Tirard's opinion concerning the influences which led to the founding of the Convention seems logical, the basis for it has never been studied in any detail. At various times since the Convention was established, eminent scholars such as Ladas,[3] Bodenhausen,[4] Ricketson,[5] Constant,[6] Pelletier,[7] Vidal-Naquet,[8] Plaisant[9] and Fernand-Jacq[10]

---

2 *Ibid.* Translation: "The pursuit of the best means to guarantee property in all forms of labour, without harm to the dissemination of scientific, industrial and artistic progress, has been for a long time an object of profound study on the part of legislators in all countries. However, the matter has already made great progress. All the world recognises today that, far from harming the advancement of science and the arts, the protection accorded to individual property rights in all branches of labour, is the most likely to further encourage progress, and build upon that which is already realised. For this reason for the last fifty years most States have, in various forms, and of which it is not necessary to discuss in detail at this moment, special legislation concerning patents, designs and industrial models, trade marks, and commercial names. ... They have thought it necessary to harmonise the progress of civilisation with the conquests of science, and that it was time, arising from the speed and ease of communications, to thoroughly protect property in labour against the audacious and criminal activities of plagiarists, forgers, and usurpers of names and trade marks. They have thought, in a word, that the protection of industrial, commercial, artistic and literary property must not be confined only to the country where this property originated, but it must be dealt with without regard to frontiers."

3 Ladas, S., *Patents, Trademarks and Related Rights; National and International Protection* (Cambridge, Harvard University Press, 1975).

4 Bodenhausen, G., *Guide to the Application of the Paris Convention for the Protection of Industrial Property* (Geneva, BIRPI, 1968).

5 Ricketson, S., *The Paris Convention for the Protection of Industrial Property* (Oxford, Oxford University Press, 2015).

6 Constant, C., *Union Internationale: Protection de la Propriété Industrielle: Texte Annoté de la Convention de Paris du 20 Mars 1883 Modifiée et Complétée par les Conférences de Rome, de Madrid et de Bruxelles* (Paris, A. Pedone, 1901).

7 Pelletier, M., and Vidal-Naquet, E., *La Convention d'Union pour la Protection de la Propriété Industrielle du 20 mars 1883 et les Conférences de Revision Postérieures* (Paris, L. Larose, 1902).

8 *Ibid.*

9 Plaisant, M., *Traité de Droit Conventionnel International concernant la Propriété Industrielle* (Paris, Sirey, 1949).

10 Plaisant, M., and Fernand-Jacq, *Les Brevets d'Invention en Droit International* (Paris, Recueil Sirey, 1931).

have examined the content of the 1883 Convention and its implications for owners of industrial property rights. Yet there is one major issue which is equally as important and has never received the scholarly attention it deserves. This issue is raised in the following interrelated questions and is the focus of this book, namely:

> In what way was the founding of the Paris Convention influenced by earlier developments at the national level? What was the role of theoretical debates in the evolution of norms of national and international industrial property protection?

In answering these questions, the book not only examines some of the early national patent laws, but, more importantly, it analyses the evolution of debate about the theoretical justification for industrial property rights in the period between 1790 and 1883. The book explains how this debate led first to reforms of national law, and then to the Paris Convention in 1883. Consequently, the first part of the book is primarily concerned with analysing the development of national law, with particular reference to the theoretical concepts which shaped the evolution of the patent systems in France and the United Kingdom from the French Revolution to the 1870s. The second part of the book examines the movement towards international protection of industrial property rights, particularly patents. At a theoretical level, the earlier national debates had prepared the way for acceptance of international industrial property protection, but agreement as to the precise terms of such protection was extremely difficult to reach. The 1883 Convention, with its establishment of unique features such as the concepts of an "Open Union", priority rights, national treatment and provision for periodic revision, was a multilateral Convention of a type which had no precedent. Just as the French Patent Law of 7 January 1791 had established a totally new concept of the patent as a "natural property right", the Paris Convention embodied another major practical and theoretical leap from national to international industrial property protection.

Although a number of modern commentators have developed various arguments concerning the theoretical basis of the patent system,[11] it is not

11 Oft-cited examples of such modern scholarship include: Boehm, K., and Silberston, A., *The British Patent System: 1. Administration* (Cambridge, Cambridge University Press, 1967), 1–38. Drahos, P., *A Philosophy of Intellectual Property* (Aldershot, Dartmouth Publishing, 1996); Machlup, F., and Penrose, E., "The Patent Controversy in the Nineteenth Century" (1950) x *The Journal of Economic History* 1; penrose, E., *The Economics of the International Patent System* (Baltimore, John Hopkins Press, 1951), 19–42; Plant, Sir A., *Selected Economic*

the purpose of this book to re-examine such scholarship. This book confines itself to a discussion of the ideas and theories (or more generally philosophies) which were developed to justify the existence of the patent system between 1790 and 1883. During the period under consideration, there were generally only two theoretical bases for the patent system: the natural property rights theory and the instrumentalist view. The word "instrumentalist" is used as a general term to encompass all those theories which stressed the importance of the underlying economic or social benefits of the patent system, as opposed to the "natural" or personal property rights of the inventor.

As a Postscript to the book, there is discussion of the on-going relevance of the debates concerning the theoretical basis of the patent system, despite the Paris Convention now having been in force for more than 130 years. In that regard, special attention is paid to the circumstances surrounding the introduction of the patent system in China in 1985. Not only is China a communist country, but in 1985 it was largely still an agrarian economy. Despite its less developed economic position at that time, the Chinese Government then realised the important role that the patent system could play in its future economic development, a prescient view that has been borne out in the subsequent decades of China's remarkable economic achievements. The example of China well illustrates the continuing importance of the patent system in the promotion of economic development, and that, as the founders of the Paris Convention realised, intellectual property protection provides important legal protections to enhance national and international prosperity.

Essays and Addresses (London, Routledge and Kegan Paul, 1974), Part Two; Schumpeter, J., *Capitalism, Socialism and Democracy* (New York, 1942); Taylor, C.T., and Silberston, Z.A., *The Economic Impact of the Patent System: A Study of the British Experience* (Cambridge, Cambridge University Press, 1973), Part One; Wright, B., "The Economics of Invention Incentives: Patents, Prizes, and Research Contracts" (1983) 73 *American Economic Review* 691.

CHAPTER 1

France – Development of Legal and Philosophical Ideas Underlying the Patent System: 1790 to 1859

> Louis etc., considérant que toute idée nouvelle, dont la manifestation ou le développement peut devenir utile á la société, appartient primitivement á celui qui l'a conçue, et que ce serait attaquer les droits de l'homme dans leur essence que de ne pas regarder une découverte industrielle comme la propriété de son auteur …[1]
>
> Preamble to the French Law of 7 January 1791 relative to useful Discoveries and to the means of ensuring the Property thereof

•••

> Toute nouvelle découverte ou invention dans tous genres d'industrie confére á son auteur, sous les conditions et pour le temps ci-aprés déterminés, le droit exclusif d'exploiter á son profit ladite découverte ou invention …[2]
>
> Extract from Art. 1 of the French Law of 5 July 1844

1 Translation: "Louis, etc., considering that every new idea, whereof the manifestation or the development may become useful to society, belongs originally to him who has conceived it; and that it would be to attack the rights of man in their essence, not to regard a discovery in industry [*in useful arts and manufactures*] as the property of its author …" Source: Regnault, T., *De la Législation et de la Jurisprudence concernant les Brevets d'Invention, de Perfectionnement et d'Importation* 135 (Paris, Antoine Bavoux, 1825).

2 Translation: "Every new discovery or invention, in all departments of industry confers upon its author, under the conditions, and for the time hereafter mentioned, the exclusive right of working for his own profit the said discovery or invention." Original and Translation derived from UNITED KINGDOM, Parliamentary Papers, *Reports by H.M. Secs of Embassy and Legation respecting Law and Practice in Foreign Countries with regard to Inventions* (1873) C. 741, vol LXVI, 483, 88.

 | DOI:10.1163/9789004470125_003

On 7 January 1791, Louis XVI signed into law the patent legislation which had been passed by the National Assembly on 30 December 1790. The essential character of the French patent system as established in 1791 remained largely unaltered until the reforms of 1844. For over 50 years the cornerstone of the French patent system was that an invention was one of the natural property rights of man,[3] and that the patent system existed merely as a legislative scheme which provided legal recognition to a pre-existing right. When the French Government adopted this concept of natural property rights in inventions as the basis for the new patent system, it amounted to a major theoretical shift from the old French system of inventor's privileges. It was especially remarkable because there was no real precedent for this concept of "natural" property rights in inventions, either in France or elsewhere. While it was true that the old system of inventor's privileges, unlike most other Royal Privileges, did often serve a useful social purpose, inventions had never before received legislative protection as natural property rights. Not only was this change important for Revolutionary France, but it had an enduring significance upon the development of the theoretical basis of the patent system throughout Europe in the nineteenth century. Other governments looked to the French system when devising their own patent laws, and French commentators entered into lively and comprehensive debates about the theoretical justifications for the patent system. Inevitably, this debate spread through to the United Kingdom, Belgium, the Netherlands, Switzerland and Prussia during the years which followed. It is apparent, therefore, that it is necessary to look primarily to France in order to understand how ideas and theories about the patent system developed between 1790 and 1860.

In the context of this discussion there are four matters which must be examined. These are as follows:

(1) Why did the drafters of the French patent law of 1791 employ the concept of natural property rights in relation to inventions?

(2) What was the significance of the fact that the French government removed the reference to natural property rights in the patent law reforms of 1844?

(3) What was the influence of private individuals and groups upon these law reforms, and how did they react to these reforms?

(4) How far did the French patent law reforms influence the development of patent legislation in other countries?

---

3 See the Preamble to the Law of 7 January 1791, reproduced above.

One more general point to note briefly at this stage is the connection between the French patent law reforms of 1791 and the movement in favour of international protection of patent rights. Although the Paris Convention was not founded until 1883, there was a striking parallel in the circumstances surrounding the passage of the Law of 1791 and the negotiations over the drafting of the Convention. Both the Law of 1791 and the Paris Convention were legal instruments without any direct precedent, and effected a significant change from what had existed before (in the first case: inventor's privileges, and in the second: bilateral treaties and domestic patent systems). In addition, the concept of "natural" property rights in inventions had a resurgence of support at the time when the preliminary work for the Paris Convention was being carried out, and was debated at length at the 1878 Paris Conference.[4]

A The Significance of the Law of 7 January 1791

(a) *Historical Background to the Enactment of the Patent Law of 1791*

The French Patent Law of 1791 is important for a number of reasons. One reason is that it represents the first example of legislative support for the notion of an invention as the "natural" property rights of the inventor. This is discussed in detail in Section (b) of this Chapter. However, the 1791 Law was also significant for other reasons. In particular, it was the first patent legislation which both abolished a system of royal privileges, and had a comprehensive statutory basis.

Royal Privileges: Introduction

Before 1790, the only State which had experimented with a patent system founded upon a statutory basis was the Republic of Venice, which had by vote of the Senate in 1474 established a patent law.[5] Various other States had established mechanisms by which industrial privileges might be granted to selected persons for the purposes of introducing and developing new manufactures, but, with the limited exception of the English patent system after the passage

4 FRANCE, Ministére de L'agriculture et du Commerce, *Comptes rendus Sténographiques publiés sous les auspices du Comité Central des Congrés et Conférences et la direction de M. CH THIRION, Secrétaire du Comité, avec le concours des Bureaux des Congrés et des auteurs de Conférences: Congrés International de la Propriété Industrielle tenu á Paris du 5 au 17 Septembre 1878* (Paris 1879).

5 Plasseraud, Y., and Savignon, F., *L'etat et L'invention: Histoire des Brevets* (Paris, La Documentation Française, 1986), 30–31.

of the *Statute of Monopolies* in 1623, these privileges could not be considered patents in the sense understood today. In essence, a privilege was a "gracious royal favour",[6] and in most systems, there was no general policy which distinguished inventor's privileges from other privileges granted by the Monarch.[7] Plasseraud and Savignon have shown that, apart from the well-established system in the United Kingdom, inventor's privileges existed in the following European countries before the mid-eighteenth century: France (from the sixteenth century), the Hapsburg Empire (from the sixteenth century), and Prussia (from the seventeenth century).[8]

Whereas the granting of monopolies by the Crown had been severely limited by the English Parliament in 1623, in France there was no such restriction upon the power of the monarch until Louis XV signed the *Declaration by the King Concerning Privileges in Matters of Commerce* of 24 December 1762.[9] However, this Declaration of 1762 was essentially different from the English *Statute of Monopolies* of 1623. The Declaration did not in any way attempt to restrict the types of privileges which the King could grant, and it was still within the prerogative of the King to determine whether or not a privilege would be awarded. The only substantial effect of the Declaration of 1762 was that privileges were henceforth to be no longer than 15 years' duration, instead of the previous usual practice of granting a privilege for an unlimited time.[10] More significantly, in 1776 Louis XVI accepted the advice of his minister, Turgot, and decreed the abolition of all privileges of the corporations (guilds), while leaving intact property rights in inventor's privileges.[11]

---

6 Savignon, F., "The French Revolution and Patents" (1989) *Industrial Property* 391, 392.

7 See for example in France – Penrose, E., *The Economics of the International Patent System* (Baltimore, John Hopkins Press, 1951), 9.

8 Plasseraud, Y., and Savignon, F., *L'etat et L'invention: Histoire des Brevets* (Paris, La Documentation Française, 1986), 43–55. Plasseraud and Savignon also note that there is an interesting early history of privileges granted in Europe in relation to the operation of gold and silver mines. Wenceslas, King of Bohemia (1271 to 1305) granted a privilege in relation to gold mines and in 1449 a privilege was granted by the Duke of Burgundy, Charles VI, to Juan de la Huerta in relation to a silver mine. It is unknown whether these privileges were granted for the introduction of new mining techniques, or simply as monopoly rewards to favoured subjects.

9 Text reproduced in Blanc, E., *L'inventeur Breveté, Code des Inventions et des Perfectionnements* (Paris, Librairie Générale de Jurisprudence de Cosse, 1852), III to IV. The *Declaration by the King Concerning Privileges in Matters of Commerce* of 24 December 1762 was said to have been made by Louis XV on the advice of the Physiocrat, Quesnay. Savignon, F., "The French Revolution and Patents" (1989) *Industrial Property* 391, 393.

10 Article 2 of the Declaration of 24 December 1762.

11 Text of the Decree of 1776 abolishing the corporations reproduced in Blanc, E., *op.cit.* v to vi. The power of the corporations was too strong to accept this Decree of 1776 without

Note on the U.S. Patent System

It is useful to note also the case of the U.S.A., which was, like France, one of the few significant countries to develop a patent system earlier than 1800. Before the American War of Independence, a limited number of the American colonies had introduced basic patent systems inspired by the *Statue of Monopolies* of 1623.[12] After the Revolution, the U.S. Constitution of 1787 placed the concept of inventors' rights on a firmer foundation.[13] This was followed by the enactment of a Patent Law on 10 April 1790,[14] which predated the French Patent Law of 1791 by less than one year. In form the Patent Law of 1790 was based upon the U.K. patent system then in operation, but in sentiment it was greatly influenced by French theories concerning the inherent or natural rights of the individual.[15] The Act of 1790 was repealed and replaced by a new Patent Act

a fight. On 23 August 1776, the King was forced to pass another Decree which reinstated the privileges of the corporations, although with limitations. The corporations were reorganised, and freedom to work was decreed in certain industries. See further: France, Chambre des Députés, *Rapport fait au nom de la Commission chargée d'examiner le project de Loi portant approbation des arrangements signés, les 14 et 15 avril 1891, entre divers états faisant partie de l'Union internationale pour la protection de la propriété industrielle* (1892), 8; Milhaud, L., *Des Brevets d'invention dans les Rapports Internationaux* (Paris, Larose et Forcel, 1892), 4; Chevalier, M., 'Les Brevets d'Invention contraires a la Liberté du Travail' (1878) *Journal des économistes* 169, 173–178.

12 Such as Massachusetts in 1641 and Connecticut in 1672. Patents for inventions were also issued in Virginia, South Carolina, New York and Rhode Island before the War of Independence. Liebesny, F., (ed) *Mainly on Patents* (London, Butterworths, 1972), 11; Plasseraud, Y., and Savignon, F., *Paris 1883: Genése du droit Unioniste des Brevets* (Paris, Litec, 1983), 21.

13 Section 8 of the Constitution of the U.S.A. states that "The Congress shall have Power To ... promote the Progress of Science and useful Arts, by securing for limited Times to Authors and Inventors the exclusive Right to their respective Writings and Discoveries". Finer, S.E., (ed) *Five Constitutions* (Bungay, Penguin, 1979), 95.

14 "The first patent granted under it was dated July 31 of the same year, for making pot and pearl ashes; and only two more patents were granted during the year. It continued in force until February 21, 1793, and only fifty-five patents were granted under it." Smith, C., 'A Century of Patent Law' (1891) 5 *The Quarterly Journal of Economics* 44, 45; See also Seely, F., "L'opinion d'un Américain sur la protection internationale de la propriété industrielle" (1893) 9 *La Propriété Industrielle* 88; "A Centenary of Patents" *New York Times,* 22 March 1891, 15

15 Particularly the philosophy of Lumiéres, which considered an invention to be a divine and natural right belonging to its creator. Plasseraud, Y., and Savignon, F., *Paris 1883: Genése du droit Unioniste des Brevets* (Paris, Litec, 1983), 21.

of 21 February 1793, with provisions clearly influenced by the French patent legislation of 1791.[16]

Privileges in France

Although the term "Royal Privilege" is commonly associated with corruption, abuse of position and unjustified advantage, it is not correct to view all types of privilege as tainted in this way. In France, the system of inventor's privileges did serve a social purpose in encouraging the introduction of new inventions, and breaking down some of the monopolies of the *corporations* (guilds). As the system of inventor's privileges was to some degree considered philosophically acceptable, its existence helped smooth the way for the later introduction of the patent law in 1791.

In France, the term "privilege" was a general term which commonly referred to the interest of any person or establishment that had been given a licence by the King.[17] There were many types of privileges granted by the French kings in addition to inventor's privileges. While it has been estimated that before the French Revolution, 270,000 French people possessed royal privileges,[18] only a very small percentage would have been inventor's privileges. For example, research carried out into the number of inventor's privileges granted in pre-revolutionary France has estimated that only 48 inventor's privileges were granted in the period between 1715 and 1760.[19] The majority of privileges granted in France would have been agricultural rights of a feudal nature, such as the rights of "banvin, banalité, péage, the monopoly of the dove-cote", and the imposition of tolls such as those of "cens, censives, carpot, champage and terrage."[20]

---

16 In relation to the French influence on U.S. policy during this early period of U.S. nationhood, see for example: Henretta, James, *The Evolution of American Society, 1700–1815* (Lexington, D.C. Heath and Co, 1973), 220–221.

17 Zeller, G., "Industry in France before Colbert" in Cameron, R., (ed), *Essays in French Economic History* (Homewood, Richard D. Irwin, 1970), 128, 132.

18 Madelin, L., *The French Revolution* (London, Heinemann, 1925), 6.

19 Plasseraud, Y., and Savignon, F., *L'etat et L'invention: Histoire des Brevets* (Paris, La Documentation Française, 1986), 41.

20 Madelin, L., *The French Revolution* (London, Heinemann, 1925), 7. Madelin defines the various agricultural privileges as follows: *Banvin* was the right of the lord of the manor to sell his wine in the parish, to the exclusion of all others, for a certain time each year. *Banalité* was the right of the feudal owner to impose a requirement for the use of facilities on his property. For example, it might be necessary for everyone within a certain radius to use his ovens for baking bread, and pay for the privilege. *Péage* was a toll on cattle or merchandise taken across the land-owner's property, or for use of bridges or roads on that property. *Cens* was a term of similar meaning to "rent". *Censives* was a special payment which might burden a farm. *Carpot* was a claim on the fruits produced by the orchards

Besides agricultural privileges, other privileges were granted to craft or manufacturing associations (both fell within the general term "corporation"). The craft association, (or *communautés de métiers*) was a closed body, exercising the monopoly of its craft, and subjecting its members to strict obligations defined in its statute.[21] As Louis Wolowski, a member of the National Assembly of France recalled in 1851, "no-one could be admitted into those guilds, and no-one could work at any of those trades without being a member of a guild, and you could only work according to the rules laid down for that guild …".[22] Although in 1581 Henry III had decreed that the guild system was compulsory for all crafts, this decree was generally not enforced, so that by the eighteenth century the great majority of crafts were not organised into guilds and therefore were not subject to such restrictions.[23] However, it was in the King's interest to encourage the creation of new guilds because when a craft association was formed, it paid a certain sum in taxation to the public authorities. In addition, no new master could practice unless he obtained the "letters of mastery" which again required the payment of a tax.[24] A *manufacture* was a "well-differentiated industrial establishment"[25] which may have been a series of workshops at one location, and placed under the direction of an entrepreneur, or it may have meant the totality of workshops in a town engaged in the manufacture of certain products, such as the silk weavers of Lyon. Besides silk weaving, it was common to find sugar refining, chocolate making, tobacco processing, lace making and metallurgy undertaken in *manufactures*.[26]

---

of a property. *Champage* were dues paid on the delimitation of the boundaries of a farm. *Terrage* were dues levied on harvests.

21 Zeller, G., "Industry in France before Colbert" in Cameron, R., (ed), *Essays in French Economic History* (Homewood, Richard D. Irwin, 1970), 128, 133. See also Coornaert, E., "French Guilds under the Old Regime" *Ibid.*, 123.

22 UNITED KINGDOM, Parliamentary Papers, *Report and Minutes of Evidence taken before the Select Committee of the House of Lords appointed to consider of The Bill, intituled, "An Act further to amend the Law touching Letters Patent for Invention" and also of The Bill intituled "An Act for the further amendment of the Law touching Letters Patent for Invention" and to report thereon to the House: Session 1851* (1851) 486 vol XVIII, 233, Evidence of Louis Wolowski at 329.

23 There has been little study of eighteenth century French crafts not subject to guilds. Zeller, G., "Industry in France before Colbert" in Cameron, R., (ed), *Essays in French Economic History* (Homewood, Richard D. Irwin, 1970), 128, 133. Penrose notes that statistics from 1673 reveal that there were only 60 corporations in Paris, and their work would have only represented a small percentage of the trades operating in that city. Penrose, E., *The Economics of the International Patent System* (Baltimore, John Hopkins Press, 1951), 9.

24 Zeller, G., *op.cit.* 137.

25 *Ibid.* 129.

26 *Ibid.* 132–134.

Much work has been done by economic historians in showing that innovation did not flourish in France under the *ancien régime,* and this was one major cause of the delay in the French industrial revolution.[27] An important reason for the lack of innovation was the strong influence of the [relatively few] corporations in blocking the introduction of new improvements. Although possessors of inventor's privileges generally sought advances in industrial development, the corporations often opposed new and more efficient modes of production, because they saw such innovations as a threat to their ancient monopolies, built around closely regulated practices. A number of nineteenth century writers recalled that before the French Revolution, the corporations were largely responsible for limiting the number of inventor's privileges granted by the King.[28] Some corporations were jealous of those who proposed to introduce new modes of production or new inventions, yet they were not themselves willing to change their own practices.[29] To ensure the maintenance of their monopoly, corporations were ready to promote secret intrigues against outsiders, and use their powerful influence with the King to ensure that inventor's privileges were not granted in their field.[30] For example, when the inventor, Argand, tried to manufacture a new type of oil lamp, he found himself vigorously pursued by many corporations, including candle-makers and tinsmiths, all claiming that his invention interfered with their monopoly privilege.[31] Argand's invention was not subject to an inventor's privilege at the time, and he was forced to suspend production of his invention for a long period. Sometimes the inventors succeeded in gaining an inventor's privilege, but almost as soon as they were registered with the *Parlement de Paris*, the corporations would apply to the King for revocation of the privilege on the ground

27 French economic historians such as Claude Fohlen argue that the industrial revolution in France covers the period from "1750 or 1770 to 1870". Even in 1851, 74.5% of the population of France lived in the countryside and in towns of less than 2000 people. Industrialisation occurred very slowly in France. Fohlen, C., "The Industrial Revolution in France" in Cameron, R., (ed) *op.cit.* 201, 203.

28 France, Chambre des Députés, *Rapport fait au nom de la Commission chargée d'examiner le project de Loi portant approbation des arrangements signés, les 14 et 15 avril 1891, entre divers états faisant partie de l'Union internationale pour la protection de la propriété industrielle* (1892), 6–9; Milhaud, L., *Des Brevets d'invention dans les Rapports Internationaux* (Paris, Larose et Forcel, 1892), 3; Chevalier, M., 'Les Brevets d'Invention contraires a la Liberté du Travail' (1878) *Journal des économistes* 169, 173–178.

29 Chevalier, M., 'Les Brevets d'Invention contraires a la Liberté du Travail' (1878) *Journal des économistes* 169, 173–178.

30 *Ibid.*

31 *Ibid.* 175.

that the invention interfered with the ancient rights of the corporation.[32] Even if the inventor's privilege was not revoked, the inventor might be driven out of business due to constant harassment by the affected corporations.[33]

It is thus apparent from the above discussion that the inventor's privilege did not operate primarily as a restriction upon the right of the public to work certain inventions. In fact, these privileges had an important social and economic function in breaking down the monopolies of the corporations and encouraging a belief that innovation and industrial development could take place outside the static structure of the corporations.[34] A similar rationale had prevailed in England in the *Statute of Monopolies* of 1623, section 6 of which recognised that patents for invention had a wider social purpose, as distinct from the offensive "monopolies of common trades".[35] Even though France retained the system of inventor's privileges at least until August 1789, (and perhaps until the date of the Patent Law of 7 January 1791),[36] this system did serve

32 France, Chambre des Députés, *Rapport fait au nom de la Commission chargée d'examiner le project de Loi portant approbation des arrangements signés, les 14 et 15 avril 1891, entre divers états faisant partie de l'Union internationale pour la protection de la propriété industrielle* (1892), 7.

33 Milhaud, L., *op.cit.* 3.

34 UNITED KINGDOM, Parliamentary Papers, *Report and Minutes of Evidence taken before the Select Committee of the House of Lords appointed to consider of The Bill, intituled, "An Act further to amend the Law touching Letters Patent for Invention" and also of The Bill intituled "An Act for the further amendment of the Law touching Letters Patent for Invention" and to report thereon to the House: Session 1851* (1851) 486 vol XVIII, 233, Evidence of Louis Wolowski, member of the National Assembly of France at 329.

35 Note, "On Reform in the Law of Patents" (1870) 28 *The Law Magazine and Review* 83, 87.

36 On the night of 4th to 5th August 1789, the National Assembly, (formerly the States General) declared that feudal rights as well as "all special privileges enjoyed by provinces, principalities, towns, guilds and corporations" were henceforth abolished. However, the "decisions of the night of 4 August had been taken verbally and had not been carefully formulated. When the question arose of giving them their due legal form, the Assembly tried to whittle down the practical effects of measures which had, after all, been passed while there was still an immediate threat of popular revolt." Soboul, A., *The French Revolution 1787–1799* (Oxford, Oxford University Press, 1976), 149. As a result, the published form of the *Decrees of 4–11 August, 1789,* did not reflect the verbal decision to abolish all the privileges noted above. In the final version of the decree, there was specific mention of the abolition of the feudal rights, and the "special privileges of provinces, principalities, pays, cantons, cities, and communities of inhabitants" but no reference was made to abolition of privileges of corporations or inventors. See Stewart, J.H., (ed) *A Documentary Survey of the French Revolution* (New York 1951), 106–110. There is therefore, weight in the argument that the Decrees of 4–11 August 1789 did not abolish either inventor's privileges or privileges of corporations, and that the abolition of the privileges of corporations was only achieved by the Law of 2 March 1791, and reinforced in the Preamble of the Constitution

a useful purpose in encouraging new invention outside the network of corporations. In addition, there was recognised to be some theoretical justification for an inventor's privilege, which made it easier to later accept the need for a patent system.

As M. Dupray de Lamahérie, an attorney and member of the 1878 Paris Conference stated, in the time of the *ancien régime* there was an essential difference between the inventor's privileges and the privileges granted to corporations. Unlike the others, an inventor's privilege was a "Privilége fondé en justice".[37] It therefore seems mistaken for later French commentators such as Michel Chevalier, (once described as a leading French economist with great influence over the Emperor Napoleon III),[38] to depict the pre-revolutionary inventor's privilege as a form of undeserved royal patronage which was at odds with the progress of French industrial development.[39] While it is true that inventor's privileges were sometimes granted in circumstances in which neither the invention itself nor the recipient deserved the privilege,[40] there is no evidence that the majority of inventor's privileges were granted because of abuse of royal authority. As in England more than one hundred years earlier, the French experiences with the system of royal privileges for invention helped to form that country's later patent system.

---

of 3 September 1791. See also "Respectueuse Pétition des Artistes-Inventeurs á l'Assemblée nationale de 2 Avril 1791" in Regnault, T., *op.cit.* 45.

37 Translation – "A privilege founded in justice". FRANCE, Ministére de L'agriculture et du Commerce, *Comptes rendus Sténographiques publiés sous les auspices du Comité Central des Congrés et Conférences et la direction de M. CH THIRION, Secrétaire du Comité, avec le concours des Bureaux des Congrés et des auteurs de Conférences: Congrés International de la Propriété Industrielle tenu á Paris du 5 au 17 Septembre 1878* (Paris 1879), 115.

38 The 1860 commercial Treaty between England and France was known in some circles as the Cobden-Chevalier Treaty, after the English and French statesmen who had been most concerned in its successful conclusion. "Free Trade in England", *New York Times,* 16 December 1891, 4. See also, "Commercial relations of England and France: Review of recent works by Chevalier, Amé and Faucher" (1860) 111 *The Edinburgh Review* 277.

39 Chevalier, M., 'Les Brevets d'Invention contraires a la Liberté du Travail' (1878) *Journal des économistes* 169.

40 For example, Mme de Maintenon, a personal friend of Louis XIV was given an inventor's privilege covering the production of hearths, stoves, ovens and chimneys, in circumstances where there is no evidence to suggest that she had invented any of these things. See Chevalier, M., *op.cit.* 176.

Political Circumstances Surrounding the Enactment of the Law of 1791

The Patent Law of 1791 was enacted during a period of political upheaval. This turbulence cannot be overlooked in any study of the theoretical basis of the reforms of 1791. It was during the period of weakening royal influence, but before the final destruction of the monarchy, that the French established the new patent system which was to remain largely intact for the next fifty years.

The collapse of the French system of absolute monarchy began on 5 May 1789, when a severe financial crisis necessitated the convening of the States-General for the first time since 1614.[41] Louis XVI's authority was successively weakened over the next three years and he was ultimately condemned to death and executed on 21 January 1793.[42]

On the night of 4 to 5 August 1789 the National Assembly, (formerly the States General) declared that the royal privileges were henceforth abolished. Mirabeau, the President of the National Assembly, later claimed in February 1791 that the intention of the National Assembly had not been to abolish inventor's privileges, because they were a right of property. He said that the "découvertes de l'industrie et des arts étaient une propriété avant que l'assemblée nationale l'eût déclaré",[43] which means that he believed that existing inventor's rights remained protected despite the Declaration of 4–5 August 1789. Considering the political turbulence of 1789, when the utopian concepts of freedom and equality for all reigned supreme,[44] it is difficult to reconcile these aspirations with an intention to retain royal privileges in inventions. The freedom to work,

---

41 Soboul, A., *The French Revolution 1787–1799* (Oxford, Oxford University Press, 1976) at 120–135; Mignet, F.A.M., *History of the French Revolution* (London, J.M. Dent and Sons, 1915), 19.

42 In relation to the general texts on this period of French history see, for example: Lefebvre, G., *La Révolution Française* (Paris 1951); Brinton, C., *A Decade of Revolution 1789–1799* (New York 1934); Cobban, A., *A History of Modern France, vol 1, Old Regime and Revolution 1715–1799* (Oxford, Oxford University Press, 1957); Soboul, A., *The French Revolution 1787–1799* (Oxford, Oxford University Press, 1976).

43 Translation: "Discoveries of industry and the arts were property rights before the National Assembly declared them to be so." Sources: "Respectueuse Pétition des Artistes-Inventeurs á l'Assemblée nationale de 2 Avril 1791" in Regnault, T., *op.cit.* 49–50; FRANCE, Ministére de L'agriculture et du Commerce, *Comptes rendus Sténographiques publiés sous les auspices du Comité Central des Congrés et Conférences et la direction de M. CH THIRION, Secrétaire du Comité, avec le concours des Bureaux des Congrés et des auteurs de Conférences: Congrés International de la Propriété Industrielle tenu á Paris du 5 au 17 Septembre 1878* (Paris 1879), Annexe 21, 529.

44 Article 1 of the *Declaration of the Rights of Man and the Citizen* of 26 August 1789 stated as follows: "In respect of their rights men are born and remain free and equal. The only permissible basis for social distinctions is public utility." Translation: Finer, S.E., (ed) *Five Constitutions* (Bungay, Penguin, 1979), 269–271.

"la liberté du travail" was a cornerstone of the new philosophies, and was emphasised in the *Declaration of the Rights of Man and the Citizen* of 26 August 1789. Liberty was to be respected by all, and "the only limitations on the individual's exercise of his natural rights" were "those which ensure the enjoyment of these same rights to all other individuals."[45] As Savignon has noted, this freedom, which encouraged competition on a level plane, was not easy to promote concurrently with the notion of any form of exclusive rights in invention.[46] However, it was also an important ideological tenet of the period that rights in property should be respected as "natural" rights, inviolable and sacred.[47] Supporters of exclusive rights in invention soon recognised that if an invention right was viewed as a "natural" right of property, it would gain protection under the new regime, but not otherwise. Accordingly, under the Patent Law of 7 January 1791, the right in invention was expressed to be one of the "natural" rights of man, and thus worthy of protection by grant of a patent.[48] As is shown below, issues of philosophical consistency, as well as political expediency, were important influences on the development of the "natural property" patent concept during the Revolution.

A number of interested parties favoured a patent system in France even before the *Declaration of the Rights of Man and the Citizen* and the abolition of royal privileges in August 1789. The model most often suggested then was that of the U.K. patent system, and little reference was made to any other justifications derived from "natural" property rights. In December 1787, for example, the Chamber of Commerce of Normandy commissioned a study of the bilateral Treaty of Commerce which had been concluded between France and the United Kingdom in 1786. In the course of this study, the Chamber of Commerce examined the U.K. patent system and concluded that a similar system should be adopted in France.[49] At the beginning of 1788, the Deputies of Commerce

45 Article 4 of the *Declaration of the Rights of Man and the Citizen* of 26 August 1789. *Ibid.*

46 Savignon, F., "The French Revolution and Patents" (1989) *Industrial Property* 391, 394.

47 Articles 2 and 17 of the *Declaration of the Rights of Man and the Citizen* of 26 August 1789. Translation: Finer, S.E., *op.cit.* 269, 271.

48 See, for example, the *Preamble to the French Law of 7 January 1791 relative to useful Discoveries and to the means of ensuring the Property thereof*, quoted at the beginning of this Chapter.

49 Sources: "Respectueuse Pétition des Artistes-Inventeurs á l'Assemblée nationale de 2 Avril 1791" in Regnault, T., *De la Législation et de la Jurisprudence concernant les Brevets d'Invention, de Perfectionnement et d'Importation* 135 (Paris, Antoine Bavoux, 1825), 47; "Exposé des Motifs, présenté le 10 Janvier 1843, á la Chambre des Pairs, par M. Le Ministre de L'agriculture et du Commerce" in Blanc, E., *L'inventeur Breveté, Code des Inventions et des Perfectionnements* (Paris, Librairie Générale de Jurisprudence de Cosse, 1852), 5.

represented to the administration that industrial progress would not advance until French inventors were induced to remain in France with their inventions instead of seeking a patent in the U.K. They advocated the adoption of a U.K.-style patent system, as did the Inspectors-General of Commerce in their Report of 13 February 1789.[50] At the same time, most of the opinions expressed by the bailliages, the cahiers of the Third-Estate (especially the representatives of the city of Paris), and the views of inventors were in favour of the introduction of some form of protection for inventions.[51]

After receiving many representations, the Committee of Agriculture and Commerce of the National Assembly appointed the Chevalier Stanislas de Boufflers, (deputy of the nobility of the bailliage of Nancy and former Governor of Senegal), to prepare a report, including any proposed legislation on the subject that might be recommended.[52] It was de Boufflers' Report, which he presented to the National Assembly on the night of 30 December 1790, which formed the basis of the French Law of 7 January 1791. De Boufflers' ardent support of the patent system was reflected in his eloquent speech in which he used nearly every possible argument to justify the system. Nevertheless, at the heart of his conception of the patent was a "natural" property right, a concept which appealed to the revolutionary creed of respect for "sacred" rights in property. Faced with this politically-charged argument, the National Assembly adopted de Boufflers' scheme with little discussion or amendment.[53]

(b) *De Boufflers' Justifications for His Proposed Patent Law*

The major difficulty that de Boufflers encountered when drafting the patent law, was to convince the National Assembly of a feasible way to reconcile patent legislation with notions of individual freedom and equality. Savignon argues that:

> [By] giving prominence to a natural property right and the idea of the inventor having control over his right, by virtue of a free agreement

50 *Ibid.*

51 *Ibid.*

52 Savignon, F., *op.cit.* 394.

53 It is interesting to note that soon after the Law of 7 January 1791 had been signed, de Boufflers was accused of having misled the National Assembly, and that he had taken advantage of the fact that many members of the Assembly were absent on the night of 30 December 1790 when his Report was presented. Naturally, de Boufflers disputed these claims. "Reponse de M. de Boufflers aux objections élevées contre la loi du 7 janvier 1791, au nom du comité d'agriculture et du commerce, imprimée par ordre de l'assemblée nationale" in Regnault, T., *op.cit.* 57.

> entered into with a free public authority, [de] Boufflers avoided drawing attention to the fact that he was advocating a plan that in many respects recalled the privileges of the *Ancien Régime.*[54]

As the drafter of the first French patent law, the reasons employed by de Boufflers to justify the legislation are important in the context of understanding the theoretical basis of this law. It is clear from his published Reports that de Boufflers stressed the importance of "natural" property rights in inventions, but did he do so for tactical reasons only? Or did he in fact see no contradiction between exclusive property rights in invention and "la liberté du travail"?[55]

In the absence of surviving personal *Memoirs* or other documents explaining de Boufflers' attitude to patent protection, modern commentators must be content to analyse de Boufflers' two Reports on the subject made to the National Assembly in 1790[56] and 1791.[57] The conclusion reached from an analysis of these Reports is that de Boufflers saw many justifications for the patent system, and that concern to protect "natural" property rights was only one issue. Although he appeared to have a genuine belief in the concept of "natural" property rights, he was equally concerned about wider social and economic advancement which could result from the introduction of a patent system.

De Boufflers' Report of December 1790

De Boufflers' first Report was written at the request of the Committee of Agriculture and Commerce of the National Assembly, and presented to that Assembly on the night of 30 December 1790. The Report was an extremely detailed document, and when later published it occupied 29 printed pages.[58] In examining the Report as a whole, it is possible to divide it into three distinct sections. The first deals mainly with the concept of natural property rights in ideas, the second considers the contractual relationship between a patentee

54 Savignon, F., "The French Revolution and Patents" (1989) *Industrial Property* 391, 395.

55 *Ibid.*

56 "Rapport fait á l'assemblée nationale par M. de Boufflers, au nom du comité d'agriculture et de commerce, dans as séance du jeudi au soir, 30 décembre 1790, sur la propriété des auteurs de découvertes et d'inventions en tout genre d'industrie" in Regnault, T., *op.cit.* 15.

57 "Reponse de M. de Boufflers aux objections élevées contre la loi du 7 janvier 1791, au nom du comité d'agriculture et du commerce, imprimée par ordre de l'assemblée nationale" in Regnault, T., *op.cit.* 57.

58 "Rapport fait á l'assemblée nationale par M. de Boufflers, au nom du comité d'agriculture et de commerce, dans as séance du jeudi au soir, 30 décembre 1790, sur la propriété des auteurs de découvertes et d'inventions en tout genre d'industrie" in Regnault, T., *op. cit.* 15–44.

and the State, and the third examines the need to encourage inventiveness in France in order to "resuscitate" French industry and make it more internationally competitive. Of these three major themes, it is apparent that de Bouffers' main concern was with the third section, namely to introduce a patent system to promote the development of French industry.

(1) *Natural Property Rights in Inventions*

Modern French commentators such as Savignon continue to point to the "natural" rights arguments for patent protection as the most important and enduring aspect of de Boufflers' report.[59] It is true that the main body of his Report begins with a discussion of the invention as a "natural" right, where appears his oft-quoted passage that the thoughts of man are a true form of property, and a type of property right which is immune to attack. He adds that "l'arbre qui naît dans un champ n'appartient pas aussi incontestablement au maître de ce champ que l'idée qui vient dans l'esprit d'un homme n'appartient á son auteur."[60] In the case of inventions, de Boufflers considers that they are the most fundamental form of property and the ownership rights of the inventor should be respected by society.[61] However, it seems that while de Boufflers favours the recognition of "natural" rights in ideas or inventions in the most absolute and unqualified sense, he is referring only to unpublished or secret ideas. Thus, he makes it clear that the inventor's absolute rights in relation to the invention end when the invention is published and made available to society.[62] While the inventor might have complete control over the terms on which the invention is revealed to society, once published, the inventor's property rights can no longer be absolute.[63]

If de Boufflers used the work of any noted philosophers in developing his concept of "natural" property rights, these sources are not presented in his Report. He was doubtless aware of the earlier work of philosophers such as John Locke, Richard Cantillon, François Voltaire, and A.R.J. Turgot, yet it

59 Savignon, F., "The French Revolution and Patents" (1989) *Industrial Property* 391, 394.

60 Translation: "No tree growing in a field belongs more indisputably to the owner of that field than the idea forming in a man's mind belongs to its author." "Rapport fait á l'assemblée nationale par M. de Boufflers, au nom du comité d'agriculture et de commerce, dans as séance du jeudi au soir, 30 décembre 1790, sur la propriété des auteurs de découvertes et d'inventions en tout genre d'industrie" in Regnault, T., *op.cit.* 16.

61 *Ibid.*

62 "Rapport fait á l'assemblée nationale par M. de Boufflers, au nom du comité d'agriculture et de commerce, dans as séance du jeudi au soir, 30 décembre 1790, sur la propriété des auteurs de découvertes et d'inventions en tout genre d'industrie" in Regnault, T., *op.cit.* 17.

63 *Ibid.*

is interesting to note that he presents the ideas in the Report as essentially his own.[64]

De Boufflers' explanation of the theoretical basis of inventor's rights is not completely consistent with the Preamble and Article 1 of the Law of 7 January 1791. The Preamble refers to the fact that:

> toute idée nouvelle … appartient primitivement á celui qui l'a conçue, et que ce serait attaquer les droits de l'homme dans leur essence que de ne pas regarder une découverte industrielle comme la propriété de son auteur. …[65]

Article 1 states that:

> [t]oute découverte ou nouvelle invention dans tous les genres d'industrie, est la propriété de son auteur. …[66]

De Boufflers' explanation of these provisions suggests that the idea itself is an essential or "natural" right of mankind, which remains as such while it is unpublished, but there are social limitations upon the exercise of this proprietary right once the invention is publicly utilised. Some later commentators certainly regarded his interpretation as authoritative.[67] However, the language used in the 1791 Law does not support any such limitation as suggested by De Boufflers and, in the course of time, his interpretation was rejected. For example, at the 1878 Paris Conference which carried out preliminary work for the Paris Convention, "natural" property rights in inventions were supported, without any restrictions associated with public use.[68]

---

64 De Boufflers might have studied the following works: Locke, J., *Two Treatises on Civil Government* (1690); Cantillon, R., *Essai sur la nature du commerce en général* (1755); Turgot, A.R.J., *Reflexions sur la formation et la distribution des richesses* (1766); Voltaire, F.M.A., *Letters on the English* (1733). See further: Martin, K., *French Liberal Thought in the Eighteenth Century* (London, Turnstile Press, 1954).

65 Translation: "every new idea … belongs originally to him who has conceived it, and that it would be to attack the rights of man in their essence not to regard a discovery in industry as the property of its author …".

66 Translation: "every discovery or new invention in all kinds of industry, is the property of its author …".

67 See, for example, Regnault, T., *op.cit.* 136.

68 See Chapter Six for further discussion of this point.

(2) *The "Social Contract"*

Although de Boufflers does not specifically mention the philosopher Jean-Jacques Rousseau, many passages in the first Report are consistent with Rousseau's concept of the "social contract". Under this theory, individual property rights are respected, but must be exercised subject to the restrictions imposed by society in the general interest.[69] In particular, the importance of the social contract to de Boufflers' theory of patent protection is made increasingly clear in the second part of the Report. It considers the contractual relationship between a patentee and the State after the decision has been made to publish the invention, and notes that the grant of a patent ensures mutual advantage to both the inventor and the wider society.[70]

On the inventor's part, de Boufflers notes that the patent assures peaceful exercise and enjoyment of the invention and this is the main reason why a patent is obtained.[71] On the part of the State, the main benefit is having access to something which was not previously disclosed.[72] If the patentee has falsely claimed an invention it is always open to the State to cancel the patent. De Boufflers also makes it clear that the patent will not be granted unless the inventor accepts two main obligations.[73] The first of these is to give the competent State authority "connaissance exacte"[74] of the invention, presumably in order that it may be worked by others after the patent has expired. The second is to pay any required patent fees during the term of the patent, and upon expiry, accept that the patented invention should be exercised by other members of the public.[75] Thus, de Boufflers justifies the patent system on the basis

69 Rousseau, J-J., *Du Contrat Social* (Paris, 1762).

70 "Rapport fait á l'assemblée nationale par M. de Boufflers, au nom du comité d'agriculture et de commerce, dans as séance du jeudi au soir, 30 décembre 1790, sur la propriété des auteurs de découvertes et d'inventions en tout genre d'industrie" in Regnault, T., *op. cit.* 17–20.

71 *Ibid.*

72 *Ibid.*

73 This tends to counteract de Boufflers' earlier statement that the inventor may enter into negotiations with society in order to arrive at mutually advantageous terms for the publication of the secret invention. In fact, inventors taking out a patent were forced to agree to standard terms of protection as set out in the Law of 7 January 1791 and the Regulations of 25 May 1791. These terms included restrictions on the duration of a patent, the necessity to pay certain fees, forfeiture clauses, etc.

74 Translation: "accurate knowledge".

75 "Rapport fait á l'assemblée nationale par M. de Boufflers, au nom du comité d'agriculture et de commerce, dans as séance du jeudi au soir, 30 décembre 1790, sur la propriété des auteurs de découvertes et d'inventions en tout genre d'industrie" in Regnault, T., *op. cit.* 18–19.

of a natural property right before publication or use, and a more instrumentalist approach later.

(3) *Patents vs Old Royal Privileges*

It is also relevant at this stage to consider the way in which de Boufflers distinguishes the concept of the patent from the old inventor's privileges. It has already been noted that there is some dispute amongst historians whether or not inventor's privileges were abolished in August 1789.[76] It is therefore arguable that the system of inventor's privileges was not officially abolished until the passage of the Patent Law of 7 January 1791.[77] Whether or not this is accepted, there is no doubt that the old system of privileges was considered odious by the members of the National Assembly, and that it was necessary for de Boufflers to do his utmost to establish clear distinctions between the inventor's privilege and a patent. This was the case even though as argued earlier in this book, the system of inventor's privileges did have social and economic advantages, and was not marked by the same degree of corruption as privileges of *corporations.*

In his discussion of the old corporate privileges, de Boufflers describes a system of artificial monopoly of objects already known to society and argues that such privileges were an attack upon the freedom of the community.[78] By contrast, he argues that a patent rewards the natural inventive gifts of mankind, and that, unlike corporate privileges, such rewards are never given for objects already known to society.[79] He also notes that society benefits from the

76 See the earlier discussion of this point under the heading "Privileges in France".

77 Article 17 of the Law of 7 January 1791 provided that royal privileges previously granted in respect of inventions and discoveries, and which satisfied the new test of patentability, would continue to be protected in the same way as any new patent. The relevant section of Article 17 provided as follows: "N'entend l'assemblée nationale porter aucune atteinte aux priviléges exclusifs ci-devant accordés pour inventions et découvertes, lorsque toutes les formes légales auront été observées pour ces priviléges, lesquels auront leur plein et entier effet; seront au surplus les possesseurs de ces anciens priviléges, assujettis aux dispositions du présent décret." Translation: "The National Assembly does not intend any violation of the exclusive privileges granted heretofore for inventions and discoveries, provided all the legal forms have been observed for those privileges, but they shall have their full and entire effect; and moreover the possessors of those former privileges shall be subject to the conditions of the present decree."

78 "Rapport fait á l'assemblée nationale par M. de Boufflers, au nom du comité d'agriculture et de commerce, dans as séance du jeudi au soir, 30 décembre 1790, sur la propriété des auteurs de découvertes et d'inventions en tout genre d'industrie" in Regnault, T., *op.cit.* 20–25. It is interesting to note that de Boufflers does not attempt to address the issue of the morality of the old inventor's privilege.

79 *Ibid.*

patented invention by gaining access to something which it has never before possessed. In a later section, he adds that the attitudes of corporations helped to distinguish the patented invention from the corporate privilege.[80] The corporations possessed a position of dangerous power (arising from their various monopolies) and they viewed independent inventors as enemies who should suffer the fate of "étouffer en naissant".[81] This antagonism towards independent inventors underlined the distinction he made between the old corporations and the individual patentee.

(4) *The Role of the Patent in Industrial Development*

Despite de Boufflers' lengthy justification of the patent as some form of "natural" or individual right with accompanying social benefits, a close reading of his first Report reveals that a very significant motivation for the Law of 7 January 1791 was to improve France's economic situation. As he was commissioned by the Committee of Agriculture and Industry of the National Assembly to write the Report, this is unsurprising, and he writes in the first sentence of an overwhelming need to "ressusciter l'industrie française".[82] Throughout the first Report, he refers to the disadvantages suffered by French manufacturers, particularly in comparison to their counterparts in the United Kingdom. He asks why the arts and industries of France had fallen behind those of comparable foreign countries, when France had equal climate, moral spirit and an intelligent population.[83]

In de Boufflers' opinion, it was the continued legacy of the old corporate system and the absence of patent legislation which was a major factor retarding the growth of French industry. In particular, he points to the fact that constant harassment by corporations, combined with limited scope for the grant of inventor's privileges, had forced unknown numbers of French inventors to leave France.[84] The social and economic structure of France had deprived

---

80 "Rapport fait á l'assemblée nationale par M. de Boufflers, au nom du comité d'agriculture et de commerce, dans as séance du jeudi au soir, 30 décembre 1790, sur la propriété des auteurs de découvertes et d'inventions en tout genre d'industrie" in Regnault, T., *op.cit.* 25.

81 Translation: – "suffocation at birth". *Ibid.*

82 Translation: "resuscitate French industry". "Rapport fait á l'assemblée nationale par M. de Boufflers, au nom du comité d'agriculture et de commerce, dans as séance du jeudi au soir, 30 décembre 1790, sur la propriété des auteurs de découvertes et d'inventions en tout genre d'industrie" in Regnault, T., *op.cit.* 15.

83 "Rapport fait á l'assemblée nationale par M. de Boufflers, au nom du comité d'agriculture et de commerce, dans as séance du jeudi au soir, 30 décembre 1790, sur la propriété des auteurs de découvertes et d'inventions en tout genre d'industrie" in Regnault, T., *op.cit.* 25.

84 *Ibid.* 31–32. Notes to de Boufflers' Report, later supplied by M. Molard, support this view. Molard gives examples of French inventions such as Briot's stamping machine for making

individual inventors of the climate in which they could make a success of their inventions, and it was no wonder that many chose to emigrate.[85]

By contrast, de Boufflers points to the situation in the United Kingdom, where it appears to him that invention is actively encouraged and patents willingly granted to foreigners.[86] He is greatly angered that the U.K. should boast superior industrial progress, since he believes that France has more natural advantages. These advantages include: (1) the superior aptitude for work, spirit, and talent of the French people;[87] (2) France's greater population than the U.K.; (3) the greater fertility of French soil; and (4) France's larger self-sufficiency in primary materials.[88] Whether or not all of these claims were true, it must be remembered that his Report was made during the period of the Eden Treaty with the U.K. of 1786–92 when there was a lessening of French economic protectionism. The Treaty anticipated a more open trading relationship between the two countries, and therefore more competition between the two markets. It is therefore unsurprising that de Boufflers and the Committee of Agriculture and Industry of the National Assembly should have been concerned to adopt new measures to encourage the competitiveness of French industry.

---

medals, a new type of grinding mill and the Nismes stocking-frame which were taken overseas to be developed. "Rapport fait á l'assemblée nationale par M. de Boufflers, au nom du comité d'agriculture et de commerce, dans as séance du jeudi au soir, 30 décembre 1790, sur la propriété des auteurs de découvertes et d'inventions en tout genre d'industrie" in Regnault, T., *op.cit.* 31, note 1.

85 In an article written in 1878 by the leader of the French anti-patent movement, Michel Chevalier, it was acknowledged that a number of French inventors had been forced to emigrate during the period prior to the enactment of the law of 1791. Chevalier referred to the case of Briot, who emigrated to England, and also Lenoir, the inventor of various improvements in the manufacture of scientific instruments. He also mentioned Réveillon, the inventor of wallpaper, who left the country after he encountered a great deal of opposition, including the vandalising of his factory in 1789. However, it was Chevalier's view that the inventors did not emigrate because of a lack of patent protection. He said that they emigrated because they wanted "la liberté de travailler" (the freedom to work), which was not available in France under the old system of *corporations*. Therefore, Chevalier believed that once the corporations were abolished, the inventors would not have asked for or required patent protection. Chevalier, M., 'Les Brevets d'Invention contraires a la Liberté du Travail' (1878) *Journal des économistes* 169, 183–184.

86 "Rapport fait á l'assemblée nationale par M. de Boufflers, au nom du comité d'agriculture et de commerce, dans as séance du jeudi au soir, 30 décembre 1790, sur la propriété des auteurs de découvertes et d'inventions en tout genre d'industrie" in Regnault, T., *op.cit.* 32.

87 *Ibid.* 38.

88 *Ibid.*

(5) *De Boufflers' Rejection of Schemes of Public Purchase of Inventions*

The National Assembly's desire to encourage the development of French industry had previously been displayed in its adoption of a scheme of public purchase of inventions. The scheme had commenced prior to 1791, and it had operated by offering sums of money for inventions which were identified as appearing to be of particular value to industry. The inventions would then be published and freely available for implementation in the particular industry.[89]

This scheme of public purchase of inventions had never been intended as a substitute for the introduction of a patent system. Although this scheme was intended to promote French industrial development, de Boufflers was sceptical about it. His Report refers particularly to the impossibility of determining whether an invention would be useful to industry if it had not yet been thoroughly tested.[90] Even if it is potentially useful, de Boufflers argues that there is no way of fairly valuing it.[91] He considers that the State has no business in interfering with the developmental stages of the inventive process, and that inventions are like babies which should be raised and nurtured under parental guidance. He also doubts whether there is a competent State authority with the ability to judge inventions.[92]

(6) *De Boufflers' Rejection of Preliminary Examination of Patent Applications*

De Boufflers' belief that the State should not interfere in the development of new inventions parallels his concern that substantive preliminary examination of patent applications should not be practised. He supports examination as to formalities only.[93] He argues that there is no Tribunal in France with the expertise to decide whether or not each application meets the criteria of patentability. He also states that it should be up to the public, rather than a Tribunal, to decide if an invention has merit.[94] It is clear that de Boufflers' philosophy is based upon the notion that a patented invention should be at the risk of market forces. His comments about the system therefore reflect the growing economic liberalism of the Eden Treaty period, and the goal of making French industry more modern and competitive. These concerns were

89 *Ibid.* 29–30.
90 *Ibid.* 30.
91 *Ibid.*
92 *Ibid.*
93 *Ibid.* 24.
94 *Ibid.*

equally as important to de Boufflers as the legal protection of "natural" property rights in inventions.[95]

Justifying the Law of 7 January 1791: De Boufflers' Second Report and the Views of the Inventors' Association

In April 1791, de Boufflers made a Second Report on the issue of patent legislation to the National Assembly.[96] This was occasioned by the controversy which surrounded the implementation of the new patent system. Although the Patent Law of 7 January 1791 had been adopted by the National Assembly largely upon the basis of his recommendations, when it came time to introduce the accompanying Regulations, many opponents of the new system came forward. Some of this opposition came from people who were ignorant about the concept of patents, and related to technical issues which were easily resolved.[97]

Although time and experience would eventually overcome many objections to the new patent system, there was a growing body of opinion, both within and outside the National Assembly, which was critical of its theoretical basis. One argument advanced was that a system of patents for inventions should not have been introduced into France because this was inconsistent with the new

95 The eminent copyright scholar, Jane Ginsburg, has drawn similar conclusions about the underlying basis of the French copyright decrees of 1791 and 1793. Although the two copyright decrees have traditionally been interpreted as profoundly "author-oriented", Ginsburg has demonstrated that the "French revolutionary sources themselves cast doubt upon the assumed author-centrism of the initial French copyright legislation. The speeches in the revolutionary assemblies, the texts of the laws, and the court decisions construing the laws, all indicate at least a strong instrumentalist undercurrent to the French decrees of 1791 and 1793." Ginsburg later adds that authors "are not securely at the core of the new literary property regime; rather, the public plays a major role. The 1791 text predominantly is preoccupied with the recognition and enlargement of the public domain." Ginsburg, J., "A Tale of Two Copyrights: Literary Property in Revolutionary France and America" (1990) 64 *Tulane Law Review* 991, 995, 1006.

96 "Reponse de M. de Boufflers aux objections élevées contre la loi du 7 janvier 1791, au nom du comité d'agriculture et du commerce, imprimée par ordre de l'assemblée nationale" in Regnault, T., *op.cit.* 56.

97 In particular, M. Roederer, a former deputy of the Third Estate to the States General, considered that there could be confusion between a *patente* for an invention, and fiscal patents, or *patentes de négoce*, which related to the operation of former wardenships and masterships. As a result of this possibility of confusion, it was agreed that Article 1 of the Patent Regulations should clearly provide for the grant of "patentes nationales sous la dénomination de *brevets d'invention* ...". It was hoped that the use of the term "brevet" would distinguish a patent for an invention from a fiscal patent. Discussed in "Respectueuse Pétition des Artistes-Inventeurs á l'Assemblée nationale de 2 Avril 1791" in Regnault, T., *op.cit.* 45, 51.

doctrine of "la liberté du travail". De Boufflers writes about this opposition in his Second Report, where he also refutes allegations that he had earlier misled the National Assembly.[98] The strength of the opposition prompted the *Société des Artistes-Inventeurs* to prepare its own Report for the National Assembly in support of de Boufflers and the patent system.[99] The Société argues in its Report that the concept of freedom is important, but denies that the granting of patent rights would have adverse consequences for the community. To those who claim that the patent is akin to the old royal privilege, the Société states that the old privileges were almost never awarded on the basis of merit, but that the patent for invention would need to have merit in order to be valid.[100] In relation to the argument that the matter of the Patent Regulations should be held over until the next session of the National Assembly, the Société comments that it would be:

> barbare et impolitique d'ajourner á la prochaine legislature ... une loi seule propre á réveiller l'industrie nationale, une loi qui a consacré la plus inviolable des propriétés, une loi que bénissent tous les artistes, une loi que la nation et les étrangers applaudissent, une loi contre laquelle personne ne réclame, une loi sur laquelle les artistes de la capitale et des provinces ont fondé leurs plus douces espérances.[101]

Although de Boufflers' Second Report raises many of the same points as the first, its most interesting feature is the stronger emphasis on the "natural" property rights of the inventor. In this later Report, economic justifications for the patent system are apparently only of secondary concern.[102] This is illustrated

98 It was alleged that de Boufflers purposely presented his First Report to the National Assembly at a date and time when many of the members were absent. See "Reponse de M. de Boufflers aux objections élevées contre la loi du 7 janvier 1791, au nom du comité d'agriculture et du commerce, imprimée par ordre de l'assemblée nationale" in Regnault, T., *op.cit.* 57.

99 "Respectueuse Pétition des Artistes-Inventeurs á l'Assemblée nationale de 2 Avril 1791" in Regnault, T., *op.cit.* 45.

100 *Ibid.*

101 Translation: "barbarous and impolitic to adjourn to the next legislature ... a law wholly proper to revive the national industry, a law dedicated to the most inviolable of properties, a law which benefits all artists, and a law which the nation and foreigners applaud, a law against which no-one protests, a law upon which artists of the capital and provinces have founded their sweetest hopes." *Ibid.* 55.

102 In terms of economic justifications for the patent system, de Boufflers' Second Report looks at two main questions. These are: (1) allegations by established manufacturers that patents are anti-competitive and would have a generally detrimental impact upon the French consumer, and (2) the effect of the patent system upon consumer prices. De

by the fact that, unlike the First Report, the Second Report does not begin with a reference to the need to reinvigorate French industry. Apparently, for tactical reasons, it opens by referring to the Law of 7 January 1791, "qui consacre le droit naturel de l'inventeur sur son invention."[103] It goes on to argue that there is a close tie between the preservation and development of French culture and promotion of the growth of industry. To de Boufflers, the protection of invention is not only a natural right of the individual, but there is a clear link between the invention, industrial progress and respect for French culture.[104] This type of argument implies that the invention is a natural property right not only of the individual inventor, but it is also some sort of intrinsic right of the community. Despite this interesting extension of de Boufflers' theory of the "natural" property right, there is little change in his explanation of how the "natural" property right of the inventor is exercised. His Second Report refers again to the right of man in his thoughts or ideas, and the fact that every person is entitled to keep his ideas secret, or to impose conditions before dissemination to the public.[105]

(c) *Conclusions Which Can Be Drawn about the Patent Law of 1791*

(i) Conclusions Drawn from de Boufflers' Reports

Although de Boufflers' Reports and the opening provisions of the patent legislation of 7 January 1791 clearly refer to the concept of the patent as a form of "natural" property right, it is apparent that this was not the sole idea or theory underlying the law of 1791. Instead, it can be seen that the need to recognise and protect "natural" property rights in invention was only one of a number of motives for the passage of the patent law. There is a great deal of evidence to suggest that concerns about finding a way to promote French industrial development were equally important. Nevertheless, the fact that there were mixed motives for the adoption of the law of 1791 does not mean that de Boufflers' arguments about "natural" property rights were merely a political tactic. Therefore, it is impossible to accept the arguments of the nineteenth century German legal scholar Hermann Rentzsch that de Boufflers acted with deliberate insincerity in propounding the artificial theory of the natural property

---

Boufflers again justifies the patent system by reference to the importance of promoting industrial development and issues of consumer choice. "Reponse de M. de Boufflers aux objections élevées contre la loi du 7 janvier 1791, au nom du comité d'agriculture et du commerce, imprimée par ordre de l'assemblée nationale" in Regnault, T., *op.cit.* 63.

103 Translation: "which conserves the natural right of the inventor in his invention." *Ibid.* 56.

104 *Ibid.* 57–58.

105 *Ibid.* 59.

rights of the inventor.[106] It is equally unfortunate that Rentzsch's interpretation of de Boufflers' motives was readily accepted by the later U.S. scholars Fritz Machlup and Edith Penrose.[107] After referring with approbation to the earlier work of Hermann Rentzsch, they stated that for "more than seventy years afterward scholars seriously debated the notion of a property in ideas, a notion first proposed, to put it bluntly, as a political ruse."[108] It has been shown above that such an interpretation is too simplistic because of the complexity of the motives for the passage of the law of 1791.

(ii) Conclusions Drawn from the Text of the 1791 Legislation

Leaving aside the general espousals of the inventor's rights in the Preamble and Article 1 of the Law of 7 January 1791, the legislation was not used merely as a vehicle to promote the "natural" property rights of inventors. In fact, the legislation represented a desire to balance the equally important interests of both inventors and society.

There were a number of basic features of the French patent law of 7 January 1791.[109] Article 1 provided that a patent could be granted for a period of 5, 10 or 15 years to the "author" of every "discovery or new invention". An invention also included an improvement upon a previously known manufacture, and thus patents for "improvements" could be obtained.[110] An "improvement" could be taken for an invention at any time during the period of the original patent, upon payment of a small fee.[111] The concept of novelty was measured only by

106 Rentzsch, H., "Geistiges Eigenthum" in *Handwörterbuch der Volkswirtschaft* (Leipzig 1866), 335. It is unsurprising that Rentzsch adopted this interpretation of de Boufflers' Report, since he was firmly of the view that there could be no property rights in ideas.

107 Machlup, F., and Penrose, E., "The Patent Controversy in the Nineteenth Century" (1950) x *The Journal of Economic History* 1, 16–17.

108 *Ibid.*

109 The French Patent Law of 7 January 1791, supplemented by the Regulations of 25 May 1791, remained in force until 1844. English translations of some of this legislation can be found in UNITED KINGDOM, Parliamentary Papers, *Report from the Select Committee on the Law Relative to Patents for Inventions* (1829) 332, vol III, 415, Appendix D (Text of the Law of 7 January 1791); UNITED KINGDOM, Parliamentary Papers, *Reports by H.M. Secs of Embassy and Legation respecting Law and Practice in Foreign Countries with regard to Inventions* (1873) C. 741, vol LXVI, 483, 88 (Text of the Law of 5 July 1844).

110 Article 2 of the Law of 7 January 1791.

111 Contrast this with the restrictive U.K. practice on the subject at that time, where it was necessary to obtain a totally new patent for any improvement. This naturally necessitated the payment of additional high fees and entailed much inconvenience. On this point, see the evidence of Mr William Newton, a patent agent, before the 1829 Select Committee of the House of Commons. UNITED KINGDOM, Parliamentary Papers, *Report from the Select Committee on the Law Relative to Patents for Inventions* (1829) 332, vol III, 415, 68.

reference to domestic experience, and it was possible to obtain a "patent of importation", which was a patent granted to the first person to bring a foreign invention into France.[112] It was not necessary that the importer should be the original inventor in the foreign country. This provision was based upon the U.K. practice, and does not appear consistent with the underlying French theory of the patent as the natural property right of its inventor.[113]

While the French Government was eager to encourage the entry of foreign inventions, it included in the legislation a draconian feature with the effect that if an invention was patented in France, and then later patented in a foreign country, the patentee would immediately forfeit his or her French patent.[114] Patents were also forfeited for insufficient description in the specification or failure to exploit the invention in France within two years of grant.[115] The patent was granted without any preliminary examination as to the substance of the application, and therefore its validity was in no way guaranteed by the government. The Law itself and the Regulations provided that specifications were public property after the patent had expired, and that during the term of the patent the specification should be open to public inspection.[116] However, in practice it was almost impossible to gain access to the specifications of either current or expired patents. A practice grew up of keeping all specifications sealed, and only opening them to scrutiny when claims of infringement, or petitions for forfeiture on the grounds of invalidity, were made before the Courts.[117]

Upon examining the main features of the Law of 7 January 1791, it is apparent that while the legislation was said to protect the natural property rights of the individual inventor, what it equally protected and promoted were the

---

112 Article 3 of the Law of 7 January 1791.

113 Savignon also argues that this provision "flagrantly contradicted" the principle of inventors' property rights. See Savignon, F., "The French Revolution and Patents" (1989) *Industrial Property* 391, 396.

114 Article 16 of the Law of 7 January 1791. However, it was said to be common practice to avoid the effects of this provision by employing an agent to take out foreign patents for the invention (in the name of the agent and not the original French patentee). See the evidence of William Newton, a patent agent, before the 1829 Select Committee of the House of Commons. UNITED KINGDOM, Parliamentary Papers, *Report from the Select Committee on the Law Relative to Patents for Inventions* (1829) 332, vol III, 415, 70.

115 Article 16 of the Law of 7 January 1791.

116 See especially Articles 10, 11, 15 and 16 of the Law of 7 January 1791.

117 See the evidence of Joseph Merry, a ribbon manufacturer of Coventry, and William Newton, before the 1829 Select Committee of the House of Commons. UNITED KINGDOM, Parliamentary Papers, *Report from the Select Committee on the Law Relative to Patents for Inventions* (1829) 332, vol III, 415, 69, 89.

domestic policies of the French nation in its industrial development. By providing for patents of importation, forfeiture for non-working or foreign patenting, and secrecy of specifications (arguably to hinder the secret from leaving the country),[118] the community interest was shown to be as important as that of the "sacred" property rights of individual inventors. Both de Boufflers two Reports, and the patent legislation, clearly displayed a mixture of theoretical justifications for the French patent system. It is not correct to argue that the protection of "natural" property rights in inventions was a paramount consideration, but neither is it accurate for scholars such as Machlup and Penrose to argue that theories of "natural" property rights were invented purely for political reasons. The idea of "natural" property rights in inventions was a cornerstone of the 1791 law, but wider economic and social interests were equally as important.

(d) *Reaction to the Patent Law after 1791*

It has been argued above that there were complex reasons why the French legislature employed the concept of natural property rights in its Patent Law of 1791. Although the drafter of the legislation, de Boufflers, appeared to genuinely believe that inventions should be protected as natural property rights, it is also true that such a concept was more politically acceptable in revolutionary France than any alternative theoretical bases for the patent system. Yet, subsequent developments after 1791 showed that the patent law did not receive immediate popular support, and its ideological foundation was subjected to close scrutiny. There are two factors which support this view. The first is that during the period of the *Directoire,* there was strong support for a weakening of patent rights. The second is that before 1844, very few French economic philosophers or legal commentators openly supported the concept of "natural" property rights in inventions. This was clear from comments made at the time of the passage of the patent law reforms of 5 July 1844. In fact, it was only ten years after the Belgian economic philosopher J.-B. Jobard introduced his concept of the *Monautopole* in 1844,[119] that some influential French commentators gave their unequivocal support to "natural" property rights in inventions. The following section discusses the first of these matters, and the second is examined in the context of Parts B and C below.

118 U.K. inventors and patent agents, such as William Newton, argued to this effect. *Ibid.*

119 Jobard, J.-B., A.-M., *Nouvelle économie sociale ou monautopole industriel, artistique, commercial et littéraire* (Paris 1844).

The Unsuccessful Reform Proposals of 1798.

In 1798 an unsuccessful attempt was made to introduce restrictions upon the grant of patents, and to establish a system of rigorous examination of all applications.[120] This proposal was put by François Eude, (an anti-patent advocate),[121] to the *Conseil des cinq-cents* on 14 pluviôse an VI (2 January 1798).[122] Although the *Directoire* was supposedly devoted to "total liberalism" in economic policies,[123] Eude's proposals were not adopted.

Although when he made his First Report, Eude was clearly not a supporter of the patent system, he realised that the government was bound by the Constitution of 1791 to provide financial protection for inventors.[124] Article 357 of the Constitution stated that "[l]a loi doit pouvoir á la recompense des inventeurs ou au maintien de la propriété exclusive de leurs découvertes ou de leurs productions."[125] Thus, although Eude's Report questions how the patent system can be reconciled with the "régime de la liberté", he realises that it would not be acceptable for the government to openly deny the effect of Article 357.[126] He also recognises that the patent system could be used to help stimulate French industrial development, but he does not think that patents should be granted so readily.[127] One reason for this is that he prefers to view the patent as a contract between the inventor and the State, rather than a "natural" property right.[128] He argues that patents are sometimes granted for worthless

120 "Rapport fait par François Eude, au Conseil des cinq-cents, sur les brevets d'invention. Séance du 14 pluviôse an VI (2 janvier 1798)" in Regnault, T., op.cit. 75. The proposals put by Eude were that each time an inventor required a patent, a special jury of 3 members would be formed which would be chosen by the Minister of the Interior. A patent would only be granted if the application received a favourable report from the special jury, and the *directoire exécutif* also agreed with the report.

121 Eude was most notable for later being President of the Royal Court of Rouen during the reign of Louis-Philippe.

122 The *Conseil des cinq-cents* (or Council of the Five Hundred), was one of the two assemblies established by the *Directoire.* Savignon, F., "The French Revolution and Patents" (1989) *Industrial Property* 391, 398.

123 *Ibid.*

124 "Rapport fait par François Eude, au Conseil des cinq-cents, sur les brevets d'invention. Séance du 14 pluviôse an VI (2 janvier 1798)" in Regnault, T., op.cit. 78.

125 Translation: "The law must provide recompense for inventors or maintain exclusive property rights in their discoveries or their productions."

126 "Rapport fait par François Eude, au Conseil des cinq-cents, sur les brevets d'invention. Séance du 14 pluviôse an VI (2 janvier 1798)" in Regnault, T., op.cit. 78.

127 *Ibid.* 79–81.

128 *Ibid.* 79.

inventions, where there is little benefit to the State, and therefore no consideration for the patent.[129]

In response to Eude's Report, de Bailleul, another member of the *conseil des cinq-cents,* presented an opposing Report to the *conseil* in which he defended the patent system as established under the law of 7 January 1791.[130] De Bailleul's Report adopts a similar position to that of de Boufflers, namely that an invention is the property of he who has made it, and moreover such a property right is inviolable.[131] As an inviolable property right, it must be protected by the full weight of the law. He strongly objects to proposals that a patent should only be granted upon the recommendation of a group of government appointees.[132] As the right to protection of an invention was enshrined in the Constitution of 1791, he argues it is not possible for the government to set onerous pre-conditions to the grant of a patent.[133]

Eude's proposals failed to receive sufficient support from the Special Committee of Inquiry which was set up by the *Conseil des cinq-cents* to examine the matter.[134] In fact, it appears that in the period between January and August 1798, Eude resiled from his own proposals and became a firm supporter of the French patent system. On 29 August 1798, he made a Second Report to the *Conseil des cinq-cents* in which he withdrew his support for the proposal to introduce a system of rigorous examination of patent applications.[135] There are two points of interest in Eude's Second Report. The first is his implied

129 On this point, Eude states "Nothing can be worse than the system of granting patents on the mere application of self-styled inventors; such a system is likely to produce a large amount of spurious patents, which are equally injurious to commerce and to the rights of those who enjoy them with fair claims. It is therefore, highly important that such grants should only be made after a mature examination, and with a thorough knowledge of the matter in hand; sound reason dictates such a course, and the interest of real inventors requires it." Translation from the original French in UNITED KINGDOM, Parliamentary Papers, *Report from the Select Committee on Letters Patent; together with the Proceedings of the Committee, Minutes of Evidence, Appendix and Index* (1872) 193, vol XI, 395, 143.

130 "Observations de Bailleul sur quelques articles du projet de resolution présenté par J.F. Eude au conseil des cinq-cents, concernant les brevets d'invention' in Regnault, T., *op. cit.* 93.

131 *Ibid.* 93.

132 *Ibid.* 94.

133 *Ibid.*

134 In relation to this Inquiry see: UNITED KINGDOM, Parliamentary Papers, *Report from the Select Committee on Letters Patent; together with the Proceedings of the Committee, Minutes of Evidence, Appendix and Index* (1872) 193, vol XI, 395, 144.

135 "Rapport fait par François Eude, au Conseil des cinq-cents, sur les brevets d'invention" (29 August 1798). Translated from the original French in *Ibid.*

acceptance of the patent as a property right of the inventor.[136] The second is his belief that little harm is done by granting a patent without previous examination, and that the likelihood of social disadvantage from spurious patents is greatly exaggerated.[137]

The fact that the proposed reforms of 1798 were aborted, demonstrates that de Boufflers' concept of "natural" property rights in inventions was finally beginning to gain more support in France.[138] Yet Eude's First Report demonstrated how the instrumentalist theory of patent protection was also gaining ground. The differences between those who supported the concept of "natural" property rights in inventions, and those who took a more instrumentalist approach gave rise to occasional comment over the next fifty years. However, there was no official consideration of the matter until 1844.

B The Significance of the Reforms of 1844

On 5 July 1844 the French legislature passed a new Patent Law. From a theoretical perspective, the most significant change was the removal of any reference to the "natural property rights" of the inventor. Under the Law of 1844, it was stated in Article 1 that the author of any new discovery or invention had an "exclusive right to exploit" the invention.[139] The question arises as to whether

---

136 Eude states that "[p]atents are nothing else than an official declaration of the inventor that the invention which he intends to utilise is his own." *Ibid.*

137 Eude notes that any "existing doubt about this might be dispelled by citing the experience gained in that respect in England, where for nearly the last century patents are granted on mere application, without such usage, in spite of its antiquity, causing any abuse; nay, the flourishing state of the factories and manufactures of that country must be chiefly attributed to that principle." *Ibid.*

138 The fact that Eude, who was originally an outspoken opponent of the 1791 patent system, became a firm supporter of the system after observing the results of the Special Committee of Inquiry, demonstrates that the philosophical basis of the 1791 law was more than a mere "political ruse". Even in his First Report, Eude does not dare to call for the abolition of the "natural" property rights provision in Article 1 of the patent law, or criticise Article 357 of the Constitution. This also lends weight to the argument that the concept of "natural" property rights in invention was more important than commentators such as Rentzsch and Machlup and Penrose realised.

139 The full text of Article 1 of the patent law of 5 July 1844 was as follows: "Toute nouvelle découverte ou invention dans tous genres d'industrie confére á son auteur, sous les conditions et pour le temps ci-aprés déterminés, le droit exclusif d'exploiter á son profit ladite découverte ou invention. Ce droit est constaté par des titres délivrés par le gouvernement sous le nom de *brevets d'invention.*"

or not the French government intended this to be seen as a rejection of the concept of "natural" property rights in inventions.

(a) *Historical Background to the Law of 5 July 1844*

Between 1791 and 1844 only minor amendments, mostly of a procedural nature, were made to the Patent Law.[140] However, as early as 1828 there was sufficient concern about the patent system to warrant the Count de Saint-Cricq, Minister of Commerce and Manufactures, establishing a Special Commission to examine the patent law.[141] This was only two years before the Revolution of July 1830, in which the Duke of Orleans, Louis Philippe, was installed on the French throne.[142] This period has been described as one in which the policies of protectionism were foremost, the Chamber of Deputies "represented with an irresistible majority the interests of the manufacturing classes: and the alliance of the two great sections of the landed and the manufacturing interests defied all the attempts which were made from time to time by successive ministers to break down this combination, and liberate the people of France from a system of heavy duties and artificial prices".[143] The new patent legislation of 1844 was clearly a product of the prevailing political and economic views of this relatively short period.

---

140 These minor amendments were introduced on 20 September 1792, 8 October 1798, 27 September 1800, 25 November 1806, 25 January 1807 and 16 August 1810. Pataille, J., and Huguet, A., *Code International de la Propriété Industrielle Artistique et Littéraire contenant les legislations Française et étrangéres et les Traités Internationaux en Matiére de Brevets d'invention, Littérature, Théatre, Musique, Beaux-Arts Dessins, Modéles, Noms et Marques de Fabrique et Concurrence Commerciale* (Paris, Marescq, 1865), 6.

141 The Commission was composed of M Girod de l'Ain, President, Count Delaborde, Baron Thénard, Molard, Ternaux, Boignet, le chevalier de Saint-Criq, Ch. Renouard, Th. Regnault, Cochaud and Guillard de Senainville. In 1831 M. Azévédo joined the Commission. Exposé des Motifs, présenté le 10 Janvier 1843, á la Chambre des Pairs, par M. Le Ministre de L'agriculture et du Commerce" in Blanc, E., *L'inventeur Breveté, Code des Inventions et des Perfectionnements* (Paris, Librairie Générale de Jurisprudence de Cosse, 1852), 46.

142 Louis Philippe was overthrown on 4 May 1848, and a Republic was declared by the National Assembly.

143 "Commercial relations of England and France: Review of recent works by Chevalier, Amé and Faucher" (1860) 111 *The Edinburgh Review* 277, 288. Karl Marx's view was that this period in French history was marked by the power of only one section of the bourgeoisie. He said that the "bankers, stock exchange kings, railway kings, owners of coal and iron mines and forests" and "landed proprietors that rallied round them – the so-called *finance aristocracy*" were the possessors of the real power at this time. He considered that the Restoration was the period of the financial entrepreneurs, and not the industrial bourgeoisie. Marx, K., "The Class Struggles in France 1848 to 1850" in Feuer, L., (ed) *Marx and Engels: Basic Writings* (New York, Fontana, 1959), 323.

(b) *Substantive Legal Changes Resulting from the 1844 Reforms*

The Law of 5 July 1844 contained many points of similarity to the previous Law of 7 January 1791. In particular, the system of granting patents without preliminary examination was retained,[144] as was the possibility of obtaining patents of improvement, for the duration of the original patent, upon payment of a small fee.[145] Patents would still be forfeited for non-working within two years of grant, or non-working for a period of two years at any time within the period of the patent.[146] However, many important changes were introduced. One of the most profound was the requirement that a patentable invention display absolute novelty, meaning that novelty was to be tested against what was already known and used in France and anywhere abroad.[147] Any less rigorous test of novelty was considered to amount to a "usurpation of the public domain".[148] At the same time, patents of importation were abolished. Foreigners were permitted to obtain patents in France for their own inventions previously patented overseas, without any requirement of reciprocity.[149] The provision in the Law of 1791 to the effect that a patent would be forfeited if a later application was made for a foreign patent was also abolished.

The reforms of 1844 had a significant impact upon foreign inventors. The requirement of absolute novelty effectively prevented many foreign inventors from patenting their inventions in France. This was because it was not usual

---

144 Article 11 of the Law of 5 July 1844. However, the issue of whether or not to introduce a system of preliminary examination of patent applications was debated at some length in the *Chambre des Pairs* on 27 and 28 March 1843. Twelve members of the Chambre spoke out on this issue, and most supported the view that it was not the role of the government to examine the legality of a patent. This matter was best left to the judicial system.

145 These were known as certificates of addition. Article 16 of the Law of 5 July 1844.

146 Article 32 of the Law of 5 July 1844.

147 Article 31 of the Law of 5 July 1844.

148 Exposé des Motifs, présenté le 10 Janvier 1843, á la Chambre des Pairs, par M. Le Ministre de L'agriculture et du Commerce" in Blanc, E., *L'inventeur Breveté, Code des Inventions et des Perfectionnements* (Paris, Librairie Générale de Jurisprudence de Cosse, 1852), 35.

149 Article 27 of the Law of 5 July 1844. However, the duration of the French patent would be only as long as the patent first taken out in the foreign country. Thus, the French patent was "dependent", rather than "independent". As to the issue of reciprocity, the original proposals of 1843 had required that patents would only be granted to foreigners if the same rights would be accorded to French nationals in the applicant's country of origin. However, the requirement of reciprocity was dropped after strong representations by the Marquis de Barthélémy. Exposé des Motifs, présenté le 10 Janvier 1843, á la Chambre des Pairs, par M. Le Ministre de L'agriculture et du Commerce" in Blanc, E., *L'inventeur Breveté, Code des Inventions et des Perfectionnements* (Paris, Librairie Générale de Jurisprudence de Cosse, 1852), 34. Plasseraud, Y., and Savignon, F., *Paris 1883: Genése du droit Unioniste des Brevets* (Paris, Litec, 1983), 89–90.

for the foreign inventor to be in the position to apply for a patent simultaneously in the country of origin and in France. In addition, the Law of 5 July 1844 introduced a new Article which provided that a patent would be forfeited if the patentee imported into France goods made abroad which were similar to those covered by the French patent.[150] The justification for this new provision was said to be to protect the national industry from competition from abroad.[151] Whether it was intended or not, the effect of these protectionist provisions was that foreign patent applications dropped from approximately 11% under the Law of 1791, to a maximum of between 2% and 6% under the Law of 1844.[152]

These reforms were, however, of an essentially practical nature. It was the removal of the reference to "natural" property rights in the Law of 1844 which directly gives rise to the question: *Why did the French Government give effect to this conceptual change?*

(c) *The Reasons for the Theoretical Reform of 1844*

It has been demonstrated above that in the decade after the passage of the patent law of 7 January 1791, there was far from unanimous support for the theory of the patent as a "natural" property right. Even de Boufflers sought to justify patent protection on a number of different bases, only one of which was the concept of the "natural" property right. In the years between the aborted reform proposals of 1798 and the reforms of 1844, there is little evidence that support in France for the "natural" property right concept became stronger. In fact, it appears that while in practical terms the patent system steadily gained favour, during this period,[153] theoretical discussion about the nature of patent protection was limited. Jean Baptiste Say was perhaps representative of the views of most other French political economists when he stated in 1803 that there was no real reason to complain about the patent system, its effect was not to harm or hinder any branch of industry, and its cost was borne voluntarily by those seeking the patented articles.[154] In other words, French commentators

150 Article 32 of the Law of 5 July 1844.

151 Exposé des Motifs, présenté le 10 Janvier 1843, á la Chambre des Pairs, par M. Le Ministre de L'agriculture et du Commerce" in Blanc, E., *L'inventeur Breveté, Code des Inventions et des Perfectionnements* (Paris, Librairie Générale de Jurisprudence de Cosse, 1852), 39.

152 Derived from patent figures from 1815 to 1883. Plasseraud, Y., and Savignon, F., *Paris 1883: Genése du droit Unioniste des Brevets* (Paris, Litec, 1983), 91.

153 This can be demonstrated by the steady growth in the number of patents granted in France from 1791 to 1844. However, it was not until 1815 that the patent statistics averaged over 100 patents granted annually. Statistics derived from Plasseraud, Y., and Savignon, F., *Paris 1883: Genése du droit Unioniste des Brevets* (Paris, Litec, 1983), 27, 70.

154 Say, J.B., *Traité d'économie politique* (Paris 1803), 263–4. One of the few French political economists who opposed the patent system in the early part of the nineteenth century

embraced the tangible advantages of the patent system, such as the perceived benefits to industrial progress, but were not particularly concerned about the theoretical basis of such protection. Thus it is unsurprising that when proposals for reform of the patent law were being drafted in 1843, the Government was more concerned to stress the practical benefits of the patent system, rather than the need to recognise the "sacred" or "natural" property rights of the inventor. France in 1843–44 was a quite different society from 1791, and the drafters of the 1844 law did not have de Boufflers' difficult task of finding a way to reconcile the patent with the *Declaration of the Rights of Man and the Citizen* and the utopian concepts of freedom and equality.

Although the Law of 5 July 1844 no longer referred to the "natural" property rights of the inventor, it is equally clear that the French Government was not attempting to make any firm statement about the theoretical basis of patent rights. In fact, both the Minister of Agriculture and Commerce, Philippe Dupin, and the Marquis de Barthélemy (a member of the Special Commission set up to examine the patent law), stated that the issue of whether a right in an invention was or was not property was a question for philosophical discussion, rather than legislation.[155] When the *Projet de Loi* was debated before the *Chambre des Pairs*, members such as Rossi and Persil continued to refer to an inventor's interest as a right of property and apparently did not see any contradiction between this view and the drafting of the provisions in the *Projet*.[156]

---

was Simonde de Sismondi. He considered that the patent monopoly was anti-competitive, and only the patentee benefited. He said that consumers and workers derived no advantage from the patent system. De Sismondi, S., *Nouveaux principes d'économie politique ou de la richesse dans ses rapport avec la population* (Paris, Delaunay, 1827), 334. Marx and Engels classified de Sismondi as one of the group of "Petty-Bourgeois" Socialists, whose philosophies favoured the proletariat. Marx, K., and Engels, F., "Manifesto of the Communist Party" (1848) in Feuer, L., (ed) *Marx and Engels: Basic Writings* (New York, Fontana, 1959), 73.

155 "Rapport fait á la Chambre des Pairs, par M. Le Marquis de Barthélemy, membre de la Commission, dans la séance du 20 mars 1843 in Blanc, E., *L'inventeur Breveté, Code des Inventions et des Perfectionnements* (Paris, Librairie Générale de Jurisprudence de Cosse, 1852), 60–61; "Exposé des Motifs, présenté le 10 Janvier 1843, á la Chambre des Pairs, par M. Le Ministre de L'agriculture et du Commerce" in Blanc, E., *L'inventeur Breveté, Code des Inventions et des Perfectionnements* (Paris, Librairie Générale de Jurisprudence de Cosse, 1852), 4–6.

156 *Chambre des Pairs,* 27 and 28 March 1843. Summary of opinions reproduced in UNITED KINGDOM, Parliamentary Papers, *Report from the Select Committee on Letters Patent; together with the Proceedings of the Committee, Minutes of Evidence, Appendix and Index* (1872) 193, vol XI, 395. The Law of 5 July 1844 was voted in the *Chambre des Pairs,* after 7 sittings, with a majority of 93 members in favour and 14 against. It was voted in the *Chambre des Députés,* after 6 sittings, with a majority of 219 members in favour and 15 against.

The Government believed that the patent legislation should be restricted to fixing the conditions of the enjoyment of the exclusive rights of the inventor, without the need to define the nature of those rights.[157] This was a quite different approach from that taken by de Boufflers in 1791, when it was considered essential that the theoretical basis of the proposed patent system should be clearly stated in the legislation.

Even if the new law was not intended to address the issue of the theoretical basis of patent protection, the avoidance of this issue gave encouragement to those who had not accepted the patent as a "natural" property right. Such an outcome was feared by at least one member of the *Chambre des Pairs* when the *Projet de Loi* was being debated on 24 March 1843. The Vicomte Dubouchage appealed to the members to include the reference to property rights in the text of the new legislation, stating that to "insert the word property is not a matter of indifference, because words may have great influence upon minds ..."[158] As Dubouchage feared, the removal of the reference to "natural" property rights in the patent legislation did lead to a re-appraisal of the theoretical basis of patent protection. This began with the speech of Dupin, the Minister of Agriculture and Commerce, when he presented the *Projet de Loi* to the *Chambre des Pairs* on 10 January 1843. In encouraging the view that a contractual relationship formed the basis of patent protection he stated that:

> [G]arantir á tout inventeur, pendant un temps donné, la jouissance pleine et entiére de sa découverte, á la condition que cet inventeur livrera cette découverte á la société après l'expiration de son privilége: tel est le contrat, simple en lui-même, que, sous les formes un peu solennelles de l'époque, les lois de 1791 ont substitué au régime arbitraire des priviléges.[159]

---

157 *Ibid.* Michel Chevalier greatly criticised the French Government for avoiding the issue of whether a patentable invention was a property right. Chevalier stated that the Government should not have avoided such "metaphysical" issues; it was in fact its task to confront such matters. Chevalier, M., 'Les Brevets d'Invention contraires a la Liberté du Travail' (1878) *Journal des économistes* 169, 191.

158 *Chambre des Pairs*, session of 24 March 1843. Translated in Machlup, F., and Penrose, E., "The Patent Controversy in the Nineteenth Century" (1950) x *The Journal of Economic History* 1, 16. See also on this point: de Molinari, G., 'De la Propriété des Inventions' (1855) *Journal des économistes* 410, 423, where de Molinari notes that some may say that if an invention confers a property right, then why was this not clearly specified in the patent law of 5 July 1844?

159 Translation: "To guarantee to every inventor, during a given time, the whole and unimpaired enjoyment of his discovery, on the condition that the inventor delivers the discovery to society after the expiration of his privilege: that is the contract, simple in itself, which, under solemn form of the period, the laws of 1791 were substituted for the arbitrary

This concept of the patent as representative of a contract seemed to become the official government position in France after the 1844 reforms. For example, in 1851, Louis Wolowski, a member of the French National Assembly, Professor of the *Conservatoire des Arts et Metiers,* and Professor of Commercial Legislation told the U.K. Select Committee on Patents that the "principle involved in this matter is not, as some think, in the nature of an acquired right to property, but it is in the nature of a contract between the inventor and the public."[160]

At least one French legal commentator, Etienne Blanc, viewed this aspect of the government's patent law reforms of 1844 as completely misguided. He stated that the effect of the 1844 reforms was to deny the special proprietary interests in invention, an outcome which had "n'a ni la vérité ni la logique pour excuse."[161] However, other legal commentators such as Michel Chevalier,[162] and Pataille and Huguet,[163] considered that the theoretical basis of the patent law remained unchanged after the reforms of 1844. As Pataille and Huguet stated, under both laws the inventor had a property right in his invention, but the 1844 reforms made it clearer that this property right was only exercised subject to the conditions imposed by government on behalf of the interests of society.[164]

---

regime of privileges." "Exposé des Motifs, présenté le 10 Janvier 1843, á la Chambre des Pairs, par M. Le Ministre de L'agriculture et du Commerce" in Blanc, E., *L'inventeur Breveté, Code des Inventions et des Perfectionnements* (Paris, Librairie Générale de Jurisprudence de Cosse, 1852), 4.

160 UNITED KINGDOM, Parliamentary Papers, *Report and Minutes of Evidence taken before the Select Committee of the House of Lords appointed to consider of The Bill, intituled, "An Act further to amend the Law touching Letters Patent for Invention" and also of The Bill intituled "An Act for the further amendment of the Law touching Letters Patent for Invention" and to report thereon to the House: Session 1851* (1851) 486 vol XVIII, 233, Evidence of Louis Wolowski at 330.

161 Translation: "Neither truth nor logic for an excuse." Blanc, E., *op.cit.* xiii.

162 Chevalier, M., 'Les Brevets d'Invention contraires a la Liberté du Travail' (1878) *Journal des économistes* 169, 179.

163 Pataille, J., and Huguet, A., *Code International de la Propriété Industrielle Artistique et Littéraire contenant les legislations Française et étrangéres et les Traités Internationaux en Matiére de Brevets d'invention, Littérature, Théatre, Musique, Beaux-Arts Dessins, Modéles, Noms et Marques de Fabrique et Concurrence Commerciale* (Paris, Marescq, 1865), 7.

164 *Ibid.* However, it should be noted that Michel Chevalier did not support the notion that the patent was a form of property right. He objected strongly to the text and the conceptual basis of both the 1791 and 1844 patent laws.

C Private Reform Proposals

It has been shown in Parts A and B of this Chapter that the concept of "natural" property rights in inventions provided an important theoretical basis for the French patent law of 1791, although this was not the sole justification which the drafter of the law, de Boufflers, or the French Government, advanced to support the patent system. Even after the reforms of 1844, there was strong evidence that the concept of "natural" property rights in inventions still endured, despite the changes in the terminology employed in the new law. Over this period, the official French Government position appeared to change from open support for the concept of "natural" property rights in inventions, to a situation where it was thought best that government should not directly endorse any one theoretical basis.

Although the official position is of primary significance, thus far, this Chapter has not discussed to any great extent the attitudes of private individuals towards this theoretical debate. Of relevance is the fact that ten years after the reforms of 1844, a number of private commentators in France and Belgium entered into a detailed theoretical debate over the nature of property rights in inventions. Although this debate had no apparent effect upon official policy relating to the French patent system, it is interesting because it demonstrated the strength of support for property rights in inventions "within natural limits". Many of the arguments used in these private debates of 1854–1856 were similar to those later raised in support of the patent system by delegates to the 1878 Paris Conference, which carried out preliminary work for the drafting of the Paris Convention.

The Nature of the Debate

Between 1854 and 1856, many articles in the French *Journal des économistes*[165] were preoccupied with a controversy concerning the nature of property rights in inventions. The essence of the debate related to the question of whether or not the property right in an invention should be considered the same as any form of property in tangible objects. If it was the same, then it should follow that the right in an invention should be a perpetual monopoly, capable of being dealt with in the same way as any other form of property. Proponents of this view developed the concept of the *Monautopole*. The alternative argument, however was that the invention was a right of property, but this right

165 This journal commenced in 1841, and was considered by the economic historians Machlup and Penrose to be the earliest and most significant "professional organ" for French economists during the nineteenth century. Machlup, F., and Penrose, E., *op.cit.* 23, note 86.

was not absolute. This argument accepted the valuable input of the individual inventor, but also accepted the fact that society contributed to the creation of the invention, and should also share some rights in the invention. This is why some argued that the patent right should be a limited monopoly.

Although this debate was largely carried on in the pages of a French journal (the *Journal des économistes*), its origins lay in Belgium. The concept of the *Monautopole* was first propounded in 1844 by the Belgian J-B. A-M. Jobard, a prodigious inventor, and long-serving Director of the Museum of Belgian Industry in Brussels.[166] At the time of Jobard's early writings, there was some debate about the concept of the *Monautopole*, but this was largely confined to Belgium.[167] However, in 1853 when the Belgian Government was considering a *Projet de Loi* to replace the patent law of 1817, the controversy surrounding Jobard's theories was rekindled, and eventually spread to France.

One of the main reasons why French commentators took such serious notice of Jobard's concept of the *Monautopole* was that at one stage in 1853 it appeared that the Belgian Parliament was going to adopt a new patent law which would incorporate Jobard's philosophy of unlimited property rights. Jobard reported that in early 1853 he had formulated a draft patent law consistent with his philosophy, and distributed the draft to all the members of the Belgian *Chambre* and *Sénat*.[168] Article 1 of this draft stated that "[l]a propriété des oeuvres de l'esprit, de l'art et de l'industrie est assimilée á la propriété ordinaire …,".[169] Although Jobard reported that the Belgian Parliament had originally been impressed by this draft,[170] it was not reproduced in the *Projet de Loi* which was presented to the *Sénat* on 29 March 1854 by M. Spitaels on behalf of the *Commissions de l'industrie, du Commerce et de l'Agriculture et de l'Intérieur réunies*.[171] Article 1 of the Belgian law adopted on 24 May 1854 stated that "[i]l sera accordé des droits exclusifs et temporaires, sous le nom de brevet

166 Jobard, J.-B., A.-M., *Nouvelle économie sociale ou monautopole industriel, artistique, commercial et littéraire* (Paris 1844).

167 For a brief history of this debate, see 'Discussion sur la Propriété des Inventions' (1862) XXXIV (2nd Series) *Journal des économistes* 72.

168 Jobard, J-B., A-M., 'Defense du Monautopole' (1854) 4 *Journal des économistes* 442.

169 *Ibid.* Translation: "Property in works of the mind, of art and of industry is assimilated to ordinary property, …".

170 *Ibid.*

171 The members of the Sénat composing this Commission were MM. De Pitteurs-Hiégaerts (President), D'Omalius, Grenier, Chevalier Bethune, Du Trieu de Terdonck, De Wouters de Bouchout, Berg and F. Spitaels. See further: UNITED KINGDOM, Parliamentary Papers, *Report from the Select Committee on Letters Patent; together with the Proceedings of the Committee, Minutes of Evidence, Appendix and Index* (1872) 193, vol XI, 395, 146.

d'invention, de perfectionnement ou d'importation, pour toute découverte ou tout perfectionnement susceptible d'être exploité comme object d'Industrie ou de Commerce."[172] As would be expected, the Belgian Parliament adopted patent legislation drafted more consistently with the model of the French law of 5 July 1844, rather than Jobard's concept of unlimited and absolute property rights.[173] Nevertheless, the prominence given to Jobard's theory of patent protection led to serious debate in France between 1854 and 1856.

(i) Jobard's Theory of the Monautopole

Although Jobard's theory of the *Monautopole* was first propounded in 1844,[174] it was not subject to serious consideration in France until 1854. By this time, Jobard had refined his views after considerable debate in Belgium with the philosophers Bastiat and Tielemans.[175] The essential features of Jobard's argument were presented in four articles which he published in the *Journal des économistes* in 1854–55.[176] Like de Boufflers, Jobard made no reference to the writings of earlier philosophers such as Locke or Turgot to support his theory, but he must have been influenced by them.[177]

---

172 Translation: "Exclusive and temporary rights shall be granted under the name of patents of invention, of improvement or of importation, for all discoveries or all improvements capable of being employed as articles of industry or of commerce." Translation derived from UNITED KINGDOM, Parliamentary Papers, *Reports by H.M. Secs of Embassy and Legation respecting Law and Practice in Foreign Countries with regard to Inventions* (1873) C. 741, vol LXVI, 483, 41.

173 The Commissioners' explanation of the *Projet* shows that the Belgian legislature viewed an inventor's right as a right which is of a limited nature, similar to the French position under the law of 5 July 1844. UNITED KINGDOM, Parliamentary Papers, *Report from the Select Committee on Letters Patent; together with the Proceedings of the Committee, Minutes of Evidence, Appendix and Index* (1872) 193, vol XI, 395, 146. For further brief historical details concerning Belgian patent legislation see Raux, R., "Adoption and Ratification by Belgium of the 1883 Paris Convention for the Protection of Industrial Property" (1984) *Industrial Property* 367–368.

174 Jobard, J.-B., A.-M., *Nouvelle économie sociale ou monautopole industriel, artistique, commercial et littéraire* (Paris 1844).

175 Jobard, J-B., A-M., 'Defense du Monautopole' (1854) 4 *Journal des économistes* 442–445.

176 Jobard, J-B., A-M., 'Defense du Monautopole' (1854) 4 *Journal des économistes* 442. Jobard, J-B., A-M., 'La Concurrence et Le Monautopole – Nouvelle Lettre de M. Jobard, en réponse a des Observations de M. Joseph Garnier' (1855) *Journal des économistes* 100. Jobard, J-B., A-M., 'La Concurrence et Le Monautopole – Nouvelle Lettre de M. Jobard, et réponse de M. Joseph Garnier' (1855) *Journal des économistes* 138. Garnier, J., 'Les Vingt Questions de M. Jobard sur la Concurrence suivies de vingt Réponses par M. Joseph Garnier' (1855) *Journal des économistes* 247.

177 See note 64 above.

The main point of Jobard's argument was that inventors were entitled to perpetual monopoly rights in relation to the application of their ideas.[178] He made it clear that the monopoly should be granted only in respect to the *application of the idea* rather than the idea itself.[179] He noted that critics of his theory pointed to the injustice of monopolising "*oeuvres de l'intelligence*",[180] but he stated that it was not his intention to allow appropriation of intelligence itself, or pure or metaphysical ideas.[181] However, once an idea had been converted into a tangible object, such as an invention, it should be considered to attract the same proprietary rights as any other tangible object.[182] Jobard stated "personne ne serait tombé dans ces subtilités différentielles entre la propriété territoriale, littéraire, artistique et industrielle."[183] If all rights of property were to be treated equally, it followed that they should all be perpetual, and capable of cession or transmission by inheritance.[184] However, although Jobard referred to all property rights as equal, he appeared to consider inventions as being particularly worthy of the benefits attached to a proprietary interest. He stated that a person has a natural property right in his creations, because those creations spring from the individual.[185] Presumably, the same argument could not be applied to support property rights in land or chattels. In justifying the argument that a patent should be a perpetual monopoly, Jobard referred also to the difficulties which arose where the monopoly was limited. He stated that it was impossible to measure, even approximately, how long an inventor would need to recoup a profit from his invention. Each case would vary. Only a perpetual patent would ensure that the inventor's just rights were respected.[186]

In relation to the concern that society should share with the inventor in the benefits of the invention, Jobard argued that this would lead to inefficient utilisation of the invention. This was largely because private ownership of property, whether of mines, land, railways or inventions, is always more efficient, and therefore better for society, than State ownership of such property.[187] If

---

178 Jobard, J-B., A-M., 'Defense du Monautopole' (1854) 4 *Journal des économistes* 442, 443.

179 *Ibid.*

180 For example, Frédéric Passy. *Ibid.*

181 *Ibid.*

182 *Ibid.*

183 Translation: "No-one should fall into tenuous differences between property which is landed, literary, artistic and industrial." *Ibid.*

184 *Ibid.*

185 Jobard, J-B., A-M., 'La Concurrence et Le Monautopole – Nouvelle Lettre de M. Jobard, en réponse a des Observations de M. Joseph Garnier' (1855) *Journal des économistes* 100, 105.

186 Jobard, J-B., A-M., 'Defense du Monautopole' (1854) 4 *Journal des économistes* 442, 446.

187 *Ibid.* 450.

an individual owns and is responsible for property, Jobard argued that there is more incentive to ensure the property is used most profitably.[188] He added that a perpetual monopoly more easily attracted investment funds, compared to a right which was only transitory.[189] Although perpetual property rights led to comparisons with the old schemes of inventor's privileges, Jobard rejected such arguments. He stated that the situation prevailing in the United Kingdom, where patent rights were granted in greater numbers than in France, showed that patents and industrial progress were inextricably intertwined.[190] He argued that in reality, there was no comparison between the economic effects of the old inventor's privileges and the patent system.[191]

Jobard's strong aversion to free trade was an important part of his concept of the *Monautopole*. He admitted that he had been an opponent of free trade for 25 years,[192] and added that "libre concurrence" was only another word for "laissez-faire".[193] He said that "laissez-faire" might result in something good and useful, but it could equally be bad and wasteful.[194] If manufacture of inventions was open to free competition, or even a restricted form of competition, society would suffer. Free competition would assist the wealthy and strong manufacturers, at the expense of the small inventor.[195] Furthermore, workers would receive greater benefits where a monopoly system was in operation. This was because where only one or two manufacturers make a particular product, there is less competition between manufacturers, leading to greater profits, part of which flows on to workers' salaries.[196] Jobard's final position was that even if France or Belgium did accept greater freedom of trade, this should not be incompatible with his theory of the *Monautopole*. International trade

188 *Ibid.* 446.

189 Garnier, J., 'Les Vingt Questions de M. Jobard sur la Concurrence suivies de vingt Réponses par M. Joseph Garnier' (1855) *Journal des économistes* 247, 251.

190 Jobard, J-B., A-M., 'Defense du Monautopole' (1854) 4 *Journal des économistes* 442, 445. De Molinari also noted that perpetual patents and inventor's privileges had a different basis. One important difference was that an inventor's privilege was only exercised "at the pleasure" of the monarch, so in theory it was revocable. De Molinari, G., 'De la Propriété des Inventions' (1855) *Journal des économistes* 410, 424.

191 *Ibid.*

192 Jobard, J-B., A-M., 'La Concurrence et Le Monautopole – Nouvelle Lettre de M. Jobard, en réponse a des Observations de M. Joseph Garnier' (1855) *Journal des économistes* 100, 104.

193 Jobard, J-B., A-M., 'Defense du Monautopole' (1854) 4 *Journal des économistes* 442, 448.

194 *Ibid.*

195 Garnier, J., 'Les Vingt Questions de M. Jobard sur la Concurrence suivies de vingt Réponses par M. Joseph Garnier' (1855) *Journal des économistes* 247, 248.

196 *Ibid.* 252.

in ordinary goods could increase, yet strong property rights in works of the intellect could still be secured by government.[197]

(ii) Responses of Other French and Belgian Commentators to Jobard's Concept of the Monautopole

(a) *Supporters of Jobard*

The main supporters of Jobard's theory of perpetual property rights in inventions during the debates of 1854–1856 were Alloury, who wrote in the *Journal des Débats*,[198] and G. de Molinari, who wrote in the *Journal des économistes*.[199] Alloury's view was that all works originating from the intellect should be granted perpetual property rights, including copyright in artistic works, and patents for inventions.[200] In support of his argument, he cited the Edict made by Turgot in 1776, (which purportedly abolished the *corporations*) in which it was stated that the freedom to work was one of the inherent rights of mankind.[201] Turgot added that the freedom to work was a form of individual property right, and that this form of property "est la premiére, la plus sacrée et la plus imprescriptible de toutes."[202] Alloury clearly believed that property in works of the intellect was one of those forms of individual right which fell within the meaning of Turgot's concept of sacred property, and was thus not amenable to the imposition of limitations upon its exercise.[203] Apart from theoretical justifications, Alloury also shared Jobard's conviction that the economic effects of the *Monautopole* would be beneficial to society. He also appeared to support Jobard's notion that perpetual patent rights would lead to more commercially-efficient uses of inventions.[204]

The most comprehensive argument in support of Jobard's theory of perpetual property rights in inventions was published in two articles written by G. de Molinari in September 1855 and January 1856.[205] De Molinari was a colleague

197 *Ibid.* 254.

198 See a critical evaluation of Alloury's writings in Passy, F., 'Lettre á M. Michel Chevalier sur deux articles parus dans le Journal des Débats touchant cette question' (1854) *Journal des économistes* 258.

199 De Molinari, G., 'De la Propriété des Inventions' (1855) *Journal des économistes* 410; De Molinari, G., 'La Propriété des Inventions' (1856) *Journal des économistes* 133.

200 Passy, F., 'Lettre á M. Michel Chevalier sur deux articles parus dans le Journal des Débats touchant cette question' (1854) *Journal des économistes* 258, 261.

201 For the text of the above Edict, see: Blanc, E., *op.cit.* v–vi.

202 Translation: "is the first, the most sacred, and the most imprescriptible of all." *Ibid.*

203 Passy, F., 'Lettre á M. Michel Chevalier sur deux articles parus dans le Journal des Débats touchant cette question' (1854) *Journal des économistes* 258, 261.

204 *Ibid.* 268–269.

205 De Molinari, G., 'De la Propriété des Inventions' (1855) *Journal des économistes* 410; De Molinari, G., 'La Propriété des Inventions' (1856) *Journal des économistes* 133.

of Jobard, being at the time of writing the articles a Professor at the Museum of Belgian Industry. His two articles are particularly interesting because, unlike Jobard, he critically analysed the concept of the *Monautopole*. His writing showed that he came to the question without strongly preconceived ideas, and he logically worked through all the arguments in support of and against perpetual patent rights.

De Molinari astutely noted that attitudes to property rights in patents were closely related to attitudes towards property rights generally.[206] Therefore, it was necessary to clarify how general property rights were perceived before turning to the specific issue of property in patents. He noted that in France and Belgium there were two distinct attitudes towards property rights. The first was that of the "économistes".[207] In general terms, most of these persons considered that property rights were founded upon issues of labour, and that the person who created something as a result of his work, was *naturally* entitled to make use of this for his own benefit.[208] This was an unlimited right to use and dispose of the result of labour, as long as the exercise of the right did not harm the rights of other members of the community.[209] Economic philosophers considered that society, as represented by government, was obliged to protect rights of property "dans ses limites naturelles",[210] and did not have the power to limit or restrain the exercise of such rights unless it was necessary to do so to prevent harm to others. They viewed property rights as the basis of the system of production and distribution of wealth, and considered that any unnecessary restraint upon free exercise of property rights would lead to economic harm.[211] The essence of their argument was that property rights were

206 De Molinari, G., 'De la Propriété des Inventions' (1855) *Journal des économistes* 410, 411.

207 References to economists during this period generally mean "economic philosophers" or persons with an interest in economic philosophy. However, economic historians make it clear that both terms can correctly be used. See for example: Fusfeld, D., *The Age of the Economist* (New York, William Morrow, 1968), viii–ix; Stigler, G., *Essays in the History of Economics* (Chicago, University of Chicago Press, 1965), 20, 156; Cannan, E., *A History of the Theories of Production and Distribution in English Political Economy from 1776 to 1848* (London, P.S. King and Sons, 1920), 379; Schumpeter, J., *History of Economic Analysis* (London, George Allen and Unwin, 1954), 476.

208 De Molinari, G., 'De la Propriété des Inventions' (1855) *Journal des économistes* 410, 411 (emphasis added).

209 *Ibid.*

210 Translation: "within their natural limits". *Ibid.*

211 *Ibid.*

not created by the law; the law merely recognised and regulated the exercise of a pre-existing natural right.[212]

According to de Molinari, a different view of property was displayed by persons he described as lawyers, socialists and communists.[213] Such groups did not consider that property was a "fruit légitime du travail; elle est le résultat d'une usurpation ou d'un vol".[214] They presumed that society was naturally invested with all material and immaterial things which were placed for the benefit of mankind, and that exclusive appropriation of such things has no justification.[215] However, society tolerated some degree of private usurpation of property, within certain limits. This was because in some situations, private exercise of property rights could be more efficient than common use. However, the rights of society were always superior to the rights of the individual, and society must always retain the option to cancel private exercise of the right.[216] The essence of their argument was that property rights were created by the law, and were not natural property rights of the individual.[217] De Molinari noted that it could be said that the French Patent Law of 5 July 1844 was motivated by socialist concerns, because the grant of property in a patented invention was made subject to artificial limitations.[218]

De Molinari's account of the opposing ideology of economic philosophers and lawyers/socialists/communists, was superficially accurate. French economic philosophers in 1855–1856 appeared to support the notion of natural property rights in patented inventions, but argued for a limitation of such rights.[219] This was the case, even though such persons also clearly supported free trade.[220] However, the attitude of the lawyers/socialists/communists group was not so clearly defined. Jobard asserted that French economic philosophers such as Joseph Garnier believed he was a socialist or communist,

212 De Molinari, G., 'La Propriété des Inventions' (1856) *Journal des économistes* 133, 136. This was a line of argument clearly influenced by the writings of John Locke. See note 64 above.

213 De Molinari, G., 'De la Propriété des Inventions' (1855) *Journal des économistes* 410, 411. See Appendix 1 – A Note on the Meaning of the Terms "Socialist" and "Communist" in the 1840s and 1850s.

214 Translation: "the legitimate fruit of labour; it is the result of a usurpation or a theft". *Ibid.* 413.

215 *Ibid.*

216 *Ibid.*

217 De Molinari, G., 'La Propriété des Inventions' (1856) *Journal des économistes* 133, 136.

218 *Ibid.*

219 See the arguments of Passy and Garnier, discussed below.

220 De Molinari, G., 'La Propriété des Inventions' (1856) *Journal des économistes* 133, 136.

merely because of his opposition to free trade.[221] However, despite his aversion to free trade, Jobard was not a socialist or communist, because his theories clearly supported natural rights in property, and elevated individual rights above those of the general community. Thus, Jobard did not fit within either of de Molinari's two groups, which displays the shortcomings of de Molinari's thesis about clearly-defined attitudes to property rights.

After having detailed the prevailing views concerning property rights generally, de Molinari turned to examine the issue of property in inventions. He identified four alternative ways that inventors' rights could be regulated.[222] The first was the communist system, where the inventor would have no right of property in the invention, as well as no right of recompense for divulging it to society. The second was the system of State rewards for inventions, where the inventor would be given some recompense for divulging the invention, but would not retain any property rights in it. The third involved the grant of a temporary property right to the inventor, in the form of a limited monopoly. The fourth was that of the perpetual property right, or *Monautopole*, as advocated by Jobard.[223]

De Molinari's view was that the most equitable approach began by assuming that inventors should have the same property rights in their inventions as owners of tangible property. This assumption should only be displaced if there was a valid reason why inventors should be treated differently from owners of tangible property.[224] He argued that the creation of an invention involved hard work, knowledge, and the injection of capital.[225] This was no different from what was required for any successful business. However, a controversial question arose regarding the contribution of society to the work of an inventor. Some of the opponents of perpetual property rights in patents had argued[226] that a person who produced a tangible object, such as constructing a house, or farming the land, had no special obligation to society because the tangible object produced was the result of his own hard work. By contrast, the inventor used the common stock of knowledge of society upon which to base the

---

221 Jobard, J-B., A-M., 'La Concurrence et Le Monautopole – Nouvelle Lettre de M. Jobard, en réponse a des Observations de M. Joseph Garnier' (1855) *Journal des économistes* 100, 101.

222 De Molinari, G., 'De la Propriété des Inventions' (1855) *Journal des économistes* 410, 429–430.

223 *Ibid.*

224 *Ibid.* 414.

225 *Ibid.*

226 For example, Passy, F., 'Lettre á M. Michel Chevalier sur deux articles parus dans le Journal des Débats touchant cette question' (1854) *Journal des économistes* 258.

invention, and thus owed an obligation to society as joint collaborator.[227] De Molinari believed that this distinction between the inventor and, for example, the householder or farmer, could not be supported. It was wrong to say that the householder or farmer owed nothing to society. Such persons benefited by the use of public amenities such as roads, in the same way the inventor benefited from the use of public knowledge.[228]

De Molinari was also concerned with the question of whether a perpetual patent monopoly would lead to economic disadvantages associated with anti-competitive behaviour. In particular, he referred to the allegation that the remuneration which could be obtained from exploitation of the invention could be far more than warranted by the amount of labour and capital invested.[229] Should the patent be of a limited duration, in order to minimise the possibility of such unwarranted windfalls? In this regard, reference was often made in France to the large fortunes made by U.K. inventors such as Watt, Arkwright, Fulton and Wheatstone.[230] However, de Molinari argued that an invention's success was also largely related to risk, and that these inventors had been at great risk in commercialising their inventions. He was also convinced that those few inventors who had made a huge profit from their inventions had made an equally large contribution to the development of society.[231]

The cornerstone of de Molinari's theory about protection for inventions was that a property right should be granted within the "limites naturelles" of an invention.[232] He recognised that inventions are superseded and are not exploited indefinitely.[233] While most patents lose their value by the time the patent expires, some have not reached their full potential by that date. Due to the difficulty of determining a defined period of protection which would be sufficient for all patented inventions, de Molinari again favoured the concept of the *Monautopole*.[234] He considered that the protection available to an invention should theoretically be of indefinite duration, subject only to the payment of fees for maintaining the patent.[235] He added that in practical terms, very

227 De Molinari, G., 'De la Propriété des Inventions' (1855) *Journal des économistes* 410, 417–418.

228 *Ibid.*

229 *Ibid.* 420–422.

230 *Ibid.*

231 *Ibid.* 422.

232 De Molinari, G., 'De la Propriété des Inventions' (1855) *Journal des économistes* 410, 425; De Molinari, G., 'La Propriété des Inventions' (1856) *Journal des économistes* 133.

233 *Ibid.*

234 De Molinari, G., 'La Propriété des Inventions' (1856) *Journal des économistes* 133, 134.

235 *Ibid.*

few patentees would see any commercial return in paying fees to maintain their patent for a longer period than the current term of patent protection.[236] However, the patentee, rather than the State, was in the best position to determine the most suitable duration of protection for each invention.[237] This was the final, and most important reason, why de Molinari considered that property rights in patented inventions should be treated the same as property rights in tangible objects.

(b) *Opponents of Jobard's Theories*

The two most vocal critics of Jobard's theory of the *Monautopole* were the economic philosophers, Joseph Garnier[238] and Frédéric Passy.[239] Garnier was the editor-in-chief of the *Journal des économistes* and a strong supporter of free trade, who considered Jobard's theories to be ill-founded. The main focus of his opposition to Jobard was in regard to the issue of free trade.[240] Although Garnier published several articles attacking Jobard's concept of the *Monautopole*, they were very simplistic and used Jobard's support for protection as a justification for ridiculing all his opinions. Jobard's lack of support for free trade was not a valid reason for Garnier's allegation that all his work was valueless. Garnier refused to publish in full letters Jobard wrote to the *Journal des économistes* trying to defend his theories.[241] This demonstrated that Garnier allowed prejudice to get in the way of sound critical thinking. However, Garnier did not deny the need for limited property rights in inventions, and he supported the patent system. His only real point of difference with Jobard or de Molinari was that

236 However, de Molinari overlooked the difficulties which can arise when a patent is used to block competition.

237 De Molinari, G., 'La Propriété des Inventions' (1856) *Journal des économistes* 133, 134.

238 Garnier, J., 'Les Vingt Questions de M. Jobard sur la Concurrence suivies de vingt Réponses par M. Joseph Garnier' (1855) *Journal des économistes* 247; Garnier, J., 'La Concurrence et Le Monautopole – Nouvelle Lettre de M. Jobard, et réponse de M. Joseph Garnier' (1855) *Journal des économistes* 138.

239 Passy, F., 'Lettre á M. Michel Chevalier sur deux articles parus dans le Journal des Débats touchant cette question' (1854) *Journal des économistes* 258; Passy, F., 'Lettre de M. Frédéric Passy, au sujet de la Défense du Monautopole' (1855) *Journal des économistes* 105; Passy, F., 'Question de la Propriété des Inventions' (1855) *Journal des économistes* 262. Jobard notes that there were other critics, such as Renouard, Coquelin, Tielemans and Odilon-Barrot, but Passy and Garnier represented particularly strident French opposition to his theory. Garnier, J., 'La Concurrence et Le Monautopole – Nouvelle Lettre de M. Jobard, et réponse de M. Joseph Garnier' (1855) *Journal des économistes* 138, 140.

240 Garnier, J., 'Les Vingt Questions de M. Jobard sur la Concurrence suivies de vingt Réponses par M. Joseph Garnier' (1855) *Journal des économistes* 247.

241 Garnier, J., 'La Concurrence et Le Monautopole – Nouvelle Lettre de M. Jobard, et réponse de M. Joseph Garnier' (1855) *Journal des économistes* 138, 139.

he did not believe that there should be perpetual property rights, as this conflicted with the goals of free trade.[242] In fact, his attitude to patents was that of the typical French economic philosopher as described by de Molinari.[243]

Frédéric Passy, an economic philosopher based in the French town of Ezy,[244] provided the most comprehensive attack upon Jobard's theory of the *Monautopole.* Although in his writings, Passy agreed with Jobard that property rights in artistic works should not be limited, he was unwilling to accept the concept of the *Monautopole* as it applied to property rights in inventions.[245] There were a number of reasons for this view. The first was that society and the inventor were joint collaborators in the invention, and it was clear to Passy that if the route to the invention was not taken by one person, it would eventually be taken by another.[246] Secondly, he believed that immaterial and abstract creations derived from ideas should not be the subject of exclusive use in any event.[247] In his view, there was a great difference between a monopoly over the use of an object and a monopoly over the application of that object in certain ways.[248]

Passy also addressed the economic implications of perpetual patent rights. He considered that society's right to take free advantage of an invention should only be prevented for as long as necessary to reward the inventor for his labour.[249] Not only did a temporary monopoly provide an opportunity to achieve this reward, but it also granted an inventor a head-start over his competitors.[250] Although Passy agreed that temporary monopolies did not always ensure that inventors achieved a reward proportionate to the merit of the invention, it was the best system available, and certainly preferable to the anti-competitive effects of the *Monautopole.*[251] Such effects would include

---

242 *Ibid.*

243 Molinari, G., 'La Propriété des Inventions' (1856) *Journal des économistes* 133, 136.

244 In 1901 he shared the Nobel Prize for Peace. He was a founding member of the International Peace League.

245 Passy, F., 'Lettre á M. Michel Chevalier sur deux articles parus dans le Journal des Débats touchant cette question' (1854) *Journal des économistes* 258, 261.

246 *Ibid.* 262.

247 *Ibid.* 264.

248 Passy, F., 'Question de la Propriété des Inventions' (1855) *Journal des* économistes 262, 265. Passy disagreed with de Molinari's analysis of the exclusive rights of the inventor in comparison to the home-owner or farmer. He stated that an inventor may harness and claim monopoly over the forces of nature in his invention, whereas a farmer never attempts to monopolise nature. *Ibid.* 264.

249 Passy, F., 'Lettre á M. Michel Chevalier sur deux articles parus dans le Journal des Débats touchant cette question' (1854) *Journal des économistes* 258, 265.

250 *Ibid.* 266.

251 *Ibid.* 266.

the self-interested inventor charging higher prices for his invention, and possibly even the re-establishment of the old *corporations*.[252] Passy feared that if strong associations of patentees were established, this would be similar to the old *corporations*, and the government could be forced to expropriate patent rights in order to combat them.[253] He considered that only freedom of competition led to constant development, and that a perpetual patent would retard this process.[254] Like Garnier, Passy did not deny the need for limited property rights in inventions.[255] He also agreed with his opponent, de Molinari, that a property right should be granted within the "limites naturelles" of the invention.[256] However, he differed from de Molinari in viewing a perpetual patent as extending beyond the natural limits of a property right, considering that a perpetual patent was an artificial extension of a right, which amounted to an unjust usurpation.[257]

The debate over the *Monautopole* in the French economic journals ended in 1856.[258] Neither supporters nor opponents of Jobard's theory clearly won the debate. However, what was important was the general consensus amongst French and Belgian commentators about the existence of property rights in inventions "within natural limits". Although there was disagreement as to what was meant by that phrase, the debate clearly demonstrated that the notion of "natural" property rights in patents had gained considerable strength in France since the patent law reforms of 1844. While this debate had no immediate, obvious influence upon the course of patent law reform in France, the ideas remained relevant and were further refined over the course of the next three decades. Ultimately, the legacy of this debate could be seen at the 1878 Paris Conference on industrial property rights, where a majority of the delegates endorsed the notion of "natural" property rights in inventions.[259]

---

252 *Ibid.* 270–273.

253 *Ibid.*

254 *Ibid.* 271.

255 Passy, F., 'Lettre de M. Frédéric Passy, au sujet de la Défense du Monautopole' (1855) *Journal des économistes* 105, 109.

256 Passy, F., 'Question de la Propriété des Inventions' (1855) *Journal des économistes* 262, 264.

257 *Ibid.*

258 However, it resurfaced again in Belgium in 1860–1861. For a brief discussion of this debate in the *Economiste belge* see Le Hardy De Beaulieu, C., 'Discussion sur la Propriété des Inventions' (1862) XXXIV (2nd Series) *Journal des économistes* 72, 78.

259 See Chapter Six for further discussion of this point.

D The International Significance of the French Patent Law of 1791

The development of the theoretical basis of patent protection in France under the laws of 1791 and 1844 was obviously a matter of great significance to French inventors and French society. Indeed, the Patent Law of 1791 was drafted with special care to ensure its conformity with the French revolutionary notions of freedom and equality. However, the influence of the French patent legislation was not confined within the borders of French territory. After 1791, many of the features of the French patent law were taken to other countries and incorporated into their patent systems. Thus, not only was the French patent system important because it was the first to enshrine the notion of "natural" property rights in inventions, but it was also significant because of its wider international role as a model for other countries to follow when establishing their own patent systems.

Evidence suggests that the French Patent Law of 7 January 1791 was the dominant model of a patent system at least until 1820. One reason for this was that during the early years of the nineteenth century, much of Western Europe was under French domination. The French patent legislation of 1791 was taken by the French armies to the Netherlands (which included Luxembourg and Belgium until 1830),[260] the Italian States, and the Rhenish Provinces (later Prussia).[261] After 1814, when these provinces won their freedom from France, many chose to retain the French patent system, including the concept of the invention as a "natural" property right. For example, on 25 January 1817, the Netherlands introduced a patent law which closely followed the French legislation of 1791, and which remained in force until the abolition of the Dutch patent system in 1869.[262] Various Italian States also followed the French example of 1791 when introducing patent legislation after 1814.[263] However, some

260 Belgium was under French rule from 1794 to 1814, and under Dutch rule from 1814 to 1830. Craeybeckx, J., "The Beginnings of the Industrial Revolution in Belgium" in Cameron R., (ed) *Essays in French Economic History* (Homewood, Richard D. Irwin, 1970), 187, 189.

261 "Coup d'Oeil rétrospectif sur la propriété industrielle" (1885) 1 *La Propriété Industrielle* 9; Plasseraud, Y., and Savignon, F., *Paris 1883: Genése du droit Unioniste des Brevets* (Paris, Litec, 1983), 50.

262 For the text of the Law of 25 January 1817 see: UNITED KINGDOM, Parliamentary Papers, *Report from the Select Committee on the Law Relative to Patents for Inventions* (1829) 332, vol III, 415, Appendix E. See also UNITED KINGDOM, Parliamentary Papers, *Reports by H.M. Secs of Embassy and Legation respecting Law and Practice in Foreign Countries with regard to Inventions* (1873) C. 741, vol LXVI, 483; Bos, J.J., "The Netherlands and the Paris Convention for the Protection of Industrial Property" (1984) *Industrial Property* 383.

263 See, for example, the Duchy of Parma and Piacenza, which continued to apply the French law of 1791. Boros, R., "Italy and the Establishment of the Paris Union for the Protection of Industrial Property" (1984) *Industrial Property* 379.

former French provinces consciously chose not to follow the French law of 1791 when they introduced their own patent systems. For example, the Prussian Laws of 14 October 1815 and 17 May 1817, which established a system of stringent examination of patent applications, were said to have been motivated by a reaction against French philosophies.[264] Lombardy, which became part of the Austrian Hapsburg Empire in 1815, was forced to accept the Austrian concept of the patent as an exclusive privilege, rather than a property right.[265] Other countries, including those outside the former French Empire, which borrowed heavily upon the French Law of 7 January 1791 when establishing their own patent systems were Russia (the Law of 17 June 1812), Spain (the Decrees of 2 October 1820 and 27 March 1826), Portugal (the Decrees of 16 January 1837 and 17 March 1868),[266] Paraguay (the Law of 20 May 1845) and Brazil (the Decrees of 28 January 1809 and 28 August 1830).[267] These laws all followed the French law of 7 January 1791 in clearly referring to the inventor's right as a form of property, and adopted many practical operating features of the French patent system. It can thus be seen that the French patent legislation, particularly the law of 1791, had a strong extra-territorial influence.

Ultimately, the French Patent Law of 1791 effected several important changes. The first was the rejection of the politically unpopular scheme of inventor's privileges and its substitution with a patent system. The second was the introduction of the concept of "natural" property rights in inventions,

---

264 Milhaud, L., *Des Brevets d'invention dans les Rapports Internationaux* (Paris, Larose et Forcel, 1892), 5.

265 On 8 December 1820, the Austrian Emperor decreed a new law for the whole Empire concerning industrial privileges. It was intended to encourage invention and its theoretical basis was that a privilege was an exclusive right. All applications were examined for general patentability (such as whether the invention was "hurtful or contrary to the law"), but there was no detailed consideration of questions of novelty. Text reproduced from UNITED KINGDOM, Parliamentary Papers, *Report from the Select Committee on the Law Relative to Patents for Inventions* (1829) 332, vol III, 415, Appendix F.

266 See a discussion of the development of Portuguese industrial property legislation in Mota Maia, J., "Development of Portuguese Industrial Property Legislation in the Light of Portugal's Ratification of the Paris Convention" (1984) *Industrial Property* 386.

267 One commentator has said that the early Brazilian patent legislation was based upon a mixture of the Laws of France of 1791, Russia of 1812 and the Netherlands of 1817, thereby emphasizing the French influence on the development of this legislation. See UNITED KINGDOM, Parliamentary Papers, *Reports by H.M. Secs of Embassy and Legation respecting Law and Practice in Foreign Countries with regard to Inventions* (1873) C. 741, vol LXVI, 483 (Report from Mr Phipps at the British Embassy in Rio de Janeiro, Brazil). A later Brazilian commentator has also acknowledged the influence of the English *Statute of Monopolies* of 1623. See Bandeira, A.C., "Brazil's Ratification of the Paris Convention of 1883" (1984) *Industrial Property* 371.

and the notion that the patent system merely guaranteed legal protection for a pre-existing right. Although de Boufflers, the drafter of the 1791 legislation, provided many additional justifications for the new patent system, there is no doubt that the most enduring conceptual legacy of this law was the notion of "natural" property rights in inventions. Although the reforms of 1844 removed any direct reference to this concept, there is no real doubt that the ideology of the French patent law remained largely unchanged even after these reforms. The debate over the issue of the *Monautopole* demonstrates that most French and Belgian commentators continued to support "natural" property rights in inventions after 1844. Thus, by the mid-nineteenth century, the French patent system had a relatively firm theoretical basis, and, in addition, it had been used as a model by many countries seeking to establish their own patent systems. France's early and significant role in the evolution of theoretical debate about the patent system foreshadowed its later prominence in the development of the 1883 Paris Convention.

CHAPTER 2

UNITED KINGDOM: Development of Ideas and Concepts about the Theoretical Basis of the Patent System: 1790–1852

> Is it not the very ground upon which a patent is granted, an exchange of benefits between the public and the inventor, by which a monopoly is given to him for a certain number of years, in return for the advantage which the public derive from knowing the nature of the invention? – Yes;[1]
>
> THOMAS BARRETT LENNARD, Chairman of the 1829 Select Committee on the Law Relative to Patents for Inventions, in a question to Charles Few, a witness before the Committee

Chapter One has explained how in France, when a new patent system was proposed in 1790, considerable discussion ensued about its theoretical basis. This question was raised again in 1798, at the time of the reforms of 1844, and in the mid-1850s it was the subject of detailed debate amongst French and Belgian commentators. The conclusion must therefore be reached that in France, understanding and discussing the theoretical basis of the patent system was as important as practical measures of law reform.

This Chapter explains that it was only from around 1851, when U.K. commentators and the U.K. Government began to display the same level of interest as the French in the theoretical basis of the patent system. Prior to 1851, there was considerable debate in the United Kingdom about the patent system, but the major concerns related to practical rather than theoretical matters. Theoretical discussion progressed little further than a general acceptance of the concept of patents for inventions as being of continuing importance to

1 UNITED KINGDOM, Parliamentary Papers, *Report from the Select Committee on the Law Relative to Patents for Inventions* (1829) 332, vol III, 415, 80.

 | DOI:10.1163/9789004470125_004

industrial development. Occasionally there was confirmation of the old theories that a contract formed the basis of the patent grant.

This Chapter focuses upon the records of evidence of the two Select Committees which were appointed in 1829 and 1851 to consider the question of patent law reform.[2] The evidence of witnesses before these Committees provides the most comprehensive record of what people with expertise in the patent system actually thought about it. In analysing this evidence, particular attention is paid to two topics of particular relevance. These relate to: (1) comments about the underlying objectives of the patent system, and (2) comments about "foreign" issues, such as the rights of foreigners to obtain patents in the United Kingdom. It is also important to note that by the late 1840s, a connection was emerging between international trade developments and U.K. patent law reform. The Great Exhibition in London of 1851 acted as a catalyst for U.K. patent law reform and may have been the point at which international protection for inventions was first considered.

A The Theoretical Basis of the U.K. Patent System: Brief Overview of Opinions before 1829

Although the earliest comprehensive examination of the U.K. patent system took place at the time of the Select Committee Inquiry of 1829, it is necessary to begin by referring to some of the theoretical discussions about the patent system which occurred before that date. It is also appropriate to refer briefly to the patent law reform movements which existed before 1829.

By 1790, the operational features of the U.K. patent system were well established. There had been no major legislative enactments affecting the patent law since the *Statute of Monopolies* of 1623. As Gomme notes, the procedure for

2 UNITED KINGDOM, Parliamentary Papers, *Report from the Select Committee on the Law Relative to Patents for Inventions* (1829) 332, vol III, 415, 80. UNITED KINGDOM, Parliamentary Papers, *Report and Minutes of Evidence taken before the Select Committee of the House of Lords appointed to consider of The Bill, intituled, "An Act further to amend the Law touching Letters Patent for Invention" and also of The Bill intituled "An Act for the further amendment of the Law touching Letters Patent for Invention" and to report thereon to the House: Session 1851* (1851) 486 vol XVIII, 233. For a detailed modern discussion of the British patent laws during the period 1700 to 1852 and the forces which shaped the evolution of these laws see Bottomley, S., *The British Patent System during the Industrial Revolution 1700 to 1852* (Cambridge, Cambridge University Press, 2014). See also generally Cornish, W., et al, *The Oxford History of the Laws of England Volume XI: 1820–1914 English Legal System* (Oxford, Oxford University Press, 2010), 931–976.

obtaining a patent was substantially the same as it had been for all grants since Henry Smyth was granted a patent for making Normandy glass in 1552.[3] The procedure was being still governed by an old Statute, "by a few orders of the Privy Council of the same period, and by various decisions of the Law Officers, and it was so cumbrous and costly, entailing independent visits to five or six separate offices", that it was surprising that the system was used at all.[4]

At a policy level, the legacies of the *Statute of Monopolies* of 1623 were the abolition of odious privileges,[5] and the introduction of the notion that the patent represented a contract between the inventor and the State.[6] Writing shortly after the passage of the *Statute of Monopolies*, Sir Edward Coke said the justification for the patent grant was:

> because the inventor bringeth to and for the Commonwealth a new manufacture by his invention, cost and charges, and therefore is reason, that he should have a privilege for his reward (and the encouragement of others the like) for a convenient time.[7]

As a result of the case of *Liardet v Johnson* in 1778,[8] it was established that a central part of this contract was the inventor's obligation to publicly disclose in the specification the description of the invention, in order that the public should have the opportunity to work the invention after the patent monopoly expired.[9] This and subsequent cases such as *Arkwright v*

3 Gomme, A.A., *Patents of Invention: Origin and Growth of the Patent System in Britain* (London, Longmans Green and Co, 1946), 13–16.

4 *Ibid.* 16.

5 See descriptions of these "odious" monopolies in "The Fallacy of Protection", *The Economist,* 16 September 1843, 34; Rose, J.A., "The principles and Policy of a Law of Patents" (1867) 11 *The Solicitors' Journal and Reporter* 159, 160 (Part One), 178 (Part Two).

6 See "On Reform in the Law of Patents" (1870) 28 *The Law Magazine and Review* 83, 88 where it is stated that the *Statute of Monopolies* brought about this change in philosophy.

7 Coke, E., *Institutes of the Laws of England* (1628–44) 3d part, c.85. See further Boehm, K., and Silberston, A., *The British Patent System: 1. Administration* (Cambridge, Cambridge University Press, 1967), 17.

8 Reported in Buller's Nisi Prius, p76, and (1778) 1 *Webster's Patent Cases* 53. Lord Mansfield set aside the patent, stating that "the law requires, as the price the patentee should pay to the public for his monopoly, that he should, to the very best of his knowledge, give the fullest and most sufficient description of all the particulars on which the effect depends."

9 Note the controversial view of Adams and Averley that enrolment of specifications was actually a requirement in England from 1711, and that the "function of the specification had always been the dissemination to the public of information about the invention." They state that from the outset, failure to enrol, or failure to enrol an adequate specification, would have been liable to render the patent void if challenged. However, there was

Mordaunt,[10] *The King v Arkwright*,[11] *Huddart v Grimshaw*,[12] *Harmer v Playne*,[13] *Bovill v Moore*,[14] and *The King v Wheeler*,[15] illustrated the emerging view of the judiciary that a contract or bargain between the inventor and the State formed the basis of patent protection. The inventor's part of the bargain was the instruction to the public evidenced in the Specification. As a reviewer of Vesey's *Reports of Cases argued and decided in the High Court of Chancery* stated in 1823, there was a strong line of cases which made clear the simple proposition that a "patentee is regarded as a contractor with the public, bound to certain terms."[16]

Although the judicial decisions show that the contract theory was the most commonly considered justification for the U.K. patent system in the years before 1829, it was not the only theory propounded. There was also some support for the view that patents were justified because they gave inventors a monopoly period of limited duration, during which the inventors had an opportunity to achieve sufficient reward for their efforts. This was the "reward by monopoly thesis".[17] Before 1829, this view was most commonly advanced by political economists such as Adam Smith,[18] and Jeremy Bentham.[19] Although U.K. political economists generally were hostile to monopolies, they made an exception for patents because they considered patents the best way to encourage invention, and thus advance industrial development. Bentham, for example, wrote that a "man will not be at the expense and trouble of bringing to maturity … invention unless he has a prospect of an adequate satisfaction."[20]

no history of successful challenges to patents on these grounds before *Liardet v Johnson*. Adams, J., and Averley, G., "The Patent Specification: The Role of Liardet v Johnson" (1986) 7 *Journal of Legal History* 156, 158–160. See also Hulme, E.W., "On the History of Patent Law in the Seventeenth and Eighteenth Centuries" (1902) 18 *Law Quarterly Review* 280.

10 (1781) *Webster's Patent Cases* 59.

11 (1785) *Davies Patent Cases* 37.

12 (1803) *Webster's Patent Cases* 230.

13 (1809) *Davies Patent Cases* 311.

14 (1816) *Davies Patent Cases* 361.

15 (1819) 1 *Carpmael's Reports* 108.

16 "Reports of Cases argued and decided in the High Court of Chancery. By F. Vesey, junior." (1823) 38 *The Edinburgh Review* 281, 289.

17 Dutton, H.I., *The Patent System and inventive activity during the industrial revolution 1750–1852* (Manchester, Manchester University Press, 1984), 18. Machlup, F., and Penrose, E., "The Patent Controversy in the Nineteenth Century" (1950) x *The Journal of Economic History* 1, 17–21.

18 Smith, A., *An Inquiry into the Nature and Causes of the Wealth of Nations* (Edinburgh 1814) vol III, 151 (first published in 1776).

19 Bentham, J., *The Rationale of Reward* (London, John and HL Hunt, 1825), 91.

20 *Ibid.*

However, there is no evidence that the U.K. Government laid emphasis on the suitability of the patent as a means of ensuring adequate reward for the results of invention. In fact, from as early as 1713, the Government showed that it did not consider that the patent system provided adequate reward for certain classes of important inventions. Between 1713 and 1813, a number of Acts were passed by Parliament to provide sums of money to certain inventors. This shows that the Government considered it necessary to go outside the patent system in order to ensure adequate reward for important inventions.

An early example of such legislative encouragement was the offer in 1713 of a public "Reward for such person or persons as shall discover methods of finding the Longitude at Sea."[21] Fourteen Acts of Parliament on the same subject were passed between 1713 and 1777,[22] and many of these related to improvements in navigation.[23] In addition, Acts were passed:

(1) In 1732 to provide 14,000 pounds to Sir Thomas Lombe for discovering and introducing the arts of making and working certain Italian machines relating to the silk trade.[24]

(2) In 1739 to provide 5,000 pounds to Johanna Stephens for her medicine for curing stones.[25]

(3) In 1813 to provide 50,000 pounds to John Palmer in relation to his plan for conveyance of mails.[26]

Parliament also granted a number of rewards to inventors without passing specific Acts. Five such rewards were granted before 1788, totalling 17,500 pounds, and another 12 such grants were made between 1788 and 1813, totalling 77,463 pounds.[27]

---

21 12 A. stat.2, c.15.

22 The more important being: Act of 1753 – 26 Geo. II, c.25; Act of 1761 – 2 Geo. III, c.18; Act of 1762 – 2 Geo. III, c.14; Act of 1765 – 5 Geo. III, c.20; Act of 1770 – 10 Geo. III, c.34; Act of 1773 – 13 Geo. III, c.77; Act of 1774 – 14 Geo. III, c.66; Act of 1777 – 17 Geo. III, c.48. A number of inventors benefited under these Acts, most particularly John Harrison, who received more than 20,000 pounds for his inventions of time-keepers and watches. UNITED KINGDOM, Parliamentary Papers, *Report from the Select Committee on the Law Relative to Patents for Inventions* (1829) 332, vol III, 415, Appendix A.

23 *Ibid.*

24 5 Geo. III, c.8.

25 12 Geo. III, c.23.

26 53 Geo III, c. 157.

27 UNITED KINGDOM, Parliamentary Papers, *Report from the Select Committee on the Law Relative to Patents for Inventions* (1829) 332, vol III, 415, Appendix A, 181. The rewards granted between 1788 and 1813 were as follows: (1) 1,000 pounds to Mr Elkinston for his method of draining land. (2) 1,000 pounds to John Davis for his method of cleaning smutty wheat (granted in 1800). (3) 800 pounds to be distributed by the Board of Agriculture for Essays on the subject of breaking up grass lands (granted in 1801). (4) 500

Apart from the Government, rewards for invention were also provided by private bodies such as the Royal Society, founded in 1662,[28] and the Society of Arts, founded in 1754.[29] Of the two Societies, the Society of Arts was clearest in making known its attitude that the patent system was not a suitable method of rewarding invention. The sole original object of the Society of Arts was:

> to promote art, industry, commerce and invention, by granting rewards and premiums for meritorious discoveries and inventions, for success in the various branches of the fine arts, for increasing the economic resources of the kingdom by the import of new or little known materials of industry, or for developing those resources by novel or improved methods.[30]

The founders of the Society of Arts considered that a patent was a bribe, rather than a reward, that patents were an injurious restriction on industry, only to be

---

pounds to Thomas Foden for his research into a substitute paste for wheat flour (granted in 1801). (5) 30,000 pounds to Dr Jenner, for his discoveries relating to vaccine inoculation (granted in 1802 and 1807). (6) 10,000 pounds to Dr Edmund Cartwright, for various mechanical inventions (granted in 1809). (7) 3,250 pounds to Captain Manby, for his device to communicate with stranded ships, and for saving the lives of ship-wrecked mariners (granted in 1810 and 1812). (8) 1,850 pounds to Mr Greathead, for his invention of a life-boat. (9) 5,000 pounds to Mr Crompton, for inventing the cotton Mule. (10) 5,258 pounds to Dr Smyth, for his discovery of nitric fumigation, to prevent communication of contagion (granted in 1813). (11) 1,305 pounds in miscellaneous rewards.

28 Christine MacLeod notes that there is evidence dating to 1673 that one of the Royal Society's aims was to encourage invention by granting appropriate rewards. Macleod, C., *Inventing the Industrial Revolution: The English Patent System, 1600–1800* (Cambridge, Cambridge University Press, 1988), 187. See also an earlier critical analysis of the work of the Royal Society in Babbage, C., *The Exposition of 1851; or, Views of the Industry, the Science, and the Government of England* (London, John Murray, 1851), Chapter XII, 149–173.

29 The Society of Arts was sometimes also known by its fuller name, *The Society for the Encouragement of Arts, Manufactures, and Commerce.* See for further details of this organisation: Wood, H., *A History of the Royal Society of Arts* (London, John Murray, 1913). Wood states that the name "Society of Arts" was first recorded as being used in the *Gentleman's Magazine* in July 1755, and it was also known as the "Society of Arts and Sciences" and "The Premium Society". The earliest known official use of the short title, "Society of Arts" was recorded in the minutes of February 1811, but the full title was still also being used in official documentation, such as the Charter of 1847. In 1908, King Edward VII granted the Society permission to add the word "Royal" to the title. *Ibid.* 17–18.

30 *Ibid.* 235. The classes under which the awards were arranged varied from time to time, but eventually they were distributed among 6 committees: (1) Polite arts, (2) Agriculture, (3) Manufactures, (4) Mechanics, (5) Chemistry, (6) Colonies and trade. The first premium list issued was in 1756. *Ibid.* 236–238.

condoned if the public could not get the benefit of a useful invention unless it bribed the inventor with a monopoly.[31] This view was expressed as early as 1765, where it was laid down in the Rules and Orders of the Society that:

> No person will be admitted a candidate for any premium offered by the Society who has obtained a patent for the exclusive right of making or performing anything for which such premium is offered.[32]

The Society expressed its opposition to the patent as a suitable means of rewarding inventors until 1845, when the Rule was finally abolished as a result of reform measures proposed by a Committee chaired by Thomas Webster.[33] Patentees were only eligible for the Society's rewards after 1845.

The Society of Arts considered that financial reward was not the only form of appropriate recognition for inventors. As early as 1756, it was proposed that certain classes of inventors, such as "Scholars, Philosophers and Gentlemen of Estate" did not invent because of the lure of financial reward.[34] Instead, it was thought that such persons sought an increase in reputation and esteem. It was for this reason that the Society introduced a system whereby the inventor could elect to receive gold, silver or copper medals, in substitution for money.[35] The first such medal was awarded in 1757.[36] These private schemes for the granting of rewards to inventors, coupled with the large number of financial rewards granted by the Government, clearly shows that as late as the early nineteenth century, there was significant uncertainty as to whether the patent system was the most suitable vehicle for rewarding inventors.

Another of the views advanced to justify the U.K. patent system before 1829 was that a patent provided an incentive to invent. Before 1829, the major proponents of the incentive theory for patent protection were the noted political economists Jeremy Bentham, and John McCulloch, as well as lesser-known theorists such as Sir William Pultney, and John Chitty. Bentham wrote that

31 *Ibid.* 244.

32 *Ibid.* 243.

33 *Ibid.* Thomas Webster later became a Q.C., an eminent patent lawyer, and an editor of patent law reports. At the time of the reforms he had lately been called to the Bar, after having acted for two years (1837–39) as Secretary of the Institution of Civil Engineers. *Ibid.* 346.

34 *Ibid.* 314–315. The Society considered that financial rewards were more appropriate for "the Mechanic, the Manufacturer, and the Planter, and to all the Multitude in whom the Desire of Gain prevails." *Ibid.* 315.

35 *Ibid.* Chapter XIV, 314–321.

36 *Ibid.*

in "new inventions, protection against imitators is not less necessary than in established manufactures" and "[h]e who has no hope that he shall reap, will not take the trouble to sow."[37] McCulloch argued that should patents be abolished, "the inducement to make discoveries would, in many cases, be very much weakened."[38] In similar terms, Chitty wrote that patents encouraged the "production of GENIUS",[39] and Pultney argued in 1791 that patents "have been one of the great causes of the important discoveries which in this country have so much improved our manufacture and trade."[40] These views were taken up and further developed by witnesses before the 1829 Select Committee.

The final rationale advanced for the patent system in this period was that of the natural property rights of the inventor. Unlike in France, there was little evidence of support for this theory in the U.K. prior to 1829. The only early supporters of the theory were the legal scholar, Dr W. Kenrick, and the political economist John McCulloch, both of whom developed their theories about rights in inventions from the earlier writings of John Locke.[41] Kenrick wrote, in a legal treatise published in 1774, that inventors and authors possessed an "equal claim to the natural rights of genius" and a "superior right to public encouragement on principles of political expediency."[42] He argued that the Government was denying to inventors the enjoyment of their natural rights, by charging large fees for the grant of patent protection, and by limiting the patent to fourteen years' duration.[43] McCulloch's argument fifty years later was similar. He stated that if "anything can be called a man's exclusive property, it is surely that which owes its birth entirely to combinations formed in his own mind, and which, but for his ingenuity, would not have existed."[44] He later added that of "all the species of property a man can possess, the fruits of his

37 Bentham, J., *A Manual of Political Economy* (1790–95).

38 McCulloch's views about the patent system had been developing since at least 1826, when he wrote an article on the subject in the *Scotsman* (26 May 1826). In 1832 he published his *Dictionary, Practical, Theoretical and Historical, of Commerce and Commercial Navigation* in which the above quotation is contained.

39 Chitty, J., *Treatise on the Law of Commerce, Manufactures and Contracts* (London, 15th ed, Sweet and Maxwell, 1909, first published 1820).

40 Quoted in Dutton, H.I., *op.cit.* 20.

41 See for example, Locke, J., *Two Treatises on Civil Government* (London, Awnsham Churchill, 1690).

42 Noted in Macleod, C., *op.cit.* 199.

43 *Ibid.*

44 *Scotsman,* 26 May 1826. Quoted in Dutton, H.I., *op.cit.* 18.

mental labours seem to be the most peculiarly his own."[45] However, there is no evidence that McCulloch's views attracted much support.

Early Patent Law Reform Movements (before 1829)

Between 1790 and 1829 there were reportedly five Bills prepared which aimed at reform of the patent system.[46] Most of the reform proposals related to matters of procedure, and did not attempt to alter the theoretical basis of the system. However, three of the Bills, if they had been successful, would have altered the terms of the contract which was widely believed to lie at the heart of the patent system.

The Bills of 1793, 1801 and 1820 all proposed the introduction of a system of concealment of specifications.[47] This issue had been debated at some length as early as the *Arkwright* cases of the 1780s.[48] As a result of the decision in these cases to cancel Arkwright's patent on the basis of the insufficiency of his specification, many patentees feared that they would soon experience the same ill treatment.[49] James Watt, one of the inventors of the improved steam engine, responded to the controversy by preparing his "Thoughts" on the patent system. One of the major changes he sought was the introduction of concealed specifications, which would not be revealed to the public until after the patent had expired.[50] This proposed reform would severely reduce or even remove the

---

45 *A Dictionary, Practical, Theoretical and Historical, of Commerce and Commercial Navigation* (1832) Quoted in Machlup, F., and Penrose, E., *op.cit.* 12.

46 These Bills were dated 1793, 1801, 1820 (two) and 1821. UNITED KINGDOM, Parliamentary Papers, *Report from the Select Committee on the Law Relative to Patents for Inventions* (1829) 332, vol III, 415, Appendix A.

47 The 1801 Bill is not mentioned in any of the Parliamentary Indices, or in the writings of historians, but it was considered a matter of record before the 1829 Select Committee. In an Appendix to the Report, it is stated as follows: "About 1819 [actually 1820], a Bill was brought before the House of Commons, to conceal the specifications of all inventions for which patents are granted, from public inspection, in order that the inventions might not be sent abroad ... A clause to the same effect had been inserted in a Bill before Parliament in 1801, on the motion of Lord Thurlow, seconded by Lord Rosslyn; but it was universally rejected, and ... Lord Eldon, thought on very proper grounds." UNITED KINGDOM, Parliamentary Papers, *Report from the Select Committee on the Law Relative to Patents for Inventions* (1829) 332, vol III, 415, Appendix A. The Bill introduced in 1820 was titled "Bill to prevent Inconvenience from Facility of procuring Copies of Specifications inrolled by Grantees of Letters Patent, for Sole Working of new Manufactures", Parliamentary Papers, (1820) 184, vol I, 285. In relation to the Bill of 1793 see: Dutton, H.I., *op.cit.* 37.

48 The cases were *Arkwright v Nightingale* (1785) 1 *Webster's Patent Cases* 60; *The King v Arkwright* (1785) *Davies Patent Cases* 37.

49 Dutton, H.I., *op.cit.* 37.

50 *Ibid.* 39–40.

threat of actions being brought against patentees for insufficiency of specifications. Watt's "Thoughts" were circulated between 1790 and 1793, with some limited result. On 9 May 1793 a private member's Bill was brought before the House of Commons with the intention of concealing specifications for the duration of a patent. It did not survive debate in the House of Lords because it was thought to conflict with the prevailing notion that the patentee had an obligation to disclose the results of his endeavours to the public.[51]

The other two Bills in 1801 and 1820, which also dealt with the contentious issue of concealment of specifications, were "universally rejected".[52] These Bills had been proposed not so much to protect patentees against vexatious claims that their specifications were insufficient, but in order to prevent specifications for U.K. patents being copied and sent abroad. As set out in the next section in the context of evidence given to the 1829 Select Committee, many early nineteenth century inventors and manufacturers considered that foreigners had a great interest in stealing U.K. inventions. They believed that the Government should take stronger steps to protect U.K. patentees from this foreign threat. Consequently, it was argued that concealment of specifications would provide some relief from this danger. However, as in 1793, the later Bills of 1801 and 1820 were rejected by Parliament because concealment of specifications was thought to undermine the basis of the relationship between the patentee and the State.[53]

B The 1829 Select Committee

(a) *Historical Background*

It is an unresolved question as to why a Select Committee was appointed in 1829 to examine the patent laws. In the preceding period there was no notable increase in agitation for patent law reform. The only two significant additions to the patent law debate during this time were the opinions expressed by a Committee of the Manchester Chamber of Commerce and the *Mechanics Magazine*.[54] The contribution of the Manchester Chamber of Commerce was not unexpected because, dating from the *Arkwright* cases, Manchester manufacturers had a history of opposition to certain aspects of the patent system.

---

51 *Ibid.*

52 UNITED KINGDOM, Parliamentary Papers, *Report from the Select Committee on the Law Relative to Patents for Inventions* (1829) 332, vol III, 415, Appendix A, 179.

53 *Ibid.*

54 Dutton, H.I., *op.cit.* 42–43.

However, while the Manchester Chamber of Commerce favoured some form of patent law reform, it made no specific proposals.[55] The Mechanics Institute, responding to some anonymous letters which had appeared in the *Mechanics Magazine*, organised a meeting in 1827 to discuss the question of patent law reform, but only six members attended.[56] Nevertheless, on 9 April 1829, Thomas Lennard introduced a motion into the House of Commons for the establishment of a Select Committee of Inquiry into the patent laws.[57] The proposal was accepted by the House, and soon after, on 8 May 1829, the Committee met under the Chairmanship of Lennard.[58]

(b) *An Analysis of the View about the Patent System Expressed by Witnesses before the 1829 House of Commons Select Committee on Patents*

(1) The Witnesses

Although some historians are of the view that in the 1830s and 1840s "the manipulation and management of select committees were common practice,"[59] there is no evidence that any of the witnesses before the 1829 Select Committee were chosen for their prejudiced opinions. Nineteen witnesses were called to give evidence before the Committee, and they represented a wide range of occupations relevant to the operation of the patent law. The professions of engineer,[60] patent agent,[61] and barrister,[62] were represented, and

55 *Ibid.*

56 *Ibid.*

57 *Ibid.*

58 UNITED KINGDOM, Parliamentary Papers, *Report from the Select Committee on the Law Relative to Patents for Inventions* (1829) 332, vol III, 415.

59 Dutton, H.I., *op.cit.* 44. David Craig, in his notes to Charles Dickens' *Hard Times* (Harmondsworth, Penguin, 1969; *Hard Times* was first published in 1854), at 327–8 comments that the "enlightened efforts of men like Peel and Shaftesbury regularly came to little because the men who had the job of carrying out legislation were often damned if they'd lift a finger unless they were forced to." He refers with approval to statements made by Edward Thompson in *The Making of the English Working Class* (1968), such as "the reports of commissions and committees of inquiry served many purposes, but reform comes low on the list ... [R]outine response to petitions ... a means of handling and channelling discontent, procrastinating, or fobbing off ill-behaved M.P.'s; or purely ... an excess of utilitarian officiousness [were reasons why the committees were established]."

60 John Farey, Marc Isambard Brunel (developer of the Thames Tunnel) and John Millington.

61 William Newton. Newton was also editor of the Second Series of the *London Journal of Arts and Sciences*, which, from 1828 had published a series of letters by "Vindicator", which criticised the costs and inconveniences of the patent system. Some argue that Newton was the author of the "Vindicator" letters. Phillips, J., *Charles Dickens and the "Poor Man's Tale of a Patent"* (Oxford, ESC Publishing, 1984), 2.

62 Benjamin Rotch.

evidence was also given by the editor of a publication which reproduced copies of enrolled specifications for sale to the public.[63] Two members of Parliament with a special interest in the question of patent reform also appeared before the Committee,[64] as did Clerks of the Patent Office,[65] and Petty Bag Office.[66] Patentees were well represented, by John Taylor, an oil-gas patentee and manufacturer, Samuel Clegg, a steam engine patentee, and Marc Brunel, Charles Few and John Macarthy (all holders of several patents). Perhaps manufacturing interests could have had greater input, since only two witnesses were called who represented that sector. These were John Merry, a ribbon manufacturer from Coventry, and Samuel Morton, a manufacturer of agricultural implements. The Committee also sought evidence of overseas practices, particularly from the U.S. Consul, Thomas Aspinwall, and a U.S. citizen who facilitated contracts between patentees and manufacturers, John Hawkins.

(2) The Issues Raised by the Witnesses

An examination of the records of evidence presented to the 1829 Select Committee clearly shows that the majority of the witnesses' evidence related to practical problems associated with the operation of the system. Very little attention was paid to theoretical issues. Although it is not within the scope of this book to examine in any detail the practical problems raised by the witnesses, they can be summarised briefly as follows:

(i) *Delay and Inconvenience*

Wyatt, editor of the *Repertory Journal*, represented the views of the majority when he noted that he had "known patents to be delayed several months waiting for His Majesty's signature, during which period the invention has been discovered by others, and the patent rendered of no effect."[67] It was also considered inconvenient and highly expensive for patent applicants to have to attend, and pay fees to, so many offices.[68] The suggested solution to some of these problems was to cut down the number of steps required to obtain a

---

63 Walter Henry Wyatt was the editor of *The Repertory*.

64 Davies Gilbert and Arthur Howe Holdsworth.

65 Moses Poole.

66 Francis Abbott.

67 UNITED KINGDOM, Parliamentary Papers, *Report from the Select Committee on the Law Relative to Patents for Inventions* (1829) 332, vol III, 415, 105. Applicants for patents sometimes resorted to following the King into the country to seek his signature. *Ibid.* Abbott at 51); See also Newton at 66 where he refers to the many times where no patents were granted for months because the King was indisposed or greatly occupied.

68 *Ibid.*

patent. This was particularly the case since several of the stages were merely formal, and there was no act done except the application of a signature.

(ii) *Lack of Security before Grant*

Possibly the greatest problem which was mentioned by nearly every witness, was the lack of legal protection for inventions before the patent was sealed. In 1829 there was no system of provisional protection in the period between application and grant. This meant that, as Taylor stated, "from the time of [the inventor] taking the first step to get a patent to the time of sealing the patent, which is the last step, any publication would vitiate the patent if proved subsequently at any period in the whole fourteen years."[69] One of the consequences of this was that it was necessary for the inventor to keep the invention secret until the patent was granted. This was often difficult to achieve, especially if he had to rely upon the secrecy of workmen.[70] The suggested answer to this problem was to provide some form of protection for the invention pending the grant of the patent,[71] although it was recognised that this reform might require the lodging of a temporary specification at the time of the application,[72] or at least making the title of the invention more precise.[73]

(iii) *Misuse of Caveat System*

A form of corruption which was endemic throughout the patent system was the misuse of caveats. Caveats were customarily entered in the Attorney-General's Office as an initial step towards a patent by parties claiming that they were working to develop inventions in certain areas. If another party applied for a patent in the same area, the party who entered the caveat would be given notice of this fact, and had the opportunity to oppose the patent.[74] While the caveat might have had some benefits in alerting legitimate inventors to the possibility that someone was seeking a patent for the same invention, there was also clear evidence of corruption. John Taylor, patentee, gave evidence that caveats were sometimes entered with the sole object of blackmail. He said that he had heard that "persons have taken caveats out upon some concealed principle; and when any patent is applied for, which they have thought might be opposed by such caveats, they have called upon the parties, and a

69 *Ibid.* 8. See also 40–41 (Aikin); 81 (Few); 82 (Poole).

70 *Ibid.*

71 *Ibid.* 120 (Holdsworth); 41 (Aikin); 46 (Few); 54 (Abbott); 116 (Rotch).

72 *Ibid.* 54 (Abbott); 66–67 (Newton); 25 (Farey); 86 (Poole); 105 (Wyatt).

73 *Ibid.* 94 (Clegg).

74 *Ibid.* 48 (Abbott).

treaty is entered into, and it sometimes follows, that a sum of money has been agreed upon to be given that the opposition should be withdrawn."[75] Several witnesses suggested that the system of caveats be abolished and a Commission of Experts should be set up to examine the novelty of every patent application, and the sufficiency of the specification.[76]

(iv) *The Lack of Patents of Addition/Improvement*

Several witnesses referred to the difficulties encountered by inventors who had applied for a patent in relation to their invention, and then later developed a useful improvement.[77] As the law then stood there was no provision for patents of addition or improvement, and the inventor needed to take out an independent patent for the improved invention. There were, however, problems with this approach, because the specification of the earlier patent was often set up against the latter as a basis of a claim of lack of novelty. Witnesses such as Rotch claimed that this problem could be solved by a scheme of patents of addition, providing that the term of the later patent expired at the same time as the first.[78]

(v) *The Problem of Patentees Who Refused to Work Their Inventions*

Some witnesses considered that patentees should be forced to work their inventions, or lose the patent.[79] The main reason for this proposed reform was to stop patentees from gaining patents merely to block their competitors, and also to ensure the public had access to new technology. Although the witnesses were aware that in France a patent could be revoked if not worked within two years of grant, they considered that two years did not give the patentee sufficient time to work the invention. Suggested periods in which the patent should be forced to start working the invention ranged from three[80] to five years.[81]

Most of the evidence presented to the Committee concerned the above five issues. However, there was some limited discussion of issues more relevant to

75 *Ibid.* 6. Abbott, Clerk of the Petty Bag Office, also acknowledged that such practices had occurred. *Ibid.* 48.

76 See for example *Ibid.* 7 (Taylor); 15 (Gilbert); 44 (Aikin); 68–72 (Newton); 101 (Millington); 83 (Poole).

77 *Ibid.* 134 (Farey); 110 (Rotch); 68 (Newton).

78 Otherwise there was the fear that a patent could be of indeterminate duration, with one improvement after another being added, and each improvement having 14 years protection. *Ibid.* 110.

79 For example, *Ibid.* 48 (Few); 72 (Newton); 116 (Rotch); 124 (Holdsworth).

80 *Ibid.* 48 (Few).

81 *Ibid.* 116 (Rotch); 124 (Holdsworth).

theoretical matters, particularly (vi) comments about the underlying objectives of the patent system; (vii) comments about the utility of the patent system; and (viii) comments about "foreign" issues, such as the patentability of inventions "communicated" from abroad.

(vi) *The Underlying Objectives of the Patent System*

Of the nineteen witnesses who appeared before the Committee, only five made direct reference to the underlying objectives of the patent system. This can be contrasted with the situation in France where, as Chapter One has demonstrated, proposals for patent law reform nearly always inspired heated debate about the theoretical basis of the system. One reason for this difference could be the fact that there was no patent system in France until 1791, and thus, being so relatively new and untested, the system was subject to greater theoretical scrutiny than in the United Kingdom. In contrast, the "modern" U.K. patent system had been in operation since 1623, people had grown accustomed to it, and did not feel the need to debate its theoretical basis.

It is thus, unsurprising, that two of the witnesses before the Committee reiterated the traditional idea that the patent system ensured public disclosure of inventions. Rotch, a Barrister with experience in patent cases, stated that "a perfect description of the specification is the only thing the public get in return for the monopoly for fourteen years …"[82] On two occasions, the Chairman of the Select Committee, Lennard, put to the witnesses his own view that "Is not the principle upon which the granting of a patent is founded, the giving a person monopoly for a limited time, for the purpose of making known to the public the nature of a beneficial invention?". On both occasions, Abbott, Clerk of the Petty Bag Office, and Few, a patentee, agreed with this assessment.[83]

Not all the witnesses shared the Chairman's view that the primary rationale underlying the patent system was to encourage disclosure of inventions. Taylor, a manufacturer and oil-gas patentee, considered that the main policy of the patent laws was to ensure adequate reward for inventors. He stated that "it seems to me just and right that some reward should attach to inventors; and there can hardly be such a reward without some monopoly …"[84] Farey, an engineer, considered that the primary objective of the patent system was "holding out an inducement and encouragement for doing what requires to be done publicly afterwards; and by ensuring a competent reward for successful

82 UNITED KINGDOM, Parliamentary Papers, *Report from the Select Committee on the Law Relative to Patents for Inventions* (1829) 332, vol III, 415, 106.

83 *Ibid.* 57 (Abbott); 80 (Few).

84 *Ibid.* 5.

exertions in bringing the invention into use."[85] He considered that the twin rationales of inducement and reward were far more important than the element of public disclosure. He was:

> [unable to accept] "the feeling with which courts of justice take up the subject of patent rights: they assume that the patent is given solely as a reward for the disclosure of a secret invention that has been concocted by the inventor in private, before he applied for his patent, and that the right granted by the patent is only conditional on the event, that the secret when disclosed in the specification, shall prove in every respect what the inventor professed it to be …"[86]

However, Farey noted that in reality in most cases, the specification in the patent grant was usually insufficiently developed to disclose anything worthwhile to the public.[87] Therefore, the so-called contract between the inventor and the State was usually voidable. He argued that the disclosure rationale was flawed because at the stage of the patent grant very little of worth was disclosed, but the patent instead granted an incentive and reward to the inventor to keep perfecting the invention and bring it into general use.[88]

Farey's views about the rationale of the patent system were also supported by Dyer, an American citizen, then settled in Manchester, who was a manufacturer of a machine for making wire cards used in wool and cotton mills.[89] He had been asked to give evidence before the Committee, but had been unable to attend due to ill-health. However, he sent a letter to the Committee, extracts from which were read. Dyer stated that he totally agreed with Farey's assessment of the policy of the patent system, "and especially with reference to the general worthlessness of first ideas of inventions (which is all that can now be secured by a patent) unless those first ideas are followed up by extended experiments, and improvements upon the first suggestions."[90]

---

85 *Ibid.* 133.

86 *Ibid.*

87 Farey stated that "in fact it almost always happens, that the inventions which ultimately come to be of great public value, were scarcely worth anything, in the crude state in which they emerged from secrecy; but by the subsequent application of skill, capital, and by well-directed exertions of the labour of a number of inferior artisans and practicians, the crude inventions are with great time, exertion and expense, brought to bear to the benefit of the community." *Ibid.*

88 *Ibid.*

89 *Ibid.* 134.

90 *Ibid.*

One of the reasons why the witnesses pointed to the crude nature of many specifications, was that in 1829 the applicant for a patent did not have any form of provisional protection between the time of presenting the petition and the time of sealing, and that sealing of the grant only took place once the specification had been enrolled.[91] For English patents, the Patent Office usually allowed only two months between petition and enrolment of the specification.[92] The short time, and the lack of provisional protection meant that most inventors "dare[d] not make a single experiment before the patent [was] granted".[93] These circumstances meant that there was much truth in Farey and Dyer's view that the public gained little benefit from access to patent specifications.

Another issue related to the theoretical basis of the patent system, was the question of the relevance of the *Statute of Monopolies* of 1623. Rotch considered that while the Statute was "extremely well calculated" for the 1600s, the words of the Statute "do not happen now at all to hit the necessities of the present period."[94] He noted that "the Judges are constantly straining the meaning of this Act to make it meet the necessity of the times" and one of the particular problems was the meaning of the term "manner of manufacture".[95] Some judges such as Lord Mansfield and Lord Tenterden had adopted a very liberal interpretation of the word "manufacture" and upheld process patents because "they are so vastly important".[96] However, other judges continued to reject all patents which were merely for processes, stating that processes were not manufactures.[97] For these reasons, Rotch considered that the patent laws required complete reform, which extended also to a reappraisal of the foundation of these laws, namely the *Statute of Monopolies* of 1623.

---

91 *Ibid.* 117.

92 If a patent was taken out also for Ireland and Scotland, the relevant period was six months. *Ibid.*

93 *Ibid.* Evidence of Rotch.

94 *Ibid.* 107.

95 *Ibid.*

96 *Ibid.* 108. It was estimated that three-quarters of all patents taken out were for processes.

97 *Ibid.* Part of this uncertainty was said to have been caused by the case of *The King v Wheeler* (1819) 1 *Carpmael's Reports* 397, where Chief Justice Abbott said that "the word manufacture ... may perhaps extend also to a new process to be carried on by known implements or elements acting upon known substances, and ultimately producing some other known substance; but producing it on a cheaper or more expeditious manner, or of a better or more useful kind ..." As Rotch stated, the "word *perhaps* sets us all at sea, and nobody can say positively what title to a patent the courts will support or will not."

(vii) *The Usefulness of the Patent System*

It is a significant fact that none of the witnesses who appeared before the 1829 Select Committee proposed the abolition of the patent system. They all thought that a well-managed patent system was potentially of great benefit to inventors and national development, but the problem was that the system was flawed in its practical application. Naturally, there was some disagreement as to the amount of change needed to ensure the proper working of the system. Brunel, an engineer and patentee, made few suggestions for improvement of the laws and agreed with the Chairman's suggestion that "[u]pon the whole … the patent laws are beneficial to the public."[98] Poole, Clerk of the Patent Office, also stated that he did "not see any defect in the present law; perhaps the specifications might be made more sure."[99] Wyatt, the editor of the *Repertory Journal*, agreed that the patent system had tended to stimulate invention, and that it had "been a greater spur to the improvement of the arts and manufactures in this country, than any other system that could be adopted …"[100] He added that the main problem was that the law was very uncertain, and that there were "great inconveniences" associated with it.[101]

The M.P. Arthur Holdsworth, agreed that "as the law is not clear with regard to patents, so many are obtained that appear defective in law, which by confusing workmen really do mischief …"[102] However, he argued that "if the law be made so clear and defined that a patent for something really useful, when taken out, would be found to be secure, then I cannot conceive that we can have too many patents, as they are the reward of men's ingenuity."[103] The manufacturers Merry and Morton both considered that they had no objection to the policy of the patent system, or the payment of fees for the obtaining of a patent monopoly, provided that the patent actually provided the security they sought.[104] Clegg, a patentee of improvements in steam-engine technology, also considered the lack of secure protection was one of the main problems of the patent system, and stated that he would be happy to pay higher patent fees if the security of his patent could be assured.[105]

98 *Ibid.* 39.
99 *Ibid.* 82.
100 *Ibid.* 104.
101 *Ibid.*
102 *Ibid.* 119.
103 *Ibid.*
104 *Ibid.* 89 (Merry); 90 (Morton).
105 *Ibid.* 94.

Another reason to support the continuation of the patent system was the view that many useful inventions would never have been developed without the opportunity to obtain a patent. Farey thought that "many great inventions would never have been brought to bear as they have been, but for the encouragement offered by a patent."[106] In making this statement, he gave an example of the case of Watt's steam engine, and referred to personal letters written by Watt at the time he was first developing his invention in 1765–76. It was clear that when Watt first conceived his idea, it was so far ahead of its time, that none of the manufacturers or investors in that kind of machinery would have assisted him in any way until he had made a prototype of his invention. However, the making of the prototype involved such a large effort and expense, that he said he would never have attempted the task unless he had obtained some legal protection. As it was, even with the benefit of a patent, Watt was "tormented with exceedingly bad health, resulting from the operation of an anxious mind, the natural consequence of staking everything upon the cast of a die …"[107] Farey also agreed with the Chairman's proposition that "many inventions are more quickly brought into general use, in consequence of a patent having been obtained for them, than they would have been if they had been left to themselves without a patent."[108] He noted that once a patent was obtained, most patentees hurried to set up workshops and train labour in the new art, with the intention of gaining the maximum advantage from the fourteen year monopoly. The only notable exception to this was in those cases where a patent was taken out with the aim of not employing the invention, and preventing others from utilising it.[109]

(viii) *Foreign Issues*

A number of issues were raised by witnesses before the Committee in the general area of patents and foreign relations. What is most notable about these opinions is the patronising attitude displayed by the witnesses towards foreign inventors and manufacturers. A general opinion prevailed that foreigners were either incompetent and unable to commercialise their own inventions,

106 *Ibid.* 140.

107 *Ibid.* 141. Extract from Watt's letter to Mr Smeaton, dated April 1776. John Farey commented that this letter was written seven years after Watt obtained his patent, during which time Watt had devoted himself entirely to the execution of his idea and that "it is not to be supposed, that anyone would have gone through all this toil, without being assured of a property in what cost such a man so much to acquire."

108 *Ibid.*

109 *Ibid.*

or that they spent a great deal of time in the United Kingdom, attempting to steal U.K. inventions. These attitudes meant that it was unlikely that anyone in the U.K. would have accepted the desirability for international protection of inventions in 1829.

(a) Fear of Advantages Taken by Foreigners

It has already been noted that some of the early proposals for patent law reform supported concealment of the specification during the period of the patent. One of the main reasons for this was that patentees feared that their inventions would fall into foreign hands, and that unless they took the trouble of obtaining foreign patents, they had no control over the exploitation of the inventions outside the United Kingdom. This issue was again raised before the 1829 Select Committee. Abbott considered that it was not advisable to print the specifications of existing patents for public use because he "generally considered it would be prejudicial to the interest of the country, … sending many valuable discoveries abroad; many of those things perhaps would be bought from English manufacturers, but if the specifications all go abroad they would be more likely to be made there than they would be if the information was not so circulated."[110] Merry agreed, stating that "there is a great evil in specifications, because they are so easily sent out of the country. I believe anyone can have a copy of the specification by paying for it, and therefore, an invention that we have here may be sent abroad with great ease."[111]

(b) Communication of Inventions from Abroad

The argument that absolute novelty should be required of all patentable inventions was not supported by any of the witnesses before the 1829 Select Committee. The general view of the witnesses appeared to be that novelty should only be tested against prior disclosures in the United Kingdom, and that use of the invention in a foreign country was not relevant.[112] In broad terms, the witnesses supported the maintenance of the legal provisions which allowed a person to gain a patent for "an invention communicated to him from a person residing abroad".[113] They thought that it was quite proper to obtain and patent foreign inventions, because foreigners usually were less technologically developed than U.K. inventors, and did not have the means to properly

110 *Ibid.* 59.
111 *Ibid.* 90.
112 *Ibid.* 153 (Farey); 108–9 (Rotch); 89 (Merry); 105 (Wyatt); 73 (Newton); 81 (Few); 160 (Hawkins).
113 *Ibid.* 153 (Farey).

exploit new inventions. Farey made this view clear. He considered that the U.K. had obtained as many new inventions from foreigners, as from amongst its own nationals,[114] and the U.K. was entitled to do this because it had a particular talent for applying new ideas to practical use.[115] He said that the:

> means of executing and applying inventions abroad are so very inferior to ours … [W]e have so much improved and perfected what was brought into this country from abroad, that although they soon become important means of national wealth to us, the foreigners made little or nothing of them by themselves. Even after they got them back again in the improved state to which we have brought them, although they received their crude ideas matured, like children sent home, after having been well educated, and become full grown, by boarding for years, without expense, at a better school than home, – still they have not been able to set them to work so extensively and profitably as we have done.[116]

Even if the invention had been perfected and brought into use in the foreign country before making its way to the U.K., Farey still considered that a patent should be granted, as it encouraged the accelerated distribution of the invention to the public in the U.K.[117] In essence, there was little dissent from the view that granting patents for inventions introduced from foreign countries served to accelerate the influx of foreign inventions into the U.K. The only point on which there was criticism of the law related to the fact that a person could not obtain a patent in the U.K. for an invention that had been communicated to him by one of his own countrymen, even if residing abroad. Many of the witnesses to the 1829 Select Committee considered that this particular rule should be abolished, and all inventions not already disclosed in the U.K. should be patentable, without regard to the nationality of the person who communicated details of the invention to the patent applicant.[118]

---

114 According to Farey, examples of foreign inventions which had not risen to importance in the countries in which they originated, but were first successfully exploited in the U.K. included: clocks and watches, the coining press, the windmill for draining land, the diving bell, the cylinder paper machine, the stocking frame, figure weaving loom, silk throwsting mill, canal-lock and turning-bridge, the machine for dredging and deepening rivers, the manufacture of alum, glass, the art of dyeing, printing, and the earliest notions of the steam engine. *Ibid.*

115 *Ibid.*

116 *Ibid.*

117 *Ibid.* 154.

118 For example, *Ibid.* 105 (Wyatt); 73 (Newton); 81 (Few); 160 (Hawkins).

(c) Views about Foreign Patent Laws

On a number of occasions, the Committee sought witnesses' views about the efficacy of foreign patent systems. It is clear that the Committee was most interested in the U.S. and French patent systems, but also asked for details about the Belgian, Austrian and Spanish systems.[119] Details about the U.S. system were provided by the U.S. Consul in London, Aspinwall, and the author of a book on the U.S. patent law, Hawkins. However, it is interesting to note that of all the foreign patent systems discussed by the witnesses, most support was given to the French patent system, rather than the U.S. system. For example, Millington, a civil engineer, stated that he thought the "French law of patents is very superior to ours",[120] a view which was echoed by Merry,[121] Newton,[122] and Poole.[123] One of the main reasons why these witnesses supported the French patent system was that its system of provisional specifications provided some security to the patentee from the moment of applying for the patent. These discussions were also interesting because they displayed a high level of understanding of the French patent system and, in some cases, practical experience in obtaining French patents.[124] Nevertheless, despite admiration for some aspects of foreign patent law, and familiarity with the difficulties inherent in obtaining foreign patents, not one witness discussed the feasibility of introducing any system of international protection of patent rights.

(3) Conclusions about the Evidence Presented before the 1829 Select Committee

After hearing the evidence of the nineteen witnesses, the Committee reported to the House of Commons that the subject of the patent laws was "in its nature so intricate and important" that, at that late stage in the Session, the Committee was only prepared to report the Minutes of Evidence.[125] It recommended that the inquiry should be resumed in the next Session,[126] but this was never done. Even though the Committee did not advise any particular amendments to the patent law, its work was important because it was the first time that an opportunity had arisen in the U.K. for so many wide-ranging views about the patent

119 *Ibid.* 131–2 and Appendices C, D, E, F, G.
120 *Ibid.* 98.
121 *Ibid.* 89.
122 *Ibid.* 67–70.
123 *Ibid.* 83.
124 For example, *Ibid.* 67 (Newton); 83 (Poole); 98 (Millington).
125 *Ibid.* 2.
126 *Ibid.*

system to be presented. In the context of the matters central to this book, there were three notable features of the evidence presented to the Committee. These included (1) the attention to practical, rather than theoretical issues; and (2) the suspicious, as well as patronising, attitude displayed by the witnesses towards foreign inventors and manufacturers. The third feature is one which is not so readily apparent from an examination of the records of the Committee. It is the fact that none of the witnesses before the Committee purported to represent any organised groups with interests in patent law reform. In reality, there is no evidence of the existence of any patent law reform groups in 1829, and interest from more general organisations, such as the Manchester Chamber of Commerce, was limited. As is noted in the next part of this work, the following two decades proved that patent law reform in the U.K. was only possible when individuals *and groups* became interested in the question.

C Overview of Movements Towards Patent Law Reform between 1830 and 1851

(a) *1830 to 1847 – The Era of Individualism*

Although the 1829 Select Committee did not publish any recommendations with respect to patent law reform, it had significant influence in increasing interest in the issue. In 1830, for example, a correspondent in the *Law Magazine* wrote that "[i]t is manifest, however, from the evidence, that the whole of this department of the law must undergo very considerable alterations."[127] Understandably, some of the evidence of the witnesses provoked controversy, particularly the proposal that a Commission be set up to examine inventions for novelty.[128] While the defects in the administration of the patent system appeared to be accepted, some thought that the witnesses' proposed solutions were "weak and shallow".[129] Yet, despite increasing interest in reform of the patent laws, it was not until 1847 that organisations began to emerge with an avowed concern to promote reform. In the interim, there were some (largely unsuccessful) proposals for reform which were promoted by certain individuals, but most failed for lack of significant support.

The first Bill incorporating proposals for patent law reform was introduced into the House of Commons in February 1833.[130] Between 1833 and 1839 there

127 "The Patent Laws" (1830) 3 *The Law Magazine* 282, 283.

128 *Ibid.*

129 *Ibid.*

130 Bill to explain and amend Laws respecting Letters Patent for Inventions, *Parliamentary Papers* (1833) 34, vol III, 169. [as amended in Committee] *Parliamentary Papers* (1833) 496

were another four Bills introduced which related to the subject of the patent laws.[131] Of these Bills, only two were passed by Parliament. The first was Lord Brougham's 1835 Bill which permitted minor amendment of specifications, and the ability to petition the Privy Council to extend patents for seven years. The second was a Bill of 1839 which dealt with minor technical matters raised by the 1835 Act. These reforms had little impact upon the problems identified by witnesses to the 1829 Select Committee.

The failure of the 1833 Bill demonstrated some of the reasons why patent law reform was largely unsuccessful in this period. It had been prepared by three solicitors, Benjamin Rotch, (who had given evidence before the 1829 Select Committee), Richard Godson, and Archibald Rosser.[132] It also had the support of Thomas Lennard, the former Chairman of the 1829 Select Committee.[133] The main problem with the 1833 Bill appeared to be that it did not address either (a) the same issues identified by the witnesses before the 1829 Select Committee, or (b) the solutions suggested by any witnesses other than Rotch.[134] The Bill was really a very individualistic approach to patent law reform, and it is unsurprising that it met with controversy, both within and outside Parliament.[135]

Lord Brougham's 1835 Bill (which became the 1835 Act), was most notable not for its contents,[136] but because it marked the first time for many years when highly-placed members of the U.K. Government began to take a personal interest in patent law reform. Lord Brougham, (who was appointed Lord Chancellor on 22 November 1830, and remained in that position until April 1835),[137] was a man of great interest in science and literature, as well as a zealous law

---

and 497, vol III, 177, 183. [clauses proposed to be added by Mr Jarvis] *Parliamentary Papers* (1833) vol III, 187.

131 Bill, intituled, Act to amend Law touching Letters Patent for Inventions, *Parliamentary Papers* (1835) 396, vol III, 597. Bill for regulating Law relating to Letters Patent for Inventions, *Parliamentary Papers* (1836) 348, vol IV, 513. Bill to amend Practice relating to Letters Patent, and for better Encouragement of Arts and Manufactures, *Parliamentary Papers* (1837) 40, vol III, 315. Bill, intituled Act to amend Law touching Letters Patent for Inventions, *Parliamentary Papers,* (1839) 506, vol IV, 371.

132 Dutton, H.I., *op. cit.* 46.

133 *Ibid.*

134 The 1833 Bill proposed to abolish the reference to the *Statute of Monopolies* 1623, and introduce a very wide definition of a patentable invention. It also proposed that any person who had received communication about an invention would be able to obtain a patent. Obviously, this would not have helped to stem some of the frauds identified by witnesses before the 1829 Select Committee.

135 Dutton, H.I., *op.cit.* 46.

136 Which were of an extremely limited, and uncontroversial nature.

137 "Lord Brougham" (1868) 25 *The Law Magazine and Law Review* 177, 214–224.

reformer.[138] Once he had taken up the subject of patent law reform in 1835, he remained active in the area until shortly before his death in 1867. It has been claimed that Lord Brougham was the "main instigator of legislative reform in the period between 1835 and 1852".[139] This is true if the comment is interpreted to refer only to the contribution of individuals, and not groups. There is clear evidence that by the late 1840s, a number of groups were emerging with a strong interest in patent law reform, and it was the influence of these groups which was primarily responsible for the extensive reforms of 1852.

(b) *The Late 1840s – The Emergence of Groups Supporting Patent Law Reform and the Relevance of Proposals for a Great Exhibition in London.*

Between 1840 and 1847 few individuals (or groups) considered the question of patent law reform. As Dutton notes, during this period free trade and working-class unrest were the major domestic issues.[140] Patent reform was "unimportant, esoteric and dull".[141] He argues that there were two reasons why in the late 1840s and early 1850s patent law reform suddenly became an issue of major importance. These reasons were (a) the influence of repeal of the corn laws and the onset of severe depression, and (b) the excitement generated by the prospect of the Great Exhibition in London.[142]

It is clear that from 1847 there was a huge increase in interest in patent law reform. The one point which distinguished this movement from earlier reformist pressures was the contribution of organisations. Although economic circumstances were no doubt relevant to the growing interest of these organisations in the patent laws, it seems more likely that it was the influence of the Great Exhibition which really inflamed public opinion about patents.[143] The

138 Besides patents, he was also especially interested in reform of the law in the following areas: abolition of slavery, defamation law and freedom of the press, education of the poor, concession to Catholic claims, the corn laws, bankruptcy law, improvements to the system of administration of justice and establishment of County Courts. *Ibid.*

139 Batzel, V.M., "Legal Monopoly in Liberal England: The Patent Controversy in the Mid-Nineteenth Century" (1980) 22 *Business History* 189, 195. Dutton, H.I., *op.cit.* 57.

140 Dutton, H.I. *op.cit.* 57.

141 *Ibid.*

142 *Ibid.* 57–58. The *Economist* attributed the zeal for patent law reform to the "coming Exhibition, which it is supposed may be dangerous to copyrights of designs if exhibited." *Economist,* 28 December 1850, 1433 (leading article).

143 By 1849 the trade situation was improving, but calls for patent law reform only became stronger. This shows that economic fluctuations were not the main reasons for the increased interest in patent law reform in this period. Charles Babbage, the inventor of the first mechanical calculator, considered that the Great Exhibition provided an opportunity

Great Exhibition may also have been the point at which international protection for inventions was first considered in the U.K.

Historical Background to the Great Exhibition

The 1851 Great Exhibition in London was the first *international* exhibition of arts and manufactures.[144] It had been preceded by a number of national exhibitions in the U.K., France and other parts of Europe.[145] The first U.K. national exhibition was organised by the Society of Arts in 1761, where prizes were presented for improvements in agricultural and other machinery.[146] Later, in 1798, an exhibition of French manufactures was held in Paris, "as a means of raising [national manufactures] from the state of decay into which they had lapsed."[147] Several similar exhibitions were held on a regular basis in France between 1798 and 1849.[148] Following the French example, a number of exhibitions of the "products of national industry" were held in various parts of Europe between 1818 and 1850.[149]

In November 1844, Francis Wishaw, the Secretary of the Society of Arts, proposed that support should be given to establishing an annual exhibition of industrial inventions.[150] In May 1845, the proposal was taken up by the Miscellaneous Matters Committee of the Society, chaired by Thomas Webster. The Committee brought the proposal to the attention of the President of the Society, Prince Albert, who directed that the matter should be subject to further examination.[151] When the Committee approached manufacturers

---

for discussion of important matters relating to the advancement of the industrial arts. He said that the law of patents was one area which called for reasoned discussion. By bringing together inventors and manufacturers from around the world, the Great Exhibition also could allow the U.K. to learn about foreign patent laws. Babbage, C., *The Exposition of 1851; or, Views of the Industry, the Science, and the Government of England* (London, John Murray, 1851), 135–136.

144 Wood, H.T., *A History of the Royal Society of Arts* (London, John Murray, 1913), 402.

145 *Ibid.*

146 *Ibid.*

147 *Ibid.* 402–3.

148 *Ibid.*

149 *Ibid.* For example, exhibitions were held in Munich (1818), Hanover (1835), Brussels (1835), Lausanne (1839), Vienna (1839), Berlin (1844), London (annually 1830–33), Birmingham (1836), Dublin (triennially 1827–50), Paris (1849).

150 *Ibid.* 403.

151 *Ibid.* 404–5. According to Wood, the "Prince Consort had, since his election as President, continuously impressed on the Society the necessity of its taking steps to improve the condition of the artistic industries of the country, then in a very backward condition, and had urged on the Society, as its proper work, the encouragement of the application of art to practical purposes."

on the subject, it was apparent that there was insufficient support for such an exhibition. However, to popularise the idea of national exhibitions, the Society decided to establish its own exhibition of "select specimens of British Manufactures and Decorative Art" which was held annually from March 1847.[152] By the third such exhibition in March 1849, the Society decided that the annual exhibitions were "only parts of a series of displays which it is proposed shall culminate every fifth year in a great national exhibition, embracing all manufactures", and it was suggested that the first of the great exhibitions should be held in 1851.[153]

Rivalry with the French also played a part in the 1849 decision to hold a great exhibition in London. Early in that year, Henry Cole, Digby Wyatt and Francis Fuller, all Committee members of the Society of Arts, visited the national exhibition held in Paris.[154] Fuller, on his return to the U.K. wrote that "it would be possible to get up in London a much better exhibition than the one in Paris".[155] Shortly after being informed of the circumstances of the Paris exhibition, and the growing support for an exhibition in London, Prince Albert decided that the 1851 exhibition should be the first to have an international character. Prince Albert stated that:

> whilst it appears an error to fix any limitation to the productions of machinery, science and taste, which are of no country, but belong as a whole to the civilised world, particular advantage to British industry might be derived from placing it in fair competition with that of other nations.[156]

Prince Albert and the members of the Society of Arts must have realised that it was only a matter of time before the French would have held the first international exhibition. The French government had seriously considered whether or not the 1849 Paris exhibition should have an international character, but the answers to circulars sent to several Chambers of Commerce throughout France had revealed that there was a general unwillingness to expose French inventions to competition from foreign inventions.[157] Nevertheless, it can be

152 *Ibid.*
153 *Ibid.* 408.
154 *Ibid.* 410.
155 *Ibid.*
156 Quoted in Sir Henry Cole's autobiography and reproduced at *Ibid.* 411.
157 Babbage, C., *op.cit.* 24–25.

seen that around the same time, both the French and the U.K. governments first considered the expediency of holding international exhibitions.

The Connection between the Great Exhibition of 1851 and Patent Law Reform

The connection between the Great Exhibition of 1851 and patent law reform was most evident in the work of the Society of Arts. It is true that one of the first organisations to become interested in patent law reform was the British Association for the Advancement of Science, which had devoted some attention to the question as early as the date of its founding in 1831.[158] However, the Society of Arts was the first organisation to set up Committees to comprehensively study the patent law.

Mention has already been made of the fact that before 1845, the Society of Arts had opposed patents, and refused to grant its awards to any patented inventions.[159] This changed in 1845 when a Committee of the Society chaired by Thomas Webster recommended that patentees should be eligible for awards. At around the same time, the Society also began to consider the question of patent law reform, and, in 1849, a Committee for Legislative Recognition of the Rights of Inventors was appointed.[160] The year 1845 was also when the

---

158 Babbage, C., *op.cit.* 16. Batzel, V.M., "Legal Monopoly in Liberal England: The Patent Controversy in the Mid-Nineteenth Century" (1980) 22 *Business History* 189, 194. Henry Cole reported to the 1851 Select Committee that the "British Association have been paying constant attention to the subject since 1836". UNITED KINGDOM, Parliamentary Papers, *Report and Minutes of Evidence taken before the Select Committee of the House of Lords appointed to consider of The Bill, intituled, "An Act further to amend the Law touching Letters Patent for Invention" and also of The Bill intituled "An Act for the further amendment of the Law touching Letters Patent for Invention" and to report thereon to the House: Session 1851* (1851) 486 vol XVIII, 233, 259.

159 See Section A of this Chapter.

160 Wood, H., *A History of the Royal Society of Arts* (London, John Murray, 1913), 382. See also Davis, I.J.G., and harrison, J., "Prelude to the United Kingdom's Accession to the Paris Convention, March 17, 1884", (1984) *Industrial Property* 395, 396. According to Wood, the "Committee published several reports" on the issue of patent law reform, and the "general tendency of the reports was rather in favour of the French system", particularly the way the French administered their system of simple registration of patents. *Ibid.* 382. Extracts from the First Report of the Committee, together with Resolutions passed to form the Heads of a Bill, dated 26 December 1850, can be found in UNITED KINGDOM, Parliamentary Papers, *Report and Minutes of Evidence taken before the Select Committee of the House of Lords appointed to consider of The Bill, intituled, "An Act further to amend the Law touching Letters Patent for Invention" and also of The Bill intituled "An Act for the further amendment of the Law touching Letters Patent for Invention" and to report thereon to the House: Session 1851* (1851) 486 vol XVIII, 233, 404–409.

Society first established a Committee to investigate the possibility of holding a "national exhibition of the products of industry".[161] Then, in 1849, the Society decided upon a definite plan for the holding of the international exhibition in 1851.[162] As Thomas Webster told the 1871 Select Committee on Patents, the "discussions about the Great Exhibition of 1851 led, in the course of the year 1850, to the subject of patents taking a very prominent place."[163] This is strong evidence establishing the connection between the Great Exhibition and calls for patent law reform.

Another point to note in this context is the argument of the later German commentators Carl Pieper and Paul Schmid, that Prince Albert not only favoured the holding of the 1851 Exhibition, but he was also one of the first persons to suggest that there should be some form of international protection for inventions.[164] As is discussed in more detail in Chapter Five, this is an interesting suggestion, but there is little firm evidence to support these views.

Growth of Organisations Supporting Patent Law Reform

Between 1847 and 1851, a large number of organisations followed the Society of Arts in turning their attention to the patent laws. Some organisations were especially established for the purpose, such as the National Association for the Reform of the Patent Laws (1847), Manchester Patent Law Reform Association (1848),[165] Art Protection Society for the amendment of the laws affecting Letters Patent (1850), Birmingham Patent Law Reform Association (1850), National Patent Law Amendment Association (1851) United Inventors Association for the amendment of the laws affecting Inventions (1851),[166] Association

161 Wood, H., *op.cit.* 404.

162 *Ibid.* 412. According to Babbage, there was little doubt that the Great Exhibition of 1851 was largely the result of the work of the Society of Arts, who first took up the proposal, and urged it upon the attention of their President, Prince Albert. Babbage, C., *op.cit.* 26.

163 UNITED KINGDOM, Parliamentary Papers, *Report from the Select Committee on Letters Patent; together with the Proceedings of the Committee, Minutes of Evidence, Appendix and Index* (1871) 368, vol X, 603, 44.

164 Pieper, C., and Schmid, P., *Geschichte der internationalen Union für den Schutz des gewerblichen Eigentums sammt Konvention und Staatsverträgen* (Berlin, Deutschen Vereins für den Schutz des gewerblichen Eigentums, 1894), 6–7.

165 This Association was first organised in 1828, but had lapsed, and in 1848 it re-organised itself under the leadership of the civil engineer and patentee, William Fairbairn, and other manufacturers and engineers. Dutton, H.I., *op.cit.* 58.

166 This was a committee composed only of patentees, including some from Manchester, Birmingham, Belfast, Dublin and Edinburgh. UNITED KINGDOM, Parliamentary Papers, *Report and Minutes of Evidence taken before the Select Committee of the House of Lords appointed to consider of The Bill, intituled, "An Act further to amend the Law touching Letters Patent for Invention" and also of The Bill intituled "An Act for the further amendment*

of Patentees and Proprietors of Patents for the protection and regulation of Patent property (1851), Society for promoting scientific inquiries with social questions: Reform on Patent Laws (1851), Patent Law League (1851),[167] and the Lambeth Patent Laws Reform Association.[168] Some of these organisations were formed largely in response to the two Bills concerning patent law reform which were introduced into Parliament on 24 March and 10 April, 1851.[169]

Apart from the organisations formed expressly for the purpose of considering proposals for patent law reform, there were many older organisations which turned their attention to the subject in or about 1851. These included the Institution of Civil Engineers, the Institution of Mechanical Engineers, the Society of Engineers,[170] the Society for promoting the Amendment of the Law (Law Society), the Society for promoting Scientific Inquiries at Dublin, the Chambers of Commerce of Liverpool, Belfast and Manchester, the London Mechanics' Institute, and the Inventors' Society.[171]

---

of the Law touching Letters Patent for Invention" and to report thereon to the House: Session 1851 (1851) 486 vol XVIII, 233, 11. (Evidence of Thomas Webster). See also the evidence of Richard Wyatt, honorary secretary of the Association at 102–3.

167 UNITED KINGDOM, Parliamentary Papers, *Report of the Commissioners appointed to Inquire into the Working of the Law Relating to Letters Patent for Inventions* (1864) 3419, vol XXIX, 321, 149.

168 Evidence of Henry Cole before the 1851 Select Committee. UNITED KINGDOM, Parliamentary Papers, *Report and Minutes of Evidence taken before the Select Committee of the House of Lords appointed to consider of The Bill, intituled, "An Act further to amend the Law touching Letters Patent for Invention" and also of The Bill intituled "An Act for the further amendment of the Law touching Letters Patent for Invention" and to report thereon to the House: Session 1851* (1851) 486 vol XVIII, 233, 259.

169 The Bill of 24 March 1851 was introduced into the House of Lords by Lord Brougham, as a private member's Bill. It was called "The Bill, intituled, An Act further to amend the Law touching Letters Patent for Inventions." The Bill of 10 April 1851 was introduced into the House of Lords by Lord Granville. This was the draft which the Government had been working on since late 1850. It was called "The Bill, intituled, An Act for the further Amendment of the Law touching Letters Patent for Inventions." UNITED KINGDOM, Parliamentary Papers, *Report and Minutes of Evidence taken before the Select Committee of the House of Lords appointed to consider of The Bill, intituled, "An Act further to amend the Law touching Letters Patent for Invention" and also of The Bill intituled "An Act for the further amendment of the Law touching Letters Patent for Invention" and to report thereon to the House: Session 1851* (1851) 486 vol XVIII, 233, 1.

170 Batzel, V.M., "Legal Monopoly in Liberal England: The Patent Controversy in the Mid-Nineteenth Century" (1980) 22 *Business History* 189, 192–193.

171 UNITED KINGDOM, Parliamentary Papers, *Report and Minutes of Evidence taken before the Select Committee of the House of Lords appointed to consider of The Bill, intituled, "An Act further to amend the Law touching Letters Patent for Invention" and also of The Bill intituled "An Act for the further amendment of the Law touching Letters Patent for Invention"*

The various organisations which turned their attention to patent law reform represented a wide variety of opinions. They were not merely vehicles to promote the interests of inventors or patentees. Henry Cole, a member of the patent Committee established by the Society of Arts, told the 1851 Select Committee that in looking generally at patent law reform associations:

> [T]he majority of all the members would be found to be inventors or manufacturers, but at the same time they represent various other classes; the Law Society chiefly represents lawyers; the Manchester Society, chiefly manufacturers; the Dublin Society, chiefly scientific men; the British Association, scientific men. With respect to the Committee of the Society of Arts, the only particular feature about it is, that, respecting generally all classes, it does not represent patent agents.[172]

Due to the diversity of the membership of these various organisations, it is unsurprising that there was disagreement amongst them as to the most pressing issues for patent law reform. Nevertheless, most agreed on certain general points. These were that the patent system needed reforming, that inventors needed better protection, and that the administration of the system needed modernising.[173]

The Emergence of the Abolition Movement

Not all, however, supported reform of the patent system. Even before the 1851 Select Committee commenced hearing evidence, a number of people had already made clear their view that the patent system should be abolished. In particular, during 1850 and 1851, the *Economist,* under the editorship of Sir James Wilson, featured articles which called for abolition of the patent system.

---

and to report thereon to the House: Session 1851 (1851) 486 vol XVIII, 233, 259 (Evidence of Henry Cole).

172 The reason for the exclusion of patent agents was said to be that in the view of the Society, "patent agents were not disinterested parties in the investigation; they were not the parties who had to pay or suffer, but the parties who gained by the present system, and lost nothing." UNITED KINGDOM, Parliamentary Papers, *Report and Minutes of Evidence taken before the Select Committee of the House of Lords appointed to consider of The Bill, intituled, "An Act further to amend the Law touching Letters Patent for Invention" and also of The Bill intituled "An Act for the further amendment of the Law touching Letters Patent for Invention" and to report thereon to the House: Session 1851* (1851) 486 vol XVIII, 233, 260–261 (Evidence of Cole).

173 Since many of the organisations sent representatives to the 1851 Select Committee, their views are discussed in that context below.

In an article in the *Economist* dated 28 December 1850, it was claimed that the "Law of Patents, like most other ancient laws, is unsuitable to our age and hostile to improvement."[174] The article further argued that before inventors established a right of property in their inventions, "they ought to give up all the knowledge and assistance they have derived from the knowledge and inventions of others."[175] As this was impossible, because inventions reflected the "mental whole of society",[176] it followed that inventors should not be entitled to any patent or other form of exclusive property right.[177]

In a later article published on 1 February 1851, the *Economist* again referred to the need to abolish the patent system, stating that the privileges granted by patents were "prohibitions on other men ... a prohibition against improvements in a particular direction, except by the patentee ... the community cannot be benefited by it".[178] The *Economist*'s arguments appeared to be based on a refutation of the oft-quoted argument that the supply of invention (which was also assumed to be the major cause of growth) would be diminished if patents were not used to protect the inventor. A reviewer in the *Edinburgh Review* of 1849 also questioned the necessity for patent protection, noting that the patent system encouraged people to undertake "enterprises so hopeless" to arrive at inventions which were often essentially useless.[179] Despite these comments, persons seeking the abolition of the patent system were clearly in the minority at this time, a point which becomes even more apparent when the evidence of the witnesses before the 1851 Select Committee is examined.

D The 1851 Select Committee

The 1851 Select Committee was appointed to conduct an enquiry into the two Bills concerning the subject of patent law reform which had been introduced into the House of Lords on 24 March and 10 April, 1851.[180] However, the Committee was not concerned merely to confine itself to an examination of the proposals set out in the two Bills. In calling evidence from thirty-two

174 *Economist*, 28 December 1850, 1433 (leading article).
175 *Ibid.* 1434.
176 *Ibid.*
177 *Ibid.*
178 *Economist*, 1 February 1851, 114–15 (leading article).
179 "The Progress of Mechanical Invention: Review of the Patent Journal and the Mechanics Magazine" (1849) 84 *The Edinburgh Review* 47, 48.
180 See note 169 above.

witnesses from many fields of experience, the Committee undertook a wide-ranging enquiry into the patent system.

An Analysis of Views about the Patent System Expressed by Witnesses before the 1851 House of Lords Select Committee on Patents

(1) The Witnesses

Amongst the witnesses examined by the 1851 Select Committee, many were persons concerned with patent legislation on a professional basis, such as patent agents,[181] barristers,[182] and solicitors.[183] In addition, the Committee also examined a large number of civil and mechanical engineers,[184] many of whom were also patentees.[185] Manufacturers were represented by the sugar refiners John Fairrie and Robert Macfie, the candle manufacturer Warren Hale, and the calico printer John Mercer. Evidence was also received from Bennet Woodcroft, Professor of Machinery at University College, London, and author of an index to Specifications of patents granted by the Patent Office. Lieutenant-Colonel Reid, Chairman of the Executive Committee of the 1851 London Exhibition also gave his opinion about the need for patent law reform. The major patent law reform associations also were represented, including the United Inventors' Association (Richard Wyatt, Secretary, and Joshua Westhead), the Manchester Patent Law Reform Association (William Fairbairn and Richard Roberts), and the Society of Arts (Henry Cole, Professor Bennet Woodcroft, and Richard Prosser). Finally, the situation for inventors in foreign countries such as Switzerland, Prussia and France was discussed by representatives from those countries.[186]

---

181 William Carpmael, Paul Hodge, Frederick Campin, William Spence and Alfred Newton.

182 Thomas Webster, Matthew Hill and John Lloyd.

183 John Duncan and Richard Wyatt.

184 Paul Hodge, William Fairbairn (later Sir William, who designed many bridges and vessels), Richard Roberts (developer of the self-acting mule and railway locomotives), Benjamin Fothergill, William Cubitt, Isambard Brunel, Richard Prosser, and James Rendel.

185 William Fairbairn, Richard Roberts, William Cubitt (inventor of the treadmill, and designer of the Southeastern railway and the Berlin waterworks), Isambard Brunel, and Richard Prosser. Other patentees who gave evidence, but who were apparently not engineers, included Sir David Brewster (the famous Scottish physicist, and inventor of the kaleidoscope, who discovered "Brewster's Law" – relating the polarising angle to the refractive index of the substance), Joshua Westhead and Charles May.

186 John Prevost, Consul-General of Switzerland, William Weddinge, of the Patent Commission of Prussia, and Louis Wolowski, Professor of Commercial Legislation, and member of the National Assembly of France.

(2) The Issues Raised by the Witnesses

There were many points of similarity in the issues raised by the witnesses before the 1829 and 1851 Select Committees. In both cases, discussion mainly revolved around practical problems associated with operation of the patent system. The problems of delay, inconvenience, lack of security before grant, the caveat system, the lack of patents of addition and the question of compulsory working again occupied most of the evidence. There was also some discussion of "foreign" issues. However, at the 1851 Inquiry, more evidence was presented concerning the underlying objectives of the patent system, and it appeared that this question was steadily receiving greater attention. One reason for this could be the fact that by 1851, there was a small, but vocal, band of persons supporting abolition of the patent system, and their arguments had prompted greater thought about theoretical issues.

(i) *Comments about the Underlying Objectives of the Patent System/ Calls for Abolition*

Unlike the witnesses before the 1829 Select Committee, nearly all those who appeared before the 1851 Select Committee gave their opinion as to the policies which lay at the heart of the patent system. In analysing this evidence, it is significant to note that only three witnesses justified the patent system on the basis of the traditional concept of the patent as a means of ensuring public disclosure of inventions.[187] However, two of these three witnesses justified the patent system upon more than one basis. The barrister, Webster, while agreeing that the disclosure of the secret was the main consideration of the patent,[188] also acknowledged that the patent system induced or stimulated invention,[189] and provided a reward for inventors.[190] Therefore, he actually used three different bases to justify the patent system. Woodcroft also stressed that the main object of the patent system was to ensure disclosure of inventions,[191]

---

187 UNITED KINGDOM, Parliamentary Papers, *Report and Minutes of Evidence taken before the Select Committee of the House of Lords appointed to consider of The Bill, intituled, "An Act further to amend the Law touching Letters Patent for Invention" and also of The Bill intituled "An Act for the further amendment of the Law touching Letters Patent for Invention" and to report thereon to the House: Session 1851* (1851) 486 vol XVIII, 233, 15 (Webster), 164 (Newton), 228, 241 (Woodcroft).

188 *Ibid.* 15.

189 Webster also stated that "if the history of the important trades of this country were carefully examined, it would be found that they had been built up upon a multiplied system of patents". *Ibid.* 13.

190 *Ibid.* 16–17.

191 *Ibid.* 228, 241.

stating that without the patent system, many inventions, especially those of a chemical nature, would be practised in secret.[192] However, he also noted that the patent system meant that there was an opportunity for inventors to obtain satisfactory financial reward from their endeavours,[193] and in many cases, acted as a stimulus for invention.[194] On the other hand, the barrister, Lloyd, argued that to justify the patent system on the basis of ensuring the disclosure of new inventions was misguided, because disclosure would eventually occur anyway.[195] He considered that most inventors enjoyed communicating their inventions; it was part of their natures to do so.[196] Even where they preferred secrecy, "there will always be found some other mind about the same time which will have hit upon the same idea, and the public will not long be deprived of the benefit."[197] Prosser, a civil engineer of Birmingham who had taken out 20 patents, favoured the abolition of the patent system, because of its limited advantages. To him, the only slight benefit from the patent system was that the publication of the specifications was a valuable record of research.[198]

It is clear, however, that the most commonly advanced justification for the patent system in 1851 was that patents acted as an inducement or incentive to invent, which in turn stimulated the inventive processes. One or more of the terms "inducement", "incentive", and "stimulus" were used by fourteen witnesses in describing the primary justification for the patent system.[199] The leading patent agent, Carpmael, agreed with the majority of witnesses when he stated that "there is a large class of cases of important inventions which have been the result of a great expenditure, partly of money and partly of time, which would not have been made without the inducement of a patent."[200]

An interesting point to note about the alleged "stimulus" of the patent system, was that it was seen to operate in different ways at a number of levels. For persons of independent means, who might not have relied upon the invention for the necessities of life, the patent brought fame and recognition, and the perception that their products were of quality. Fairbairn, the civil engineer,

192 *Ibid.* 232.
193 *Ibid.*
194 *Ibid.* 231.
195 *Ibid.* 362.
196 *Ibid.*
197 *Ibid.*
198 *Ibid.* 315.
199 *Ibid.* 146 (Fairrie), 153 (Macfie), 324 (Brewster), 347 (Westhead), 172 (Fairbairn), 32, 35, 38 (Carpmael), 88–9, 92 (Hodge), 370 (May), 283, 354, 278 (Hill), 113 (Campin), 288 (Mercer), 187, 189 (Roberts), 211 (Fothergill), 231 (Woodcroft).
200 *Ibid.* 38.

patentee and member of the Manchester Committee and the United Inventors' Association, said:

> [T]he great and powerful stimulus is to rise to distinction as an inventor ... [the patent] gives me the precedence over all parties who are not inventors of the same article, whereby, as a matter of trade, customers would come to me, in the first instance, for the machine I have invented, rather than go to the copyist.[201]

A similar view was expressed by Westhead, Chairman of the Inventors' Association for the Amendment of the Patent Laws.[202] At the other extreme of the social spectrum, Mercer, a calico printer, referred to the necessity to provide easy access to patent protection for ordinary people. He argued that the "greatest number of inventions are made by plain, and often poor people, but they have no encouragement to invent under the present patent laws" because the cost of obtaining a patent was too high.[203] He considered that patents should be made cheaper and easier to obtain, and this would stimulate ordinary people to be more inventive.

There were also some witnesses who continued to support the patent system upon the basis of the need to reward the inventor. Woodcroft agreed that, in a "large majority of cases", if the patent law did not exist, and no artificial protection were granted, there would be many instances in which an inventor would be deprived of profits which others would reap from his invention.[204] Carpmael, a patent agent, agreed that provision of reward was an important aspect of the patent system.[205] Roberts, the holder of "13 or 14" patents, including the gas-meter and the self-acting mule, stated that without the patent system, he would not have brought some of his inventions into use, because there would not have been sufficient advantage to compensate him for the unavoidable expense incurred.[206] An opposing opinion was given by the Master of the Rolls, Sir John Romilly, who thought that it was "a wrong principle to reward inventions by giving a monopoly".[207] This was largely because he considered

201 *Ibid.* 172.
202 *Ibid.* 347.
203 *Ibid.* 288. Charles Dickens wrote a scathing comment on the limited access of average people to the patent system in his short story: *"A Poor Man's Tale of a Patent"* (1850). For a commentary upon this work see: Phillips, J., *Charles Dickens and the "Poor Man's Tale of a Patent"* (Oxford, ESC Publishing, 1984).
204 *Ibid.* 232.
205 *Ibid.* 32.
206 *Ibid.* 195.
207 *Ibid.* 390.

that the patentee was usually a person who took a known principle, and made small additions to bring it into use. The person who discovered the important principle rarely gained patent protection.[208]

Perhaps the most interesting theoretical debate concerning the patent system emanated from the Society of Arts, which presented to the Select Committee a copy of *Extracts from the First Report on the Rights of Inventors,* together with the *Resolutions of the Committee for Legislative Recognition of the Rights of Inventors* (dated 26 December 1850).[209] Within the period of five years between 1845 and 1850, the Society had not only come to accept the benefits of the patent system, but it also strongly supported the French concept of natural property rights in inventions. In its First Report, the Society stated that:

> [E]very one must feel that inventive labour has its rights, which are not only entitled to equal recognition, but, being intellectual, are entitled, if possible, to a higher kind of recognition than other kinds of human labour. It may be called, for want of a more comprehensive phrase, a *natural* right, the exercise of which should be left perfectly free, and recognised as peculiarly sacred.[210]

The Society added that:

> [I]t must be conceded that inventors are entitled as fully to a positive recognition of their labours as *property*, as any other description of working people in the commonwealth.[211]

It was a necessary part of the Society's argument that there should be no pregrant examination of patent applications as to questions of validity. The property right could not be subject to any pre-conditions, and issues relating to the merit of the invention should be left for market forces to determine.[212] As the Committee for Legislative Recognition of the Rights of Inventors comprised a large number of influential people, such as the Marquis of Northampton, the

---

208 *Ibid.*
209 *Ibid.* Appendices C and D.
210 *Ibid.* 405.
211 *Ibid.*
212 *Ibid.* 405. The Society did accept, however, the proposition that patent monopolies should be of limited duration. It was necessary to do this to ensure that the public's interest and the inventor's interest both benefited from the patent.

Earl of Radnor, Dr Lyon Playfair, John Farey,[213] the author Charles Dickens,[214] and the potter Herbert Minton, their statements in support of natural property rights in inventions were quite remarkable. It is probably the earliest published example of significant U.K. support for natural property rights in inventions. Cole,[215] told the Committee that the Report:

> fairly embodies the views of the whole of the members named as constituting the committee. I do not think there were more than one or two divisions, and there was generally a great harmony of opinion among them upon the subject. It also embodies the views of the Council to whom it was reported, and who published it. And all the evidence which has subsequently come before the Council of the Society of Arts, shows that it is pretty generally approved of by the members at large.[216]

Abolition of the Patent System

In contrast to the arguments advanced by the Society of Arts, some witnesses argued that the patent system was a false stimulus to invention, and in many

---

213 This is the same John Farey who had given so much important evidence on the patent system to the 1829 Select Committee.

214 On 19 October 1850, Dickens had published his short story entitled *A Poor Man's Tale of a Patent*. Its main theme was to expose the costs, delays and inconveniences associated with obtaining a patent. It is not clear where Dickens derived his interest in patent law reform. It has been argued that Dickens' association with Henry Cole may have been a factor of influence. Dickens joined the Society of Arts in 1849 and had been in correspondence with Cole since 1847. Jeremy Phillips argues that "Cole invited Dickens to join the Society for the specific purpose of harnessing his literary talents and broad access to the general public, the better to state the case for patent law reform." Phillips, J., *Charles Dickens and the "Poor Man's Tale of a Patent"* (Oxford, ESC Publishing, 1984), 2–5.

215 Henry (later Sir Henry) Cole, is most famous for his involvement in the introduction of the penny post system, and for his work in establishing the Great Exhibition of 1851. He was Chairman of Council of the Society of Arts in 1852. He wrote a treatise on "Jurisprudence [in] connection with Inventions" and on 14 March 1849 he directed the attention of the Council of the Society of Arts to patent law reform. Phillips, J., *Charles Dickens and the "Poor Man's Tale of a Patent"* (Oxford, ESC Publishing, 1984), 2–5.

216 UNITED KINGDOM, Parliamentary Papers, *Report and Minutes of Evidence taken before the Select Committee of the House of Lords appointed to consider of The Bill, intituled, "An Act further to amend the Law touching Letters Patent for Invention" and also of The Bill intituled "An Act for the further amendment of the Law touching Letters Patent for Invention" and to report thereon to the House: Session 1851* (1851) 486 vol XVIII, 233, 259. Cole's own view was that the rights of the patentee should be considered the same as any other owner of property. Frederick Campin, a patent agent, (whose occupation excluded him from the Society of Arts) also made similar statements about property in inventions. *Ibid.* 113.

cases, patents obstructed development. Not all these witnesses advocated abolition of the system, but as a minimum they identified the need for extensive reforms. Cubitt, President of the Institution of Civil Engineers, doubted its benefits, believing that inventive persons would invent without regard to whether or not patents existed.[217] While he acknowledged that the patent system was useful in early times, in "a rude and infant state of society, where there is very great room for improvement,"[218] there was less value in patents "the more improved society becomes".[219] He believed that the U.K. had reached a stage where the patent system was no longer necessary to stimulate invention. He also stated that patents obstructed development, because of the monopoly granted to the patentee for fourteen years.[220]

Other persons also spoke of their concerns about the obstruction to development caused by the patent monopoly.[221] Ricardo, Chairman of the Electric Telegraph Company, told the Committee that the patent system should be abolished because it was encouraging a multiplicity of patents in various areas, which were being used as artificial blocking devices and subjecting legitimate inventors and manufacturers to costly litigation to defend their activities.[222]

Both Reid, Chairman of the Executive Committee of the 1851 Great Exhibition, and the barrister, Lloyd, considered that the patent system should be abolished. They argued that many persons who were not of a naturally inventive nature, were given a "false stimulus" by the patent system and had been encouraged to spend their time in pursuing worthless inventions.[223] Others also denied the "stimulus" provided by the patent system and spoke more generally of the beneficial effects which would flow from abolition of patents. Brunel, a civil engineer and famous inventor,[224] (whose father had given evidence at the 1829 Select Committee), considered that patents were

217 *Ibid.* 217.

218 *Ibid.* 219.

219 *Ibid.*

220 *Ibid.* 218.

221 *Ibid.* 92 (Hodge), 149–50 (Fairrie), 154–55 (Macfie), 246 fwd (Brunel), 307 (Reid), 393 (Ricardo).

222 Ricardo's evidence appears as an Appendix to the main part of the Report. *Ibid.* 399. (This is not the political economist, David Ricardo, who died in 1823.)

223 *Ibid.* 308 (Reid). Lloyd stated that "you incite them in pursuit of a shadow, which is continually apparently within their grasp, but continually eludes it; I find, in fact, that for one inventor, or supposed inventor, who succeeds, there are 50, or perhaps 100 who fail". *Ibid.* 361.

224 He designed the Clifton Suspension Bridge, the Royal Albert Bridge, the first trans-Atlantic wooden steamship, and the first iron-hulled screw-driven steamship. His father, Marc, had designed the first tunnel under the River Thames.

"productive of almost unmixed evil with respect to every party connected with them", including both the patentee and the public.[225] He disagreed with the proposition that the patent law encouraged inventions, stating that it "practically discourages them".[226] The reason for this was his belief that the state of development of the U.K. in 1851 was such "that a good invention now is rarely a new idea".[227] He added that the inventions then being patented were largely merely improvements upon old ideas, and patent protection was not justified. Furthermore, he argued that patents obstructed improvement in many fields, and gave an example of the case of the Electric Telegraph Company, who "were obliged to buy up everybody's inventions, good or bad, that interfered technically with theirs".[228] This had caused the expenditure of large sums of money, and public detriment by preventing the rapid distribution of electric telegraphs throughout the country.[229] Brunel also argued that the patent system did not benefit ordinary inventors, because their financial situation generally compelled them to sell the invention before it was put to public use.[230] Wealthy capitalists and industrialists were the main people who benefited from the patent system.[231] He added that in his view, the U.K. would suffer no real international detriment if the patent system was abolished. He agreed that there would be "greater inducements to parties making discoveries to take them to America or France, where patent laws do exist", and "for a year or two" those foreign countries would have "a priority in the use of discoveries".[232] However, he argued that this advantage would only be temporary, because the invention could easily be obtained from the foreign country and brought back

---

225 UNITED KINGDOM, Parliamentary Papers, *Report and Minutes of Evidence taken before the Select Committee of the House of Lords appointed to consider of The Bill, intituled, "An Act further to amend the Law touching Letters Patent for Invention" and also of The Bill intituled "An Act for the further amendment of the Law touching Letters Patent for Invention" and to report thereon to the House: Session 1851* (1851) 486 vol XVIII, 233, 246.

226 *Ibid.*

227 *Ibid.* 246.

228 *Ibid.* 249. He added that he believed that the Company had refrained from adopting many good improvements, because of fear of infringing other patents which it had not been able to purchase.

229 *Ibid.*

230 *Ibid.* 248.

231 Other witnesses also agreed that the inventor was usually not the person who benefited most from the patent. It was acknowledged that most good inventions were sold to "capitalists" who then proceeded to arrange the financing for commercialisation. *Ibid.* 210 (Fothergill), 179–180 (Fairbairn), 271 (Hill), 397–98 (Ricardo).

232 *Ibid.* 253.

to the U.K. free of charge. In addition, it was likely that once the U.K. had abolished the patent system, France and America would do the same.[233]

Cubitt also agreed that abolition of the patent system would probably force some inventors overseas, but that their inventions could easily be obtained, and brought back to the U.K. in a short space of time.[234] He added that the price of goods made in the U.K. would be cheaper because there would be no need to pay royalty fees to the patentee.[235] The Consul-general for Switzerland, Prevost, also gave his opinion that abolishing the patent system would not cause any long-term economic loss.[236] Although Switzerland had no patent system, he argued that it did not suffer any detriment. Instead, when a patent was obtained in France or the U.K. which had any relevance to Swiss manufactures,[237] the invention was soon discovered by the Swiss, and introduced into that country.[238]

The 1851 Select Committee hearings provided the first opportunity for those favouring abolition of the patent system to make their views known in an official forum. Until that time, very little had been published in the U.K. on the question of abolition, possibly because the wider subject of patent law reform had not received much attention since the earlier Select Committee of 1829. After 1851 there was a steady increase in the volume of publications favouring abolition of patents, although as is argued in the next Chapter, these views always remained in the minority.

(ii) *Foreign Issues*

The witnesses before the 1851 Select Committee appeared to be more aware than their 1829 counterparts of foreign issues associated with patent rights. This was possibly due to the fact that the Great Exhibition was being held in the same year. There was also a growing interest in protection of the rights of foreign inventors.

(a) Communication of Inventions from Abroad

The concept that the novelty of an invention should be tested only against prior disclosures in the United Kingdom, was supported by all the witnesses before the 1829 Select Committee, and it clearly retained support in 1851.

233 *Ibid.*
234 *Ibid.* 220.
235 *Ibid.*
236 *Ibid.* 293.
237 Mainly watchmaking and jewellery. *Ibid.*
238 *Ibid.* 293.

Most thought that inventions should remain patentable even if they had been communicated from abroad, with the knowledge of the foreign inventor.[239] Despite improvements in international communications, many witnesses still argued that laws permitting communication of inventions from abroad served to ensure the early introduction into the U.K. of inventions which had the potential to be highly beneficial to the country.[240] Some therefore argued that the interests of the public in ensuring development outweighed the interests of the foreign inventor.[241] It was also stated that as most countries besides France and the U.S.A. permitted patents of importation, the U.K. should adopt the course of the majority, and not put itself in a disadvantageous position.[242] However, in relation to cases where people made "a trade of importing to the prejudice of the foreign inventor",[243] a large number of witnesses argued that this practice should be stopped.[244] They argued that "the rights of the original inventor abroad should be preserved."[245] This might be accomplished by ensuring that the permission of the foreign inventor was sought before any patent was granted in the U.K., or requiring the foreign inventor to be the person who applied for the patent in the U.K.[246] Hodge, a patent agent, suggested that foreign inventors should be given a grace period of one year from the date of patenting in their country of origin in which to apply for a patent in the U.K., otherwise the invention would become public property.[247] These changing attitudes to foreign inventors were quite significant, and there were far fewer patronising remarks about foreign inventors and manufacturers than in 1829. Foreigners were no longer seen merely as trading enemies, trying to steal U.K. inventions.

---

239 For example, *Ibid.* 188–9 (Roberts).

240 *Ibid.* 142 (Spence), 315–7 (Prosser), 158 (Newton), 344–5 (Westhead), 283 (Hill), 71 (Carpmael).

241 *Ibid.* 104 (Wyatt), 118 (Campin).

242 *Ibid.* 118 (Campin).

243 *Ibid.* 189 (Roberts). Hodge called patent importers "a parcel of people who have no character of their own, and who do not care what they do. The persons introducing foreign patents without proper authority are generally men of no reputation." *Ibid.* 101.

244 *Ibid.* 180–1 (Fairbairn), 372 (May), 339 (Rendel), 326 (Brewster), 307 (Reid), 270 (Cole), 366 (Lloyd), 150–1 (Fairrie), 217 (Cubitt).

245 *Ibid.* 19 (Webster).

246 *Ibid.* 213 (Fothergill).

247 *Ibid.* 101. Hodge had practised as a patent agent in the U.S.A. for 16 years, and his proposal was based upon U.S. law.

(b) Views about Foreign Patent Laws

As in 1829, the Committee sought witnesses' views about the efficacy of foreign patent systems, and called evidence from French, Swiss, Prussian and U.S. patent experts.[248] Although the members of the Committee questioned the foreign witnesses closely, it was apparent that their greatest interest was in the systems of preliminary examination of specifications practised in the U.S.A. and Prussia. Their interest in the French patent system did not appear as great as in 1829, possibly because they wanted to look for alternatives beyond the French system of simple registration of patents. In regard to the Swiss evidence, the Committee found it useful to obtain a description of an economy without a patent system, but it was sceptical about the relevance of the Swiss experience in a major manufacturing country like the United Kingdom. Neither the witnesses or the Committee members discussed the feasibility of introducing any system of international protection of patent rights.

E The Aftermath of the 1851 Select Committee – The Reforms of 1852 and Their International Significance

(a) *The Passage of the 1852 Act*

After hearing the evidence of the witnesses, the Select Committee eventually decided that it would recommend to the House that neither of the two Bills be adopted, but that a third Bill should be drawn up. This Bill, which was introduced into the House of Lords in June 1851, was drawn up by Thomas Webster,[249] but *The Times* newspaper alleged that it was in reality Earl Granville's bill.[250] *The Times* stated that "the inquiries respecting it had been conducted by him, and all the provisions it contained were thus stamped with the approval of the Government."[251] As the President of the Board of Trade, Henry Labouchére, stated in the House of Commons on 5 August 1851, the members of the 1851 Select Committee had seriously considered recommending abolition of the

248 John Prevost, Consul-General of Switzerland; William Weddinge, of the Patent Commission of Prussia; Louis Wolowski, Professor of Commercial Legislation, and member of the National Assembly of France; and Paul Hodge, a patent agent who had practised for 16 years in the U.S.A.

249 Dutton, H.I. *op.cit.* 62.

250 At that time, Earl Granville was the Vice-President of the Board of Trade, and had been the Chairman of the 1851 Select Committee.

251 *The Times*, 21 August 1851, 4 (leading article).

patent system, but had finally decided against this course.[252] He reported that Earl Granville had:

> expressed an opinion, shared by the majority of the Lords' committee, that the principle of patent laws was vicious and ought to be discarded; but he and all the committee held it most desirable that this bill, remedying monstrous and glaring evils in the present system, should pass into law at once, and they thought that the public opinion of this country was not ripe for so great a change as the abolition of patents.[253]

Since an analysis of the views of witnesses before the 1851 Select Committee shows that a majority did not support abolition of the patent system, this comment about informed "public opinion" not seeking patent abolition was quite correct. Writers in the mainstream press, such as *The Times*, criticised any moves to limit patent protection, stating that the patent system should be reformed, rather than abolished.[254] It was really only the *Economist* which came down firmly in support of Early Granville's view that the patent system should be abolished.[255]

(b) *The Content of the 1852 Act*

The fact that the 1851 Select Committee seriously considered abolition of the patent system is probably more interesting than the actual provisions of the Patent Law Amendment Act 1852. As the Attorney-General told the House

---

252 Reported in *The Times*, 6 August 1851, 4.

253 *Ibid.* The *Economist* also reported that Earl Granville wished to abolish the patent system. It said in a leading article on 26 July 1851, 811 that it read "with great pleasure, Earl Granville's manly declaration, that 'he had gone into the committee with some doubt, and he was sorry to say, such was the obstinacy of his nature, that all the evidence in favour and against had sent him forth confirmed in the belief that it was inadvisable for the public, of no advantage for the inventor, and wrong in principle, to have any patents for inventions at all.' "

254 See *The Times*, 1 August 1851, 4; 7 August 1851, 4; and 21 August 1851, 4 (leading articles). *The Times* stated that the twin rationales for the patent system were to ensure disclosure of inventions to the public and to provide just reward to inventors.

255 The *Economist* stated that "we agree with the Noble Lord … that the principle of the law is erroneous, that the system of patents is altogether wrong, and that no possible good can ever come of a Patent Law, however, admirably it may be framed." (26 July 1851, 812 – leading article). U.S. commentators viewed the results of the 1851 Select Committee with interest. An article in the *New York Times* praised Earl Granville's view that the patent system should be abolished, but recognised that this goal would not be achieved for some time. (*New York Times*, 22 May 1852, 2 – leading article).

of Commons on 4 August 1851, the fact was that "scarcely any of the clauses related to the substantive law of patents, but simply to the machinery by which patents were to be obtained."[256] The 1852 Act was not the same as Webster's 1851 Bill, because that Bill was not able to be returned to the House of Lords in the 1851 Session.[257] Another two Bills were introduced after the change of government in February 1852,[258] and it was the government Bill which became the 1852 Act.

There was little distinction between the 1851 Webster Bill and the 1852 Act. The main difference was that all the 1851 Bills had provided for some form of compulsory preliminary examination of patents as to issues of novelty, whereas such an examination was at the commissioners' discretion under the 1852 Act.[259] Other features of the 1852 Act included the introduction of a single patent for the United Kingdom, in place of the three separate patents for England, Scotland and Ireland. The patent fee was not significantly lowered: in fact, under the new system the fee for a patent was set at 180 pounds.[260] However, a scheme for periodical payment of fees was introduced, and so it was no longer necessary for patentees to suffer the economic hardship of paying the full fee at the beginning of the patent term. A single Patent Office, under the Commissioners of Patents, was established, in place of the various offices which had previously had jurisdiction over patents. The patenting of inventions which had been "communicated from abroad" also continued, although a new section provided that a U.K. patent for an invention previously patented abroad could not continue in force after the expiry of the foreign patent.[261] The most useful change was the introduction of a provision that patent rights should commence as from the date of application rather than the

256 Reported in *The Times*, 5 August 1851, 3.

257 Evidence of Thomas Webster – UNITED KINGDOM, Parliamentary Papers, *Report from the Select Committee on Letters Patent; together with the Proceedings of the Committee, Minutes of Evidence, Appendix and Index* (1871) 368, vol x, 603, 44.

258 A private Bill was again introduced by Lord Brougham, and a government Bill was introduced by Lord Colchester. *Ibid.*

259 *Ibid.* Patent Law Amendment Act 1852, section 8. Thomas Webster told the 1871 Select Committee (at 46) that it was a matter of some concern that none of the promoters of the 1852 Act had been members of the 1851 Select Committee, or had been actively involved in patent law reform in 1851.

260 This was higher than the previous fee for an English patent, but lower than a fee for a patent which covered the three kingdoms. See Patent Regulations of 1 October 1852, made under the Patent Law Amendment Act 1852.

261 Patent Law Amendment Act 1852, section 25.

date of sealing, although it became necessary for the applicant to file either a Provisional or Complete Specification at the date of application.[262]

(c) *The International Significance of the Reforms of 1852*

In Chapter One it was noted that the French patent legislation, and particularly the Law of 7 January 1791, was used as a model by many countries who subsequently decided to introduce or modernise their patent systems. The same could be argued of the U.K. patent legislation after the reforms of 1852.

The influence of the United Kingdom patent law was particularly apparent when patent systems were introduced into many British colonies in the mid-nineteenth century.[263] Within ten years after the passage of the U.K. Act of 1852, it was estimated that approximately one-half of all British colonies had enacted their own patent legislation, using the Act of 1852 as the appropriate model.[264] These included most of the larger colonies such as Victoria,[265] New South Wales (including Queensland),[266] Tasmania,[267] South Australia,[268] India,[269] Ceylon,[270] Cape of Good Hope,[271] New Zealand,[272] and British Honduras.[273]

---

262 Patent Law Amendment Act 1852, sections 3 and 6. If a Provisional Specification was filed, it was necessary to ensure that the nature of the invention was described sufficiently in order that the same invention could be ascertained in the subsequent Complete Specification.

263 Patents granted under the Great Seal prior to 1 October 1852 were said to extend to England, the Channel Islands, the Isle of Man, the Colonies and Plantations abroad, but not to extend to Scotland or Ireland, (for these latter countries separate patents were granted.) Under the U.K. Patent Laws Amendment Act of 1852, patents granted from 1 October 1852 extended only to the United Kingdom of Great Britain and Ireland, the Channel Islands and the Isle of Man, the decision having been taken to no longer extend U.K. patents to any of the Colonies. However, as far back as 1829, there were questions whether the Colonial legislatures were obliged to recognise patents granted in the United Kingdom. Thomas Lennard, Chairman of the 1829 Select Committee noted that "[i]t has been stated, that a patent taken out for the colonies, does not avail a party in those colonies that have legislatures of their own, unless it is recognized by those legislatures …" UNITED KINGDOM, Parliamentary Papers, *Report from the Select Committee on the Law Relative to Patents for Inventions* (1829) 332, vol III, 415, 103.

264 UNITED KINGDOM, Parliamentary Papers, *Report of the Commissioners appointed to Inquire into the Working of the Law Relating to Letters Patent for Inventions* (1864) 3419, vol XXIX, 321, Evidence of Woodcroft, Superintendent of Specifications at the Patent Office in London at 4, Evidence of Edmunds, Clerk of the Patents, Patent Office, London at 30.

265 Patent Act 1854 (Vic).

266 Patent Act 1852 (N.S.W.).

267 Patent Act 1858 (Tasmania).

268 Patent Act 1859 (S.A.).

269 Patent Act 1856 (India).

270 Patent Act 1859 (Ceylon).

271 Patent Act 1860 (Cape of Good Hope).

272 Patent Act 1860 (N.Z.).

273 Patent Act 1862 (British Honduras). General details about these various Acts are derived from: UNITED KINGDOM, Parliamentary Papers, *Report from the Select Committee*

The U.K. Act of 1852 also had some influence outside the British colonies. Examples of countries whose patent systems appear to have some notable points of similarity to the U.K. model (so far as mechanical matters are concerned) included the Austrian Law of 15 August 1852, the Belgian Law of 24 May 1854,[274] the Colombian Law of 13 May 1869, and the Swedish and Norwegian Laws of 19 August 1856.[275] The French and U.K. traditions of leadership in the development of patent law continued into the second half of the nineteenth century, and it was consistent with this tradition that the governments and individuals of these two countries led the movement towards international protection of industrial property rights.

The Patent Law Amendment Act of 1852 was certainly not the kind of Act which was sought by witnesses before the 1851 Select Committee. It did little to address the problems raised by the majority of witnesses, who clearly desired a major reconstruction of the patent system. *The Times* saw the Bill which came to the Commons in August 1851 as "mutilated and transformed" compared to the original proposals, upon which there had been "bestowed so much patient attention."[276] The 1852 Act was seen as a temporary measure only, which would remedy some of the worst defects,[277] but was not a final solution.[278]

It is probable that the failure comprehensively to address the problems identified by the witnesses before the 1851 Select Committee encouraged the

on Letters Patent; together with the Proceedings of the Committee, Minutes of Evidence, Appendix and Index (1872) 193, vol XI, 395, Evidence of Woodcroft, Chief Clerk of the Patent Office in London at 76 and Appendix (A). UNITED KINGDOM, Parliamentary Papers, *Correspondence respecting International Arrangements for Assimilation in Law and Practice in regard to Letters Patent of Inventions* (1874) C. 999, vol LIV, 211.

274 Although the influence of the French Law of 5 July 1844 was also evident.

275 This information has been obtained from examining the texts of the relevant laws and commentaries in UNITED KINGDOM, Parliamentary Papers, *Reports by H.M. Secs of Embassy and Legation respecting Law and Practice in Foreign Countries with regard to Inventions* (1873) C. 741, vol LXVI, 483; Pataille, J., and Huguet, A., *Code International de la Propriété Industrielle Artistique et Littéraire contenant les legislations Française et étrangéres et les Traités Internationaux en Matiére de Brevets d'invention, Littérature, Théatre, Musique, Beaux-Arts Dessins, Modéles, Noms et Marques de Fabrique et Concurrence Commerciale* (Paris, Marescq, 1865).

276 *The Times,* 21 August 1851, 4 (leading article). Further changes were incorporated in the 1852 Bill.

277 *The Times,* 1 August 1851, 4 (leading article).

278 See also Dutton, H.I., *op.cit.* 64.

growth of the patent abolition movement over the next twenty years. However, this Chapter has shown that regardless of the later abolition debate, by 1851 there was a strong body of opinion in the U.K. that the patent system had the potential to achieve valuable objectives. Although the system had many practical problems, most thought it better to have a defective system, rather than no system at all. Many witnesses before the 1851 Select Committee adopted an instrumentalist approach in justifying the existence of the patent law. In their opinion, the patent law served a useful social purpose, by stimulating invention, rewarding the inventor, and/or discouraging secrecy. This was quite different from the oft-quoted opinion in France, which saw the objective of the patent system as being the protection of "natural" property rights in inventions. Yet, as was shown in Chapter One, even in France there was in reality a mixture of theoretical justifications for the patent system. Similarly, this Chapter notes that although U.K. commentators in the early nineteenth century might have restricted their theoretical discussions to a brief acknowledgement of the contractual relationship between the inventor and the State, these opinions became more thoughtful and were refined as the century progressed. The 1851 Select Committee saw a more detailed discussion of these issues than had been the case in 1829. How these theoretical debates were further developed in the U.K. during the next twenty years is the subject of Chapter Three.

CHAPTER 3

UNITED KINGDOM: Development of Ideas and Concepts about the Theoretical Basis of the Patent System: 1853–1872

> The entire abolition of a system which does not benefit the inventor, which hampers the producer, and taxes the purchaser, would, in the words of a great inventor, Sir Isambard Brunel, be 'an immense benefit to the country'.[1]

∴

Chapter Two has demonstrated that U.K. commentators showed no great interest in the theoretical basis of the patent system until 1851. This was in contrast to the situation in France, where in both 1790–1 and 1843–4, proposals for patent law reform had prompted significant discussion of this issue. However, suddenly, in 1851, and prompted by the proposals for a Great Exhibition in London, patent law reform became an important concern in the United Kingdom. Along with issues of a practical nature, some commentators began to look closely at the theoretical basis of the patent system. The study of theoretical questions began in earnest when organisations, as well as individuals, became interested in the patent law.

This Chapter examines the ideas and opinions about the patent system which developed in the U.K. in the twenty years after the passage of the Patent Law Amendment Act 1852. In an article published in 1950,[2] the U.S. economic historians Fritz Machlup and Edith Penrose wrote that from 1850 to 1875 a "controversy" raged between supporters and opponents of the patent system in a number of countries (chiefly the U.K., France, Germany, Holland and Switzerland).[3] They argued that at "the end of the 1860's the cause of patent protection seemed completely lost."[4] The main focus of this Chapter is to

---

1 *The Times*, 15 August 1864, 8 (leading article).

2 Machlup, F., and Penrose, E., "The Patent Controversy in the Nineteenth Century" (1950) x *The Journal of Economic History* 1.

3 *Ibid.* 1.

4 *Ibid.* 4.

 | DOI:10.1163/9789004470125_005

demonstrate that Machlup and Penrose's arguments were misguided, and that there was no significant threat to the continued existence of the patent system in the U.K. during this period.

During the twenty years after the 1852 Act, the level of debate about patents in the U.K. varied significantly. There was not constant discussion about the system, but there were certain periods in which a published article, speech or report would focus public attention on it. However, there were some discernible trends in public opinion towards patents, and these trends occupied three distinct periods of time. In the first period, from 1853 up to 1864 (the end of the 1862–1864 Select Committee Inquiry on Letters Patent for Inventions),[5] there was very little support for the abolition of the patent system in the U.K.: in general, those who examined the matter asked only for removal of practical difficulties associated with the administration of the patent law. In the second period, following the publication of the Select Committee's Report in July 1864, until early 1871, a significant number of individuals (but not organisations) supported the abolition of the U.K. patent system. However, by the third period, which coincided with the work of the 1871–1872 Select Committees,[6] the majority opinion, (of both individuals and organisations), was that the patent system remained a necessary stimulus to invention and that U.K. trade advantages depended upon its continued existence.

There were three main reasons why the patent abolition movement failed in the United Kingdom. These were:

(1) The lack of any suitable alternative to the patent system, and in particular, perceived problems associated with various proposed schemes for State rewards.

(2) The fact that most patent abolitionists were individuals who fell within a limited range of professions. They were usually lawyers, economic philosophers or intellectuals, who did not necessarily share the same perspective on the problem as practical users of the patent system such as patent agents,[7] inventors, manufacturers and their workmen.

---

5 UNITED KINGDOM, Parliamentary Papers, *Report of the Commissioners appointed to Inquire into the Working of the Law Relating to Letters Patent for Inventions* (1864) 3419, vol XXIX, 321.

6 UNITED KINGDOM, Parliamentary Papers, *Report from the Select Committee on Letters Patent; together with the Proceedings of the Committee, Minutes of Evidence, Appendix and Index* (1871) 368, vol X, 603; UNITED KINGDOM, Parliamentary Papers, *Report from the Select Committee on Letters Patent; together with the Proceedings of the Committee, Minutes of Evidence, Appendix and Index* (1872) 193, vol XI, 395.

7 Although it must be noted that patent agents would have had a vested interest in maintenance of the patent system.

(3) The fact that even at the height of the attack upon the patent system, very few professional, commercial and cultural organisations supported abolition. The patent abolitionists were generally individuals and thus did not have the influence which they needed to secure their desired reforms.

It should also be explained at this stage why this Chapter does not examine U.K. theoretical debates about the patent system after 1872. The main reason is that by 1872 the U.K. Government began to turn its attention to the possibility of an international agreement in relation to patents, and this evolving policy was completely inconsistent with any notion of abolishing the domestic patent system. In addition, in 1873 the first International Patent Congress was held in Vienna[8] and that coincided with a great decrease throughout Europe in agitation for abolition of patents.

A U.K. Attitudes to the Patent System from 1853 until 1864

(a) *Overview of Debates – 1853 to 1863*

The immediate consequence of the Patent Law Amendment Act 1852 was a temporary cessation of calls for patent law reform. Bennet Woodcroft, who in 1852 became Superintendent of Specifications in the Patent Office, gave evidence before the 1862–64 Select Committee on Letters Patent,[9] that of nine societies which had been formed between 1848 and 1851 with the express purpose of effecting reform in the patent laws, not one was still in existence in 1862.[10] He asserted that this was "proof of the general satisfaction given by the working of the new law ..."[11]

Very few articles were published or speeches made on the subject of patent law reform between 1853 and August 1861. The only major examination of the patent system which occurred before the 1862–64 Select Committee was the *Report of the Committee of the British Association and of the Social Science Association on the Amendment of the Patent Laws* (1861).[12] This Report resulted

8 Pieper, C., *Der Erfinderschutz und die Reform der Patentgesetze. Amtlicher Bericht über den Internationalen Patent-Congress zur Erörterung der Frage des Patentschutzes. Mit einer Einleitung von Dr. C.W. Siemens F.R.S.* (Dresden, Commission der Schulbuchhandlung, 1873). See Chapter Five for further details on the work of this Congress.

9 UNITED KINGDOM, Parliamentary Papers, *Report of the Commissioners appointed to Inquire into the Working of the Law Relating to Letters Patent for Inventions* (1864) 3419, vol XXIX, 321.

10 *Ibid.* 149 (Appendix 1).

11 *Ibid.*

12 Reproduced in UNITED KINGDOM, Parliamentary Papers, *Report of the Commissioners appointed to Inquire into the Working of the Law Relating to Letters Patent for Inventions*

from the work of a Committee formed in 1859 which was composed of members of both the British Association for the Advancement of Science, and the National Association for the Promotion of Social Science. The work of this joint committee, which came out firmly in favour of the continued existence of the patent system, illustrates that the patent abolition movement had difficulty attracting support from important scientific and cultural organisations. Without this support, the movement had little hope of success.

(i) Organisations and Patent Abolition – The Work of the British Association for the Advancement of Science and the National Association for the Promotion of Social Science: 1859 to 1861

It was not long after the founding of the National Association for the Promotion of Social Science in 1857 that the issue of patent law reform was brought to its attention. This was unsurprising, since the President of the Association was the noted patent-reformer, Lord Brougham, and it also contained members such as Lord Stanley, Thomas Webster and Robert Macfie, who were at the forefront of the debate over the patent system.[13] Stanley, later the Chairman of the 1862–64 Select Committee on Patents, and Macfie, an influential Liverpool sugar refiner (and later M.P. for Leith) subsequently became two of the strongest supporters of the patent abolition movement.

The Constitution of the Association provided that law reform was one of its clear aims.[14] On the suggestion of Macfie at the Liverpool Congress in October 1858, the Association resolved that one of the first areas of law which should be studied was the patent system.[15] Consequently, at the Association's November 1859 meeting in Bradford:

(1864) 3419, vol XXIX, 321, 174 (Appendix to evidence of Thomas Webster). Also discussed in 'Report of the Special Committee on the Patent Laws' (1861) *Transactions of the National Association for the Promotion of Social Science* 229.

13 See generally, "The National Association for the Promotion of Social Science" (1858) 4 *The Law Magazine and Law Review* 145.

14 The Constitution provided that the Association should "aid the development of social science … to guide the public mind to the best practical means of promoting the amendment of the laws … and the diffusion of sound principles on all questions of social economy." *Ibid.* 159.

15 See Macfie, R.A., 'The Law of Patents for Inventions' (1858) *Transactions of the National Association for the Promotion of Social Science* 147. "The National Association for the Promotion of Social Science; Congress at Liverpool, October 15, 1858" (1858–9) 6 *The Law Magazine and Law Review* 117, 155.

> [A] Committee was appointed to co-operate with a Committee of the British Association, held at Aberdeen in the same year, to consider and report on the best means to be adopted for affording better protection and security to property in inventions, and for obviating the objections made to the operation and working of the Patent Laws.[16]

Like the social science Association, the British Association for the Advancement of Science had also shown an interest in patent law reform since its foundation. At its first conference in York in 1831, the aims of the Association were discussed and it was agreed that patent law reform was "one of the objects specially deserving the attention of a scientific association ..."[17] Although on various subsequent occasions the Association did undertake limited studies of the practical effects of the patent system,[18] it was not until the annual meeting in Aberdeen in 1859 that the attention of the Association widened to examine more generally the inadequacies of the patent laws. Aware that the National Association for the Promotion of Social Science had also been discussing this question, the British Association proposed that a joint committee of the two Associations should be established to report upon the matter.[19]

In examining the Report of the joint Committee which was presented to the members of the two Associations in 1861, it is clear that there was overwhelming support for the continuance of the patent system. This result was a victory for Webster, who, as an active member of both Associations, and a member of the joint Committee, had lobbied his fellow committee members to take a firm stance in favour of the concept of patents for inventions.[20] In a paper

16 UNITED KINGDOM, Parliamentary Papers, *Report of the Commissioners appointed to Inquire into the Working of the Law Relating to Letters Patent for Inventions* (1864) 3419, vol XXIX, 321, 174 (Appendix to evidence of Thomas Webster). The actual Resolution was moved by Webster, and seconded by Macfie, and read as follows: "That the Council be requested to appoint a Committee to consider the question of improvements in the law of patents, and to co-operate with the Committee of the British Association for the same object." (1859) *Transactions of the National Association for the Promotion of Social Science* 273.

17 "Report of the Special Committee on the Patent Laws" (1861) *Transactions of the National Association for the Promotion of Social Science* 229.

18 For example, between 1854 and 1859 the Association considered what should be done with the large sum of money raised by patent fees. It finally resolved that the money should be used more directly for "the reward of meritorious inventors, and the advancement of practical science." *Ibid.*

19 "Report of the Special Committee on the Patent Laws" (1861) *Transactions of the National Association for the Promotion of Social Science* 229.

20 Webster, T., "On the Protection of Property in Intellectual Labour as embodied in Inventions, Books, Designs and Pictures, by the Amendment of the Laws of Patent-right

published at the time, Webster stated that all discussion of patent law reform should take place under the assumption that the "protection to property in the products of intellectual labour" was "consistent with natural justice and good policy".[21] He urged his fellow members to support the argument that intellectual labour could give rise to a right of property when embodied in a visible or tangible form, although he would not go so far as to present this as a "natural" property right.[22]

Webster's concept of the theoretical basis of the patent system was adopted by the joint Committee. It agreed that inventors had rights of property in their inventions, which were essentially rights arising from "the product of their own brains."[23] It considered that the benefits of the patent system should remain available to all inventors.[24] Nevertheless, it could not deny that a number of practical problems existed.

The major concern was the proliferation of patents granted since the 1852 amendments came into operation. The Report noted that under the 1852 Act, the cost of obtaining patents was greatly reduced, and:

> now it is that too many are granted; that the cost is so small, and the facility of obtaining so great, that claims of all kinds, however frivolous or absurd, ... are made the subject of Patent privilege.[25]

The consequence of this was that the community was:

> deluged with invalid and worthless Patents, which serve no other purpose than to harass the public, obstruct the progress of invention, encourage litigation, and in some cases serve as instruments of oppression.[26]

---

and Copyright" (1859) *Transactions of the National Association for the Promotion of Social Science* 237, 244.

21 *Ibid.*

22 *Ibid.* 238.

23 *Report of the Committee of the British Association and of the Social Science Association on the Amendment of the Patent Laws* reproduced in UNITED KINGDOM, Parliamentary Papers, *Report of the Commissioners appointed to Inquire into the Working of the Law Relating to Letters Patent for Inventions* (1864) 3419, vol XXIX, 321, 174 (Appendix to evidence of Thomas Webster).

24 *Ibid.*

25 *Ibid.*

26 *Ibid.*

The Report of the joint Committee identified two main ways in which the problems associated with the excessive numbers of patents could be resolved. It did not think it would be justified to return to the old system where fees were so high that few patents were granted. This was because of the Committee's conviction that inventions gave rise to property rights, and that legal protection for these rights should remain available to all inventors.[27] However, the Committee proposed that all applications for patents should be subject to a compulsory examination before a special Tribunal of a judge and assessors in regard to issues of novelty, originality, or utility. If an application was found to fail one or more of these tests, the applicant would be advised not to pursue the application.[28]

The second way to resolve the problems associated with the large numbers of patents was to introduce a form of compulsory licensing, somewhat similar to the proposals made by Macfie in 1858.[29] The Committee noted that "[o]ne argument of those who object to the whole system of Patent grants for inventions, is, that such a system tends to obstruct the progress of invention; ... that the case is exceptional where any great stride is made in invention" and because of this, the grant of a patent could cause other inventors following close behind in the same area to be prevented from pursuing their improvements.[30] It proposed that this problem could be overcome by a system of compulsory licensing. Although the Committee realised that this proposal called into question the nature of the property rights belonging to the inventor, it was a necessary compromise solution. It had evidently been urged by some members of the Committee that if an inventor was compelled to grant a licence, this meant that he would not have "that full power over the creation of his genius to which he is entitled".[31] However, the Committee finally adopted a more instrumentalist approach in its recommendation in favour of compulsory licensing. It considered the interest of the public as well as the inventor, and accepted that there was no reason why the State should bind itself to create an absolute

27 *Ibid.*

28 *Ibid.* However, if the applicant rejected the advice, he could still obtain the patent, but only at his own peril.

29 See Macfie, R.A., 'The Law of Patents for Inventions' (1858) *Transactions of the National Association for the Promotion of Social Science* 147.

30 *Report of the Committee of the British Association and of the Social Science Association on the Amendment of the Patent Laws* reproduced in UNITED KINGDOM, Parliamentary Papers, *Report of the Commissioners appointed to Inquire into the Working of the Law Relating to Letters Patent for Inventions* (1864) 3419, vol XXIX, 321, 176 (Appendix to evidence of Thomas Webster).

31 *Ibid.* 177.

interest where a more limited one, equally securing the interests of the public, would suffice.[32]

The recommendations of the joint Committee were clearly in favour of the continuance of the patent system, although it was recognised that major reforms were required. It has been noted that in the "years following, this document became a charter of reform aspiration",[33] and it is clear that the work of the joint Committee helped the 1862–1864 Select Committee in determining which issues were of most concern. The joint Committee's recommendations were also closely studied by other bodies interested in the patent system.[34] Far from being a document which could be used to advance the interests of the patent abolition movement, the Report reaffirmed the importance of the patent system.

(ii) Individuals and Patent Abolition – 1861 to 1864

The release of the joint Committee's Report coincided with a resurgence of support for the abolition of the patent system. Articles severely critical of the system appeared in the mainstream press and in specialist economic and law journals from August 1861. Some of these articles advocated the abolition of the patent system; others wanted severe limitations to be placed upon its operation. Although the authors were very strident in making known their views, the opinions they presented were not those of the majority. The number of articles published in support of abolition was not great, and most authors came from only one or two professional groups (lawyers or economic philosophers). They

---

32 *Ibid.*

33 Batzel, V.M., "Legal Monopoly in Liberal England: The Patent Controversy in the Mid-Nineteenth Century" (1980) 22 *Business History* 189, 194. In 1863 a commentator wrote that the membership of the joint Committee was such that "no body of men could be found whose judgment is likely to carry more weight with the public; ... the chairman was Lord Stanley; Mr Joseph Napier, General Sabine, Mr Grove, Mr Webster, Mr Heywood and other eminent men, were amongst its active members; its report was prepared with great care, and was based on resolutions carried after anxious inquiry and discussion." "The Patent Law" (1862–3) 14 *The Law Magazine and Law Review* 94, 97.

34 See for example, *Report of the Sub-Committee appointed at a Meeting of the General Committee of the Manchester Patent Law Reform Association held at the Town Hall, January 31st, 1862, to consider the Resolutions proposed by a Committee of the British Association for the Reform of the Patent Laws, and to report to the General Committee on the Merits of such Resolutions, and also to suggest any other Alterations in the present Laws which the said Sub-Committee may consider necessary or desirable.* Reproduced in UNITED KINGDOM, Parliamentary Papers, *Report of the Commissioners appointed to Inquire into the Working of the Law Relating to Letters Patent for Inventions* (1864) 3419, vol XXIX, 321, 211.

were generally not inventors or manufacturers: the people who had the greatest interest in the operation of the patent system.

One of the few inventors who supported abolition of patents was Sir William Armstrong, who was also President of the Mechanical Engineers' Society. In August 1861 he gave an address before the Society in which he made a strong attack upon the patent system. The speech was reported in *The Times*, and led to considerable debate.[35] The essence of his argument was that the patent system should be abolished, because inventors were being constantly obstructed in their work by a multitude of patents. He considered it was inappropriate to grant monopoly rights in relation to "primary ideas" which are "capable of useful application" and which "ought to be the common property of all".[36] Another inventor of lesser note, C.W. Strickland of Whitby, wrote in support of Armstrong, stating that his main objection to the patent system was that it was "opposed to the true principles of free trade."[37] In addition, he argued that one of the main policies which lay at the heart of the patent system was to ensure that inventors reaped a pecuniary advantage from their invention, but in reality, this object was not being met.[38] He stated that, in his large experience of patents and patenting, the inventors of the most valuable inventions reaped very little reward, because their rights were constantly infringed, and they were forced to either suffer the infringement, or spend large sums of money in pursuing litigation.[39] Shortly after, John Ricardo, M.P., who had given evidence in support of abolition of patents before the 1851 Select Committee, reasserted his earlier views, and called for the establishment of a Parliamentary Committee to examine the specific issue of abolition of the patent system.[40] These speeches and letters published in *The Times* were indicative of the limitations of the early patent abolition movement. Each writer gave different reasons for abolition, either a denial of property rights in inventions (Armstrong), support for free trade (Strickland), or practical problems with the working of the system (Strickland and Ricardo). It is clear that the abolition movement

35 *The Times*, 20 August 1861.

36 *Ibid.*

37 In reply, the correspondent "A.V.N." (probably Alfred Vincent Newton, a strong supporter of the patent system), stated that Armstrong did not have full understanding of the practical benefits of the patent system. These benefits included the stimulus to development provided by patents, and the fact that under the patent system, new ideas were converted into "tangible property", without which security there would be little inducement to invest in new inventions. *The Times*, 26 August 1861 (letter).

38 *Ibid.*

39 *Ibid.*

40 *The Times*, 29 May 1862 (letter).

could not gain ground unless there was more coherence and consistency in the arguments of its supporters.

Several lawyers and economic philosophers tried to develop a more secure theoretical base for the abolition movement during 1863 and 1864. *The Law Magazine and Law Review* was particularly active in publishing articles which were critical of the patent system. At this stage, these critics focused on the alleged property rights in inventions. They challenged this notion in varying degrees. One group argued that inventions gave rise to only limited property rights, and that there should be a severe reduction in the circumstances in which patents could be granted. The other group alleged that inventions could not give rise to property rights, and that the patent system should be abolished. Although these debates over the nature of property rights were clearly influenced by the earlier scholarship of economic philosophers such as Locke and Voltaire, none of the commentators made direct reference to these writings.[41]

Those who supported the first, less extreme view, began by acknowledging the right of an inventor to the products of his own brain. One commentator noted, for example, that:

> Up to a certain point, indeed, the privilege is of natural law; for of all acquired rights, that of an inventor to his own creation may be most truly called his own; so long as he keeps it to himself he possesses that property which the first occupant by common consent of mankind possesses in the subject of his occupancy; he may enjoy it in secret or he may give it when he chooses to the public.[42]

While it was true that the analogy between property in inventions and property in tangible objects was accurate up until the point of disclosure to the public, proponents of the first view argued that the so-called property rights in inventions must be severely limited after disclosure.[43] It was no longer correct to refer to natural property rights in inventions, but rather to recognise that the inventor's rights extended only so far as positive law and municipal regulation permitted.[44] Thus, the instrumentalist view prevailed: that the patent was essentially a contract between the inventor and the State, rather than a

41 See: Locke, J., *Two Treatises on Civil Government* (1690); Voltaire, F.M.A., *Letters on the English* (1733).

42 "The Patent Law" (1862–3) 14 *The Law Magazine and Law Review* 94, 95.

43 *Ibid.*

44 *Ibid.*

property right. It was further argued that society's interest favoured a more restricted access to patents.[45]

The second view advanced was that an invention could never be the subject of a right of property, and that the patent system should be abolished. It was argued that "[p]roperty is necessarily that which *is capable of appropriation*", and inventions did not meet this requirement.[46] This was the view expressed by the Reverend J.E.T. Rogers, Professor of Political Economy in the University of Oxford, and Professor of Economic Science and Statistics at King's College, London. Rogers argued that to be appropriated, property must be distinguishable, and no two or more persons could have the same right of property in the same single object or single utility.[47] It was also essential that equal protection should be accorded to equal or similar kinds of property. Although Rogers admitted that it did not necessarily follow that all property should be of a material character, he did not think that inventions satisfied the tests of property. He argued that the notion of property rights in inventions was really no more than "squatting, transferred to the industrial centres ... and of squatting upon materials and powers which are the property, not of individuals, but of the human race."[48]

Rogers' opinion that the inventor was in reality a squatter was based on two factors. He stated that when people invented, the invention was either the result of a sudden conception, or the elaboration of well-known and general natural laws.[49] Unless it could be asserted that the genius in the invention could be shared by no other person, or that no other person could have followed the same logical sequence which led to the invention, there could be no intrinsic property right in the invention.[50] Although the law might grant a property right to an applicant for a patent, (just as the law might allow any other privilege which invaded the liberty of others), he argued that this right had a "factitious and not a natural origin".[51] Calling for the abolition of the patent system, Rogers went on to deny the stimulus to invention allegedly provided by patents, and stated that "all economists I believe are convinced that [patents] are nugatory, mischievous, unwholesome."[52]

45 *Ibid.*

46 Rogers, J.E.T., "On the Rationale and Working of the Patent Laws" (1863) 26 *Journal of the Statistical Society of London* 121, 123. This paper was first read before the Statistical Society of London on 17 February 1863.

47 *Ibid.*

48 *Ibid.* 124.

49 *Ibid.* 125.

50 *Ibid.*

51 *Ibid.*

52 *Ibid.* 129.

Another commentator who argued that it was a misplaced notion to refer to property rights in inventions was William Hawes, Chairman of Council of the Society of Arts. Like Rogers, he also argued that the "seeds of invention" which already existed in the stock of public knowledge, "are the nuclei of most modern discoveries and improvements, and legislative interference will neither produce them nor stimulate their growth."[53] He argued for the abolition of the patent system, stating that new processes or new mechanical combinations derived from information freely and gratuitously published must be public property, and could not belong exclusively to those who merely adopted that public knowledge and gave it a practical form.[54] Hawes also based his argument upon the notion that in earlier days some form of artificial stimulus might have been required to ensure the introduction of new inventions into England, but this was no longer necessary.[55] Competition and better communications meant that any new inventions would quickly be introduced. Furthermore, he asserted that most patents were no longer being granted for new and useful improvements, but for purposes of obstruction, to obtain indirect extension of older patents, and as a valuable means of "puffing" or of attracting public attention in advertisements.[56] He also argued that the principles of natural law which maintain freedom of thought and action, as well as principles of free trade, were inconsistent with the continued existence of the "mischievous" and "unwholesome" patent laws.[57]

Despite the fact that by 1864 there was clear evidence of more publicity being given to anti-patent sentiment, the number of persons who were actually recorded as favouring abolition was not large. As a commentator stated in the *Law Magazine and Law Review* in 1864, "[t]he number of recent publications on the question of the policy of patents is but limited."[58] There is insufficient evidence to support the assertions of Machlup and Penrose that there was a significant patent abolition movement in the U.K. before 1864.[59] The records

53 Hawes, W., "On the Economical Effects of the Patent Laws" (1863–4) 16 *The Law Magazine and Law Review* 61, 64–5. This paper was first read before the National Association for the Promotion of Social Science at Edinburgh on 9 October 1863. See also Hawes, W., "Patent Law Amendment" (1863–4) 16 *The Law Magazine and Law Review* 355.

54 *Ibid.*

55 *Ibid.* 67.

56 *Ibid.* 73.

57 *Ibid.* 75–76.

58 "The Policy of Patents" (1864) 17 *The Law Magazine and Law Review* 315.

59 Machlup, F., and Penrose, E., "The Patent Controversy in the Nineteenth Century" (1950) x *The Journal of Economic History* 1, (particularly their statement that "the controversy was at its height between 1850 and 1875").

of the evidence given by witnesses to the 1862–64 Select Committee on Patents also reinforces this fact.[60]

b) *The 1862–64 Select Committee on Patents*

(i) Historical Background

Unlike the previous two Select Committees which had examined the working of the patent system, the 1862–64 Select Committee was not the result of Bills which had been introduced into Parliament calling for the amendment of the patent laws. Instead, the main factor which prompted the Solicitor-General, Sir Hugh Cairns, to propose the establishment of the Select Committee in 1862 was his interest in the recommendations for patent law reform which had been proposed in 1861 by the joint Committee of the British Association and the National Association for the Promotion of Social Science.[61] This explains why there was a close correlation between the topics raised in the 1861 Report, and the questions asked of the witnesses before the Select Committee.

Witnesses before the Committee were asked to give their opinion on twelve common questions.[62] These questions focused upon practical problems associated with the operation of the patent system. The question of the abolition of patents was not specifically referred to the Committee,[63] but some witnesses commented upon this matter in the course of giving their evidence.

(ii) An Analysis of Views about the Patent System Expressed by Witnesses before the 1862–64 Select Committee on Patents.

(1) *The Witnesses*

The 1862–64 Select Committee can be criticised for its narrow choice of persons who were asked to give oral evidence. Of the 21 witnesses orally examined,

---

60 UNITED KINGDOM, Parliamentary Papers, *Report of the Commissioners appointed to Inquire into the Working of the Law Relating to Letters Patent for Inventions* (1864) 3419, vol XXIX, 321.

61 *The Times*, 29 May 1862 (leading article).

62 UNITED KINGDOM, Parliamentary Papers, *Report of the Commissioners appointed to Inquire into the Working of the Law Relating to Letters Patent for Inventions* (1864) 3419, vol XXIX, 321, 178. The questions are listed in Appendix Two of this book.

63 See the evidence of William Grove, Q.C., before the 1871 Select Committee into the patent laws. Reflecting upon his role as one of the Commissioners in the 1862–64 inquiry, he stated that although the question of abolition of the patent system had been considered important by some members of the Committee, they could not directly address the issue in their 1864 Report because the question had not been referred to them. UNITED KINGDOM, Parliamentary Papers, *Report from the Select Committee on Letters Patent; together with the Proceedings of the Committee, Minutes of Evidence, Appendix and Index* (1871) 368, vol X, 603, 26.

5 attended on behalf of the Admiralty, Navy or War Offices, and were concerned only to ensure that the Crown gained greater rights in relation to use of patented inventions.[64] Amongst the other witnesses, the greatest number were persons concerned with patent legislation on a professional basis. There were three patent agents,[65] three barristers,[66] two persons who worked in the Patent Office,[67] and the Registrar of the Privy Council.[68] Only 7 witnesses were inventors,[69] and/or manufacturers.[70] However, in addition to the 21 witnesses who appeared in person before the Committee, a further 32 individuals and 16 organisations responded to the Committee's request to submit their written comments on the questions.[71] This written evidence largely originated from inventors and manufacturing and business organisations (especially Chambers of Commerce). When this is studied in addition to the oral evidence, it is apparent that the records of the 1862–4 Select Committee provide an extremely comprehensive range of views about the U.K. patent system.

(2) *The Issues Raised by the Witnesses*

The Policy of the Patent System

It is unfortunate that the 1862–64 Select Committee did not directly ask the witnesses what they thought was the underlying theory or policy of the patent

64 These witnesses were the Duke of Somerset, (of the Admiralty), Rear Admiral R.S. Robinson (Comptroller of the Navy), Brigadier-General J.H. Lefroy (of the War Office), Charles Clode (Solicitor to the War Department), and Frederick Abel (head of the Chemical Department of the War Office).

65 William Carpmael (who had been a patent agent for 40 years), William Spence (who had been a patent agent for 23 years), and Alfred Newton (who had been a patent agent for "a considerable number of years").

66 William Grove, Q.C. (who was also a member of the Select Committee), Montague Smith Q.C. (also a member of Parliament) and Thomas Webster.

67 Bennet Woodcroft, (Superintendent of Specifications), and Leonard Edmunds (Clerk of the Patents).

68 Henry Reeve.

69 John Scott Russell (inventor of the "wave-line" system of shipbuilding), John Platt (also a manufacturer), Sir William Armstrong (President of the Mechanical Engineers Society), Richard Roberts (inventor of the self-acting spinning mule), and Sir Francis Crossley (carpet manufacturer and member of Parliament).

70 John Platt (a large manufacturer of Oldham and also a patentee), Robert Macfie (an influential Liverpool sugar refiner and later M.P. for Leith), and Matthew Curtis (a large manufacturer in Manchester).

71 UNITED KINGDOM, Parliamentary Papers, *Report of the Commissioners appointed to Inquire into the Working of the Law Relating to Letters Patent for Inventions* (1864) 3419, vol XXIX, 321, 178. A full list of individuals/companies and organisations who made written submissions to the Select Committee is included in Appendix Two of this book.

system, and whether or not the system achieved its aims. It also did not ask the witnesses whether they thought the patent system should be abolished. Nevertheless, if in the course of answering any of the set questions, the witness raised any of the more general policy issues, the Committee was willing to pursue these matters. In addition, some of the questions, (such as those relating to public inconvenience from the multitude of patents, trifling patents, proposals for compulsory licences, or patents for foreigners), often extracted responses relating to the general policy of the patent system. The issue of inconveniences and trifling patents also gave abolitionists the opportunity to make their views known.

There is no doubt that the majority of witnesses considered that many practical inconveniences arose from the operation of the patent system. This was despite the reforms of 1852. The most common complaints related to the large increase in the number of patents being granted,[72] the trifling nature of many patents,[73] the perception that inventors were obstructed in their endeavours by pre-existing patents,[74] and the risk of innocent infringement of patents.[75] However, most witnesses did not suggest that these problems were sufficient to warrant abolition of the patent system.

The Majority View – Faith in the Underlying Policy of the Patent System

A question arises as to why the majority of witnesses before the Committee did not advocate the abolition of the patent system, especially since most identified many problems with the practical working of the patent laws. The answer to this question is to point to the fact that witnesses perceived the underlying policy of the patent system as still very important, even if the laws were flawed. As the patent agent, William Spence, told the Committee, a patent was a special monopoly of a limited type, it was more of the nature of a contractual undertaking between the inventor and the public, by which the public

72 For example, see *Ibid.* paras 273–274 and 339 (Carpmael), 965 (Grove), 1670 (Webster), 1116 (Armstrong), 1243 (Smith), pages 178 (Romilly), 180–81 (Palmer), 213 (Blair), 183 (Leeds Chamber of Commerce), 189 (Macfie and Sons), 191 (Bristol Chamber of Commerce), 184 (Nottingham Chamber of Commerce), 185 (Holden), 205 (Cowper), 196 (Wolverhampton Chamber of Commerce), 192 (Fairrie), 201 (Hunt), 202 (Henry), 202 (Ronald), 202 (Pattison), 205 (Philosophical Society of Glasgow).

73 *Ibid.* Witnesses who referred to the large number of patents being granted also argued that many of those patents were frivolous or trifling.

74 *Ibid.* para 758 (Russell), 1137 (Armstrong), 1243 (Smith), 978 (Grove), 872 (Platt).

75 *Ibid.* The obstructive effect of pre-existing patents upon later research was usually mentioned together with the risk of innocent infringement of a pre-existing patent.

benefited by gaining access to new inventions.[76] William Grove, a member of the Committee, noted that the rationale of the patent law was that by granting a temporary monopoly, "you secure in the long run more new inventions to the public."[77] Although he considered that "the minor class of inventions" would be perfected without the benefit of the patent system, major inventions needed its stimulus and reward in order to be developed.[78] Without the patent system, the inventor would not have any form of security to fund his expenses, and he would not gain finance from capitalists.[79] Furthermore, in relation to some trades, the inventor would have difficulty in forcing his invention to the attention of the public, as he would not be able to resist the pressures of opposition from trade interests.[80] Richard Roberts, the inventor of the self-acting mule, agreed with Grove's assessment of the benefits of the patent system, and stated that he would never have received finance for his invention without the security of a patent.[81] Similar evidence was provided by Bennet Woodcroft.[82] E.A. Cowper, a consulting engineer in London, also pointed to the stimulus to invention provided by the patent laws, and the fact that inventors were induced to spend time and money in perfecting their inventions, resulting in "constant progress in the industry of the country".[83]

The only time when witnesses spoke of "property" in inventions was in connection with the proposal of the 1861 joint Committee of the British Association and the National Association for the Promotion of Social Science that compulsory licensing should be introduced to overcome the situation where a multitude of patents were found to be blocking further development in certain fields. Although a number of witnesses before the Select Committee supported the joint Committee's proposal,[84] there was also some strong objection. John Platt, for example, stated that a scheme for compulsory licensing would be

76 UNITED KINGDOM, Parliamentary Papers, *Report of the Commissioners appointed to Inquire into the Working of the Law Relating to Letters Patent for Inventions* (1864) 3419, vol XXIX, 321, paras 683–686.

77 *Ibid.* para 1722. Thomas Webster appeared to agree with this assessment.

78 *Ibid.* para 1023.

79 *Ibid.*

80 Grove gave the example of noxious trades, where this problem might be particularly relevant. *Ibid.*

81 *Ibid.* paras 1395–1402.

82 *Ibid.* para 148.

83 *Ibid.* 205.

84 *Ibid.* paras 681–692 (Spence), 725, 740 (Scott Russell), 1182 (Armstrong), 1894 (Newton), 2067 (Webster). Correspondents: *Ibid.* 180–215: Leeds Chamber of Commerce, Potter, Halifax Chamber of Commerce, Leather, Fletcher, Rankine, Hunt, Richardson, Henry, Pattison, Wingate, Philosophical Society of Glasgow.

"interfering with a man's own property".[85] He added that he did not think it possible that any tribunal would have the skills to accurately assess the value of an invention, and might seriously damage the pecuniary interests of inventors.[86] Another inventor, Sir Francis Crossley, agreed with the Chairman of the Select Committee, Lord Stanley, that there were cases where a patentee might be "perverse or foolish enough to shut up his Patent from others".[87] However, this should be considered as "any other case of an abuse of private property, not to be interfered with without greater inconvenience than the interference would avert".[88] Despite these assertions that the patent system protected property rights, the reason why most witnesses supported its continued existence was because of the social benefits which flowed to both the inventor and the community. These benefits included security and reward for inventors, and public access to new inventions. In essence, the majority of witnesses adopted a strongly instrumentalist justification for the patent system.

The Minority View – Advocating Abolition of the Patent System

Only three of the witnesses who appeared before the Committee considered that the patent system should be abolished, and one of the written responses also clearly gave this opinion. The arguments most frequently used to justify the abolition (or alternatively, the severe restriction) of the patent system included (1) a rejection of the need for an artificial stimulus for invention; and (2) an assertion that a system of financial rewards would be preferable to the patent system.

Armstrong, whose 1861 campaign against the patent system was noted above, advocated the abolition of the system because he considered that there was no need for an artificial stimulus for invention. As an inventor, he believed that most inventions would be discovered without the existence of the patent system.[89] He stated that there was no need to "adopt a system of monopoly for the purpose of eliciting [inventions]; they turn up simply in the ordinary and natural course of things."[90] While he agreed that the patent could bring some financial reward to the inventor, he said that this did not mean that the patent system had to be retained. He preferred that a scheme of "artificial rewards" should be adopted.[91] Armstrong also made some interesting comments about

85 *Ibid.* para 917.
86 *Ibid.* para 921.
87 *Ibid.* para 1690.
88 *Ibid.*
89 *Ibid.* para 1108.
90 *Ibid.*
91 *Ibid.* paras 1112, 1162.

the distinction between copyright and patents. Like most of the patent abolitionists, he did not suggest that the copyright system should also be abolished. The reason for this was that there was no difficulty in defining the subject of copyright, whereas the subject of the patent was often imprecise.[92] It was this lack of precision in the patent system which led to confusion, threats of infringement, costly litigation and all the other problems he had identified.[93]

J. Spence of Liverpool, also shared Armstrong's view that there was no need for the artificial stimulus of the patent system. He was "of the opinion that the Patent system, on the whole, is of more injury than benefit to the community."[94] He added that in the past, when the "arts were in a barbarous condition", it was expedient to employ a patent system to "lure men's minds in the direction of inventions".[95] However, he considered that in 1863, the patent system was not required as "every pathway of science has been explored, and the arts are brought to such a point that great Inventions are at an end, and the business of the patentee now is to contrive modifications, often little more than mere differences of a pattern."[96]

Scott Russell also favoured the abolition of the patent system. He stated that he "should be very glad to see the Patent Laws entirely removed …"[97] However, he later qualified his statement when he noted that if the patent laws were abolished, this could lead to injustice because "you could not altogether do away with the right of a man to the benefit of the fruit of his own brains."[98] For this reason, he advocated the adoption of a new form of patent, which would entail a right to remuneration only, and not a right to control the use of the patented invention.[99] Since there was no absolute right to a patent, and it was only a contractual bargain between the inventor and the Crown, he argued that the Crown should dictate a "small limited sum" which the patentee could charge for the use of the invention.[100]

---

92 *Ibid.* para 1156.

93 Armstrong stated as follows: "In the case of copyright the thing claimed is distinctly defined. There is no possibility of two persons writing the same book or producing the same work of art, but two persons may and do constantly conceive the same invention. That is because the invention is not of that defined character that the subject of copyright is; there is a vagueness about it, a comprehensiveness which renders it very objectionable as a subject of monopoly, because you cannot grant a monopoly without excluding other persons who are working upon the same subject." *Ibid.*

94 *Ibid.* 191.

95 *Ibid.*

96 *Ibid.* This was clearly a naïve view, proved incorrect by later industrial development.

97 *Ibid.* para 722.

98 *Ibid.* paras 722–723.

99 *Ibid.* paras 733–734, 746–748.

100 *Ibid.*

Macfie, the most vocal of the sugar refiners of Liverpool, had a personal conviction that the patent system should be abolished.[101] However, he said that despite this opinion, he had "very little hope of seeing it".[102] This comment demonstrates that in 1863 a strong critic of the patent system such as Macfie, found it unlikely that there would ever be sufficient public support for its abolition. Macfie added that it would be more realistic to seek its reform, and proposed the adoption of one of two possible new systems. The first proposal consisted of a short patent monopoly of three years, after which the patented invention would be valued, and the patent cancelled once royalties to the amount of the stated value had been received. The alternative proposal was that the "nation should purchase every invention which any inventor thought proper to make known," and that the Chancellor of the Exchequer should be empowered annually to put forward a sum of money to a committee of patentees, for division amongst inventors.[103] This second proposal might or might not operate in conjunction with a short patent monopoly of three years.[104] He considered that a system of state rewards, such as in accordance with his second proposal, would provide "some sort of honourable recognition that would please and stimulate parties cognizant of improvements, and would contribute to their success in promoting the sale of the articles, the novelty and merit of which should be thus certified."[105] These aims appeared to mirror some of the traditional justifications for the patent system.

Foreign Issues

The Committee received some comments that the policy of the patent system should be re-evaluated in the light of free trade issues. The Liverpool Chamber of Commerce, for example, was strongly of this opinion.[106] The main reason why it raised this issue was the influence of the sugar refiners, particularly Macfie. As Macfie told the Committee in his oral evidence, sugar refining had suffered since the introduction of free trade measures, because sugar refined in foreign countries could be imported into the U.K. in competition with the U.K. product.[107] Many of the foreigners who refined the sugar were able to "steal" U.K. inventions, and use them overseas without paying patent royalties.

101 *Ibid.* para 1962.
102 *Ibid.*
103 *Ibid.* para 1963.
104 *Ibid.*
105 *Ibid.* para 2000.
106 *Ibid.* 190.
107 *Ibid.* para 1957.

This had been the case, for example, in relation to sugar refined in the West Indies.[108] Macfie had earlier advised the 1851 Select Committee that he feared this result, and it had been one reason why he had unsuccessfully urged that U.K. patents should automatically apply to all of the colonies.[109]

Many other witnesses considered that the U.K. laws relating to the patenting of foreign inventions were unsatisfactory, but mainly for the reason that foreign inventors were not accorded the same level of protection as U.K. inventors. This was a major shift in attitude from the earlier 1829 Select Committee, where many witnesses viewed with suspicion the activities of foreign inventors and manufacturers. The 1862–4 Select Committee records also include the first clear proposal for an international agreement in connection with the operation of the patent system.

Only two witnesses, Harrison Blair of Manchester, and William Armstrong, considered that foreigners should not have the benefit of patenting their inventions in the United Kingdom.[110] Blair argued that the granting of patents to foreigners was not consistent with free trade. Armstrong asserted that because of improved facilities for communication between countries, it was no longer necessary to provide for patenting of foreign inventions. Any invention would eventually make its way to the U.K., and it was not likely that inventions would be lost without the patent system.[111] However, he admitted that abolishing the ability to patent foreign inventions could lead to problems for U.K. inventors wishing to patent their inventions abroad. He agreed that foreign countries might move to apply reciprocal sanctions against U.K. inventors, and that this could lead to disadvantage.[112] He was forced to agree that if the patent system was maintained "it may, perhaps, be expedient as a matter of reciprocation to allow foreign inventions to be patented."[113]

---

108 *Ibid.*

109 UNITED KINGDOM, Parliamentary Papers, *Report and Minutes of Evidence taken before the Select Committee of the House of Lords appointed to consider of The Bill, intituled, "An Act further to amend the Law touching Letters Patent for Invention" and also of The Bill intituled "An Act for the further amendment of the Law touching Letters Patent for Invention" and to report thereon to the House: Session 1851* (1851) 486 vol XVIII, 233, Macfie at 151–153.

110 UNITED KINGDOM, Parliamentary Papers, *Report of the Commissioners appointed to Inquire into the Working of the Law Relating to Letters Patent for Inventions* (1864) 3419, vol XXIX, 321, paras 1220–1234 (Armstrong), 214 (Blair).

111 *Ibid.*

112 *Ibid.* paras 1230–1234.

113 *Ibid.* para 1232.

In general, however, most witnesses before the Committee, as well as most correspondents, supported the granting of patents to foreign inventors.[114] Most of these also considered that the law which allowed the patenting of inventions imported from abroad by a person other than the inventor should be abolished.[115] The records of evidence show a growing interest in ensuring justice to foreign inventors, and a conviction that the patenting of an invention by anyone other than the inventor or his nominee was tantamount to "stealing". As Spence told the Committee, the custom of permitting patents of importation had led to annoyance on the part of the Americans, who had observed persons being encouraged "to prowl about the Patent Office at Washington" in search of an invention to take back to the U.K. to patent.[116]

Some of the witnesses also considered the international ramifications if the U.K. abolished its patent system. Edmunds, Clerk of the Patents since 1833, noted that in 1861 approximately one-quarter of patent applications were made by foreigners, mostly French and Americans.[117] These inventions were being brought to the U.K. because it was a country in which inventions were given "the highest value".[118] He was convinced that "[w]ere England to abolish protection of inventions, inventors would carry their inventions to other countries", just as Swiss inventors customarily did.[119] He asserted that if the patent system was maintained only for U.K. inventions, and the legal reforms were limited to denying protection to foreign inventions, then U.K. inventors would suffer some form of foreign sanctions.[120] Crossley, a patentee, agreed that if foreign inventions were not patentable in the U.K., "foreign nations would probably reciprocate" and U.K. inventors would find themselves without any means of protecting their inventions overseas.[121] Instead, the more rational approach was to ensure that foreign inventors were fully protected in the U.K.,

114 For example, *Ibid.* paras 928 (Platt), 1094 (Grove), 1539 (Curtis), 809 (Scott Russell), 1613 (Crossley); Pages 180 (Chelmsford), 180 (Palmer), 179 (Romilly), 186 (Henry), 184 (Huddersfield Chamber of Commerce), 185 (Holden), 185 (Leather), 182 (Leigh), 182 (Hughes), 188 (Halifax Chamber of Commerce).

115 The following persons or groups wished to see the continuance of the law relating to importation of inventions from abroad by a person other than the inventor or his/her nominee: *Ibid.* para 701 (Spence), 1613 (Crossley), 1900 (Newton): Page 182 (Hughes), 186 (Henry), 184 (Nottingham Chamber of Commerce), 180 (Chelmsford), 214 (Blair), 215 (Birmingham Chamber of Commerce), 210 (Cowper).

116 *Ibid.* para 616.

117 *Ibid.* para 576.

118 *Ibid.*

119 *Ibid.*

120 *Ibid.*

121 *Ibid.* para 1626.

and by this means, encourage other countries to introduce comprehensive patent laws which would benefit U.K. inventors.[122] The most ambitious view was that of the Chamber of Commerce of Huddersfield, which considered that the U.K. government should negotiate international arrangements regulating the grant of patents.[123] It is unclear whether the Chamber of Commerce sought a series of bilateral treaties between the U.K. and foreign countries, or a multilateral treaty. At that time, the U.K. government had recently entered into several bilateral commercial treaties which included provisions relating to the protection of trade marks and designs, but not patents.[124] Nevertheless, the suggestion to negotiate international arrangements respecting patents was ignored by the Committee, and the subject did not receive official attention in the U.K. until 1870–71.

(iii) The Report of the Select Committee

Having sat intermittently to take evidence between November 1862 and June 1864, the Committee finally made its Report on 29 July 1864.[125] In this, the Committee referred to the fact that "one of the main grounds of defence" of the patent system was said to be "the stimulus it offers to invention".[126] However, it accepted the evidence of "the majority of witnesses", who considered that the objectives of the patent system were not being achieved, because of "practical

122 *Ibid.* 198 (Letter of James Thomson and William Hancock). It was certainly true that U.K. inventors had cause for grievance concerning some foreign patent systems. In France, for example, it was a requirement of the patent legislation that all patentees should manufacture the patented article in France. Platt told the Committee that this law was "much to our disadvantage", and U.K. inventors had "made very great complaint" to the French about the law, but the complaints had been unsuccessful. *Ibid.* para 946. Platt also complained about the patent system in Prussia, where very few patents were granted, and applications refused for spurious reasons. He told the Committee that "[a]s to Prussia, I do not know that I ever knew of a Patent granted, for every application that I ever sent there has been refused." *Ibid.* para 876.

123 *Ibid.* 184.

124 See Appendix Three for a select list of some of these treaties.

125 The Report was made in the name of nine members of the Committee: Lord Stanley, Lord Overstone, Sir William Erle, Sir William Page Wood, Sir Hugh Cairns Q.C., M.P., Horatio Waddington, William Grove Q.C., W. E. Foster M.P., and William Fairbairn. One member of the Committee, W.M. Hindmarsh, dissented from the Report, and submitted his own Report on 29 September 1864. The main point on which he differed from the rest of the Committee was that he supported the extension of the duration of some patents beyond 14 years. UNITED KINGDOM, Parliamentary Papers, *Report of the Commissioners appointed to Inquire into the Working of the Law Relating to Letters Patent for Inventions* (1864) 3419, vol XXIX, 321, v-xviii.

126 *Ibid.* v.

inconvenience from the multiplicity of Patents."[127] The Committee accepted that the existence of the multitude of patents:

> embarrasses the trade of a considerable class of persons, artizans, small tradesmen, and others, who cannot afford to face the expense of litigation, however weak the case against them may seem to be. [In addition,] "particular manufactures and branches of invention" [were] "so blocked up by Patents, that not only are inventors deterred from taking them up with a view to improvement, but the manufacturer in carrying on his regular course of trade, is hampered by owners of worthless Patents, whom it is generally more convenient to buy off than to resist.[128]

The Committee also accepted that there was a considerable problem with a number of persons in the same trade combining together to buy up all the patents relating to it, and financing legal attacks upon subsequent improvements.[129]

The Committee suggested a number of reforms to reduce the problems associated with the operation of the patent system. Its main suggestion was that the Law Officers should have a greater role in the granting of patents, and that they should conduct a careful inquiry "as to whether there has been any previous documentary publication of the invention".[130] If there was evidence of such prior publication, the patent application should be refused.[131] The Committee also refused to accept the need for a system of compulsory licensing. In doing so, it stated that even if there were occasions where a patentee refused to grant licences to work an invention, this did not "justify a peculiarly sweeping interference with rights to which the law has assigned the character of property."[132] In addition to the theoretical objections to compulsory licensing, the Committee noted many practical difficulties, such that "no rule can be laid down for estimating the value of a Patent, or the amount of charge which may be reasonably imposed on those using it."[133]

On the question of foreign inventions, the Committee recommended the abolition of patents of importation. International communications were

127 *Ibid.* ix.
128 *Ibid.*
129 *Ibid.*
130 *Ibid.* xiii.
131 *Ibid.*
132 *Ibid.* xxiii.
133 *Ibid.*

such that useful foreign inventions were quickly introduced into the United Kingdom, and there was no need to provide special monopolies for mere importers of foreign inventions.[134] The law also encouraged theft of inventions from the legitimate foreign owner.[135] The Committee agreed that patents should be granted to foreign applicants or their agents or nominees, but would not enter into the issue of whether this right should be exercised only subject to reciprocal arrangements being made with foreign countries. It also did not determine whether the law should require the foreigner to work the patented invention in the United Kingdom.[136]

Even if all the Committee's recommendations were implemented, it warned that the inconveniences associated with the patent system would not be completely removed. Although it had not been asked to consider the question of abolition of the patent system, it stated that the problems which had been identified were "inherent in the nature of a Patent Law, and must be considered as the price which the public consents to pay for the existence of such a law."[137] This statement shows that the Committee did not express unqualified support for the patent system. However, by listening to the oral evidence of the witnesses, and reading the written submissions, the Committee must have realised that abolition of the patent system was not a viable option at that time. It simply did not have sufficient support.

B U.K. Attitudes to the Patent System from August 1864 until Early 1871

The strongest support for the abolition of the U.K. patent system occurred in the years from 1864 until 1870. During this period there was a marked increase in the amount of published material which favoured abolition. Although the issue was the subject of wider public debate, it is clear, however, that there was very little likelihood that the patent abolitionists would succeed in achieving their aim. This was because most patent abolitionists remained part of limited occupational groups, such as lawyers, economic philosophers and a few members of Parliament. Most inventors, engineers, manufacturers and workmen continued to support the patent system. Although the patent abolitionists tried to attract the support of scientific and cultural organisations, they failed

134 *Ibid.* xii.
135 *Ibid.*
136 *Ibid.*
137 *Ibid.* xiv.

miserably. This was largely because abolitionists did not offer any practical alternative to the patent system.

(a) *The Minority View – Advocating Abolition of the Patent System*

Although the Select Committee reported in July 1864, the Government made no attempt to implement the Committee's recommendations.[138] There was, however, a significant increase in the number of published speeches and articles supporting abolition of the patent system. Many of these appeared in *The Times*, whose editorial policy appeared to favour the abolitionists.

In August 1864, Lord Stanley, (who had acted as Chairman of the Select Committee), made a speech at Liverpool in which he explained the Committee's recommendations. The most interesting part of his speech was his reference to the fact that the alterations in the "details" of the patent law could not overcome some of the problems which were inherent in a patent system.[139] This comment provoked a strong response in *The Times*. In an editorial published on the same day as the report of Stanley's speech, *The Times* "ventured to suggest" that the only remedy for the "evils" associated with the system was that of "abolition of Patents altogether."[140] *The Times* recognised that such a suggestion would provoke opposition, particularly from patentees, who would see a threat to the security of their property rights.[141] However, it did not accept "any supposed natural right of an inventor as the basis of our existing legislation", and argued that the State should refuse to enter into any further disadvantageous bargains with inventors.[142]

One of the arguments often used to defend the patent system against abolitionists was to assert that copyright and patents should attract the same legal treatment.[143] *The Times* rejected such arguments. It said that there were "many arguments" which could be "advanced in favour of the expediency of

138 The only patent Bills introduced into Parliament during this period were three private members Bills which were first presented to the House of Lords in February 1865. These Bills, known as the Shepard, Wright and Spencer Patent Bills after their proponents, related to the narrow area of restoration of patents where patent renewal fees had not been paid on time. None of these Bills obtained a second reading. UNITED KINGDOM, *Parliamentary Debates*, House of Lords, 24 and 27 February 1865. See also *The Times*, 25 and 28 February 1865.

139 *The Times*, 15 August 1864.

140 *Ibid.*

141 *Ibid.*

142 *Ibid.*

143 See for example, the arguments of Edmund Pontifex, (a "well-known engineer and machine-maker") whose letter supporting the patent system was published in *The Times* on the same day as the above editorial.

copyright in literature which are inapplicable to Patent Right in arts."[144] *The Times* asserted that it was unfair that two persons might invent something independently of each other, but could not both have a valid patent for the same invention. In contrast, copyright was a much fairer system because "no two men ever invented the same book, and the copyright of one author cannot derogate from the rights of a second."[145] *The Times* also rejected the argument that patents provided a necessary stimulus to invention. It argued that the "instinct of economy is too strong in man to require any inducement to call it into exercise."[146] In addition, the financial rewards associated with the patent system did not go to those who most deserved them. *The Times* asserted that an inventor was, in most cases, "a poor working engineer employed in some great manufactory" who "was compelled to sell the Patent almost before he obtained it."[147]

The Times returned to the issue of the abolition of patents after the publication of the Select Committee's Report in February 1865.[148] On 10 February 1865 (the day after the publication of the Committee's Report) another editorial appeared in *The Times* calling for the abolition of the patent system. Stating that there were few who could testify to the benefits of the patent system, *The Times* again referred to the "hindrance to manufacturing progress" caused by the multiplicity of patents, and reiterated most of the arguments it had made against the system in August 1864.[149]

Patent abolitionists such as Robert Macfie recognised that the support of the newspapers was essential if they wished to influence public opinion in favour of their cause. Between 1865 and 1869, Macfie and other individuals who favoured patent abolition[150] attempted to win the support of the large scientific and cultural organisations such as the National Association for the Promotion of Social Science. This was unsuccessful,[151] and the patent abolitionists were forced to reassess their tactics. Instead of trying to win over the organisations, and with them their membership of influential inventors,

144 *Ibid.*

145 *Ibid.*

146 *Ibid.*

147 *Ibid.*

148 The Select Committee's Report was published in full in *The Times* on 9 February 1865.

149 *The Times*, 10 February 1865.

150 Besides Macfie, the most famous patent abolitionists were: Professor Thorold Rogers, Sir William Armstrong, Sir Roundell Palmer, the Liverpool Chamber of Commerce and the Newcastle and Gateshead Chamber of Commerce.

151 For a discussion of the attitude of the scientific and cultural organisations towards abolition of patents see: (*b*) *The Majority View – Supporting the Patent System* below.

manufacturers and engineers, the abolitionists turned to the general public. In 1869, a campaign was organised to bring the matter to the attention of the public by a combination of newspaper articles in *The Times* and the *Economist*, and the introduction of a Bill into Parliament which called for the abolition of patents.[152]

On 28 May 1869, Macfie, being the member for Leith, moved in the House of Commons a Resolution to the effect "[t]hat in the opinion of this House the time has arrived when the interests of trade and commerce, and the progress of the arts and sciences in this country, would be promoted by the abolition of Patents for inventions."[153] This motion was contained in a petition made in the name of the Newcastle and Gateshead Chamber of Commerce. The motion was seconded in the House of Commons by Sir Roundell Palmer,[154] and subjected to intense debate, although it was ultimately withdrawn on the same day through lack of support.

In the House of Commons, speeches in support of Macfie's motion were made only by Palmer and the former Foreign Secretary, Lord Stanley. Other members of the House, including Lord Elcho, and Messrs Samuda, Denman, Howard, Mundella, and Stapleton, either entirely opposed the motion or considered that it was far too premature.

In moving the Resolution, Macfie referred generally to the practical inconveniences associated with the operation of the patent system. He stated that these practical inconveniences had been expressed by the majority of the witnesses before the 1862–64 Select Committee, yet nothing had been done since that Report. He proposed that the House either adopt his motion to abolish patents "*simpliciter* or ... call upon the Government to issue a Royal Commission, so that the question might no longer be postponed."[155] In seconding the motion, Palmer stated that the time had come for the abolition of the patent system, asking whether anyone could doubt "that in this advanced

---

152 Macfie, R.A., (ed), *Recent Discussions on the Abolition of Patents for Inventions in the United Kingdom, France, Germany, and the Netherlands: evidence, speeches and papers in its favour* (London, Longmans and Co, 1869) "Preface".

153 The most complete record of the text of the motion, accompanying personal notes written by Macfie, together with the speeches of Macfie, Palmer and Stanley in the House of Commons are contained in *Ibid.* 8–115. See also UNITED KINGDOM, *Parliamentary Debates*, House of Commons, 28 May 1869; and *The Times*, 29 May 1869.

154 Sir Roundell Palmer was a former Solicitor-General and Attorney-General, and was later Lord Chancellor (1872–4 and 1880–85).

155 Macfie, R.A., (ed), *Recent Discussions on the Abolition of Patents for Inventions in the United Kingdom, France, Germany, and the Netherlands: evidence, speeches and papers in its favour* (London, Longmans and Co, 1869), 92.

era of knowledge the public would gain, on the whole, by the abolition of the patent laws".[156] He denied that an inventor had any special moral or natural right to the "fruit of his brain", and noted that there were wide philosophical differences between copyright and patents.[157] To those who argued that abolition of the patent system would encourage inventors to keep their inventions secret, Palmer stated that such instances would be rare and insignificant. Similar remarks were made by Lord Stanley, who had acted as Chairman of the 1862–64 Select Committee. Stanley stated that he had been a supporter of the patent system but after hearing the evidence before the Select Committee, he saw the "practical abuses and inconveniences of the existing system, and how difficult it would be to remedy them".[158] Gradually he had come to realise "the evil was really irremediable, being inherent in the principle itself."[159] His three main objections to the patent system were:

(1) you could hardly ever secure the reward going to the right man [; (2)] you could not establish any proportion between the public service rendered and the value of the reward received [; and (3)] you … could not prevent very great inconvenience and injury being inflicted upon third parties.[160]

When other members of the House rose to debate the motion, it was clear that the proposal for the abolition of the patent law did not have a hope of success. The most that could be anticipated was the appointment of another Select Committee, but this was not matter of priority. Members such as Howard stated that to abolish the patent system would remove a strong stimulus to invention, and deny an inventor his property rights.[161] He argued that an attack upon the patent system was equally an attack upon copyright, as both were of a common origin. Mundella, a patentee and manufacturer, also agreed that there was no fundamental difference between copyright and patents, and said he had personal knowledge that the patent system provided a great stimulus to invention.[162] He added that working men had a great interest in the

156 *Ibid.* 93–4.
157 *Ibid.* 95.
158 *Ibid.* 110.
159 *Ibid.*
160 *Ibid.* 111.
161 It is interesting that none of the speeches in opposition to the motion were reprinted in Macfie, R.A., (ed), *Recent Discussions on the Abolition of Patents for Inventions in the United Kingdom, France, Germany, and the Netherlands: evidence, speeches and papers in its favour* (London, Longmans and Co, 1869). However, the text of the opposing speeches can be found in UNITED KINGDOM, *Parliamentary Debates,* House of Commons, 28 May 1869; and *The Times*, 29 May 1869.
162 UNITED KINGDOM, *Parliamentary Debates,* House of Commons, 28 May 1869.

preservation of the patent laws, and feared that abolition would lead to the emigration of inventors to France and America. Stapleton agreed that unless the labourer "had a patent law for his protection, [he] would go unrewarded for his time and trouble."[163] Elcho, Denman, and Samuda also reflected the views of the majority when they stated their readiness to accept the alleged problems and inconveniences of the patent system, but thought the system should not be abolished without a full inquiry.

Although the failure of Macfie's motion made it abundantly clear that any proposal for patent abolition would not be seriously considered by the House, the debate in Parliament brought the issue to the attention of the public. On 29 May 1869, an editorial appeared in *The Times* which praised the motion proposed by Macfie, and derided his opponents as lacking in judgment.[164] It again alleged that the patent laws "inflict the most grievous injustice on innocent persons."[165] Characterising the patent laws as "legislation based upon no such obligation as underlies the ordinary laws of property", and which must be justified "as gratuitous creations of the Legislature", *The Times* stated that the patent laws could not satisfy the necessary requirement of national benefit.[166] It alleged that invention would abound if the patent system was abolished.

On 5 June 1869 an editorial in the *Economist* suggested that "[i]t is probable enough that the Patent-Laws will be abolished ere long",[167] although it criticised the way in which the abolitionists had presented their case to the House. It considered that the patent system was outmoded, and that patents were no longer needed as an inducement either to inventors or capitalists.[168] It also referred to the obstructive effects of the patent laws. An editorial in the *Spectator* noted that there was a lack of evidence as to the true effect of the working of the patent law,[169] but considered that it was unlikely that evidence could be produced to show that patented "inventions are overwhelmingly valuable, so as to compensate for all the injury a Patent-Law must do".[170]

Apart from sections of the press and a minority of the members of Parliament, Macfie's motion for the abolition of patents also gained the support of a number of prominent individuals. Professor J.T. Rogers, the economic

163 *Ibid.*
164 *The Times*, 29 May 1869 (editorial).
165 *Ibid.*
166 *Ibid.*
167 *Economist*, 5 June 1869 at 656 (editorial).
168 *Ibid.*
169 *Spectator*, 5 June 1869 (editorial). The *Spectator* noted that the 1862–64 Select Committee had not received evidence from "workmen".
170 *Ibid.*

philosopher, wrote a letter to Macfie dated 29 July 1869 in which he alleged that the patent laws were of a type which "can confer a right on one person only by inflicting a wrong on a number of other persons, it is intrinsically vicious, and cannot be defended on the grounds of its intentional goodness."[171] William Armstrong also wrote a letter to Macfie, advising of his support, and reiterating his well-known views about the "monstrous" and "indiscriminate" patent system.[172] Andrew Johnson, M.P., a manufacturer, also wrote to Macfie that it was his "firm conviction" that the patent laws should be abolished,[173] as did John Thomson, "a notable inventor".[174] A detailed explanation of the abolitionist view was presented to the Glasgow Chamber of Commerce by James Stirling, who stated that the notion of "property in ideas" was a "double fallacy that thought can and should be appropriated."[175] He argued that a patent was no less than a monopoly of thought, and seen in that light, common sense revolted against it.[176] He further argued that the patent law could not be justified on the ground of expediency, for there was no evidence that invention required artificial stimulus.[177] Similar arguments that the patent laws had no sound basis were also presented to the Liverpool Chamber of Commerce by E.K. Muspratt, in July 1869.[178] After hearing Muspratt's paper, the Chamber of Commerce resolved to press for the appointment of a Select Committee to examine the policy of the patent laws.[179]

It will be seen from the above discussion that even at the height of the patent abolition debate in 1869, the opposition to the patent system in the U.K. was mainly confined to a few Chambers of Commerce, a select group of individuals (including a few members of Parliament), together with occasional support from sections of the press. There is no evidence that large numbers of people who were really interested in the working of the patent system supported abolition. In fact, the reverse is true. There is significant evidence that inventors, manufacturers and workmen continued to support the patent system despite the arguments of the abolitionists. This is particularly apparent

171 Macfie, R.A., (ed), *Recent Discussions on the Abolition of Patents for Inventions in the United Kingdom, France, Germany, and the Netherlands: evidence, speeches and papers in its favour* (London, Longmans and Co, 1869), viii.
172 Letter dated 13 May 1869. Reproduced in *Ibid.* 237.
173 Letter dated 7 July 1869. Reproduced in *Ibid.* 239.
174 *Ibid.* 238.
175 Reproduced in *Ibid.* 116–123.
176 *Ibid.*
177 *Ibid.*
178 Paper of E.K. Muspratt reproduced in *Ibid.* 231–236.
179 *Ibid.*

upon examination of the attitudes to the patent system of some of the larger scientific and cultural organisations who often had a strong membership of inventors and manufacturers.

(b) *The Majority View – Supporting the Patent System*

As early as March 1865, the patent abolitionists, headed by Macfie, had attempted to convince the annual Congress of the National Association for the Promotion of Social Science that the Association should support the abolition of the patent system. Macfie later stated that he had hoped that the Association would "lend important aid to the cause."[180] To provoke interest in the question, Macfie presented a paper in which he spoke of the alleged injurious effects of the patent system.[181] His argument rested on two bases. First, he stated that he did not dispute that an inventor had a right of use or property in his invention, but he did not agree that this should be an *exclusive* right. He argued that to give one inventor an exclusive right subverted or denied the right of use of all others, when such other inventors might be as original or hardworking as the patentee, but had delayed submitting their application to the Patent Office.[182] He further argued that the State ought not give a right of exclusive property (and with it a "power to meddle with others, and forbid them to use their valuable knowledge"), except in cases where common use and enjoyment would diminish public wealth or harm a previous possessor.[183] Since "God" had drawn a distinction "between things material or measurable ... and things mental" it was clear that the first could be subject to exclusive rights of property, whereas the second could not be appropriated "without loss to our race".[184]

Macfie's second argument was that the patent system was adverse to free and fair trade.[185] Free and fair trade meant it was not right to tax one manufacturer and let another "go free", but Macfie argued that this was precisely the effect of the patent system. As he had earlier told the 1862–64 Select Committee, he

180 *Ibid.* 249.

181 Macfie, R.A., "Long Restrictions on the Use of Inventions, and Obligation to make heavy Payments to Patentees, incompatible with free and fair trade" (1865) *Transactions of the National Association for the Promotion of Social Science* 260–261.

182 Macfie, R.A., (ed), *Recent Discussions on the Abolition of Patents for Inventions in the United Kingdom, France, Germany, and the Netherlands: evidence, speeches and papers in its favour* (London, Longmans and Co, 1869), 243.

183 *Ibid.*

184 *Ibid.*

185 See also Macfie's earlier work: Macfie, R.A., *The Patent Question Under Free Trade* (London, Longmans, Green, Reader and Dyer, 1863) which was first read before the National Association for the Promotion of Social Science in Edinburgh in October 1863.

argued that it was not right that U.K. manufacturers had to pay heavy patent fees, when they were subject to open competition with all the world.[186] Most foreign rivals were not paying those same patent fees, and Macfie asked, how could "any statesman, or member of a Chamber of Commerce, defend or palliate such gross and grievous inequalities"?[187] He referred again to his proposal for the abolition of exclusive patent monopolies, and suggested the introduction of schemes of State rewards.[188]

Besides his own support for abolition, Macfie also tried to convince the Association that many other influential persons shared his opinion. He referred to the support of the Liverpool Chamber of Commerce and Lord Stanley.[189] He also alleged that Sir Hugh Cairns had developed doubts about the merits of the patent system, as had many other persons of influence (whom Macfie failed to name).[190] He referred to growing support for patent abolition on the Continent, and mentioned the names of "M. Chevalier, Swiss statesmen ... and the German Congress of Political Economists".[191]

Macfie's attempt to convince the Association of the merits of the abolition movement failed from the outset. His speech at the 1865 Congress was immediately challenged by another member, Robert Wilson, a solicitor, who spoke strongly in support of patents.[192] He warned that:

> [A]n ill-judged surrender of the patent law might involve an irreparable loss ... [T]he inventor's privilege rests on a long-continued tradition; it subsists, with some dissent but general approval, as an institution sound in principle, and, on the whole, beneficial in effect: it is supported at home by powerful interests.[193]

186 Macfie, R.A., (ed), *Recent Discussions on the Abolition of Patents for Inventions in the United Kingdom, France, Germany, and the Netherlands: evidence, speeches and papers in its favour* (London, Longmans and Co, 1869), 245.

187 *Ibid.*

188 *Ibid.* 247.

189 *Ibid.*

190 *Ibid.* He did, however, describe them as persons "on the other side of the Speaker's chair, ... law officers of the Crown, ... and Radicals".

191 *Ibid.*

192 Wilson, R., "On the Report of the Patent Law Commissioners" (1865) 19 *The Law Magazine and Law Review* 139. Webster described Wilson as having "the largest experience in patent cases that anybody ever had". UNITED KINGDOM, Parliamentary Papers, *Report from the Select Committee on Letters Patent; together with the Proceedings of the Committee, Minutes of Evidence, Appendix and Index* (1871) 368, vol x, 603, 87 (Evidence of Thomas Webster).

193 *Ibid.* 158.

Wilson urged the Association to "attend for the present to the question of reformation" of the patent law, and "adjourn the question of abolition."[194] That is exactly what the Association did.

It is possible that one of the reasons why few of the important industrial, scientific or cultural organisations in the U.K. favoured abolition of the patent system was because of the influence of certain well-connected individuals who remained committed to the patent system. Two such individuals, the barrister Thomas Webster and the patent agent Alfred Newton, figured prominently in the debates over the patent laws in a number of these Associations. Both never wavered in their strong support for the patent system. Webster held influential positions at various crucial times in the Institution of Civil Engineers, the Society of Engineers, the National Association for the Promotion of Social Science (which merged in 1864 with the Law Amendment Society), the British Association and the Society of Arts.[195] Newton was influential in the Institution of Civil Engineers and the National Association for the Promotion of Social Science.[196]

It has already been mentioned in the previous Chapter that in 1845 Webster had persuaded the Society of Arts to abolish the rule that patentees could not be eligible for the Society's prizes. In 1855–6 he was a member of the patent law reform Committee of the British Association for the Advancement of Science. Between 1859 and 1861 he had been a member of the Joint committee of the British Association and the National Association for the Promotion of Social Science which examined the patent law. In 1865 he led the Society of Engineers in its decision to reject the proposals of Howels Davies that the Society should support the abolition of patents.[197] It is unsurprising, therefore, that within the National Association for the Promotion of Social Science, the combined influence of Webster, Newton and Wilson, should have succeeded in minimising the effects of the arguments of patent abolitionists such as Macfie.

As a result of the debates at the 1865 Sheffield Congress, the Association decided to re-convene the Sub-Committee on the Patent Law. The membership of the Sub-Committee comprised Webster, Newton, Wilson, Frederic Hill

194 *Ibid.*

195 Batzel, V.M., "Legal Monopoly in Liberal England: The Patent Controversy in the Mid-Nineteenth Century" (1980) 22 *Business History* 189, 193.

196 *Ibid.*

197 This point is made by Victor Batzel, who has studied the work of the Society of Engineers, and noted the contribution of Webster. Batzel states that the "position finally adopted by the Society was set by Thomas Webster …, who noted that the problem was one of 'abuses or administration rather than matters of principle'." *Ibid.*

(an inventor and senior official of the Post Office), F.J. Bramwell (an engineer), William Newmarch (a banker, accountant and actuary), and Dr R.M. Pankhurst (a barrister).[198] Manufacturers were not represented on the Sub-Committee,[199] and significantly, Macfie was not a member. The Sub-Committee's support for the continued existence of the patent system was apparent from the first Resolution presented in its March 1866 Report. That Resolution stated that "it is expedient that there should be a Patent Law."[200] The Report noted that the main reason for this view was that the opponents of the patent system had been unable to suggest a practicable substitute for it.[201] It is also clear that the Sub-Committee believed that abolition of the patent system would be an attack upon property rights of individuals. The Report affirmed that the invention was a right of property and that the "claims or rights of the inventor to own such property may be likened to those of the first finder or first occupant, and rest upon the same principle as other property".[202] The Sub-Committee did not accept that the invention was a "natural right" of the inventor, stating that this issue had been "long ago settled in the negative".[203] However, it stated that the right of an inventor was a property right created by municipal law. The Sub-Committee also supported the patent system because it considered that patents were "the only means hitherto derived for stimulating invention, and rewarding the inventor."[204]

Although the Sub-Committee's Report was never formally adopted by the membership of the Association, Macfie's arguments gained no additional support in subsequent Congresses. In 1868, both William Spence and Alfred Newton read papers before the Association in which they urged their fellow members to recognise the essential benefits of the patent law. Spence noted "the importance of treating patents … as channels of industry".[205] He added that U.K. industry could improve in terms of application of new inventions and opening up new sources of manufacture, and the patent system could play a

---

198 The Report of the Sub-Committee is included in UNITED KINGDOM, Parliamentary Papers, *Report from the Select Committee on Letters Patent; together with the Proceedings of the Committee, Minutes of Evidence, Appendix and Index* (1871) 368, vol X, 603, 195 (Appendix 1).

199 This point was noted with interest by the 1871 Select Committee. *Ibid.* 87.

200 *Ibid.* 195.

201 *Ibid.*

202 *Ibid.*

203 *Ibid.* 196.

204 *Ibid.*

205 Spence, W., "Patents as Channels of Industry" (1868) *Transactions of the National Association for the Promotion of Social Science* 256, 260.

vital role in this area.[206] He agreed with the argument often advanced by patent abolitionists that scientific men would invent regardless of the existence of the patent law, but thought that legal protection was needed to ensure that the inventions were brought to the attention of financiers and adapted for commercial use.[207] However, both Spence and Newton[208] considered that it was "most important for the interests of society to remove all existing impediments to the effective administration of patent law."[209]

In 1869, Macfie made a final attempt to interest the National Association in the abolition of the patent system. He read a paper to the Association in which he again attacked the notion of exclusive property rights in inventions, and spoke of the alleged disadvantages caused to U.K. manufacturers forced to pay royalties in a climate of free trade.[210] However, the Association again largely ignored Macfie's arguments. In a paper read in opposition to Macfie, Henry Dircks noted that Macfie's paper was full of unsubstantiated allegations, and that he had no statistics to prove any connection between patents and losses to U.K. manufacturers from foreign competition.[211] Furthermore, Dircks alleged that there was not one instance on record "of the public at large being placed otherwise than advantageously through the intervention of patented engines, machines, and new manufactures."[212] In fact, he argued, the public benefited from new inventions, which generally led to cheaper goods. Newton, Webster and Spence joined Dircks in attacking Macfie's paper.[213] Newton argued that Macfie represented a sectional interest, and that the majority of the public was in favour of patents. In particular, Newton alleged that from his own observations, "among working men there was never a stronger feeling than at present of the advantage of patents."[214] Spence "urged that if the patent law were abolished on account of the difficulty of administering it, many other laws must

206 *Ibid.*

207 *Ibid.*

208 Newton, A.V., "On our System of Patent Law Adjudication, with Suggestions for Removing the Evils arising therefrom" (1868) *Transactions of the National Association for the Promotion of Social Science* 249.

209 Spence, W., *op.cit.* 260.

210 Macfie, R.A., "Some of the Objections to Patents for Inventions" (1869) *Transactions of the National Association for the Promotion of Social Science* 177.

211 Dircks, H., "On the Policy of a Patent Law" noted in (1869) *Transactions of the National Association for the Promotion of Social Science* 185. Dircks was a lawyer, and author of a book published in 1867 called *Inventors and Inventions*.

212 *Ibid.*

213 *Ibid.* 186–188.

214 *Ibid.* 187.

share the same fate."[215] Both he and Webster thought that the proposed abolition of patents in the Netherlands and Germany would be a good thing, for those inventors would relocate to the United Kingdom.[216] Frederic Hill noted Macfie's concerns about the relationship between patents and free trade, but said that any hardship to U.K. manufacturers could be overcome by "the introduction of international patents".[217] The above discussion shows that whenever patent abolitionists such as Macfie attempted to seek the Association's support for their cause, they were met with an immediate hostile response. It is therefore unsurprising that the abolitionists were forced to look elsewhere for support.

The patent abolitionists had very little success in influencing other organisations to support their quest. Macfie's 1869 Parliamentary motion to abolish the patent system brought the issue to the attention of many organisations, but most rejected the proposals for abolition. For example, on 22 June 1869, the Inventors' Institute held a meeting "to consider the action to be taken in opposition to the measures now in progress for the abolition of patent rights."[218] The Institute, which had 700 members, held the opinion that "it was not desirable to abolish the existing patent laws, though they were willing to admit all useful and appropriate amendments."[219] The members unanimously supported four resolutions concerning the patent law. These were:

(1) That the inventor was entitled to remuneration for his labour, expenditure and skill as much as the author or artist of a copyright work.
(2) That capital would not be embarked in promoting inventions unless profitable return for such capital was assured by operation of law.
(3) That a good system of patent law tends to foster the trade and industry of the country, and to maintain its industrial position against the pressures of foreign competition.
(4) That working men were particularly supportive of the patent system.[220]

Other professional organisations also reacted to Macfie's motion by reaffirming their strong support for the patent system. On 17 June 1870, a meeting of

215 *Ibid.*
216 *Ibid.*
217 *Ibid.* 186. Note, however, that Newton "regarded international patents as impracticable, for no two countries were in the same position." *Ibid.* 187.
218 *The Times*, 23 June 1869.
219 *Ibid.*
220 *Ibid.*

the Society of Engineers unanimously resolved that "the granting of exclusive privileges of limited duration for the encouragement and reward of inventors tends largely to promote the industrial progress and commercial prosperity of Great Britain."[221] On 4 January 1870, the Manchester Institution of Engineers unanimously resolved that "this meeting considers that the trade in inventions, which is founded upon the grant of patents, is of great advantage to the country in promoting its industrial prosperity, and that any abuses which exist in the present patent system may be rectified by available amendments."[222] A similar resolution was carried unanimously by the London Association of Foremen Engineers and Draughtsmen, at a meeting held on 6 May 1871.[223] The Association resolved that "the recognition of property in inventions contributes most materially to the wealth of the community, and that the abolition of such property would be most injurious to the industrial progress of the nation."[224]

Since there is no evidence that the patent abolitionists ever had significant support from the government or organisations representing inventors, engineers and manufacturers, this means that there was never any real threat to the continued existence of the patent system in the United Kingdom. After 1869–70 the patent abolitionists began to abandon their cause when they realised that they would never achieve their goals because of the lack of this essential support.

Another, secondary reason for the decline of the abolition movement was the attitude of the press. Although the abolitionists had the clear support of *The Times* and the *Economist*, other newspapers and journals rejected their cause. An editorial in the *Saturday Review*, for example, considered that the patent laws were "extremely unsatisfactory" but argued they should be reformed rather than abolished.[225] It argued that if it could be ensured that only meritorious inventions received patent protection then "no one would dream of questioning the moral claim of an inventor to this peculiar kind of

221 Reproduced in UNITED KINGDOM, Parliamentary Papers, *Report from the Select Committee on Letters Patent; together with the Proceedings of the Committee, Minutes of Evidence, Appendix and Index* (1872) 193, vol XI, 395, 159. The Society further resolved that "the abuses which attend the present patent system, as now administered, are capable of removal by suitable amendments in the laws, and that, therefore, all practicable means should be adopted for obtaining the important object."

222 *Ibid.* 164.

223 *Ibid.* 163.

224 *Ibid.*

225 *Saturday Review*, 5 June 1869.

property".[226] The *Saturday Review* further argued that abolition would lead to injustice, and that copyright would then become vulnerable to attack.

Slightly later, an editorial in the *Pall Mall Gazette* also claimed that "of all the forms of property the one most clearly traceable to human endeavour, and the one most distinctly devolving on the person who has used that endeavour, is property in invention."[227] It added that there was a strong analogy between patent rights and other kinds of private property and alleged that the patent abolition movement was "the socialism of very rich men, impatient of the impediments put in their way by unimportant people" such as ordinary inventors.[228] An editorial in a professional journal, the *Engineer*, asserted that the patent system should be retained, because the system provided a useful record of invention.[229] It argued that encouraging the dissemination of knowledge about both successful and unsuccessful inventions was an often overlooked benefit of the patent system.[230]

Articles also appeared in the *Law Magazine and Review* strongly supporting the retention of the patent system. The correspondent "C.S.D." wrote that if the public desired the use of new inventions, it must pay for them, and "until some better scheme can be suggested than has yet been suggested, for the regulation of the relations between inventors and the public, it would be inexpedient to abolish the contract made by Letters Patent."[231] John Lascelles, a barrister, stated that "in addition to being unjust to inventors, the abolition of the patent laws would be highly impolitic."[232] He added that the discovery of a new art or manufacture was the result of labour and expense, "and if exclusive property has any ethical foundation at all, its foundation is that universally admitted right, which every man is considered to have, to enjoy the fruits of his own ability and industry."[233] He also thought that the patent laws were essential as an incentive to inventors.[234]

All this evidence demonstrates that there was no significant threat to the U.K. patent system in the period from 1864 to early 1871. While there was an

226 *Ibid.*

227 Reproduced as "Property and Patents" (1871) 5 *The Irish Law Times and Solicitors' Journal* 169.

228 *Ibid.*

229 *Engineer*, 9 July 1869.

230 *Ibid.*

231 "On Reform in the Law of Patents" (1870) 28 *The Law Magazine and Review* 83, 98.

232 Lascelles, J., "Our Patent Laws: Their Origin and Policy, with suggestions for their Amendment" (1870–1) 30 *The Law Magazine and Review* 1, 8.

233 *Ibid.* 6.

234 *Ibid.*

abolition movement, it was largely ineffective. It never received the support of government, and organisations representing inventors, manufacturers and engineers. Important sections of the press were unsympathetic to the abolitionists. Most agreed that what was needed was reform of the patent system, rather than its abolition. To this end, another Select Committee was appointed to examine the patent law in March 1871.

C The 1871–72 Select Committees on Patents

On 7 March 1871, a Select Committee was appointed by the House of Commons to carry out inquiries into the operation and effect of the patent law.[235] The Committee was appointed in response to a patent reform Bill introduced into the House of Commons on the same date by Hinde Palmer.[236] The appointment of such a Committee had also been moved by Macfie in the House of Commons on 21 February 1871.

The 1871 Select Committee was chaired by Bernhard Samuelson and met several times between 16 March 1871 and the date of its Report in the following July.[237] The Report was inconclusive, because the members considered that further inquiries needed to be conducted. Upon the motion of Samuelson on 8 February 1872, the Committee was re-convened, held further meetings, and made its final Report on 8 May 1872.[238]

The 1871–72 Select Committees were quite unlike the 1862–64 Select Committee where the topics discussed were highly circumscribed and little direct reference was made either to the policy of the patent system, or its abolition. The later Committees encouraged a wide ranging discussion of policy

---

235 UNITED KINGDOM, Parliamentary Papers, *Report from the Select Committee on Letters Patent; together with the Proceedings of the Committee, Minutes of Evidence, Appendix and Index* (1871) 368, vol X, 603, ii.

236 *Bill to amend Law relating to Patents for Invention:* UNITED KINGDOM, Parliamentary Papers, (1871) 65, vol IV, 419. This Bill was later withdrawn by Hinde Palmer on 2 August 1871. See also: *The Times,* 3 August 1871.

237 The Report was dated 20 July 1871. The members of the 1871 Select Committee were the Attorney-General, the Chancellor of the Exchequer, Colonel Wilmot, Captain Beaumont, and Messrs Gordon, Arthur Peel, George Gregory, Hinde Palmer, Stewart Hardy, Macfie, Cawley, Platt, Hick, Mundella, Mellor, James Howard, Elliot, Joshua Feilden, Dillwyn, Orr Ewing, Pim, Laird, Lopes and Andrew Johnston.

238 UNITED KINGDOM, Parliamentary Papers, *Report from the Select Committee on Letters Patent; together with the Proceedings of the Committee, Minutes of Evidence, Appendix and Index* (1872) 193, vol XI, 395, iii–v. The members of the 1872 Select Committee were largely the same as those of the 1871 Select Committee.

issues. Although the records of evidence of the 1871–72 Committees demonstrate that the witnesses considered there were several underlying theoretical justifications for the patent system, most took an instrumentalist approach in relation to these policy issues. A clear majority rejected any suggestion for abolition of the patent system. Apart from these theoretical considerations, the 1871–72 Committees are also important because both the witnesses and the Committee members were strongly in favour of some form of international agreement respecting the operation of the patent laws. This was the first time that this issue received such support in the U.K. and it helps explain why only one year later, in 1873, the U.K. Government took great interest in the work of the international patent Congress of Vienna.

(a) *An Analysis of the Views about the Patent System Expressed by Witnesses before the 1871–72 Select Committees on Patents*

(1) The Witnesses

During their two periods of operation, the 1871–72 Committees received evidence from 30 witnesses. A far wider range of occupations and professions were represented than had been the case before the 1862–64 Committee. As previously, lawyers were well represented,[239] and evidence was also received from Sir Roundell Palmer, former Attorney-General and former Solicitor-General, and Lord Romilly, Master of the Rolls. Peter Henson, the clerk to the Attorney-General, gave evidence, as did Bennet Woodcroft, Chief Clerk of the Patent Office and William Michell, 1st Class Clerk of the Patent Office. Lucius Chittenden, a U.S. lawyer and former Register of the U.S. Treasury gave evidence as to the working of the U.S. patent laws. Patent agents were also well represented.[240]

An interesting fact about the 1871–72 Committees was the large number of manufacturers and patentees who gave evidence. The manufacturers included some notable persons such as Eugene Schneider, the Managing Partner of the Creuzot Steel works in France, and former President of the *Corps Legislatif*; Isaac Holden, a large-scale woollen manufacturer; Sir William Armstrong; Robert Macfie; James Howard, a manufacturer of agricultural machinery; John Wright, a manufacturer and Chairman of the Birmingham Chamber of Commerce; and Edmund Muspratt, an alkali manufacturer and former

239 William Robert Grove, Q.C., Thomas Webster Q.C., Theo Aston (Barrister), John Johnson (solicitor and patent agent), Frederick Campin (Barrister, and formerly a patent agent), Arthur Bower (solicitor).

240 Alfred Newton, John Johnson, William Carpmael, George Haseltine, William Wise (who also spoke on behalf of the Society of Engineers).

President of the Liverpool Chamber of Commerce. Patentees who gave evidence included Henry Bessemer, the inventor of the Bessemer process in steel metallurgy and at least 100 other inventions; James Nasmyth, the inventor of the steam hammer; Anthony Mundella, inventor of steam powered hosiery making machines; and Captain Beaumont, inventor of the rock tunnelling machine. Other witnesses included William Siemens, President of the Institute of Mechanical Engineers; and Christian Allhusen, President of the Newcastle and Gateshead Chamber of Commerce.

(2) The Issues Raised by the Witnesses

Policy of the Patent System

In examining the evidence of the witnesses before the 1871–72 Committees, it is clear that there was overwhelming support for the policy of the patent system. Most witnesses thought that the patent system was intrinsically beneficial, but criticised the inconvenience which arose from its practical working in the United Kingdom. This was precisely the kind of opinion which had been given about the patent system by witnesses before the earlier Select Committees in 1829, 1851 and 1862–64. Only five witnesses before the 1871–72 Committees clearly desired the abolition of the patent system.[241] A further four witnesses thought the availability of patents should be severely reduced, or speculated that it might be necessary to abolish the patent system at some indeterminate future date.[242] At most, less than one-third of the witnesses before the Committees supported the abolition movement in any way.

The majority of witnesses adopted an instrumentalist approach to the policy of the patent system. They believed that the patent system existed to benefit both inventors and the community. Many witnesses considered that the patent system stimulated invention, and this was its primary justification. As Aston stated, "it is beyond question, that the grant of patents, or the grant of some statutory right of property in an invention in some form necessarily stimulates persons to make inventions."[243] It was also thought that the

---

241 Romilly, Schneider, Armstrong, Macfie and Allhusen.

242 Grove, Palmer, Muspratt and Samuelson.

243 UNITED KINGDOM, Parliamentary Papers, *Report from the Select Committee on Letters Patent; together with the Proceedings of the Committee, Minutes of Evidence, Appendix and Index* (1871) 368, vol X, 603, 98. Similar remarks were also made at 151 (Holden); and in the 1872 Select Committee, 18 (Newton), 23 (Siemens), 44 (Howard), 112–113 (Mundella), 58–9 (Wright), 76 (Woodcroft), 80 (Haseltine), 128 (Samuelson). UNITED KINGDOM, Parliamentary Papers, *Report from the Select Committee on Letters Patent; together with the Proceedings of the Committee, Minutes of Evidence, Appendix and Index* (1872) 193, vol XI, 395.

patent system encouraged a more rapid development of new manufactures, and thus increased national wealth.[244] Famous inventors such as Nasmyth and Bessemer agreed that the patent system acted as a stimulus to invention.[245] Bessemer stated that he would never have developed his steel manufacturing process without the patent laws to protect him. He was induced to keep working on his process and expending 20,000 pounds on its development, because he knew he had the security of a patent behind him.[246]

A number of witnesses also stated that there were different types of inventors, some of whom more likely required the stimulating effect of the patent laws. For example, Howard claimed that most inventors were "men engaged as draughtsmen and foremen, or in some other subordinate capacity", not wealthy persons, and not usually "born inventors".[247] He agreed that "born inventors" did not require the stimulus of the patent system, because they would invent in any circumstances, but said that these were in a minority.[248] Wright agreed that "working men" needed the stimulus of the patent system, and added that in his area, Birmingham, the working men and manufacturers were in favour of the patent system.[249] A number of other witnesses agreed that the class of inventors most commonly benefited by the patent system were "artisans".[250]

Those witnesses who questioned the value of the patent system generally argued that inventions would be produced regardless of whether or not the patent system was retained. For example, Samuelson argued that human ingenuity was in itself a stimulus to invention,[251] a point also made by Palmer,[252] Schneider,[253] Armstrong,[254] and Macfie.[255] However, some who were attracted to the abolition movement, agreed that the patent system needed to be retained in relation to "great" or "exceptional" inventions. Grove,[256] Schneider,[257]

244 46 (Webster) (1871 Select Committee).
245 179 (Nasmyth), 139, 147 (Bessemer) (1871 Select Committee).
246 134 forward (Bessemer) (1871 Select Committee).
247 44 (Howard) (1872 Select Committee).
248 *Ibid.*
249 58 (Wright) (1872 Select Committee). Several witnesses were of the opinion that "working men" supported the patent system, and would object to its abolition. Such witnesses included 113 (Mundella), 97 (Muspratt), 55 (Howard), 64–66 (Campin) (1872 Select Committee).
250 91 (Webster), 82 (Palmer), 27 (Grove) (1871 Select Committee).
251 125 (Samuelson) (1872 Select Committee).
252 74–75 (Palmer) (1871 Select Committee).
253 129–130 (Schneider) (1871 Select Committee).
254 173–4 (Armstrong) (1871 Select Committee).
255 186 (Macfie) (1871 Select Committee).
256 7, 14, 23 (Grove) (1871 Select Committee).
257 133 (Schneider) (1871 Select Committee).

Palmer,[258] and Muspratt,[259] all acknowledged that some important inventions might need the stimulus of patent laws.

The second major justification for the patent system was that it provided a form of financial reward for inventors. It is interesting that this point was mentioned more frequently by witnesses before the 1872 Committee, where a greater number of patentees and manufacturers gave evidence. Siemens told the Committee that he had migrated to the U.K. because there was no patent system in his country of origin (Germany), and he sought "some security" for his efforts.[260] Beaumont agreed that the thought of reaping financial reward from his invention induced him to spend large sums in developing his diamond drill for boring tunnels.[261] Howard and Muspratt made similar comments about the importance of the prospective financial benefit from a patent,[262] although Muspratt considered that some minor inventions received too much reward from the patent system.[263]

Most of those who favoured the abolition movement agreed that it was important to provide some reward for inventors. To that end, a number of witnesses supported the introduction of schemes of State rewards to replace the patent system. Macfie had earlier proposed schemes of State rewards to the 1862–64 Select Committee, and he had then suggested they should be operated in conjunction with a limited form of patent. However, in 1871 he proposed that the patent system should be completely abolished, and replaced with a new system involving "certificates of merit", "medals", an "honour conferred by the Queen", and/or "rewards of a pecuniary kind".[264] Romilly and Armstrong also agreed that the patent system should be abolished and replaced by a system of State rewards.[265] However, most witnesses opposed the introduction of a scheme of State rewards. Bessemer considered that a system of State rewards would never provide the same stimulus to invention as the patent system, because inventors would have no confidence that the value of their inventions would be appreciated by the body responsible for the awards. He had made 50,000 pounds from his steel process, and did not think that the awarding body

258 77 (Palmer) (1871 Select Committee).
259 88 (Muspratt) (1872 Select Committee).
260 22, 27 (Siemens) (1872 Select Committee).
261 119–120 (Beaumont) (1872 Select Committee).
262 44, 52–54 (Howard), 88 (Muspratt) (1872 Select Committee).
263 93 (Muspratt). Allhusen also made this point at 106–7. (1872 Select Committee) Grove made this point before the 1872 Select Committee at 28.
264 186 (Macfie) (1871 Select Committee) (1871 Select Committee).
265 40 (Romilly), 172 (Armstrong) (1871 Select Committee).

"would have voted a purse of 50,000 *l.* for a man who was totally unknown in the trade, and who had apparently the wildest notions."[266]

It is unsurprising that supporters of the patent system such as Webster,[267] Siemens,[268] Howard,[269] Wright,[270] Mundella,[271] and Nasmyth,[272] should have joined with Bessemer in rejecting outright any proposals relating to schemes of State rewards, but it is a significant point that several of those who tended towards abolition also rejected State rewards. Grove, for example, stated that:

> [T]he notion of Government rewards is quite out of the question; to make political interest for inventors would be simply to have that man rewarded who was the most ingenious beggar ... instead of having inventors attending to their own business we should have them running about the corridors of the House of Commons trying to obtain rewards for their inventions.[273]

Schneider also made the point that a system of State rewards would be impractical. He said such rewards "might not be granted at all, because there would be a fear of burdening the public funds, or they would be granted very badly, because a political assembly cannot be a good judge of the amount to be granted in such cases."[274] Samuelson considered that a scheme of State rewards would be "absolutely chimerical".[275]

Some of the witnesses before the 1871–72 Committees referred to a third justification for the patent system: namely, the contractual relationship between the inventor and the State, and the importance of disclosure of inventions. Haseltine,[276] Grove,[277] and Aston,[278] for example, referred to the "bargain" between the inventor and the State, as the basis of the patent system. Howard stressed the importance of disclosure, stating that "one of the greatest

266 145 (Bessemer) (1871 Select Committee).
267 94 (Webster) (1871 Select Committee).
268 27–28 (Siemens) (1872 Select Committee).
269 44 (Howard) (1872 Select Committee).
270 58 (Wright) (1872 Select Committee).
271 117 (Mundella) (1872 Select Committee).
272 181–2 (Nasmyth) (1871 Select Committee).
273 7 (Grove) (1871 Select Committee).
274 132 (Schneider) (1871 Select Committee).
275 127 (Samuelson) (1872 Select Committee).
276 82 (Haseltine) (1872 Select Committee).
277 28 (Grove) (1871 Select Committee).
278 98 (Aston) (1871 Select Committee).

advantages is that we thereby indirectly get a record of inventions".[279] Even Armstrong, a strong opponent of the patent system, stated that the patent evidenced a "bargain, in which the public, in consideration of submitting to the disadvantages of a monopoly, are to acquire the use of a valuable invention which would otherwise be lost to them."[280]

Even though the notion of disclosure as a basis for the patent system had become less important than the consideration of stimulating invention, it remained relevant to many witnesses. A number believed that a consequence of the abolition of patents would be an increase in secretly worked inventions. Webster, for example, made this point,[281] as did Aston,[282] Schneider,[283] Grove,[284] Nasmyth,[285] Siemens,[286] and Palmer.[287] However, most witnesses considered that the extent of secret practise of inventions would still be limited, because it was difficult to keep inventions secret.[288] This was particularly true of patented products, although patented processes might be kept secret without too much difficulty.[289] Romilly, for example, said he knew of "many cases" where inventions were worked in secret, including "some places at Swansea where chemical discoveries are kept secret."[290] Bessemer stated that he had a number of inventions which he had not patented, and preferred to work in secret.[291]

The fourth justification for the patent system was that an invention was the property of the inventor. Most witnesses agreed that there was no "natural" property right in an invention, but they considered it public policy for the

279 44 (Howard) (1872 Select Committee). Aston made the same point. 100 (Aston) (1871 Select Committee).

280 172 (Armstrong) (1871 Select Committee). Palmer made a similar comment at 75 (1871 Select Committee).

281 93 (Webster) (1871 Select Committee).

282 98, 125 (Aston) (1871 Select Committee).

283 132 (Schneider) (1871 Select Committee).

284 13 (Grove) (1871 Select Committee).

285 179 (Nasmyth) (1871 Select Committee).

286 35 (Siemens) (1872 Select Committee).

287 75 (Palmer) (1871 Select Committee).

288 See especially 177 (Armstrong), 190 (Macfie) (1871 Select Committee).

289 13, 30 (Grove), 50 (Webster), 75 (Palmer), 132 (Schneider) (1871 Select Committee); 95 (Muspratt) (1872 Select Committee).

290 41 (Romilly) (1871 Select Committee).

291 140, 147 (Bessemer) (1871 Select Committee). Bessemer said his secret inventions included one for the manufacture of bronze, and one which used secret machinery, which had been practised for 28 years.

State to grant a temporary property right.[292] Webster, for example, stated that it was a:

> matter of public policy that property should be in the hands of certain individuals; that property which people have created by labour, whether physical or mental labour, should be theirs, if not in perpetuity, yet for a limited time … [He added that] the restriction of the right of copying which is what creates the property … is a municipal right regulated by expediency.[293]

Webster also used the term "intellectual property" to describe property rights in inventions, as well as copyright works.[294] Holden agreed that rights in inventions were property rights, and that to refuse to grant property rights in inventions would be as "disastrous in its effects as the want of protection to property in general".[295] Mundella considered that "the laws of every civilised country ought to recognise property in that which is the creation of a man's hand or brain; whether it is brain labour or hand labour, it is all the same."[296] Campin, who spoke on behalf of an association of working men called the *Labour Representation League*, argued that the patent abolitionists were influenced by Communist propaganda, because "a man who denies property in the fruits of a man's intellect, must necessarily deny all rights of property."[297] However, patent abolitionists such as Muspratt,[298] Palmer,[299] Armstrong,[300] and Macfie,[301] rejected the concept of property rights in inventions, on the basis that there could be no exclusivity in knowledge. Palmer, for example, stated that knowledge, unlike material things, was capable of being possessed and used by the whole world at the same time, and was not diminished by

292 One notable person who still believed that an inventor had a "natural" right in his invention was Woodcroft, Chief Clerk of the Patent Office. 72 (1871 Select Committee). Haseltine also considered that the inventor had a right to a patent, which was not based merely upon a question of public policy. 81 (1872 Select Committee).

293 89 (Webster) (1871 Select Committee).

294 65 (Webster) (1871 Select Committee).

295 150 (Holden) (1871 Select Committee).

296 116 (Mundella) (1872 Select Committee).

297 66 (Campin) (1872 Select Committee).

298 94 (Muspratt) (1872 Select Committee).

299 77 (Palmer) (1871 Select Committee).

300 172 (Armstrong) (1871 Select Committee).

301 186 (Macfie) (1871 Select Committee).

simultaneous use.[302] Therefore, he asserted, inventions, which were derived from knowledge, should not be appropriated.[303]

Most of the supporters of the patent system saw no real distinction between the policy of patents and the policy of copyright.[304] However, some of those who favoured abolition considered that copyright was acceptable, but patents were not. Schneider, for example, drew "a considerable distinction between the creations of art and literature, and what are called industrial inventions."[305] A copyright work was "the soul, the spirit, the personality, of the man who invents it" whereas an invention was only "a solution of a problem which has presented itself to everyone, and which anyone else might have hit upon".[306] Armstrong stated that copyright did not involve any monopoly of ideas, and the field of authorship was not narrowed by copyright. He asserted that in contrast, patents monopolised ideas and limited the field of invention.[307]

International Considerations

International Effect of Abolition of Patents in the United Kingdom

The 1871–72 Committees were greatly interested in the witnesses' views about the international effect of any proposals to abolish the patent system in the United Kingdom. There were a number of conflicting opinions.

A significant number of witnesses believed that if the U.K. abolished the patent system, inventors would leave the U.K. and take their inventions to countries where the patent system still existed. Therefore, it was feared that U.K. manufacturers would have less access to new inventions, and U.K. industry would fall behind its competitors.[308] Siemens, for example, said that his experience demonstrated what would happen if there was no patent system. He said that the "fact of there being no properly understood and regulated Patent Law in Germany induced me to come over to this country, and make this my real home."[309] He also noted that German manufacturers had slower access to new inventions than their U.K. competitors, and he said that this was the result of their limited patent system.[310] He stated that German inventors

302 78 (Palmer) (1871 Select Committee).
303 *Ibid.*
304 See for example, 63 (Wright), 119 (Beaumont) (1872 Select Committee).
305 128 (Schneider) (1871 Select Committee).
306 *Ibid.*
307 172 (Armstrong) (1871 Select Committee).
308 See generally, for example, 62 (Wright), 74 (Woodcroft), 112–3 (Mundella) (1872 Select Committee); 148 (Bessemer), 61–2 (Webster) (1871 Select Committee).
309 22 (Siemens) (1872 Select Committee).
310 *Ibid.* 26, 34.

were willing to pay voluntary royalties to him, in order to gain access to knowledge about his inventions.[311] Howard, an exporter, agreed that inventors would leave the U.K. if the patent system was abolished,[312] and also stated that the situation in Austria and Germany demonstrated the disadvantages which would result if the patent system was abolished. He asserted that Prussia and Austria "are generally six or seven years behind us, and in that way we command the trade of the world."[313] Haseltine also stated that there was "very much less" invention in Prussia, than in the U.K. or the U.S.A.[314] Nevertheless, his experience in the U.S.A. had shown that Prussian inventors who migrated were just as ingenious as the Americans, and they had taken out large numbers of patents in the U.S.A.[315]

Holden also believed that "one of the reasons why industry has made so little progress in Prussia has been owing to the difficulty of obtaining patents."[316] He added that the situation in Switzerland was no better. The lack of a patent system meant that there was little stimulus for people to invent, and in fact, there were no persons "worthy of the name of an inventor" in Switzerland.[317] He asserted that in Switzerland "industry makes no progress".[318] In contrast, Mundella believed that there had been inventors in Switzerland, but the lack of a patent system had caused them to leave their country in order to exploit their inventions.[319] Another opinion was presented by Grove, who believed that it was of little consequence that Switzerland and the Netherlands had no patent system, since their manufacturing industries were on such a small scale.[320]

An opposing argument was advanced by some witnesses who believed that countries without patent systems (such as Switzerland or the Netherlands), or countries with limited patent systems (such as Germany), were in an advantageous position. This opinion was usually based on principles of free

---

311 *Ibid.* 34.

312 45 (Howard) (1872 Select Committee).

313 *Ibid.* Haseltine further stated that although the Germans had free access to U.K. inventions, the state of the art in Germany, in for example, sugar-refining, was far below the situation in the United Kingdom. 84 (1872 Select Committee).

314 79 (Haseltine) (1872 Select Committee). Haseltine was a citizen of the U.S.A. but had practised as a patent agent in the U.K. for 16 years.

315 *Ibid.*

316 151 (Holden) (1871 Select Committee).

317 *Ibid.* 152.

318 *Ibid.*

319 116 (Mundella) (1872 Select Committee).

320 14 (Grove) (1871 Select Committee).

competition. Muspratt, for example, said that under the regime of free trade, manufacturers in the U.K. were being brought into greater competition with foreign manufacturers, and it was increasingly the case that foreign manufacturers were making "enormous strides" in embracing new developments.[321] He gave an example from his own area, the chemical trade. He believed that German chemical manufacturers had almost caught up to U.K. manufacturers in terms of development, yet they did not have to bear the burden of paying patent royalties.[322] He also asserted that countries without patents were advantaged because industries were taken to those countries, to avoid the patent laws. For example, French producers of analine had taken their factory to Switzerland to avoid French patent laws.[323]

Macfie also believed that industries were taken to Switzerland, the Netherlands or Germany to avoid paying patent royalties.[324] He reiterated his earlier arguments that under free trade, countries without a patent system would compete at a very great advantage compared to those countries which maintained a patent system.[325] Both Armstrong[326] and Allhusen[327] also agreed that the introduction of free trade had caused difficulties for manufacturers in competing with foreign producers who were not subject to patent royalties. Samuelson, who believed that the patent system retained some usefulness, but would not predict its survival beyond another 10 or 20 years, said that the real problem for U.K. manufacturers lay in neutral markets.[328] He stated that there was little prospect of damaging foreign competition in the home market, but considered that in neutral markets such as "the South of Germany, and the North of Italy", U.K. manufacturers were suffering from intense competition from manufacturers situated in countries without patent laws.[329] He referred particularly to the Swiss spinning industry, as being highly competitive in the markets adjacent to Switzerland.[330] Some of those who favoured abolition considered that if one large and influential country such as the U.K. gave up its patent system, others would quickly follow.[331]

---

321 93 (Muspratt) (1872 Select Committee).

322 *Ibid.*

323 96 (Muspratt) (1872 Select Committee).

324 189 (Macfie) (1871 Select Committee).

325 *Ibid.*

326 176 (Armstrong) (1871 Select Committee).

327 Allhusen was the President of the Newcastle and Gateshead Chamber of Commerce. 103 (1872 Select Committee).

328 126–7 (Samuelson) (1872 Select Committee).

329 *Ibid.* 124.

330 *Ibid.*

331 28–30 (Grove), 189 (Macfie), 75 (Palmer) (1871 Select Committee).

Proposals for International Assimilation of Patent Laws/ International Treaty

It has already been noted that as early as the 1862–64 Select Committee, the majority of witnesses supported the granting of patents to foreigners. By 1871–72, witnesses were unanimous that foreign inventors should not be treated any differently to nationals. Statistics of patent applications made during the years 1867 to 1869 demonstrate that by this time, a large number of U.K. patent applications were being made by foreigners.[332] Consistent with these facts, many witnesses took the further step of suggesting that there should be some international arrangements for the assimilation of patent laws, or at least some form of international patent treaty.

Most of the witnesses before the 1871–72 Select Committees supported international assimilation of patent laws, but foresaw that this goal would be difficult to achieve. Even patent abolitionists such as Allhusen, Muspratt, Macfie, Armstrong and Romilly supported international assimilation, largely because it would be one method of addressing the alleged problems for U.K. manufacturers caused by the introduction of free trade.[333] By the term "assimilation" was meant an agreement amongst all the U.K.'s major trading partners to establish patent systems upon certain defined bases. It was then asserted that this would alleviate most of the problems associated with unfair foreign competition. The fact that U.K. patent abolitionists so strongly supported international assimilation of patent law has often been overlooked by later commentators such as Machlup and Penrose.[334] It is certainly clear that as interest in international patent assimilation or patent treaties grew, calls for abolition waned. Thus, by 1873, when the international patent Congress was held in Vienna,[335] the abolition movement in the U.K. had almost totally disappeared. As will be seen in the next Chapter, a similar pattern emerged in Germany. In respect to the U.K., it is clear that the patent abolition movement was declining by 1871–72, and one reason for this decline was the fact that the abolitionists had failed to win the support of government or important scientific, professional and cultural

332 For example, during that period, 2480 U.K. patent applications were made by persons resident in London, and 966 applications were made by persons resident in Paris. 203 (Appendix 4) (1871 Select Committee).

333 103 (Allhusen), 93 (Muspratt) (1872 Select Committee); 190 (Macfie), 176 (Armstrong), 38 (Romilly) (1871 Select Committee).

334 Machlup, F., and Penrose, E., "The Patent Controversy in the Nineteenth Century" (1950) x *The Journal of Economic History* 1.

335 Pieper, C., *Der Erfinderschutz und die Reform der Patentgesetze. Amtlicher Bericht über den Internationalen Patent-Congress zur Erörterung der Frage des Patentschutzes. Mit einer Einleitung von Dr. C. W. Siemens F.R.S.* (Dresden, Commission der Schulbuchhandlung, 1873).

organisations. However, it is also quite probable that the U.K. patent abolitionists abandoned their quest when they saw serious efforts being made towards international assimilation of patent laws. Such proposals addressed their concern to make the patent system more consistent with principles of free trade.

Although most witnesses supported in theory the idea of international assimilation of patent laws,[336] many believed this would be too difficult to achieve in practice.[337] Grove, for example, stated that the patent laws were too complex to permit international assimilation.[338] He referred to the example of the extradition law, which he described as relatively simple, yet it was extremely difficult to regulate at an international level.[339] Howard considered that the only way that international assimilation of patent laws could occur would be if the U.K. reformed its patent system, and other countries then copied the U.K. model.[340] He also considered that the issue of international copyright was more important than international patents, and thought any proposals for assimilation should be deferred.[341] Siemens suggested that one way of achieving international protection of patents would be for the countries in Europe and North America to establish an "International Patent" which would cover the whole of their territories.[342] All the participating countries would be bound to give effect to the patent when it was granted by one member State.[343]

(b) *The Report of the 1872 Select Committee*

On 8 May 1872, the Select Committee made its Report to the House of Commons.[344] Despite the fact that Macfie was a member of the Committee, the Report was firmly in favour of the continuation of the patent system. The

336 See especially 121 (Beaumont) 102 (Wise), 86 (Haseltine), 43 (Johnson), 66 (Campin), 26–29 (Siemens), 45 (Howard), 74 (Woodcroft) (1872 Select Committee); 127 (Aston), 38 (Romilly), 144 (Bessemer), 190 (Macfie), 176 (Armstrong), 168 (Chittenden) (1871 Select Committee).

337 *Ibid.*

338 28 (Grove) (1871 Select Committee).

339 *Ibid.*

340 45–6 (Howard) (1872 Select Committee).

341 *Ibid.*

342 27 (Siemens) (1872 Select Committee).

343 *Ibid.* This was a particularly visionary suggestion. It was not until 1973 that the European Patent Convention was signed, and it was followed in 1975 by the Community Patent Convention. Of the two, the Community Patent Convention was closer to Siemen's proposals, since it was intended to operate as a unitary patent for the territory of the European Community. However, the Community Patent system was still not operational at the date of writing.

344 iii–v (1872 Select Committee).

Report made three major statements about the beneficial effects of the patent system. These were:

(1) THAT the privilege conferred by letters patent promotes the progress of manufactures, by causing many important inventions to be introduced and developed more rapidly than would otherwise be the case.

(2) THAT the same privilege leads to the introduction and publication of numerous improvements, each of a minor character, but the sum of which contributes greatly to the progress of industry.

(3) THAT in the absence of the protection of letters patent, the competition of manufacturers amongst themselves would, doubtless, lead to the introduction of improved processes and machinery, but that it would probably be less rapid than under the stimulus of a patent law.[345]

These statements indicated that the Committee had accepted that the major theoretical justification for the patent system was as a means to stimulate invention. A secondary justification was the importance of publication and disclosure of new improvements. In addition, the Committee rejected proposals regarding the introduction of schemes of State rewards, stating that "it does not appear that the granting of pecuniary rewards could be substituted, with advantage to the public interest, for the temporary privilege conferred by letters patent."[346]

The Committee also addressed the issue of international assimilation of patent laws, reporting that it was:

> of opinion that there should be an assimilation in the law and practice in regard to inventions amongst the various civilised countries of the world, and that Her Majesty's Government be requested to inquire of Foreign and Colonial Governments how far they are ready to concur in international arrangements in relation thereto.[347]

Despite the views of most witnesses that international assimilation of patent laws would be extremely difficult to achieve, this recommendation made it

345 *Ibid.* iii.
346 *Ibid.*
347 *Ibid.* v. Such investigations were undertaken. See: UNITED KINGDOM, Parliamentary Papers, *Reports by H.M. Secs of Embassy and Legation respecting Law and Practice in Foreign Countries with regard to Inventions* (1873) C. 741, vol LXVI, 483.

very clear that the Committee believed it inappropriate for a large manufacturing nation such as the U.K. to contemplate the abolition of patent laws. Instead, in the Committee's view, the future lay in increased penetration of the patent system around the world and greater international co-operation regarding the working of the patent laws.

On 23 May 1872, an editorial in *The Times* commented upon the Report of the 1872 Select Committee.[348] Its comments clearly demonstrated its acceptance that there was now little likelihood of abolition of the patent system. It stated that this outcome was apparent from the overwhelming evidence laid before the Committee by the witnesses, and also the recommendations in the Report. *The Times* noted that although the patent system "has been assailed by very powerful opponents, popular opinion is certainly not ripe for its total abolition."[349] Moreover, it asserted that the majority of inventors were not men of capital, but were artisans, who needed the stimulus of the patent system to exercise their "inventive genius".[350] It noted that the abolition movement might have been successful if most inventors were men of wealth who could withstand open competition, yet the contrary was more commonly the case.[351]

These comments are especially significant because, as set out earlier in this Chapter, between 1864 and 1869 *The Times* had published a number of editorials which called for the abolition of the patent system. By 1872, *The Times* and other commentators who once favoured abolition, were reassessing their attitude to the question. In fact, this Chapter has shown that there never was a serious threat to the patent system in the U.K. during the 1850s to 1870s. The abolitionists were at all times in the minority and never gained the support of a majority of informed public opinion.

There has always been some difficulty in explaining why the U.K. embraced movements towards international protection of industrial property rights during the 1870s and 1880s, when it was supposed during a part of this time there was a strong anti-patent movement in its own territory. This Chapter demonstrates that there was no such influential anti-patent sentiment, and therefore no inconsistency between the U.K.'s policy on patent protection in the domestic, and later, international, spheres. Evidence also suggests that U.K. patent abolitionists supported, rather than opposed, the notion of international assimilation of patent law. In fact, it is likely that the abolition movement, already in severe decline, collapsed altogether because of the work of

348 *The Times*, 23 May 1872.
349 *Ibid.*
350 *Ibid.*
351 *Ibid.*

the 1873 international patent Congress in Vienna.[352] As is set out in the next Chapter, a similar pattern can be seen in Prussia (later Germany) during the same period, despite the fact that the Prussian patent abolition movement was stronger than in the United Kingdom.

352 See further Chapter Five.

CHAPTER 4

Overview of Patent Abolition Debates

France, the Netherlands and Prussia 1860s and 1870s

> The Royal Prussian Government is therefore of opinion that steps should be taken for the total abolition of the patent system throughout the whole range of the Federal Power, a measure recommended by the theory of social science and already sufficiently prepared for in public opinion ...[1]
>
> COUNT VON BISMARCK, 10 December 1868

Chapter Three has challenged traditional opinions concerning the extent of support for the patent abolition movement in the U.K. during the period 1850 to 1872. It has shown that support for abolition was much less than previous scholarship suggests. This Chapter examines the strength of the patent abolition movement in three other countries: France, the Netherlands and Prussia. Of these three countries, only France was similar to the U.K. in having a significant patent system in operation before 1860. Yet it was in the other two countries, (the Netherlands and Prussia), where the abolition movement was strongest.

This Chapter starts in Section A by examining the abolition movement in France, and demonstrates the similarities between the course of this movement and the abolition movement in the United Kingdom. In both countries, the movement floundered because it lacked the support of scientific and cultural organisations, inventors, manufacturers and government. In Section B,

1 *Motion in the Federal Council of the North German Confederation by the Chancellor of the Confederation, Count von Bismarck, with the grounds thereof,* (10 December 1868), translated from the original German in UNITED KINGDOM, Parliamentary Papers, *Return of any Public Official Documents received at the Foreign Office, exhibiting Reasons why Count Von Bismarck and the Government of Prussia, and Mr Fock, the Minister of the Interior of the Netherlands, and the Dutch Government, have recommended, and the Chambers of the latter Country have resolved on, the Abolition of Patents for Invention* (1870) 41, vol LXI, 527, 11.

 | DOI:10.1163/9789004470125_006

attention is focused on the situation in the Netherlands, where the patent system was abolished in 1869.[2] In this case, the abolitionists were successful because they were easily able to convince the government as well as inventors and manufacturers, of the practical, (rather than theoretical), disadvantages associated with the operation of the patent laws. In Section C, attention is focused upon the situation in Prussia (later Germany), showing that the abolition movement had more support from government, economic philosophers and business groups than in the United Kingdom. However, it failed to win the support of practical users of the patent system. Ultimately, as in the case of the U.K., the patent abolition movement in Germany collapsed after 1873.[3]

A The Patent Abolition Movement in France

Chapter One has examined the debate concerning the theoretical basis of the patent system which was a subject of interest to a number of French and Belgian commentators during the 1840s and 1850s.[4] This debate revolved around whether the inventor should have a perpetual property right in the invention, (a *monautopole*), or whether a more limited proprietary right was more appropriate. It was noted in that Chapter that none of the opponents of the *monautopole* supported the complete abolition of the patent system. They only required the imposition of what they saw as reasonable limitations upon the exercise of the patent, in consideration of the public interest.

From 1862, however, some French commentators began to question the continued need for a patent system. There were two reasons for this change. The first was the adoption of freer trade policies in France after the signing of the series of bilateral commercial treaties beginning in 1860. As a consequence of these new policies, some commentators believed that the patent system was allied to the discredited system of protectionism, and should be abolished. The second factor was the abolitionist stance taken by some French commentators as a consequence of their attendance at the Universal Exhibition held in London in 1862.

2 The Netherlands abolished its Patent Act of 25 January 1817 (*Staatsblad, No 6*) on 15 July 1869 (*Staatsblad, No 126*).

3 Prussia, and the North German Confederation, did not abolish their patent laws. Instead, on 25 May 1877, a new patent law was passed with effect throughout the whole of the German Reich.

4 See Chapter One, C Private Reform Proposals.

(a) *Background to the Debates*

(i) The Bilateral Commercial Treaties of the 1860s

Until the treaties of commerce in the 1860s, the French patent system was perceived as an acceptable part of the protectionist economy.[5] Michel Chevalier, a prominent French advocate of free trade, argued that the patent system was less oppressive than the "monstrueux"[6] powers conferred upon the Customs Office, particularly "les visites domiciliaires, la confiscation, la dénonciation soldée, les visites á corps, outrage á la morale publique et á la pudeur."[7] While such practices occurred, the patent system was not likely to be criticised.[8] However, after the commercial treaties of the 1860s, many of the allegedly objectionable activities associated with protectionism were abandoned, and the patent system was exposed to greater scrutiny.[9]

Many French economic philosophers questioned whether the continued existence of the patent monopoly was consistent with the new trade policies. There were basically two schools of thought which emerged in France and Belgium on this question during the 1860s and 1870s. The first (and most extreme) opinion was that patents for inventions were monopolies without social benefit, and should be abolished along with all forms of protectionism. The second was that a degree of competition in trade was necessary, but sometimes the State should step in to grant and protect exclusive rights. Those holding this opinion considered that some forms of labour, such as creating a new invention, were of such benefit to society that there was a place for the continued existence of monopoly rights.[10]

5 Chevalier, M., 'Les Brevets d'Invention contraires a la Liberté du Travail' (1878) *Journal des économistes* 169, 188.

6 Translation: "monstrous" *Ibid.*

7 Translation: "home visits, confiscation, paid informants, bodily searches, outrage to public morals and decency." *Ibid.*

8 *Ibid.*

9 A commercial treaty of 1860 between France and the U.K. was followed by similar treaties between France and the other main European powers. A commercial treaty was concluded with Belgium in 1861, with Prussia in 1862 (in 1864 this was extended to the whole of the Zollverein), with Italy in 1863, with Switzerland in 1864, with Sweden, Norway, the Grand Duchy of Mecklenburg, Spain and the Netherlands in 1865, with Austria in 1866, and with Portugal and the Papal States in 1867. All of the above treaties contained a "most favoured nation clause" – effectively a conventional tariff applicable without distinction to all products from the contracting parties. Rist, M., "A French Experiment with Free Trade: The Treaty of 1860" in Cameron, R., (ed), *Essays in French Economic History* (Homewood, Richard D Irwin, 1970), 286.

10 For a detailed discussion of these views, see (c) below.

(ii) The Effect of the 1862 Universal Exhibition in London, and the Writings of Michel Chevalier

Although the adoption in 1860 of freer trade policies was probably the major factor which influenced a re-assessment of the policy of the patent system in France, the favourable results of the commercial treaties were not seen in France until after 1863.[11] Therefore, perceptions about the benefits which arose from freer trade cannot alone explain why criticism of the patent system began to develop during the years 1862–1863. There is strong evidence that the more immediate reason for the debate was French participation at the Universal Exhibition in London in 1862. Just as the 1851 Great Exhibition in London had influenced U.K. commentators and government to re-examine the policy and procedures associated with their patent system,[12] some French commentators who had seen the 1862 exhibition were led to believe that the patent system was of doubtful use.

In 1869, Rolin-Jaequemyns, an advocate in Gand, explained that the upsurge in French and Belgian criticism of the policy of the patent system during the years 1862 and 1863 was primarily the result of the Universal Exhibition of 1862.[13] He thought that the spectacle presented at the Exhibition of many similar products being invented by a variety of persons in all corners of Europe at the same time, made it clear to those who attended that no one person could honestly lay sole claim to an invention.[14] He added that the Exhibition showed that most discoveries which had been attributed to one person, were really the result of the combined work and research of many persons, and thus it was not equitable for only one person to claim exclusive rights of ownership of these inventions.[15]

Chevalier, President of the French Section of the International Jury of the 1862 Exhibition, (and author of the Introduction to the Report of the members of the French section), was convinced that the patent system was no longer suited to the needs of French industry.[16] He stated that he was in favour of unconditional abolition of the patent system, adding that:

---

11 Rist, M., "A French Experiment with Free Trade: The Treaty of 1860" in Cameron, R., (ed), *Essays in French Economic History* (Homewood, Richard D Irwin, 1970), 307.

12 See Chapter Two above.

13 Rolin-Jaequemyns, G., "De Quelques Manifestations Récentes de l'Opinion Publique en Europe au Sujet des Brevets d'Invention" (1869) 1 *Revue de droit International et de Législation Comparée* 600.

14 *Ibid.* 604.

15 *Ibid.*

16 Chevalier, M., "Introduction" in *Rapports des membres de la section française du jury international sur l'ensemble de l'exposition universelle de Londres de 1862* (Paris, 1862) quoted in *Ibid.*

> On seeing at the Exhibition in London, at a few paces from each other, the same machines, the same tools, new productions, invented or discovered a thousand miles apart by men who arrived at the same result, sometimes by different ways, legislators and magistrates felt themselves bound to ask to what principles of justice and equity could one of these inventors appeal that he might obtain a temporary monopoly, rendering abortive the efforts and experiments on the part of ten other inventors as persevering, as conscientious, and as intelligent as himself.[17]

Chevalier claimed that the patent system hindered French industrial development, and was particularly damaging to export industries.[18] He suggested that it should be replaced with a system of special rewards for ingenious persons who rendered useful services to society by developing new inventions.[19]

Chevalier's 1862 Report was debated at some length at a meeting of the French *Académie des Sciences morales et politiques* in 1863.[20] At that meeting, he was joined by other members of the *Académie*, Odilon Barrot, de Lavergne, and Pellat, in arguing that the patent system was damaging to French industry, and did not afford any real advantages to the public.[21] This argument was refuted by the well-known economic and legal commentators, Wolowski, Renouard and Dupin, who claimed that equity and public utility necessitated a patent system.[22] Dupin also stressed the philosophical similarities between rights in tangible and intellectual property.[23]

---

17 Translated into English in UNITED KINGDOM, Parliamentary Papers, *Return of any Public Official Documents received at the Foreign Office, exhibiting Reasons why Count Von Bismarck and the Government of Prussia, and Mr Fock, the Minister of the Interior of the Netherlands, and the Dutch Government, have recommended, and the Chambers of the latter Country have resolved on, the Abolition of Patents for Invention* (1870) 41, vol LXI, 527, 2.

18 *Ibid.*

19 Chevalier, M., "Introduction" in *Rapports des membres de la section française du jury international sur l'ensemble de l'exposition universelle de Londres de 1862* (Paris, 1862) quoted in Macfie, R.A., (ed), *Recent Discussions on the Abolition of Patents for Inventions in the United Kingdom, France, Germany, and the Netherlands: evidence, speeches and papers in its favour* (London, Longmans and Co, 1869), ii.

20 Verge, M., *Compte-Rendu des séances de l'Académie des Sciences morales et politiques* (vol 63, 1863) (Institut impérial de France), 235–242. Discussed in Rolin-Jaequemyns, G., *op. cit.* 604–5.

21 *Ibid.*

22 *Ibid.*

23 *Ibid.*

Chevalier's strong convictions about the merits of free trade greatly influenced all his writings on the patent system.[24] His essential point was that "[t]ous les brevets d'invention constituent un monopole, or, il est incontestable que le monopole est la négation même de la liberté du travail."[25] For Chevalier, free trade, and freedom of the individual to work unencumbered by unnecessary restrictions, were synonymous. Patents clearly interfered with freedom of labour.[26] While his views were simply and clearly presented, (and partly for this reason he gained supporters both in France and the U.K.),[27] his writings did not contain a great deal of theoretical insight. The most comprehensive and detailed articles written in support of abolition of patents in France during the 1860s and 1870s were those of T.N. Benard, editor of the *Journal des économistes*. Benard was joined in his campaign against patents by other eminent commentators such as P. Vermeire, Paul Coq and A. Boudron.

(b) *The Theories of the Patent Abolitionists*

As early as November 1862, Benard had drawn attention to what he perceived were some insurmountable problems of the patent system.[28] In various later articles written between 1863 and 1869 he developed and expanded his views. Other French commentators such as Auguste Boudron and Paul Coq agreed generally with the issues raised by Benard. In addition, there were a number of foreign commentators who favoured abolition of patents, and who had some impact upon the course of the debate in France. Close attention was paid to the course of the patent reform movements in the U.K., and Chevalier

---

24 Chevalier, M., 'Les Brevets d'Invention contraires a la Liberté du Travail' (1878) *Journal des économistes* 169.

25 Translation: "all patents for inventions constitute a monopoly, but, it is incontestable that monopoly amounts to the negation of freedom of work." SOCIETE D'ECONOMIE POLITIQUE, "Réunion du 5 Juin 1869" (1869) *Journal des économistes* 446 (Chevalier at 455).

26 *Ibid.*

27 Chevalier's work opposing the patent system was cited with approval by U.K. commentators such as Macfie and Hawes. Macfie and Chevalier also corresponded with each other. See letter from Chevalier to Macfie reproduced in Macfie, R.A., (ed), *Recent Discussions on the Abolition of Patents for Inventions in the United Kingdom, France, Germany, and the Netherlands: evidence, speeches and papers in its favour* (London, Longmans and Co, 1869), 81. Hawes, W., "On the Economical Effects of the Patent Laws" (1863–4) 16 *The Law Magazine and Law Review* 61, 75.

28 Benard, T.N., "The Results of a Bad Law", *Avenir Commercial*, 1 November 1862. (Translated by the author into English and reproduced in Macfie, R.A., (ed), *Recent Discussions on the Abolition of Patents for Inventions in the United Kingdom, France, Germany, and the Netherlands: evidence, speeches and papers in its favour* (London, Longmans and Co, 1869), 175. See further Benard's article on the subject of financial advantages gained by patent lawyers, in *Avenir Commercial*, dated 28 June 1863, and also reproduced in *Ibid.* 180–184.

and Benard were in correspondence with U.K. abolitionists such as Macfie.[29] A meeting of 5 June 1869 of the *Société d'Economie Politique*[30] framed its topic of discussion around the Motion introduced into the House of Commons by Macfie on 28 May 1869, which called for the abolition of patents in the United Kingdom.[31] French commentators also paid close attention to the writings of the Belgian economist, P. Vermeire, and the Spanish Professor of political economy, Gabriel Rodriguez.

One argument often raised against the patent system was that patents were too easily obtained by persons who had not undertaken any work to justify such a right, and French industry was suffering as a result. Benard, for example, asserted that "[c]ommon sense and equity would join to say that when a scientific man indicates a discovery or an invention, that invention or discovery remains at the disposal of every one if the finder does not claim the exclusive right to work it."[32] However, the law did not mirror common sense, for it allowed a person who was not the inventor to patent the discovery, and thus claim exclusive rights to it. Benard noted that Hofmann, the inventor of red aniline, had communicated his technique to the French *Académie des Sciences* in 1858, and had chosen not to take out a patent. However, a French manufacturer had taken Hofmann's technique, patented it, and claimed exorbitant sums in licensing fees. As a result, many French manufacturers of colouring-stuffs were forced to leave France, and establish factories across the border in Switzerland and Belgium.[33] A related argument was advanced by Rodriguez, who asked why a person who had arrived at a certain result independently, should be prevented from using that invention, just because he was not the first person to patent it.[34] Both Benard and Rodriguez considered that patents

---

29 There are a number of extracts from the correspondence between Macfie and Chevalier and Benard in Macfie, R.A., (ed), *Recent Discussions on the Abolition of Patents for Inventions in the United Kingdom, France, Germany, and the Netherlands: evidence, speeches and papers in its favour* (London, Longmans and Co, 1869).

30 SOCIETE D'ECONOMIE POLITIQUE, "Réunion du 5 Juin 1869" (1869) *Journal des économistes* 446.

31 See Chapter Three, Section B, (a) *The Minority View – Advocating Abolition of the Patent System.*

32 Benard, T.N., "The Results of a Bad Law", *Avenir Commercial*, 1 November 1862. (Translated by the author into English and reproduced in Macfie, R.A., (ed), *Recent Discussions on the Abolition of Patents for Inventions in the United Kingdom, France, Germany, and the Netherlands: evidence, speeches and papers in its favour* (London, Longmans and Co, 1869), 177.

33 *Ibid.* 179.

34 Rodriguez, G., "De la Propriété des Inventions" (1862) XXXIV (2nd Series) *Journal des économistes* 79, 81.

were often granted to those who did not deserve the benefit, while at the same time, hard-working persons were denied legal protection for their inventions.

Abolitionists often argued that there was a fundamental distinction between exclusive property rights in inventions, and property rights in tangible objects.[35] Benard, for example, argued that an inventor should not be granted an exclusive property right. He stated that:

> nous ne saurions admettre, … que l'application nouvelle d'un principe déjá connu, que la découverte d'un agent naturel inconnu jusqu'alors, ou de nouvelles propriétés ou d'autres modes d'action d'agents naturels, ou de matériaux précédemment découverts, soient des inventions.[36]

Benard did not deny property rights in inventions. However, he stated that the property right in an invention should not be defined in the same way as a property right in land.[37] He considered that an invention should be public property and should not be privately or exclusively owned.[38] Some advocates of the patent system such as Le Hardy de Beaulieu[39] had argued that exclusive ownership of industrial property did not lessen social capital,[40] largely because the inventor increased the sum of human knowledge and experience. However, Benard rejected this argument outright, stating that all invention was built upon earlier knowledge, and that the true reward, or "rent" should be paid to the descendants of the first inventors (presumably the public at large).[41] Similar points were made by Boudron,[42]

35 Benard, T.N., "Les Inventions: sont-elles une propriété?" (1868) XI (3rd Series) *Journal des économistes* 47.

36 Translation: "we cannot admit … that the new application of a principle already known, that the discovery of a natural agent hitherto unknown, or of new properties of other modes of action of natural agents, or of materials previously discovered, are inventions." *Ibid.* 49.

37 Benard, T.N., "Les Inventions: sont-elles une propriété?" (1868) XI (3rd Series) *Journal des économistes* 47, 52.

38 *Ibid.*

39 See further below, under the heading (*c*) *The Theories of Supporters of the Patent System.*

40 For example, Le Hardy De Beaulieu, C., "Les Progrés Techniques et économiques dans les Houilléres et les Brevets d'Invention" (1866) *Journal des économistes* 238.

41 Benard, T.N., "Les Inventions: sont-elles une propriété?" (1868) XI (3rd Series) *Journal des économistes* 47, 53.

42 Boudron, A., "On Perpetuity of Patent-Right" reproduced in Macfie, R.A., (ed), *Recent Discussions on the Abolition of Patents for Inventions in the United Kingdom, France, Germany, and the Netherlands: evidence, speeches and papers in its favour* (London, Longmans and Co, 1869), 281.

Rodriguez,[43] and Vermeire.[44] Vermeire's opinions were more extreme than the rest, since he advocated the abolition of all forms of intellectual property, including copyright. He argued that an idea which formed the basis of a product of manufacture could not be considered an object of exclusive property rights, because some other person could come into possession of that idea without robbing the man who had first conceived it.[45] He believed that "the monopolies of sale and enterprise called 'intellectual property' must be given up."[46]

Several abolitionists followed Chevalier in arguing that there was a close association between patents and protectionism. Vermeire, for example, said that patents were not only opposed to freedom of trade, but also liberty of labour.[47] He argued that "anti-economical monopolies violate the liberty of labour, and, if they could be worked on an important scale, would cause to society more loss than the spirit of invention could bring it advantage."[48]

Another argument advanced was that the French government should take a more empirical approach to any assessment of the patent system. Benard, for example, argued that property rights should only be recognised when they tended to the general good, and were useful in advancing the interests of the human race.[49] He stated that the granting of exclusive property rights to inventors did not advance this aim, and in most cases, the patent system allowed the right of the inventor to prevail over the interest of society. This was a reversal of the natural situation where "le *droit* de la société doit prévaloir sur l'intérêt d'un seul".[50]

Abolitionists also rejected the argument that inventors needed the reward of special monopoly rights. Benard, for example, noted that many other occupations involved intelligence, hard work, difficulty and perseverance, yet no special property rights were granted to reward those persons. A good factory

---

43 Rodriguez, G., "De la Propriété des Inventions" (1862) XXXIV (2nd Series) *Journal des économistes* 79, 81.

44 Vermeire, P., *Libre Travail, ou l'Abolition de la Propriété Intellectuelle* (Paris, 1864). Extracted and reviewed in "The Policy of Patents" 17 (1864) *Law Magazine and Law Review* 315.

45 *Ibid.* 317.

46 *Ibid.* 321.

47 *Ibid.*

48 *Ibid.* See also Benard, T.N., "Les Inventions: sont-elles une propriété?" (1868) XI (3rd Series) *Journal des économistes* 47, 57.

49 Benard, T.N., "Les Inventions: sont-elles une propriété?" (1868) XI (3rd Series) *Journal des économistes* 47, 48, 57.

50 Translation: "the right of the community ought to prevail over the interest of the individual." *Ibid.* 58. See also Coq on this point. SOCIETE D'ECONOMIE POLITIQUE, "Réunion du 5 Juin 1869" (1869) *Journal des économistes* 446, 454 (Paul Coq).

manager who delivered quality goods at cheap prices, a farmer who by superior ploughing increased the yield of his field, or a sailor, who found the means of shortening voyages by using certain currents or winds, all rendered a signal service to society, but were not granted a property right.[51] Rodriguez made a similar point, and asserted that the inventor's head-start over his competitors was a form of natural monopoly (although limited.)[52]

Benard and Rodriguez also disputed the necessity for patents as a means to stimulate invention. Benard argued that many of the most important inventions such as the hammer, plough, screw, needles, smelting ore, manufacture of pottery, porcelain, paper, ink and boats, all occurred without the help of a patent system.[53] Rodriguez added that it was in the nature of men to invent, and agreed that many important inventions had arisen without being patented.[54]

Benard, Boudron, Coq and Rodriguez all agreed that there were many additional practical disadvantages associated with the patent system. These included an alleged (but unsubstantiated) increase in prices associated with the monopoly right, and the possibility that patentees used their rights to obstruct further improvements.[55] Benard and Rodriguez argued that intelligent workers were entranced by the prospect of reward from the patent system, and many wasted their time racing after delusions.[56]

Although the writings of the abolitionists demonstrated a considerable amount of insight into the policy and practical effect of the working of the patent system in France, they were not able to achieve any significant practical result. In France, as in the U.K., the abolitionists remained a small group of individuals, compared to the large number of supporters of the patent system.

---

51 Benard, T.N., "Les Inventions: sont-elles une propriété?" (1868) XI (3rd Series) *Journal des économistes* 47, 51.

52 Rodriguez, G., "De la Propriété des Inventions" (1862) XXXIV (2nd Series) *Journal des économistes* 79, 84.

53 Benard, T.N., "Les Inventions: sont-elles une propriété?" (1868) XI (3rd Series) *Journal des économistes* 47, 54.

54 Rodriguez, G., "De la Propriété des Inventions" (1862) XXXIV (2nd Series) *Journal des économistes* 79, 85.

55 Benard, T.N., "Les Inventions: sont-elles une propriété?" (1868) XI (3rd Series) *Journal des économistes* 47, 55, 56. Boudron, A., "On Perpetuity of Patent-Right" reproduced in Macfie, R.A., (ed), *Recent Discussions on the Abolition of Patents for Inventions in the United Kingdom, France, Germany, and the Netherlands: evidence, speeches and papers in its favour* (London, Longmans and Co, 1869), 281–282. SOCIETE D'ECONOMIE POLITIQUE, "Réunion du 5 Juin 1869" (1869) *Journal des économistes* 446, 453 (Paul Coq).

56 Benard, T.N., "Les Inventions: sont-elles une propriété?" (1868) XI (3rd Series) *Journal des économistes* 47, 62; Rodriguez, G., "De la Propriété des Inventions" (1862) XXXIV (2nd Series) *Journal des économistes* 79, 85.

(c) *The Theories of Supporters of the Patent System*

French advocates of the patent system generally believed that the process of inventing was of such benefit to society that there was a place for the continued existence of monopoly rights. Although by the 1860s most of the supporters of the patent system no longer accepted the theory of the *monautopole*, they did recognise a connection between rights in individual labour and the creation of property interests.

The most uncompromising view about the need for strong property rights in inventions was voiced by Ch. Le Hardy de Beaulieu, Professor of Political Economy at the Belgian Museum of Industry, whose writings were widely published in French economic journals.[57] His papers formed the major target for the patent abolitionists such as Benard, largely because he considered that there was no material distinction between property rights in inventions, and rights in tangible property. In presenting his arguments, he drew upon a wide range of sources, including the works of the philosophers Adam Smith, Samuel Smiles, J.-B. Say, Florez Estrada, Louis Leclerc, and Frédéric Bastiat.

In Beaulieu's earliest writings on the subject of patents in 1862,[58] he stated that work was part of the human personality, and that it was essential that some form of State recognition should be given to the results of such labour.[59] If a person had invented something as a result of his labour, it was not equitable that he should be liable to lose the advantage of that invention to a person who merely copied it. Beaulieu was clearly of the opinion that property was most efficiently managed in the hands of private individuals,[60] and it was largely for this reason that he also supported the notion of the *monautopole*.[61] He commented that it was ridiculous to fear the effect of perpetual property rights in inventions, because in practical terms, all inventions would eventually become obsolete, and thus there was a natural limit to this type of monopoly.[62] Even where an inventor abused his exclusive right, and refused to allow

57 See, for example, Le Hardy De Beaulieu, C., "Discussion sur la Propriété des Inventions" (1862) XXXIV (2nd Series) *Journal des économistes* 87; Le Hardy De Beaulieu, C., "La Propriété des Inventions est une Propriété comme une autre" (1868) XII (3rd Series) *Journal des économistes* 251; Le Hardy De Beaulieu, C., "Les Progrés Techniques et économiques dans les Houilléres et les Brevets d'Invention" (1866) *Journal des économistes* 238.

58 Le Hardy De Beaulieu, C., "Discussion sur la Propriété des Inventions" (1862) XXXIV (2nd Series) *Journal des économistes* 87.

59 *Ibid.* 87.

60 *Ibid.* 90.

61 Hardy De Beaulieu, C., "Les Progrés Techniques et économiques dans les Houilléres et les Brevets d'Invention" (1866) *Journal des économistes* 238, 244–247.

62 *Ibid.* 250.

others use of the invention, Beaulieu believed that this would result in minor inconvenience, and would actually encourage further useful work in "inventing around" the invention, in order to avoid the monopoly.[63] He also advanced the theory of "service for service".[64] This meant that when a person had rendered to society a particular service, such as creating a new invention, society should assure to that person an equivalent recompense.[65] An inventor would not receive his just recompense if there was no patent system.

A number of other commentators spoke in favour of patent rights, although they adopted a less extreme position than Beaulieu and did not advocate the adoption of the *monautopole*. Jules Pautet, a French political economist, considered that the discovery of a new process for simplifying human labour constituted a true or natural right of property.[66] Like Beaulieu, he recognised a close connection between labour and property rights in the results of such labour.[67] Although he advocated free trade, he thought that the concept of granting patents could be reconciled with the new economic policies by offering only limited and temporary monopolies.[68] Professor Batbie of the Faculty of Law of Paris added that there was no intrinsic difference between property rights in inventions and property in land, although the State had customarily limited the duration of the patent monopoly.[69]

Supporters of the patent system argued that the abolitionists did not understand the important distinction between the idea itself and its formulation or presentation.[70] Joseph Garnier, who was, like Chevalier, a strong supporter of free trade,[71] strongly argued this point. He asserted that an inventor could not

63 *Ibid.* See also a reiteration of this point in Le Hardy De Beaulieu, C., "La Propriété des Inventions est une Propriété comme une autre" (1868) XII (3rd Series) *Journal des économistes* 251, 255.

64 Le Hardy De Beaulieu, C., "La Propriété des Inventions est une Propriété comme une autre" (1868) XII (3rd Series) *Journal des économistes* 251, 257.

65 *Ibid.*

66 SOCIETE D'ECONOMIE POLITIQUE, "Réunion du 5 Juin 1869" (1869) *Journal des économistes* 446 (Jules Pautet at 455).

67 *Ibid.*

68 *Ibid.*

69 SOCIETE D'ECONOMIE POLITIQUE, "Réunion du 5 Juin 1869" (1869) *Journal des économistes* 446 at (Batbie at 460).

70 SOCIETE D'ECONOMIE POLITIQUE, "Réunion du 5 Juin 1869" (1869) *Journal des économistes* 446 (Garnier at 451).

71 Garnier had previously been editor-in-chief of the *Journal des économistes*, and in 1855 had violently attacked Jobard's theory of the *monautopole*. See Chapter One above.

claim a right of property in scientific ideas, but only in mechanical, physical or chemical processes arising from the use of those ideas.[72]

The patent advocates saw many other justifications for the granting of monopoly rights to inventors. One benefit of the patent system was that consumers rather than the State had the task of valuing the worth of the invention.[73] Any system of State rewards would be bound to fail, since the State was incompetent to appreciate the value of an invention.[74] Patents were also a means of developing production and encouraging new discoveries, and there was serious doubt as to whether this would continue if total liberty in the use of inventions was adopted.[75] Louis Wolowski, another political economist in Paris, agreed with the majority of the patent advocates that each service rendered by a person was entitled to sufficient recompense, and there was no reason why an inventor should be excluded from this proposition.[76] It was only equitable that in exchange for revealing his new process or product to society, the inventor should be granted a temporary monopoly right.[77]

(d) *The Outcome of the Patent Debate in France*

The lack of success of the French patent abolitionists is demonstrated by the fact that the French Government never took seriously any proposals to abolish the patent laws. The patent system as established in France under the Law of 5 July 1844 remained in force until 1 January 1969,[78] and during the period between 1844 and the establishment of the Paris Convention in 1883, only minor amendments were made to the French patent laws.[79] However, amongst French lawyers there was clearly some dissatisfaction with the

72 SOCIETE D'ECONOMIE POLITIQUE, "Réunion du 5 Juin 1869" (1869) *Journal des économistes* 446 (Garnier at 452).

73 *Ibid.*

74 *Ibid.*

75 SOCIETE D'ECONOMIE POLITIQUE, "Réunion du 5 Juin 1869" (1869) *Journal des économistes* 446 (Batbie at 461).

76 SOCIETE D'ECONOMIE POLITIQUE, "Réunion du 5 Juin 1869" (1869) *Journal des économistes* 446 (Wolowski at 465).

77 *Ibid.*

78 Plasseraud, Y., and Savignon, F., *L'etat et L'invention: Histoire des Brevets* (Paris, La Documentation Française, 1986), 99.

79 These were as follows: Law of 21 October 1848 concerning the application of the Law of 5 July 1844 to various French colonies. Decree of 5 June 1850 concerning the application in Algeria of the Law of 5 July 1844. Law of 20 May 1856 which modified Article 32 of the Law of 5 July 1844 (concerning forfeiture of rights). Law of 23 May 1868 relating to the protection of inventions eligible to be patented and of designs displayed at public exhibitions. Source: (1885) 1 *La Propriété Industrielle* 11–15.

practical working of the patent laws. This was exemplified by the statement of De Lavergne that "[i]l n'y a pas de matiére plus litigieuse que celle des brevets d'invention" and "que la législation est défectueuse et qu'il serait trés difficile, sinon impossible de l'améliorer".[80] The main reason for this dissatisfaction was that there was no system of substantive examination of patent applications before grant, which led to the problem of competing claims over one invention. In an attempt to reduce the consequent large amount of patent litigation, in 1858 the Government proposed a *Projet de Loi* which would have replaced the Law of 5 July 1844.[81] The major innovation of this *Projet* was not to introduce a system of substantive examination of patent applications, but rather to provide for a tribunal before which a patentee could contest the novelty and originality of his invention against the combined claims of any other persons who alleged a prior right to the invention.[82] However, shortly after these proposals were made, the *Projet* was allowed to lapse because the Government became preoccupied with other matters and no longer thought the reform was necessary.[83]

One of the major reasons why proposals for abolition of patents were not taken seriously by the French Government was doubtless because there was not perceived to be any realistic alternative to the patent system. This point was made by Edmond Picard in 1871,[84] and was similar to the arguments employed against the abolition of patents in the United Kingdom. As Picard noted, there were generally perceived to be two alternatives to the patent system. These were (1) abolishing the patent system and leaving inventors to the mercy of market forces or the vulnerable protection gained from keeping the invention secret; or (2) abolishing the patent system and giving to the

80 Translation: "There is no matter more litigated than that of patents for inventions" and "that the legislation is defective and it would be very difficult, if not impossible, to ameliorate." De Lavergne made this point in 1863 at a meeting of the *Académie des sciences morales et politiques de France.* Quoted in Rolin-Jaequemyns, G., "De Quelques Manifestations Récentes de l'Opinion Publique en Europe au Sujet des Brevets d'Invention" (1869) 1 *Revue de droit International et de Législation Comparée* 600, 609.

81 *Moniteur universel,* 5 July 1858.

82 *Ibid.* See further Rolin-Jaequemyns, G., "De Quelques Manifestations Récentes de l'Opinion Publique en Europe au Sujet des Brevets d'Invention" (1869) 1 *Revue de droit International et de Législation Comparée* 600, 608.

83 *Ibid.*

84 Picard, E., "Suppression des Brevets d'Invention" (1871) 3 *Revue de Droit International et de Législation Comparée* 391. Picard was an advocate before the Court of Appeal of Brussels and co-author with Olin of a work entitled *Traité des brevets d'Invention*, published in Paris and Brussels in 1869.

State the ability to grant public rewards to inventors of notable inventions.[85] However, Picard believed that both alternatives were "insuffisantes ou dangereuses",[86] the first because it would engender a culture of fear amongst inventors that their inventions would be usurped before they had gained sufficient financial advantage to make the task of inventing worth the effort, and the second because the government was incompetent to determine the value of inventions.[87] He also made the point that as the government used the argument of its own incompetence in order to justify not conducting substantive examination of all patent applications, it could hardly claim it was in a position to judge the value of inventions for the purpose of granting State rewards.[88]

There were two main reasons why the patent abolition movement had minimal influence in France. First, the debate was mainly confined to the writings of economic philosophers. Few inventors, manufacturers or engineers had any interest in the question. As in the U.K., the abolitionists had little or no support from government and cultural or scientific organisations. The second reason why the abolition movement failed so dismally in France was possibly because of the enduring belief that there were natural property rights in inventions and abolition of the patent system would have amounted to an attack upon fundamental property rights. This concept of natural property rights in inventions had been a cornerstone of the French patent system since 1791 and the patent abolitionists could not overcome this theoretical hurdle. The strength of French attachment to the concept of natural property rights in inventions was later made abundantly clear at the Paris Conference in 1878.[89]

---

85 *Ibid.* 393.

86 Translation: "insufficient or dangerous" *Ibid.*

87 *Ibid.* 393–394.

88 *Ibid.* Picard claimed that if the French or Belgian governments did wish to abolish the patent system, there was one alternative that they had not investigated. This was the action of unfair competition, established under Article 1382 of the Code of Napoléon. There had been in France a long history of protection against unfair competition in relation to trade marks, indications of origin and commercial names, and at the Brussels Revision Conference of the Paris Convention in 1900, the French government actively supported the introduction into the Convention of a provision to protect against unfair competition generally. (Article 1, para VI of the Additional Act of Brussels of 1900, which became Article 10*bis* of the Convention). See further BUREAU INTERNATIONAL DE L'UNION POUR LA PROTECTION DE LA PROPRIETE INDUSTRIELLE, *Conférence de Bruxelles: Decémbre 1897 et Décembre 1900* (Berne 1901) (Michel Pelletier, French delegate at 187–188).

89 FRANCE, Ministére de L'agriculture et du Commerce, *Comptes rendus Sténographiques publiés sous les auspices du Comité Central des Congrés et Conférences et la direction de M. CH THIRION, Secrétaire du Comité, avec le concours des Bureaux des Congrés et des auteurs de Conférences: Congrés International de la Propriété Industrielle tenu á Paris du*

B The Patent Abolition Movement in the Netherlands

On 15 July 1869, the legislature of the Netherlands passed a Law which provided that patents for inventions were no longer to be granted.[90] This Law repealed the patent legislation of 25 January 1817. The Netherlands was the only country to abolish its patent system as a result of the patent abolition debates of the 1850s to 1870s. Why did the abolition movement succeed here, but in no other country? In answering this question, it should be noted that practical, rather than theoretical considerations were predominant factors leading to the abolition of the Dutch patent system. In addition, the Dutch patent abolition movement was widely supported by government, inventors, manufacturers and the public. This was quite different from the situation in the United Kingdom or France.

(a) *General Historical Background to the Patent Abolition Debate*

Although Dutch criticism of the patent system was largely directed to the patent Law of 25 January 1817, there was a much longer history of protection for inventions in the Netherlands. A. Huet, Professor of the Polytechnic of Delft, noted in an article written in 1888,[91] that there was evidence of the grant of rights called "*octrois*" in relation to the use of inventions since the fifteenth century, although this protection was granted by government privilege or favour, rather than as of right.[92] These "*octrois*" remained available in the Netherlands until 8 November 1810, the date when the French patent law of 7 January 1791 became operative in the Netherlands. After the restoration of its independence from France in 1813, the Netherlands passed its own patent Law, dated 25 January 1817.[93]

---

5 au 17 Septembre 1878 (Paris 1879). See further discussion of the work of the 1878 Paris Conference in Chapter Six below.

90 The Law of 15 July 1869 provided that: (1) From the date of its promulgation, (1 January 1870), no more patents for inventions would be granted except to persons who had made application before the date of operation of the Law. (2) Patents already granted under the Law of 25 January 1817 would continue in force, and could be renewed for a maximum of 15 years. See further Rolin-Jaequemyns, G., "De Quelques Manifestations Récentes de l'Opinion Publique en Europe au Sujet des Brevets d'Invention" (1869) 1 *Revue de droit International et de Législation Comparée* 600, 615–616.

91 Huet, A., "Aperçu Historique de la Législation sur les Brevets d'Invention dans les Pays-Bas" (1888) 4 *La Propriété Industrielle* 86.

92 *Ibid.*

93 See also Bos, J.J., "The Netherlands and the Paris Convention for the Protection of Industrial Property" [1984] *Industrial Property* 383.

Opposition to the Netherlands Patent Law of 1817 first occurred much earlier than 1869. In 1854, a three member Committee[94] of the *Nederlandsche Maatschappij ter bevordering van Nijverheid* (Netherlands Industrial Association) investigated the working of the patent laws, and subsequently the Association presented a petition to the King demanding a complete abolition of the patent system.[95] Shortly after, at the International Congress for Tariff Reform in Brussels in 1856, Professor Ackersdijk of the University of Utrecht noted the connection between patents and protectionism, and declared that "après avoir abattu les barriéres qui s'opposent au libre échange des produits du commerce et de l'industrie il faudrait supprimer les entraves que les Brevets apportent á la liberté du travail."[96] These reports, petitions and statements were said to have had a great effect upon the public mind in the Netherlands,[97] and the perception of the disadvantages of the patent system was further reinforced by the writings of the French political economist Michel Chevalier,[98] and two Dutch critical commentaries which appeared in 1867 and 1868.[99]

(b) *Reasons for the Abolition of the Patent System in the Netherlands in 1869.*

Two striking aspects of the abolition of patents in the Netherlands are the overwhelming support for the measure and the haste with which the reform was accomplished. The motion for the repeal of the patent law of 1817 was drawn up by the Dutch government in early 1869, was passed by the Second Chamber

---

94 Composed of the following members: J. Faber van Riemsdyk, G. Simons and J. Ackersdijk.

95 Huet, A., *op.cit.* 87.

96 Translation: "After having abolished the barriers opposed to free trade in the products of commerce and industry, one should remove the fetters by which patents have shackled the freedom of labour." Quoted in Milhaud, L., *Des Brevets d'invention dans les Rapports Internationaux* (Paris, Larose et Forcel, 1892), 6.

97 Huet, A., *op.cit.* 87.

98 G. Rolin-Jaequemyns stated that the Government's explanatory memorandum to the Dutch Law of 1869 had been heavily influenced by the writings of Michel Chevalier. Rolin-Jaequemyns, G., "De Quelques Manifestations Récentes de l'Opinion Publique en Europe au Sujet des Brevets d'Invention" (1869) 1 *Revue de droit International et de Législation Comparée* 600, 616. In the debates in the Second Chamber on 22 June 1869, Fock, Secretary of State for Home Affairs, referred with approval to the writings of Chevalier. Source: Macfie, R.A., (ed), *Recent Discussions on the Abolition of Patents for Inventions in the United Kingdom, France, Germany, and the Netherlands: evidence, speeches and papers in its favour* (London, Longmans and Co, 1869), 220.

99 The first was that of a doctoral thesis published by E. Star Busman in 1867, and the second a study of intellectual property published by J. Freseman Vietor in 1868. A reference to the contribution of the work of Star Busman appeared in the explanatory memorandum of the Law of 1869 abolishing the patent system. Huet, A., *op.cit.* 87.

in June 1869 after two days' debate,[100] and less than a month later was passed by the First Chamber.[101] The ease with which the reform was achieved in the Netherlands contrasted with the situation in the U.K. where there were a number of official inquiries into the patent system over a considerable period of time, yet no significant reform occurred until the Patents, Designs and Trade Marks Act 1883 (U.K.).

There seem to be four principal reasons why the Netherlands abolished its patent law in 1869. In descending order of importance these were:

(i) The small number of patents granted each year and the fact that they were primarily granted to foreigners;
(ii) Dutch admiration of the Swiss system, where no patents were granted;
(iii) Other practical difficulties relating to the operation of the patent system, particularly the law of infringement; and
(iv) Theoretical objections.

(i) Inactive Patent System/Resentment of Foreigners

The most important reason for the abolition of the patent system in the Netherlands was the general perception that foreign industrialists, rather than Dutch nationals, were its major beneficiaries. Huet notes that at the time of the passage of the Law of 1869, an average of only 16 patents were granted to Dutch nationals each year, with 124 being granted to foreigners.[102] One of the main reasons why only a small number of patents were granted to Dutch nationals was thought to be the high fees associated with obtaining a patent. It cost 10,500 florins for a patent for 15 years, a fee which most Dutch inventors or manufacturers could not afford to pay.[103] Therefore, most Dutch patentees

---

100 The debate in the Second Chamber took place on 21 and 22 June 1869, and the motion was passed by that Chamber by a majority of 49 to 8. The dissentients were Bichon, Blussé, Vader, Hofmann, Heemskerk Azn, Van Wassenaer, and Van Zinnicq Bergmann. Source: Macfie, R.A., (ed), *Recent Discussions on the Abolition of Patents for Inventions in the United Kingdom, France, Germany, and the Netherlands: evidence, speeches and papers in its favour* (London, Longmans and Co, 1869), 225. See also UNITED KINGDOM, Parliamentary Papers, *Return of any Public Official Documents received at the Foreign Office, exhibiting Reasons why Count Von Bismarck and the Government of Prussia, and Mr Fock, the Minister of the Interior of the Netherlands, and the Dutch Government, have recommended, and the Chambers of the latter Country have resolved on, the Abolition of Patents for Invention* (1870) 41, vol LXI, 527.

101 The Motion was passed by the First Chamber by a majority of 29 to 1. The Law abolishing the patent system was dated 15 July 1869. Source: Macfie, R.A. *op.cit.* 280.

102 Huet, A., *op.cit.* 86.

103 *Ibid.*

were large foreign manufacturing concerns, which were the subject of resentment by smaller Dutch firms.[104]

During the debates in the Second Chamber, the issue of alleged foreign advantage was discussed on a number of occasions. Heemskerk Azn, a strong supporter of the patent system, member for Gorinchem, and former Minister of the Interior under the previous (conservative) Government, noted that there had been proposals that only patents for the introduction of inventions from foreign countries should be abolished.[105] It was then argued by abolitionists that if patents for foreigners were abolished, they would be left with so few domestic applicants, that it would not be worth maintaining the patent system.[106] However, Heemskerk Azn and another conservative, Van Zinnicq Bergmann, replied that foreign patents contributed to Dutch industrial development, because they "encourage[d] the introduction into our own country of inventions already carried out abroad."[107] Heemskerk Azn also considered that the abolition of patents would result in political embarrassment to the Netherlands in its future foreign relations. He envisaged the introduction of some form of international agreements in the area of copyright, trade marks, designs and patent law, and stated that it would be wrong for the Dutch to "abolish patents here with the intention that Netherlanders should apply for patents in foreign countries, and in their own country should set up the dishonourable, immoral industry of imitation."[108] Van Zinnicq Bergmann made the same point, believing that there was a serious question "whether the passing of the Law now before the House might not involve the country in international troubles."[109]

(ii) The Influence of the Swiss Model

In supporting the abolition of the patent system, the Dutch government viewed with admiration the situation in Switzerland, and was generally unconcerned

---

104 *Ibid.* 87.

105 UNITED KINGDOM, Parliamentary Papers, *Return of any Public Official Documents received at the Foreign Office, exhibiting Reasons why Count Von Bismarck and the Government of Prussia, and Mr Fock, the Minister of the Interior of the Netherlands, and the Dutch Government, have recommended, and the Chambers of the latter Country have resolved on, the Abolition of Patents for Invention* (1870) 41, vol LXI, 527, 4 (Heemskerk).

106 *Ibid.* (Remarks attributed to de Bruyn Kops).

107 *Ibid.* 4 (Heemskerk Azn).

108 *Ibid.* 7. In 1851 another Dutch commentator, A.J.B. Stoffels, had published a detailed study on the patent laws, in which he recommended the adoption of a system of international patent legislation. Huet, A., *op.cit.* 87.

109 Macfie, R.A, (ed) *op.cit.* 198.

about possible future international ramifications.[110] Patents had existed in Switzerland between 1798 and 1800, under the *République helvétique* but disappeared with the enactment of the unitary constitution.[111] A number of proposals for the re-establishment of a patent system had been made between 1848 and 1864, but these had not been adopted by the legislature.[112]

The *Bureau International de l'Union pour la Protection de la Propriété Industrielle* explained that there were three main arguments which had been used by opponents of a patent system in Switzerland.[113] These were (1) the belief that absolute liberty in manufacture was of more advantage to the national industry; (2) those who supported the doctrine of common rights did not admit the need for special privileges or monopolies; and (3) many thought that the restrictions and expenses which would be applied to industrial activities by the introduction of patents, far outweighed the meagre benefits to inventors in a small country such as Switzerland.[114]

A Commission of the National Council was established in 1864 to examine the question of proposals for a patent law, but it rejected the idea. The Commission found that without patent laws, the Swiss had achieved the position of the third richest economy in Europe (in comparison with the size of its population), and there was apparently no need for a patent system.[115] Rivier (a Professor at the University of Brussels), argued that Swiss industry generally showed a rapid adoption of new improvements, which was probably due to free access to new inventions. He also argued that the Swiss were as inventive as any other nation.[116]

Rivier's opinions were shared by prominent members of the Dutch legislature such as Godefroi, the member for Amsterdam,[117] who also considered

---

110 It was only during and after the Paris Conference in 1880 that the Dutch government began to feel politically embarrassed about its lack of a patent system. Even so, it was not until 7 November 1910 that the Netherlands adopted another patent law, (which did not come into force until 1 June 1912). FRANCE, Ministére des Affaires étrangéres, *Conférence Internationale pour la protection de la propriété Industrielle* (Paris 1880). (See particularly the attitude of the Dutch delegate, H.C. Verniers van der Loeff, at 21 and 146).

111 Rivier, A., "Note sur la Question des Brevets d'Invention en Suisse" (1869) 1 *Revue de droit International et de Législation Comparée* 617.

112 *Ibid.* 617–618.

113 BUREAU INTERNATIONAL DE L'UNION POUR LA PROTECTION DE LA PROPRIETE INDUSTRIELLE, "Bulletin de la Propriété Industrielle" (1885) 1 *La Propriété Industrielle* 25.

114 *Ibid.*

115 Rivier, A., "Note sur la Question des Brevets d'Invention en Suisse" (1869) 1 *Revue de droit International et de Législation Comparée* 617, 620.

116 *Ibid.*

117 Godefroi was described by Vice Admiral Harris, British consul in the Hague, as "an able lawyer" and a "leading member of the Liberal party". UNITED KINGDOM, Parliamentary

that there was little likelihood of any international arrangements respecting patents. This was because countries such as the U.K., France, Belgium and Germany would no doubt recognise the evils of the patent system, and join with Switzerland and the Netherlands in abolishing their own patent laws.[118]

Heemskerk Azn was the only member of the Dutch legislature who clearly rejected the suggestion that Switzerland was a model to follow. In his view, Swiss industrialists had the benefit of patents in foreign countries, yet in their own country they were merely a race of imitators, operating in a "pirate state".[119] Outside the Netherlands, Heemskerk's opinion about Switzerland was shared by many others. Americans considered that the Swiss were a race of copyists, even in relation to their specialities of manufacture such as watchmaking and shoe design. W.C. Dodge told the 1878 U.S. Congressional Committee on Patents that the Swiss had pirated most developments in watch manufacture from other countries, and that "nearly every valuable improvement in time-keepers has originated in England, France and the United States."[120] Similar points were made by witnesses before the U.K. 1871 and 1872 Select Committees on Patents.[121]

Even some Swiss began to lobby for the introduction of a patent system. As early as 1865, the Swiss Federal Council proposed to partially amend the Constitution to give the Federal government power to legislate on intellectual and industrial property matters.[122] However, the voters failed to pass the amendment.[123] By the 1870s there was developing in Switzerland a strong movement in favour of a patent system. This movement was headed by Bally,

Papers, *Return of any Public Official Documents received at the Foreign Office, exhibiting Reasons why Count Von Bismarck and the Government of Prussia, and Mr Fock, the Minister of the Interior of the Netherlands, and the Dutch Government, have recommended, and the Chambers of the latter Country have resolved on, the Abolition of Patents for Invention* (1870) 41, vol LXI, 527, 1.

118 *Ibid.* 1–4.

119 UNITED KINGDOM, Parliamentary Papers, *Return of any Public Official Documents received at the Foreign Office, exhibiting Reasons why Count Von Bismarck and the Government of Prussia, and Mr Fock, the Minister of the Interior of the Netherlands, and the Dutch Government, have recommended, and the Chambers of the latter Country have resolved on, the Abolition of Patents for Invention* (1870) 41, vol LXI, 527, 7 (Heemskerk).

120 UNITED STATES OF AMERICA, Congressional Papers, *Arguments before the Committee on Patents of the Senate and House of Representatives, in support of, and suggesting amendments to, the Bills, (S. No. 300 and H.R. 1612) to amend the Statutes in relation to Patents, and for other purposes* (1878) 45th Congress, 2nd Session, Senate 1788, Misc Docs 50, 70–71 (Dodge). See also evidence of J.J. Storrow to the same effect at 319–320.

121 See Chapter Three above.

122 (1885) 1 *La Propriété Industrielle* 89.

123 *Ibid.*

the shoe manufacturer.[124] After undertaking a tour to the U.S.A. as a Swiss Commissioner to the 1876 Philadelphia Exhibition, Bally addressed a paper to Swiss manufacturers in which he noted that all Swiss manufactures were "more or less a simple copy".[125] He argued that the "absolute want of [patent] protection will never awaken in a people the spirit of invention, but, on the contrary, accustoms them to copy more and more that which belongs to their neighbours, and that is not to the honor of the country."[126]

The 1878 Paris Conference was the catalyst for change to the law in Switzerland.[127] The Federal Government again proposed the amendment of the Constitution to include a power to enact patent legislation. This proposal was put to a popular referendum on 30 July 1882.[128] Once again, it did not succeed, largely because it was coupled with a proposal for stronger governmental control over epidemics.[129] Although the cotton and chemical industries were hostile to patents, many other inventors and manufacturers favoured some form of legal protection for inventors. In 1884, a special society was established (The Swiss Society for the Protection of Inventions and Industrial Designs) to lobby for Constitutional amendment.[130] The work of this society was largely responsible for the success of the Constitutional amendment concerning patent law, which was passed by popular referendum on 10 July 1887.[131] On 29 June 1888, Switzerland finally enacted a Patent Law.[132]

Although the Dutch legislature used the case of Switzerland as a model which should be followed, the above discussion shows that the Swiss government, and particularly the Federal Council, was not convinced that its no-patent policy was appropriate. By 1869, moves had begun in Switzerland which

124 Source: UNITED STATES OF AMERICA, Congressional Papers, *Arguments before the Committee on Patents of the Senate and House of Representatives, in support of, and suggesting amendments to, the Bills, (S. No. 300 and H.R. 1612) to amend the Statutes in relation to Patents, and for other purposes* (1878) 45th Congress, 2nd Session, Senate 1788, Misc Docs 50, (Appendix at 449).

125 *Ibid.*

126 *Ibid.*

127 (1885) 1 *La Propriété Industrielle* 89.

128 (1885) 1 *La Propriété Industrielle* 25.

129 (1885) 1 *La Propriété Industrielle* 89. The vote was 156658 against the amendment, with only 141616 supporting it. Only 7 full Cantons and one *Demi*-Canton supported it (from a total of 21 full and 2 *Demi*-Cantons). (1887) 3 *La Propriété Industrielle* 59.

130 (1885) 1 *La Propriété Industrielle* 25.

131 The vote was 203809 in favour of the amendment and 57630 against it. The proposal failed to gain a majority in only two areas: the Canton of Uri and the *Demi*-Canton of Appenzell. (1887) 3 *La Propriété Industrielle* 49.

132 (1889) 5 *La Propriété Industrielle* 77; (1893) 9 *La Propriété Industrielle* 58, 70.

favoured the introduction of patent laws. The Dutch legislature seemed to overlook this fact in its zeal to justify its policy of patent abolition.

(iii) Practical Problems Associated with the Dutch Patent Law of 1817

Bos has noted that there were many practical difficulties associated with the operation of the Law of 25 January 1817.[133] During the nineteenth century, the Dutch Supreme Court had interpreted the patent law "in an unfortunate way by ruling that reproducing, for one's own business, a device patented by someone else but not selling it, did not constitute infringement."[134] Thus, it was not unexpected that many Dutch inventors and manufacturers questioned the worth of a patent, especially when it was also realised that the patent was granted without any government guarantee as to its validity. As Godefroi stated, "if a government is not in a position to decide whether the claimant of a patent has a right to it, can it be sanctioned in granting a privilege blindfold[ed], which establishes a temporary monopoly?"[135] De Bruyn Kops, a noted political economist and advocate of free trade, also argued that the lack of guarantee given to the inventor by the patent made many question the law's effectiveness, and these points were of particular concern to "leading industrial organs, such as the Chambers of Commerce and Factories, the Industrial Society, the Union for Promoting Mechanical and Manual Industry, and the Nederlandsche Industrieel" who had "unanimously ... declared against Patents".[136] Although the abolitionists claimed that the question of reform of the patent system had been examined, they were of opinion that the practical defects were so great that "a good law on patents is an impossibility".[137] Godefroi added that this

---

133 Bos, J.J., "The Netherlands and the Paris Convention for the Protection of Industrial Property" (1984) *Industrial Property* 383.

134 *Ibid.*

135 UNITED KINGDOM, Parliamentary Papers, *Return of any Public Official Documents received at the Foreign Office, exhibiting Reasons why Count Von Bismarck and the Government of Prussia, and Mr Fock, the Minister of the Interior of the Netherlands, and the Dutch Government, have recommended, and the Chambers of the latter Country have resolved on, the Abolition of Patents for Invention* (1870) 41, vol LXI, 527, 4. See also "L'avant-Projet de Loi Hollandais sur les Brevets d'Invention (1893) 9 *La Propriété Industrielle* 130, 131 which also makes a similar point about the practical difficulties noted by Godefroi.

136 Macfie, R.A., (ed), *Recent Discussions on the Abolition of Patents for Inventions in the United Kingdom, France, Germany, and the Netherlands: evidence, speeches and papers in its favour* (London, Longmans and Co, 1869), 203.

137 UNITED KINGDOM, Parliamentary Papers, *Return of any Public Official Documents received at the Foreign Office, exhibiting Reasons why Count Von Bismarck and the Government of Prussia, and Mr Fock, the Minister of the Interior of the Netherlands, and the Dutch Government, have recommended, and the Chambers of the latter Country have resolved on,*

conviction was reinforced by an examination of foreign patent laws, where there was "not a single good one among them, nor one which does not give rise to difficulties which hitherto have been found to be insurmountable."[138]

The few supporters of the patent system such as the conservatives Heemskerk Azn and Van Zinnicq Bergmann did not pretend that the patent law was perfect. Indeed, Heemskerk Azn "cordially agreed" with the patent abolitionists such as Godefroi that "the law of 1817 [was] faulty",[139] but he disagreed that this necessarily meant that the patent system should be abolished. He stated that the motion for abolition of patents had been brought before the Chamber with undue haste, and believed that the industrial classes, represented by the Industrial Association (*Nederlandsche Maatschappij ter bevordering van Nijverheid*), the Workmen's Association (*Maatschappij van Handwerlsnijverheid*), and the Industrial Committee (*Vereeniging van en voor Industrielen*), would have preferred the matter to have been thoroughly debated at the Congress of Industry at Groningen which was to be held in the following July.[140] Van Zinnicq Bergmann agreed that the Chamber should be more cautious, and stated that even if one gave credence to the "doctrines" of fervent critics of the patent system such as Michel Chevalier, "[c]ould such difficulties not be obviated through a *reform* of the Patent-Law?"[141]

(iv) Theoretical Objections

It will be seen from the above discussion that the primary reasons for the abolition of patents in the Netherlands in 1869 related to practical issues such as high fees, the over-representation of foreigners amongst patentees, the lack of security in a patent, and judicial interpretation of patent infringement. Theoretical objections did exist, but they were of minor importance. In this respect, the Netherlands differed from France, (and to a lesser extent, the U.K.) where there was a great deal of theoretical discussion about patents during this period, although leading to no significant patent law reform.

Some Dutch abolitionists used free trade theories as a justification for their cause. Many government (liberal party) members approached the issue purely from an economic point of view, considering that promotion of free trade

---

the Abolition of Patents for Invention (1870) 41, vol LXI, 527, 3 (Godefroi); Macfie, R.A., (ed), *op.cit.* 205 (Van Houten).

138 UNITED KINGDOM, Parliamentary Papers, *Return of any Public Official Documents received at the Foreign Office* etc. at 4 (Godefroi).

139 *Ibid.* 5.

140 *Ibid.*

141 Macfie, R.A., (ed), *op.cit.* 198.

was more important than property rights in inventions or international legal relations. Van Houten, the liberal member for Groningen, observed that the proposals for the abolition of patents were "closely connected with the historical development of society, and the liberation of labour and industry."[142] Fock, the Secretary of State for Home Affairs, stated that "[p]atents are great impediments to industry and free trade, and that it is in the public's interest that they should be abolished."[143] De Bruyn Kops, a noted political economist, advocated "entire freedom and removal of all impediments",[144] and another liberal party member, Gefken, favoured "free competition".[145]

Dutch abolitionists also discussed the differences between patents and copyright. There was an awareness that some might see an attack upon patents as also being an attack upon copyright. Thus, Godefroi stated that the major theoretical objection to the patent system was the fact that it presumed to grant a right of exclusive use over something which was really amenable to use by more than one person.[146] Copyright was not based upon a system of exclusive rights of occupation, and therefore it was not objectionable.[147] Van Houten further explained the difference between copyright and patents, stating that "the law providing for Copyright does by no means prevent anybody from applying any published work to further development of science."[148] However, the supporters of the patent system did not acknowledge any such distinction between copyright and patents, and alleged that "[i]f Patents be abolished, we shall logically have to come to repealing Copyright as well".[149] Heemskerk Azn argued that a "counterfeited edition" was "nothing else than the imitation of an object of industry; the writer is an author, but the inventor is no less an author."[150]

At a more general level, a small number of patent abolitionists argued that the inventor had no property rights in his invention because of the limited nature of the right customarily granted. De Bruyn Kops asserted that if an invention gave rise to a right of property, that right should be unlimited in duration.[151] Van Houten observed that the "so-called" right of the inventor was "on

142 *Ibid.* 207.
143 *Ibid.* 220.
144 *Ibid.* 223.
145 *Ibid.* 224.
146 UNITED KINGDOM, Parliamentary Papers, *Return of any Public Official Documents received at the Foreign Office* etc. at 1.
147 *Ibid.*
148 Macfie, R.A., (ed), *op.cit.* 207.
149 *Ibid* 200 (Heemskerk Azn).
150 *Ibid.*
151 *Ibid.* 203–204.

no very solid basis" for it was only temporary, and could be taken away through expropriation.[152] He also considered that the patent system gave rewards to undeserving persons, because most patentees were not true inventors, but merely imitators.[153] A similar point was made by Van Voorthuysen, another liberal member, referring with approval to the opinions of Lord Stanley in support of Macfie's 1869 motion to abolish the patent system in the United Kingdom.[154]

In response to the attacks upon the notion of property rights in inventions, Heemskerk Azn argued that his opponents did not appreciate the well-established principles which he defended. The origin of patents lay "in the cultivation of a free spirit, and the ennobling of labour; and of these, the right of protection existed since time immemorial."[155] He noted that patents had been respected in two of the "most freedom-advocating of constitutions", namely the U.S.A. and France.[156] There were also significant reasons why property in inventions should be protected. Rejecting the notion that most patentees were merely imitators, Heemskerk Azn claimed that the real injury to society would arise "in the case when all protection is refused to the inventor; when he cannot bring his invention forward without its being imitated; and another man who has not taken the least trouble about it enjoys the fruits of his invention."[157] If patents were abolished there would be a return to the "barbarous age" before patents, where inventors had to work in secret, and there was a danger that important inventions could be lost to society.[158]

Despite the attempts by members of the opposition (conservative) party to persuade the government members in the Chamber to reassess their policy of abolition, the anti-patent feeling was such that the motion was easily passed.[159] However, the government's opinion that it was leading the way in a world-wide movement to abolish the patent system was misguided. The Netherlands had a small economy and an inactive and flawed patent system. It could abolish its patent laws without significant ramifications, but it was in a very different

---

152 *Ibid.* 205.

153 *Ibid.*

154 *Ibid.* 218. See further Chapter Three on this point.

155 *Ibid.* 199.

156 *Ibid.*

157 UNITED KINGDOM, Parliamentary Papers, *Return of any Public Official Documents received at the Foreign Office* etc. at 6.

158 *Ibid.* Heemskerk Azn understood that an important German invention to preserve gunpowder from exploding spontaneously had been lost to society because the inventor had died without revealing its secret.

159 See further details at notes 100 and 101 above.

position from the larger, more industrialised countries of France, the United Kingdom and Prussia/Germany.

On 7 November 1910, the Dutch legislature finally enacted a patent law to replace the system abolished in 1869. Although the Netherlands was without a patent system for more than 40 years, for the last 25 years of this period there was a significant movement in the Netherlands favouring the reintroduction of the patent system. As early as 1886, there was formed in the Netherlands a "*Société des partisans d'une législation sur les brevets pour les Pays-Bas*",[160] which was composed mainly of engineers, and which lobbied the Dutch government for the reintroduction of a patent system.[161] By 1893, the Dutch government accepted that a patent system would have to be adopted. The Minister of Foreign Affairs, Van Tienhoven, stated that the Netherlands was "moralement obligé"[162] to pass patent legislation following its delegate's representations to the 1890–91 Madrid Conference of the International Union for the Protection of Industrial Property.[163] Shortly after, the Minister of Waterstaat, Commerce and Industry, prepared draft patent legislation which was widely distributed for comment.[164] However, between 1895 and 1908 the Dutch government's interest in patent legislation waned, and it was only after strong lobbying by the Association for the Development of Industry and Manufacture in the Netherlands,[165] and the Industrial Society of the Netherlands,[166] that patent legislation was finally passed in 1910.

C The Patent Abolition Movement in Prussia

On 10 December 1868, Count von Bismarck, Chancellor of the North German Confederation, introduced into the Federal Council of that Confederation a Motion in which he called for the abolition of the patent system.[167] Speaking

160 (1886) 2 *La Propriété Industrielle* 89.
161 *Ibid.*
162 Translation: "morally obligated".
163 (1893) 9 *La Propriété Industrielle* 130.
164 *Ibid.*
165 (1901) 17 *La Propriété Industrielle* 195.
166 (1908) 24 *La Propriété Industrielle* 108.
167 Motion of 10 December 1868 translated and reproduced in UNITED KINGDOM, Parliamentary Papers, *Return of any Public Official Documents received at the Foreign Office, exhibiting Reasons why Count Von Bismarck and the Government of Prussia, and Mr Fock, the Minister of the Interior of the Netherlands, and the Dutch Government, have recommended, and the Chambers of the latter Country have resolved on, the Abolition of Patents for Invention* (1870) 41, vol LXI, 527, 9.

on his own behalf, and also on behalf of the Royal Prussian Government, von Bismarck argued that the North German States should set an example to the South German States by abolishing patents, and hoped that patents would eventually be abolished throughout the whole extent of the Zollverein.[168] Besides the U.K., France and the Netherlands, Prussia was the only other important country where significant debate about the value of its patent system took place during the 1860s and 1870s. Why did the abolition movement ultimately fail in Prussia (and the German Reich after its formation in 1871) despite the support of von Bismarck and many important German economic philosophers and business associations?

(a) *General Historical Background to the Patent Abolition Debate*

Patent legislation had existed in Prussia since 14 October 1815,[169] and was subject to the limitations imposed by certain regulations agreed upon by the States of the Zollverein in Stuttgart in 1841, and which came into effect on 21 September 1842.[170] The cornerstone of the Prussian patent system was the

168 *Ibid.* 11. The Zollverein was a customs and commercial union established on 21 September 1842 between 25 States of the Germanic Confederation, namely: The Kingdoms of Hanover, Bavaria, Prussia, Saxony, and Wurttemberg, the Grand-Duchies of Baden, Hesse, Saxe-Weimar-Eisenach, the Duchies of Anhalt-Bernburg, Anhalt-Dessau, Anhalt-Coethen, Nassau, Saxe-Altenburg, Saxe-Coburg-Gotha, Saxe-Meinengen-Hildburghausen, the Electorate of Hesse, the Principalities of Hohenzollern-Herlingen, Hohenzollern-Sigmaringen, Reuss Major, Reuss Minor, Schwartzburg-Rudolstadt, Schwartzburg-Sondershausen and Waldeck, the Landgraviate of Hesse-Homburg and the Free State of Frankfort am-Mein.

169 For the text of the Law of 14 October 1815 see: von Kleinschrod, C. TH., *Die Internationale Patentgesetzgebung nach ihren Prinzipien nebst Vorschlägen für ein Künftiges Gemeines Deutsches Patentrecht* (Erlangen, Verlag von Ferdinand Enke, 1855), 169–171.

170 For a detailed discussion of these limitations see: Report by Evan Baillie, British Consul in Darmstadt (Baden), January 1873. Reproduced in UNITED KINGDOM, Parliamentary Papers, *Reports by H.M. Secs of Embassy and Legation respecting Law and Practice in Foreign Countries with regard to Inventions* (1873) C. 741, vol LXVI, 483, 9–15. See also: DEUTSCHEN PATENTAMT, *Hundert Jahre Patentamt: Festschrift Herausgegeben vom Deutschen Patentamt* (Munich, Carl Heymanns Verlag, 1977), 352–355. The limitations imposed by membership of the Zollverein were as follows: (1) Patents were to be granted only for novel inventions. An invention previously practised within the Zollverein area was not to be patentable. (2) The patent right was to extend to the right of exclusive manufacture or practice of the invention in question. It extended also to a right to introduce a new process or method of manufacture or to apply exclusively new machines or implements for manufacture. Therefore, the patentee could prohibit the use of the method or the use of the patented machines by all those who had not acquired the right from him. (3) Once a patent had been granted to a person in one State, only that person or his legal successor could apply for the same patent in another State of the Zollverein. (4) Every State within the Zollverein retained the power to decide whether a patent ought to be granted,

requirement that all applications for patents be subject to rigorous examination as to novelty by the Technical Deputation for Industrial Matters of the Ministry of Commerce.[171] A patent was only considered novel if no description of it had been previously published either in Prussia or anywhere else in the world and no use had been previously made of it in Prussia. This requirement that all applications be subject to substantive examination, coupled with the requirement of universal novelty, meant that very few patents were granted in Prussia. For example, in 1870, of 551 applications made for patents in Prussia, only 74 patents were granted.[172] It was rare for a foreigner to be granted a patent in Prussia, largely because such persons could not satisfy the strict requirements as to novelty. As the U.K. Consul in Berlin stated in 1872, the novelty requirement:

> materially affects British inventors, and is a cause of constant vexation to them. Every patent which is granted in England is published with all its details in London in the official journal of the Patent Office. This, as well as every mechanical and industrial newspaper or periodical of any consequence published in the world, is regularly read at the Department in Berlin which is charged with the administration of the Patent Laws.[173]

The U.K. Consul in Berlin added that once the journals and periodicals had been read by the Department in Berlin, the "principal points [were] entered into ledgers for future reference" and if it were found that any invention the subject of a patent application had previously been published "officially or unofficially", the application was "invariably refused".[174] It was to be expected, then,

---

independent of the outcome of an application in any other Zollverein State. (5) The patentee's right did not extend to any right to limit the importation of articles made overseas by use of the patented invention. Also, the patentee could not control the sale or disposal in trade of such articles or their use or consumption.

171 Report of T.N. Plunkett, British Consul in Berlin, 12 December 1872. Reproduced in UNITED KINGDOM, Parliamentary Papers, *Reports by H.M. Secs of Embassy and Legation respecting Law and Practice in Foreign Countries with regard to Inventions* (1873) C. 741, vol LXVI, 483, 128–135.

172 *Ibid.* 135. Bismarck noted in 1868 that "in Prussia during the last 10 years, on the average, 87 per cent of the applications sent in for patents have been rejected, and only between 50 and 100 patents have been granted." UNITED KINGDOM, Parliamentary Papers, *Return of any Public Official Documents received at the Foreign Office, exhibiting Reasons why Count Von Bismarck and the Government of Prussia, and Mr Fock, the Minister of the Interior of the Netherlands, and the Dutch Government, have recommended, and the Chambers of the latter Country have resolved on, the Abolition of Patents for Invention* (1870) 41, vol LXI, 527, 11.

173 *Ibid.* 130.

174 *Ibid.* 131.

that U.K. as well as U.S. inventors complained bitterly about what amounted to a lack of patent protection in Prussia.[175] In reflecting upon his experiences of the Prussian patent system before the reforms of 1877,[176] the U.S. inventor J.J. Storrow told the 1878 U.S. Congressional Committee on Patents that the Prussian patent law "exposed the public to sufficient annoyance, and it was neither framed nor administered so as to reach or encourage inventive talent everywhere. It was not, in effect, a patent system, as we understand it."[177]

Von Bismarck agreed that the strict requirements of the Prussian patent law meant that there was a "proportionally lesser diffusion of the patent system" in Prussia, as compared to countries such as the U.K., France, Belgium and North America/U.S.A.[178] He also considered that of the patents granted in Prussia, "but a small number have been so successful as to be worth mentioning."[179] For this reason, Prussia was in quite a different position from the U.K. or France in respect to the issue of abolition of patents. While the latter countries had strong patent systems which were seen to have definite impact upon industrial

175 See Chapter Three for further details in regard to U.K. complaints about the lack of availability of patent protection in Prussia.

176 On 25 May 1877, the Reichstag adopted a patent law for the whole of the German Reich. The law came into effect on 1 July 1877. Many commentaries on the legislative history and content of this law were published at the time. See for example: Goldenberg, A., *Ueber das Projectirte Patentgesetz für das Deutsche Reich; November 1876* (Strassburg, G. Fischbach, 1876). Andre, W., *Der revidirte Entwurf eines Patentgesetzes für das deutsche Reich* (Chemnitz, S.C.F. Bidenhabn, 1876). Landgraf, J., *Das deutsche Reichsgesetz betreffend den Schutz von Erfindungspatenten* (Stuttgart, Julius Maier, 1877). Lenz, O., *Entwurf eines Patentgesetzes vom Reichskenzleramt veröffentlicht* (Berlin, Julius Springer, 1877) Alexander-Katz, R., *Bemerkungen zu dem Entwurf eines Patentgesetzes* (Berlin, Carl Heymann's Verlag, 1877). Sieber, E., *Kurze Bemerkungen zum Entwurf eines deutschen Patentgesetzes* (Berlin, Dümmlers Verlagsbuchhandlung, 1877). Morillot, A., *De la Protection accordée aux Oeuvres d'art, aux Photographies, aux Dessins et Modéles Industriels et aux Brevets d'Invention dans l'Empire d'Allemagne* (Paris, Cotillon et Cie, 1878). Gareis, C., *Ueber das Erfinderrecht von Beamten, Angestellten und Arbeitern* (Berlin, Carl Heymann's Verlag, 1879). Knoblauch, H., *Das Patentgesetz für das Deutsche Reich vom 25 Mai 1877* (Berlin, Eugen Grosser, 1880).

177 UNITED STATES OF AMERICA, Congressional Papers, *Arguments before the Committee on Patents of the Senate and House of Representatives, in support of, and suggesting amendments to, the Bills, (S. No. 300 and H.R. 1612) to amend the Statutes in relation to Patents, and for other purposes* (1878) 45th Congress, 2nd Session, Senate 1788, Misc Docs 50, 319.

178 UNITED KINGDOM, Parliamentary Papers, *Return of any Public Official Documents received at the Foreign Office, exhibiting Reasons why Count Von Bismarck and the Government of Prussia, and Mr Fock, the Minister of the Interior of the Netherlands, and the Dutch Government, have recommended, and the Chambers of the latter Country have resolved on, the Abolition of Patents for Invention* (1870) 41, vol LXI, 527, 11.

179 *Ibid.*

development,[180] in Prussia, the patent system was perceived to have made little contribution to the economy. It is unsurprising that in 1868, many Prussians supported von Bismarck's proposals for the abolition of a useless organ, "so confessedly full of defects".[181]

(b) *Von Bismarck's Arguments in Support of the Abolition of Patents*

In his Motion of 19 December 1868, von Bismarck provided a number of reasons why the patent system should be abolished. He made reference to both practical and theoretical justifications for his position.

Von Bismarck's theoretical objections primarily took the form of a denial of the existence of any natural property rights in inventions. He argued that it was:

> settled that the securing of an exclusive right to the profitable use of industrial inventions is neither enjoined by a natural right of the inventor's, which is to be protected by the State, nor to be deduced from the sequence of general economic principles.[182]

The lack of such a natural property right in inventions was essential to von Bismarck's argument, for he alleged that the maintenance of the patent system depended upon "proof of a special internal principle of justification."[183] As there was no such special internal principle, the whole system was based upon an extremely vulnerable foundation. As a secondary point, he also opposed any notion that a patent was needed to provide a reward for inventors.[184] He believed that inventors had sufficient reward from obtaining a natural headstart over their competitors, and they could also use secrecy to maintain their advantage.[185] It was clear that his primary concern was the maintenance of free trade policies, which he called "free industrial production",[186] and he did not consider the patent system compatible with these policies.

Although von Bismarck made some reference to theoretical objections, his real focus was the perceived practical difficulties associated with patents.

---

180 Either negatively or positively, depending upon the perception of the individual.

181 UNITED KINGDOM, Parliamentary Papers, *Return of any Public Official Documents received at the Foreign Office*, etc. at 11.

182 *Ibid.* 9.

183 *Ibid.*

184 *Ibid.*

185 *Ibid.* 9, 11.

186 *Ibid.*

Some of these difficulties had been experienced in Prussia, but many were more readily associated with the simple registration systems operating in France and the United Kingdom.

Of the difficulties which had been experienced in Prussia, von Bismarck was most concerned with the problem of operating a system of substantive examination. Although the Technical Deputation for Industrial Matters had a "comparatively excellent auxiliary apparatus", for carrying out examinations of patent applications, nevertheless, it was almost impossible to decide if an article sought to be patented had already been produced or made known elsewhere.[187] It was not only the case that the reference material was "superabundant", but there was a great difficulty in "carrying out of fixed principles" in reference to the criteria of novelty.[188]

One of the suggested remedies for this problem was for Prussia to switch to the "so-called announcement system" (simple registration system) which operated in France and the United Kingdom.[189] However, von Bismarck rejected this system, stating that it gave rise to "abuses", and "obstacles", and in particular trades there was great suffering from "the mass of patents taken out,, mostly for the purpose of swindling speculation."[190] He added that the large number of legal proceedings to prosecute for infringement and defend against competing claims, had "brought about a reaction in the public opinion [in France and the U.K.] ... which demands the abolition of that system."[191] He asserted that it was only a matter of time before France and the U.K. abolished their patent systems, although he acknowledged that "there is the apprehension that the country which first proceeds to it will suffer great injury in regards to the others."[192] He also questioned whether the patent system had really been of great benefit to the industrial development of "England, Belgium, France and North America".[193] Pointing to the case of Switzerland, he alleged that economic development could occur without a patent system, and he asserted that industrial progress in the major trading nations might have been even faster if they had been freed earlier from anti-competitive practices such as patents.[194]

187 *Ibid.* 9.
188 *Ibid.* 10.
189 *Ibid.*
190 *Ibid.*
191 *Ibid.*
192 *Ibid.*
193 *Ibid.*
194 *Ibid.*

(c) *Supporters of von Bismarck's Proposals to Abolish the Patent System*

In 1950, Machlup and Penrose wrote that in the attacks upon the patent system which occurred in Germany in the 1860s and 1870s, "free trade arguments were used more than they were in England, and economists were almost unanimous in the condemnation of the system."[195] They added that trade associations and chambers of commerce were almost unanimous in their abolitionist stance, but that many lawyers, engineers, industrialists and inventors continued to support the patent system.[196] In general terms, Machlup and Penrose are correct in their assessment of the groups which advocated the abolition of patents in Germany (and particularly Prussia), although they do not sufficiently highlight the extent of opposition to von Bismarck's proposals by the engineering and legal professions.

It has been noted above that von Bismarck was a strong advocate of competition, and used free trade as a justification for his belief that patents should be abolished. He was not the only person in government to hold this opinion.

When von Bismarck spoke out against patents in 1868 he was also representing the attitude of certain influential Ministers and the officials of the Prussian patent office – the Technical Deputation for Industrial Matters of the Ministry of Commerce. Until at least 1859, the Prussian patent officials were clearly not opponents of the patent system. For example, in 1851, Johann Wilhelm Wedding, a member of the Prussian Board of Trade and Commerce and member of the Technical Deputation, gave evidence before the United Kingdom Select Committee on Patents to the effect that patents were desirable, and should be made easier to obtain in Prussia.[197] He considered that the Prussian patent examiners were too strict in carrying out the novelty examination, and were too ready to reject applications. He also suggested that it would be desirable if all States of the Zollverein adopted a patent law.[198] Shortly afterwards, on 8 July 1853, a government inquiry to consider reform of the patent system was set up in Prussia, under the auspices of the Ministerial Director of the

195 Machlup, F., and Penrose, E., "The Patent Controversy in the Nineteenth Century" (1950) x *The Journal of Economic History* 1, 4.

196 *Ibid.* See also on this point Penrose, E., *The Economics of the International Patent System* (Baltimore, John Hopkins Press, 1951), 14.

197 UNITED KINGDOM, Parliamentary Papers, *Report and Minutes of Evidence taken before the Select Committee of the House of Lords appointed to consider of The Bill, intituled, "An Act further to amend the Law touching Letters Patent for Invention" and also of The Bill intituled "An Act for the further amendment of the Law touching Letters Patent for Invention" and to report thereon to the House: Session 1851* (1851) 486 vol XVIII, 233, 302 (In the Report, Wedding is called William Weddinge).

198 *Ibid.* 302–303.

Ministry of Commerce, von der Heydt.[199] As part of this inquiry, the Ministry investigated the attitudes of District administrations (*Bezirksregierungen*) and Chambers of Commerce (*Handelskammern*) to the patent system.[200] The results of this survey showed that only 4 District administrations and 5 Chambers of Commerce favoured the abolition of the patent system, while 18 and 22 respectively wished to retain it.[201]

After 1858, however, this position began to change, following the appointment of Rudolf Delbrück as Prussian Minister of Commerce in 1859.[202] Heggen describes Delbrück as a zealous advocate of free trade, who was very critical of the patent system.[203] It was clear that most Prussian economic philosophers at that time favoured free trade, and in doing so, rejected the concept of patent monopolies. Delbrück, and later von Bismarck, adopted what was perceived at the time to be enlightened economic thought.

Of the many economic philosophers who came to prominence in Prussia during the 1850s and 1860s, the most influential in the debates over free trade were probably John Prince-Smith, Karl Braun, Otto Michaelis, Arwed Emminghaus, Max Wirth, Albert Schäffle, Hermann Rentzsch, the Swiss Viktor Böhmert, and the Frenchmen Michel Chevalier and Jules Faucher.[204] In 1846, Faucher had joined Prince-Smith in forming the first "Free Trade Society" [*Freihandels-Verein*] in Berlin,[205] and they were later influential in the establishment in 1858 of the first of the annual *"Volkswirtsschaftliche"* Congresses, and in 1863 the journal entitled *Vierteljahrschrift für Volkswirthschaft und Culturgeschichte*.[206] This structured programme of meetings, together with the new economic journal, gave German economic philosophers the opportunity to debate free trade and the patent system in some detail. Of the ten important economic philosophers noted above, only Max Wirth clearly supported the patent system. This probably represents the general level of support for the patent system amongst all German economic philosophers at the time.

199 von Kleinschrod, C. TH., *Die Internationale Patentgesetzgebung nach ihren Prinzipien nebst Vorschlägen für ein Künftiges Gemeines Deutsches Patentrecht* (Erlangen, Verlag von Ferdinand Enke, 1855), 172.

200 See further: Heggen, A., *Erfindungsschutz und Industrialisierung in Preussen 1793–1877* (Göttingen, Vandenhoeck und Ruprecht, 1975), 55–57.

201 *Ibid.* 56.

202 *Ibid.* 76.

203 *Ibid.*

204 *Ibid.* 72–73. See also Prince-Smith, J., "Ueber Patente für Erfindungen" (1863) *Vierteljahrschrift für Volkswirthschaft und Culturgeschichte* 150.

205 Heggen, A., *op.cit.* 73.

206 *Ibid.*

For example, at the annual *"Volkswirtsschaftliche"* Congress in Dresden on 14 September 1863, a resolution was adopted by an overwhelming majority to the effect that patents hindered the progress of invention, hampered the prompt general utilisation of useful inventions, were a deceptive form of compensation to inventors, and were generally injurious to common welfare.[207]

Prince-Smith was the most outspoken German economic philosopher who rejected the patent system largely because of its perceived anti-competitive characteristics. Nineteenth century commentators pointed to Prince-Smith as the leader of the Prussian anti-patent movement, allied also with Schäffle.[208] It was at the *"Volkswirtsschaftliche"* Congress in 1863 that Prince-Smith presented a paper calling for the abolition of the patent system.[209] This paper was the first to provide any detailed consideration of the theoretical objections to patents.

A central focus of Prince-Smith's writings was his rejection of any concept of property rights in inventions. He considered that private property rights should only be accorded for a good social purpose, and protecting inventions did not meet this criteria.[210] He also argued that the invention sprung from an idea or concept, which, unlike a tangible article, was something which should not be exclusively appropriated by any one person.[211]

Prince-Smith also rejected the other common theoretical justifications for the patent system. He argued that patents did not secure just reward to inventors, and, in fact, led more frequently to losses rather than gains.[212] He considered that open competition would be more likely to provide inventors with opportunities to obtain reasonable recompense for their work. Part of this would be because they would have freedom to make use of the prior inventions of others.[213] He also rejected the notion that patents promoted inventive activity. He argued that the patent system encouraged persons to leave their

207 Rolin-Jaequemyns, G., "De Quelques Manifestations Récentes de l'Opinion Publique en Europe au Sujet des Brevets d'Invention" (1869) 1 *Revue de droit International et de Législation Comparée* 600, 610; Heggen, A., *op.cit.* 73; Machlup, F., and Penrose, E., *op.cit.* 4.

208 See, for example, the writings of Professor Klostermann, particularly Klostermann, R., "Zur Reform der Patentgesetzgebung" in *Die Patentgrage: Sechs Breisschriften über Reform der Patent-gesetzgebung. Prämiirt durch den Verein deutscher Ingenieure* (Köln, Verlag von Eduard Heinrich Maher, 1876), 17. Rolin-Jaequemyns also considered these two economists to be the main instigators of the anti-patent movement in Prussia. Rolin-Jaequemyns, G., *op.cit.* 610.

209 Prince-Smith, J., "Ueber Patente für Erfindungen" (1863) *Vierteljahrschrift für Volkswirthschaft und Culturgeschichte* 150 .

210 *Ibid.* 156–158.

211 *Ibid.* 157–158.

212 *Ibid.* 161.

213 *Ibid.*

usual fields of production and pursue the dream of "inventing" along often uneconomic pathways.[214] He further questioned whether the patent system actually achieved the expressed goal of encouraging the dissemination of new knowledge. It was his view that the patent system led to "das heimliche und isolirte Arbeiten"[215] which was not conducive to free exchange of ideas.[216] If the patent system was abolished, he predicted a situation where inventors would hasten to publish their ideas, and would enter into more co-operative arrangements with other inventors.[217] This would generally lead to a faster development and utilisation of new inventions. Although it had often been argued that patent protection enabled an inventor to obtain financial backing for expensive research and development, he proposed that "[w]o aber wirklich kostspielige Vorbereitungsversuche gemacht werden müssten, da wäre es ein Leichtes, mit Hilfe der Oeffentlichkeit, freiwillige Beiträge aus öffentlichem Interesse zu schaffen."[218]

Many of the points made by Prince-Smith were later taken up by other economic philosophers. Most of these commentators also supported the abolition of the patent system, as evidenced by the abovementioned resolution of the "*Volkswirtsschaftliche*" Congress in September 1863. The most interesting writings related to the issue of property rights in inventions. Böhmert, for example, (a Professor of Political Economy at Zurich Polytechnic, whose work was respected in Prussia), thought it misguided to believe that the inventor or society was in any way benefited by the grant of exclusive property rights in an invention.[219] After stating that he had carried out a detailed investigation into the history of protection for inventions in the U.K., Prussia and Switzerland, he concluded that a patent system retarded economic growth. He argued that the greater the use of patents, the greater the detrimental impact upon economic growth.[220] It should be noted, however, that Böhmert's conclusions as set out in his article, were largely based upon an examination of the U.K. patent system,

214 *Ibid.* 161.

215 Translation: "clandestine and isolated work".

216 Prince-Smith, J., "Ueber Patente für Erfindungen" (1863) *Vierteljahrschrift für Volkswirthschaft und Culturgeschichte* 150, 160.

217 *Ibid.*

218 Translation: "where it should be necessary to make expensive preparatory experiments, it would be easy with good publicity to obtain voluntary contributions in the public interest." *Ibid.*

219 Bohmert, V., "Die Erfindungspatente, nach volkswirthschaftlichen Grundsätzen und industriellen Erfanrungen; mit besondrer Rüchsicht auf England und die Schweiz" (1869) *Vierteljahrschrift für Volkswirthschaft und Culturgeschichte* 28, 30.

220 *Ibid.* 79.

and particularly upon his selective reading of the evidence given before the 1862–1864 U.K. Select Committee on Patents. As was shown in Chapter Three, it is difficult to see how these conclusions could have been supported by reliance upon evidence of the 1862–1864 Select Committee.

Other economic philosophers such as Otto Michaelis, the editor of the Berlin "National-Zeitung" (and after 1867 a member of the North German Reichstag), agreed with Prince-Smith and Böhmert that it was absurd to suggest that intellectual labour produced property in ideas in the same way that manual labour created property in tangible objects.[221] Albert Schäffle also disagreed with the notion of intellectual property, stating that the right amounted to "control of a market", which was by its nature anti-competitive and objectionable.[222] Hermann Rentzsch agreed that "[p]roperty in ideas, once published, is an insoluble contradiction" and added that an idea could not be the subject of exclusive appropriation because the same idea could be possessed by many people at the same time.[223]

Of all the influential economists in Prussia, only Max Wirth clearly supported the patent system. Yet even he did not support property rights in inventions. Wirth was originally a journalist on economic matters. From 1865 he was Manager of the Swiss Statistical Bureau, and during the mid-1870s he began a publishing career in Berlin.[224] As a journalist, who later became a publisher, Wirth was particularly interested to ensure the protection of literary works, and perhaps for this reason he diverged from most other economists when he supported the general concept of intellectual property rights. However, he believed that inventions were "emanations of the current state of civilisation and, thus, common property".[225] The State could grant a temporary monopoly to encourage research and exploitation of inventions, but in the absence of State intervention, there was no fundamental right of property in inventions.

---

221 Michaelis, O., "Zur Selbstkritik des Patentschutzes" in (1870) 8 *Vierteljahrschrift für Volkswirthschaft und Culturgeschichte* 100–121. Discussed in Heggen, A., *op.cit.* 73–74.

222 Schaffle, A., *Die nationalökonomische Theorie der ausschliessenden Absatzverhältnisse* (Tübingen, 1867) discussed in *Ibid.* and Machlup, F., and Penrose, E., *op.cit.* 12.

223 Rentzsch, H., "Geistiges Eigenthum" in *Handwörterbuch der Volkswirtschaft* (Leipzig, 1866) translated in Machlup, F., and Penrose, E., *op.cit.* 12.

224 Wirth, M., "Bericht über die Verhandlungen des sechsten Kongress Deutscher Volkswirthe zu Dresden" (1863) *Vierteljahrschrift für Volkswirthschaft und Culturgeschichte* 222. Heggen, A., *op.cit.* 74.

225 Wirth, M., "Bericht über die Verhandlungen des sechsten Kongress Deutscher Volkswirthe zu Dresden" (1863) *Vierteljahrschrift für Volkswirthschaft und Culturgeschichte* 222, translated in Machlup, F., and Penrose, E., *op.cit.* 13–14.

Some influential German lawyers also followed the economic philosophers in rejecting private property rights in inventions. For example, in May 1863, Fr. Bitzer, (one of seven members of a Commission of Experts set up to examine suggestions for a new patent law by Resolution of the Federal Assembly of the North German Confederation on 24 July 1862),[226] wrote that it was taken as accepted that property rights were interlinked with material things, and thus there were no such property rights in inventions.[227] From a reading of the Report of the Commission, it can be seen that the members paid most attention to practical issues such as the means by which the various patent laws of the German States could be more closely assimilated, rather than entering into a detailed study of theoretical justifications for the patent system. Nevertheless, the notion that the patent was granted by the State to encourage or reward invention, rather than to protect fundamental property rights, was inherent in the Commission's recommendations.[228]

As most German economic philosophers, and some lawyers, appeared to reject any notion of private property rights in inventions, this made the patent system vulnerable to attack. Then, as free trade became more strongly accepted in Prussia and the Zollverein during the 1860s, an abolition movement began. In 1863, the Prussian Government refused to accept the recommendations of the Commission of Experts which made several proposals for a uniform patent system for the North German Confederation,[229] and instead instigated its own Inquiry into whether or not the patent system in Prussia should be completely abolished.[230] In the course of the Inquiry the Minister of Trade, von Itzenplitz, asked each Chamber of Commerce to report whether it considered that there were insurmountable obstacles associated with the continuance of the patent system.[231] Thirty-one Chambers of Commerce advised that they wished to see its abolition, while only sixteen believed it should be reformed and improved.[232] Of the 31 Chambers of Commerce which

226 At that time, the Confederation comprised Austria, Prussia, Bavaria, Saxony, Wurtemburg, Hanover, and the two Hesses.

227 Bitzer, F., *Vorschläge für ein Deutsches Patentgesetz, beantragt durch die von der hohen deutschen Bundesversammlung durch Beschluss vom 24 Juli 1862 einberfene Commission von Fachmännern, met Erläuterungen und einer Ausführung über die principielle Rechtfertigung des Patentschutzes* (Stuttgart, August Schaber, 1864), 122.

228 *Ibid.* See particularly the Introductory section to the above Report, "Gutachten", 1–48.

229 See above note 226.

230 Rolin-Jaequemyns, G., "De Quelques Manifestations Récentes de l'Opinion Publique en Europe au Sujet des Brevets d'Invention" (1869) 1 *Revue de droit International et de Législation Comparée* 600, 610.

231 Heggen, A., *op.cit.* 80–81.

232 *Ibid.*

favoured the abolition of the patent system, the views of Cologne were representative.[233] Clearly influenced by the arguments advanced by Prince-Smith, the Cologne Chamber of Commerce wrote that the patent was "a monopoly ... subject to all the disadvantages in its consequences which are common to all monopolies."[234] Not only was it objectionable, but it had a retarding effect upon industrial development. Some inventors found that their "endeavours to compete in the sphere of inventions are suddenly checked by Patents", while other inventors wasted their time "watch[ing] with jealousy possible infringements of others on their monopolies."[235] It was also argued that many persons chased the dream of a patent, when they should have applied themselves to "regular industry".[236] The Cologne Chamber also believed that patents led to higher consumer prices during the term of the patent.[237] It considered that the patent system should be abolished and replaced by a scheme of State rewards for meritorious inventions.[238]

Given the strength of opposition to the patent system by economic philosophers and business associations, it was unsurprising that the Prussian Government should have sought the abolition of patents. Von Bismarck's Motion presented to the Federal Council in December 1868 clearly had the support of important interest groups. The Council of the North German Confederation also thought the Motion had merit, and the matter was referred to a Committee for further evaluation.[239] No definite plan of action had been adopted at the time of the formation of the German Reich on 18 January 1871.

On 10 May 1872, the Reichstag found it necessary to consider how the patent laws would be administered under the new political regime.[240] This matter was brought to the attention of the Reichstag by a Petition which had earlier been

233 Report of the Chamber of Commerce of Cologne, dated 15 September 1863. Reproduced and translated in Macfie, R.A. (ed), *Recent Discussions on the Abolition of Patents for Inventions in the United Kingdom, France, Germany, and the Netherlands: evidence, speeches and papers in its favour* (London, Longmans and Co, 1869) 272–275.

234 *Ibid.* 272.

235 *Ibid.* 273.

236 *Ibid.*

237 *Ibid.*

238 *Ibid.* 274.

239 Heggen, A., *op.cit.* 103.

240 Article 4(5) of the Imperial Constitution of 15 May 1871 declared that questions concerning patents and patent laws were reserved to the Reichsrath, and were no longer to be dependent upon the different Governments which composed the German Empire. UNITED KINGDOM, Parliamentary Papers, *Reports by H.M. Secs of Embassy and Legation respecting Law and Practice in Foreign Countries with regard to Inventions* (1873) C. 741, vol LXVI, 483, 128 (Report of T.N. Plunkett, British Consul in Berlin).

presented to the *Petitionskommission* by a Berlin merchant, C.F. Wappenhaus.[241] The Petition had been remitted to the Reichstag by the *Petitionskommission,* and it was presented with the strong support of the Prussians Prince-Smith and Delbrück, as well as Von Bismarck.[242] Von Bismarck's position was that it would be desirable "if the Parliament would use the opportunity of the discussion to express itself in favour of the full abolition of patent protection."[243] In the course of that same year, many impartial observers predicted that patent laws throughout the new German Reich would soon be abolished.[244] These observers underestimated the strength of the interest groups who opposed the need for abolition.

(d) *Supporters of the Patent System*

Most of the support for the pro-patent movement in Prussia (and later, the German Reich), came from the engineering and legal professions. The engineering profession also encompassed many of the most important inventors and manufacturers, such as Werner Siemens. In 1872, the Reichstag did not adopt the Prussian proposals for the abolition of patents, largely because of

241 Heggen, A., *op.cit.* 107.

242 *Ibid.*

243 Translated in Kronstein, H., and Till, I., "A re-evaluation of the International Patent Convention" (1947) 12 *Law and Contemporary Problems* 765, 767.

244 See, for example, the Report of Evan Baillie, U.K. Consul in Darmstadt, Duchy of Baden, dated January 1873. He stated that "the opinion in this country entertained generally by the Government and the manufacturing classes, is that the institution of patents is one which has outlived itself, and has ceased to be generally useful". He added that there "was every probability that the present system will shortly either be greatly modified, or done away with altogether". UNITED KINGDOM, Parliamentary Papers, *Reports by H.M. Secs of Embassy and Legation respecting Law and Practice in Foreign Countries with regard to Inventions* (1873) C. 741, vol LXVI, 483, 15. In his Report from Berlin dated 12 December 1872, T.N. Plunkett, U.K. Consul in Berlin stated that it was to be expected that "whenever the question is mooted again, a very strong push will be made to induce the Reichsrath to settle it once and for all in a summary and conclusive manner, by repealing the various existing patent laws, without passing any new one in their place." He further added that "it would seem more than probable that ultimately the opponents of the patent system will obtain the solution for which they have so long contended." *Ibid.* 129, 135. In his Report from Dresden dated 28 December 1872, J. Hume Burnley, U.K. Consul in Saxony, stated that the opinion of Saxon manufacturers was much less in favour of patents than it used to be, and that three of the five Chambers of Commerce (Leipzig, Zittau and Plauen) had voted to abolish patents. The Dresden Chamber of Commerce was also "more against patents than in favour of them." Only the Chemnitz Chamber, which chiefly represented owners of iron foundries, was in favour of patents. He added that the Saxon Government would be ready to support any movement by the Imperial Government to abolish the patent laws. *Ibid.* 139–140.

the belief that public opinion would not favour abolition.[245] In particular, it was felt that the interests of the Society of German Engineers could not be ignored, because the Society had "repeatedly and actively come out in favour of patent protection."[246]

In a history of the German Patent Office written in 1977 to celebrate the one hundredth anniversary of its foundation in 1877, it was noted that the first proposal for a uniform patent legislation for all the German States had originated with a discussion in the *Verein Deutscher Ingenieure* (V.D.I.) in 1861.[247] In fact, this is incorrect, because as early as 1855 von Kleinschrod had published a long treatise on German and foreign patent laws, in which he made certain proposals for a uniform patent law for all members of the Zollverein.[248] In addition, in 1858, the general meeting of the V.D.I. discussed in some detail proposals for a thorough revision of the patent laws.[249] Nevertheless, it is true that after 1861, the V.D.I. became very active in connection with patent law reform. The most influential of its members were the engineers Werner Siemens and Carl Pieper,[250] and the lawyers W. André,[251] and

245 Kronstein, H., and Till, I., *op.cit.* 768.

246 *Ibid.*

247 DEUTSCHEN PATENTAMT, *Hundert Jahre Patentamt: Festschrift Herausgegeben vom Deutschen Patentamt* (Munich, Carl Heymanns Verlag, 1977), 357. Note: *Verein Deutscher Ingenieure* refers to the Society of German Engineers.

248 von Kleinschrod, C. TH., *Die Internationale Patentgesetzgebung nach ihren Prinzipien nebst Vorschlägen für ein Künftiges Gemeines Deutsches Patentrecht* (Erlangen, Verlag von Ferdinand Enke, 1855).

249 Heggen, A., *op.cit.* 88.

250 Pieper was a civil engineer based in Dresden. He wrote several publications on the patent question and was a member of the Executive Committee and the Secretary of the 1873 Vienna Patent Congress. His publications included: Pieper, C., *Der Erfinderschutz und die Reform der Patentgesetze. Amtlicher Bericht über den Internationalen Patent-Congress zur Erörterung der Frage des Patentschutzes. Mit einer Einleitung von Dr. C.W. Siemens F.R.S.* (Dresden, Commission der Schulbuchhandlung, 1873); Pieper, C., *Zur Reform des Patentgesetzes und des Gebrauchs-Musterschutzes* (Berlin, Polytechnische Buchhandlung, 1890); Pieper, C., *Sind die Industrie-Schutzgesetze verbessert? – nach dem stenographischen Bericht und den Protocollen der Conferenz für den Schutz des gewerblichen Eigentums* (Berlin, Puttkammer und Mühlbrecht, 1891); Pieper, C., and Schmid, P., *Geschichte der internationalen Union für den Schutz des gewerblichen Eigentums sammt Konvention und Staatsverträgen* (Berlin, Deutschen Vereins für den Schutz des gewerblichen Eigentums, 1894).

251 Based in Osnabrück and Chemnitz, Saxony, W. André was trained as a lawyer, but had taken an early interest in the concerns of engineers and the patent system. He was a member of the *Deutsche Patentschutz-Verein*. He was a member of the Preparatory Committee of the 1873 Vienna Patent Congress and was also the author of works on the patent system, such as Andre, W., *Der revidirte Entwurf eines Patentgesetzes für das deutsche Reich* (Chemnitz, S.C.F. Bidenhabn, 1876).

R. Klostermann[252] who later established the *Deutsche Patentschutz-Verein* which operated between 1874 and 1877, seeking the passage of a uniform German patent law.[253] Other German engineers who were active in the cause of patent reform included Herman Grothe,[254] Eugen Langen,[255] F. Philippson,[256] Franz Grashof,[257] and E. Kayser.[258] Of these influential persons, Werner Siemens appears to have been the most important, possibly because he operated in Berlin and he was famous for his discoveries in the fields of telegraphy and electro-industry.[259] His contemporaries such as André considered him to have been the founding father of the German patent law,[260] and it is indeed true that the V.D.I.'s 1873 Draft Patent Law[261] which Siemens so heavily promoted, significantly influenced the work of the Commission of Experts who drafted the patent legislation which was finally passed in 1877.[262]

---

252 A Professor of Mining Law in Bonn, Klostermann was the only noted German to adopt the French concept that labour gave rise to property rights, and that while manual labour resulted in tangible property, intellectual labour gave rise to property in ideas. He sought a complete assimilation between copyright and patents as well as an assimilation of all international intellectual property laws. Klostermann, R., *op.cit.* 35–72.

253 Heggen, A., *op.cit.* 116–117.

254 Grothe operated in Berlin, where he was the editor of the *Polytechnischen Zeitung*. He was a member of the Preparatory Committee of the 1873 Vienna Patent Congress and was also the author of Grothe, H., *Der Internationale Patent-Congress in Wien (4–9 August 1873)* (Berlin, Julius Springer, 1873).

255 Langen was based in Cologne, where he was President of the V.D.I. He was a member of the Preparatory Committee of the 1873 Vienna Patent Congress.

256 Philippson worked as an engineer in Berlin. He was later the author of Philippson, F., *Die Reform der Patent-gesetzgebung, beartbeitet im Auftragedes handels-und Gewerbe-Vereins für Rheinland und Westphalen* (Düsseldorf, Schaubsche Buchhandlung, 1890).

257 Grashof was a Professor at Karlsruhe and Director of the V.D.I.

258 Kayser was an engineer in Breslau.

259 Werner Siemens was the elder brother of William Siemens who was also a famous inventor in the fields of electricity and the use of heat. William Siemens had moved to the U.K. early in his life, to take advantage of its more liberal patent laws, and as noted in Chapter Three, he played a part in patent law reform in the U.K. Both William and Werner Siemens were members of the Executive Committee of the 1873 Vienna Patent Congress. In 1847, Werner Siemens joined J.G. Halske in forming a company called Siemens and Halske, which made telegraphic equipment. It was extremely successful. Plasseraud, Y., and Savignon, F., *Paris 1883: Genése du droit Unioniste des Brevets* (Paris, Litec, 1983), 144.

260 Andre, W., *Der revidirte Entwurf eines Patentgesetzes für das deutsche Reich* (Chemnitz, S.C.F. Bidenhabn, 1876), 1.

261 *Sketch of a Patent Law for the German Empire* (Cologne, 1873).

262 Morillot, A., *De la Protection accordée aux Oeuvres d'art, aux Photographies, aux Dessins et Modéles Industriels et aux Brevets d'Invention dans l'Empire d'Allemagne* (Paris, Cotillon et Cie, 1878), 52–53; See further Bojanowski, *Ueber die Entwickelung des Deutschen Patentwesens in der zeit von 1877 bis 1889* (Leipzig, Verlag von Arthur Felix, 1890), Chapter 1.

Siemens' opinions about the value of the patent system were the same as many other members of the V.D.I. In response to the resolutions of economic philosophers who condemned patents at the "*Volkswirtsschaftliche*" Congress in September 1863, Siemens wrote an opinion, dated 13 October 1863, in which he spoke of the practical advantages to be gained from a strengthened and improved patent system.[263] The opinion was divided into two parts; the first recognising the difficulties which had arisen from the working of the seriously defective Prussian patent system, and the second examining in some detail the theoretical justification for patents.

Siemens believed that most of the practical defects of the Prussian patent system stemmed from the system of preliminary examination. He considered that the examination was undertaken in a mysterious and inconsistent manner, and therefore the work of the Technical Deputation for Industrial Matters did not inspire public confidence.[264] This problem could only be overcome if there was some proof given of the quality of the invention. He also pointed to the difficulties associated with patent specifications which were often not accurate, and which led to the problem of uncertainty in determining the precise field of the patent.[265] The question of patent infringement was also not adequately dealt with under the Prussian patent laws.[266]

Although acknowledging practical problems associated with the Prussian patent system, Siemens believed that the system had definite value, and should be reformed, rather than abolished. He considered that there were four main justifications for a patent system and these were as follows:

(1) The traditional argument that the patent system stimulated invention with its promise of reward to the inventor. This stimulatory effect led to greater technical progress.[267]

(2) While a patent had the characteristic of a monopoly, this was open to licensing and in this way persons other than the patentee gained the right to use the invention.[268]

(3) The patent system encouraged inventors to reveal their secrets to society, and thus led to greater diffusion of knowledge.[269]

263 Noted in Heggen, A., *op.cit.* 92–93.
264 *Ibid.*
265 *Ibid.* 92.
266 *Ibid.*
267 *Ibid.* 93.
268 *Ibid.*
269 *Ibid.*

(4) A patent allowed an inventor some economic security in relation to his invention, and because of this security he was in a better position to obtain financial support to commercialise the invention.[270]

(e) *The Collapse of the Anti-patent Movement in Germany*

As late as 1872 there was a widely-held opinion that the Reichstag would abolish all patent systems then operating in the German Reich. In fact, no such move took place, and, on 25 May 1877 a patent law was passed which applied throughout Germany. Why did the abolition movement collapse?

The first reason was the Great Depression in Europe which began suddenly in 1873, and lasted for a considerable period. In Germany, the depression was particularly severe, with conditions only gradually improving up until 1887 when a new boom period began.[271] The famous German economist, Dietzel, noted that the crash of 1873 had affected the whole of Europe but that Germany had particular difficulties in emerging from the slump. Germany was greatly affected by the dumping of cheap U.K. goods in its domestic market, which led to depressed prices for domestic goods.[272] Thus, he stated that "this circumstance aided admirably the protectionist propaganda, which of course, in spite of the victory of the free-trade people, had remained ever active. Above all, the smelting and textile industries called for greater protection."[273] By 1879, the German Government was ready to renounce its former free trade policy, and it introduced a series of tariffs to protect German industry, particularly the steel industry.[274] The Government also encouraged the growth of cartels, which, with tariffs, "were the main pillars of a structure that restrained competition from both foreign and domestic sources. The tariffs functioned chiefly to block the potential flow of imports ... [and] the cartels restrained competition between their members in the agreed-upon product lines."[275] This emergence of protectionism necessarily involved a rejection of the ideals of free-traders such as Prince-Smith, and paved the way for the adoption of stronger patent laws in 1877.[276]

---

270 *Ibid.*

271 Dietzel, H., "The German Tariff Controversy" (1903) 17 *The Quarterly Journal of Economics* 365, 385–387.

272 *Ibid.* 385.

273 *Ibid.*

274 Webb, S., "Tariffs, Cartels, Technology, and Growth in the German Steel Industry, 1879 to 1914" (1980) 40 *Journal of Economic History* 309.

275 *Ibid.* 312.

276 For further discussion of the connection between the economic crisis and the movement in favour of patent law reform see: DEUTSCHEN PATENTAMT, *Hundert Jahre*

The second reason for the failure of the anti-patent movement in Germany was an increase in nationalism which occurred from the beginning of the 1870s. Both Machlup and Heggen have noted that by the 1870s, the technological gap between Germany and the U.K. was fast closing, particularly in the chemical and electrical industries.[277] Due to this fact, German workers in these fields began to see themselves as innovators, rather than merely copyists, and this growing sense of pride and nationalism led to calls for greater legal protection for their inventions. This point was well illustrated in a work written by Noah Jacobsohn in 1876 entitled *Patentfrage und Krisis*.[278] In this, the author undertook a detailed study of the connection between nationalism, innovation, and economic development, and argued that a stronger patent system was needed for Germany to overcome the legacy of its recent economic crisis.

The third reason for the failure of the anti-patent movement was the relative strength of the pro-patent lobby, particularly the engineering profession which formed the backbone of the V.D.I. Although most German economic philosophers were strong abolitionists, their numbers were small compared to the V.D.I. In Germany, as in the U.K., the abolitionists' failure was inevitable because they never won the support of influential associations representing inventors and engineers. Although in Germany more Chambers of Commerce favoured abolition, this was insufficient without further, more general, support from manufacturing groups. In addition, although some influential members of the Prussian government supported abolition, they did not represent the views of all State governments of the German Reich. The Government of Wurtemburg, for example, did not support the Prussian proposals, even in 1872. Dr Steinbeis, the President of the Board of Trade of Wurtemburg, told George Petre, U.K. Consul in Stuttgart, that he did not think his Government, or "the majority of practical men here" would agree to abolish patents, because "such a step would remove all incentive to the exercise of inventive talent, and would be highly injurious to industry in general".[279]

The final reason for the collapse of the abolition movement in Germany was the influence of the 1873 Vienna International Patent Congress. This issue is discussed in detail in the following Chapter, but it is relevant to note

---

Patentamt: Festschrift Herausgegeben vom Deutschen Patentamt (Munich, Carl Heymanns Verlag, 1977), 357–359.

277 Machlup, F., "Patentwesen" (1964), discussed in Heggen, A., *op.cit.* 100–101.

278 Jacobsohn, N., *Patentfrage und Krisis* (Berlin, Puttkammer und Mühlbrecht, 1876).

279 Report of George Petre, dated 15 December 1872. UNITED KINGDOM, Parliamentary Papers, *Reports by H.M. Secs of Embassy and Legation respecting Law and Practice in Foreign Countries with regard to Inventions* (1873) C. 741, vol LXVI, 483, 281.

here the large number of members of the V.D.I. who were appointed to the Executive Committee of that Congress.[280] There were also a large number of general German delegates to the Vienna Congress, who spoke favourably about patents, and particularly the concept of international assimilation of patent laws. As in the U.K., German abolitionists began to consider that international assimilation of patent laws could overcome many of their objections. For all these reasons, it became increasingly clear to the German Government after 1873 that it would be necessary to reach some form of compromise with the pro-patent lobby, and the patent law of 1877 was the eventual result.[281]

Both this Chapter and Chapter Three have demonstrated that the patent abolition movement did not succeed in countries with large economies, which led in the fields of industry and innovation, or had pretensions to do so in the future. In the U.K., France and Prussia (later Germany) individual inventors, engineers and manufacturers did not generally support abolition, and neither did their professional organisations. These groups believed that the patent system was essential to continued economic development, although there were many disparate opinions as to the theoretical justifications for the system.

The year 1873 represented a turning point in perceptions about the patent system. Until that time, debates were largely confined to the domestic arena. As a purely domestic matter, it was easier to accept proposals for abolition of patents. However, after the international patent Congress in Vienna in 1873, many began to realise that the patent laws had international significance. Instead of trying to abolish patents, it was preferable to seek international agreement for the regulation of the patent laws. Thus, the initial debates over international protection of patents had the effect of strengthening the domestic patent systems of leading industrial countries such as the U.K. and Germany. This in turn led to greater respect for the objectives of the patent laws, and a firm desire for an international agreement. The following three Chapters show how the Paris Convention of 1883 arose from these circumstances.

280 Pieper, C., *Der Erfinderschutz und die Reform der Patentgesetze. Amtlicher Bericht über den Internationalen Patent-Congress zur Erörterung der Frage des Patentschutzes. Mit einer Einleitung von Dr. C.W. Siemens F.R.S.* (Dresden, Commission der Schulbuchhandlung, 1873), 4–5.

281 See further Heggen, A., *op.cit.* 100.

CHAPTER 5

Stepping into the International Arena

The Vienna Congress 1873

> In Anbetracht der grossen Ungleichheit der bestehenden Patentgesetzgebungen und in Anbetracht der Veränderten internationalen Verkehrsbeziehungen der Jetztzeit liegt das Bedürfniss für Reformen vor und es ist dringend zu empfehlen, dass die Regierungen sobald wie möglich eine internationale Verständigung über den Patentschutz herbeizuführen suchen.[1]
>
> Resolution III of the Vienna Congress 1873

∴

In the earlier chapters of this book, it has been shown how the theoretical basis of patent protection was developed and refined in various national systems between 1790 and 1872. In the course of this discussion, particular emphasis has been placed upon explaining the contrast between the French concept of natural property rights in inventions, and the more instrumentalist approach taken in countries such as the United Kingdom and Prussia/Germany. During the 1860s and early 1870s, all these patent systems were challenged by abolition movements, but they survived because, regardless of their varying theoretical bases, they were seen to be institutions of enduring significance for inventors, manufacturers and general economic and industrial development.

---

1 Translation: "Considering the great differences in present patent administration and considering the altered international commercial relations, the necessity of reform is evident, and it is of pressing moment that Governments should endeavour to bring about an international understanding upon patent protection as soon as possible." Original German text located in Pieper, C., *Der Erfinderschutz und die Reform der Patentgesetze. Amtlicher Bericht über den Internationalen Patent-Congress zur Erörterung der Frage des Patentschutzes. Mit einer Einleitung von Dr. C.W. Siemens F.R.S.* (Dresden, Commission der Schulbuchhandlung, 1873), 260. English translation from UNITED STATES OF AMERICA, Congressional Papers, *Report of the Commissioners appointed to Revise the Statutes relating to Patents, Trade and other Marks, and Trade and Commercial Names under Act of Congress approved June 4, 1898* (1900) 56th Congress, 2nd Session, Senate document 20, 225.

 | DOI:10.1163/9789004470125_007

By the 1870s, strong support emerged for the introduction of some form of international patent protection. This Chapter commences with an explanation of why there was seen to be a need for such protection in the years before the Vienna Congress of 1873. It then examines the work of the Vienna Congress, which was the first international meeting solely devoted to patent law. This Congress was important to the development of the 1883 Paris Convention for two main reasons. First, it established a goal of international assimilation of patent laws. Second, it contributed to the collapse of the patent abolition movement in the United Kingdom and Germany.

A Early Proposals for International Patent Protection

It is commonly known that the first conference devoted to the question of international patent law was the Vienna Congress of 1873. Subsequently, one further private conference and two diplomatic conferences were held in Paris in 1878, 1880 and 1883. These Paris Conferences were directly responsible for the drafting of the Paris Convention of 1883.

It is not so well known that the earliest movement toward international protection of patent rights began in the United Kingdom. This point was acknowledged by the first Secretary of the International Bureau of Industrial Property, B. Frey-Godet, in a Report he made to the Second A.I.P.P.I. Congress in London in 1898.[2] He noted the work of the various U.K. Select Committees on Patents and the influence of individuals such as Bessemer, Armstrong and Siemens, who spoke of the need for an international understanding on patent law.[3]

Frey-Godet's opinions are consistent with the conclusions which have already been reached in this book. Chapter Two briefly discussed the possibility that international patent protection was promoted in the U.K. as early as the 1850s. In a short history of the Paris Convention and its preparatory conferences written in 1894, Carl Pieper (General Secretary and member of the Preparatory Committee of the 1873 Vienna Congress), and Paul Schmid, (who with Pieper was an influential member of the *Deutschen Vereins für den Schutz des gewerblichen Eigentums*),[4] traced the origins of the international movement to the year 1851. They asserted that it was Prince Albert, Consort of Queen

2 Frey-Godet, B. "*Comparaison du texte de la Convention et de la législation britannique correspondante*" (1898) *Annuaire de l'association Internationale pour la Protection de la Propriété Industrielle* 151–152.

3 *Ibid.*

4 See further Chapter Four for more details on this Association.

Victoria, who had first suggested international protection for inventions at the time of the Great Exhibition in London in 1851.[5] They further suggested that Prince Albert merely adopted proposals which had previously been circulating in the German States, although they did not specify in any detail the origin of such proposals.[6] Subsequently, these statements of Pieper and Schmid were adopted without question by the modern commentators Plasseraud and Savignon, who added that Prince Albert's suggestions were dismissed by the U.K. Government, because such international arrangements were not seen to be in the U.K.'s economic interest.[7]

It is doubtful whether Pieper and Schmid were correct in their statements about Prince Albert's contribution to the history of international patent protection. If Prince Albert had made such proposals in 1851, it is strange that no mention of this fact was made by any witness before the 1851, 1862–1864 or 1871–1872 Select Committees. Indeed, it was previously mentioned in Chapter Two that neither the witnesses before the 1851 Select Committee, or the Select Committee members themselves, discussed the feasibility of introducing any system of international protection of patent rights.[8] What is more likely is that Prince Albert spoke in favour of proposals to introduce temporary legal protection for inventions exhibited at the Great Exhibition in London in 1851,[9] and this was later mistakenly viewed by Pieper and Schmid as support for more comprehensive international patent protection.

During the 1850s, there were, however, indications that a small number of persons in the U.K. had turned their minds to the general issue of international patent protection. In their 1984 review of the circumstances of the U.K.'s accession to the Paris Convention, the then Comptroller-General of Patents,

5 Pieper, C., and Schmid, P., *Geschichte der internationalen Union für den Schutz des gewerblichen Eigentums sammt Konvention und Staatsverträgen* (Berlin, Deutschen Vereins für den Schutz des gewerblichen Eigentums, 1894), 6–7.

6 *Ibid.*

7 Plasseraud, Y., and Savignon, F., *Paris 1883: Genése du droit Unioniste des Brevets* (Paris, Litec, 1983), 121.

8 There is also no mention of such proposals in any books written about the 1851 Great Exhibition. One work, for example, pays great attention to the contribution of Prince Albert, as President of the Exhibition, but does not mention his desire to establish international patent protection. See: Babbage, C., *The Exposition of 1851; or, Views of the Industry, the Science, and the Government of England* (London, John Murray, 1851). See also Wood, H., *A History of the Royal Society of Arts* (London, John Murray, 1913), Chapter XVII, 401–416, concerning Prince Albert's contribution to the 1851 Exhibition.

9 This was the first time that such a scheme had been introduced anywhere in the world. See *Protection of Inventions Act* (1851) (U.K.) and *Act for extending Term of Provisional Registration of Inventions under Protection of Inventions Act 1851* (1852) (U.K.).

I.J.G. Davis, and retired Principal Examiner, J. Harrison, noted that some of the early U.K. patent law reform societies such as *The Association of Patentees and Proprietors of Patents* had a specific objective to secure international treaty arrangements for the mutual recognition of the rights of inventors.[10] However, when such societies referred to international patent protection, what they really envisaged was a series of bilateral treaties, and not a multilateral treaty such as the Paris Convention. International arrangements were also of secondary importance when compared to the compelling need for domestic patent law reform at that time.

The earliest U.K. proponent of international assimilation of patent laws was Bennet Woodcroft, Superintendent of Specifications at the U.K. Patent Office, who in 1856 was reported to have "personally visited various continental states to arrange the plans for such assimilation".[11] The precise nature of Woodcroft's proposals have not been recorded in any official documents, although Thomas Webster, U.K. delegate to the 1873 Vienna Congress, noted that Woodcroft's proposals were "the result of his own considerations and inquiries into the patent systems of other countries."[12]

While it appears that nothing immediate came of Woodcroft's proposals, in 1858 three members of the U.K. Parliament introduced a Private Members' Bill "To make Provisions to secure International Patent Right".[13] The object of this Bill was to grant to foreign patentees the rights of U.K. patentees, although the duration of the U.K. patent term was linked to the duration of any prior foreign patent. The applicability of the provisions of the Bill was also limited by the fact that only nationals of States designated by Order in Council could apply for protection, which would have probably depended upon some degree of reciprocity.[14] Although the Bill was not passed, and its proposed benefits to foreign inventors were limited, nevertheless it was an early example of U.K. concern to promote international protection of inventions.

---

10 Davis, I.J.G., and Harrison, J., "Prelude to the United Kingdom's Accession to the Paris Convention, March 17, 1884" [1984] *Industrial Property* 395, 397.

11 Pieper, C., *Der Erfinderschutz und die Reform der Patentgesetze. Amtlicher Bericht über den Internationalen Patent-Congress zur Erörterung der Frage des Patentschutzes. Mit einer Einleitung von Dr. C.W. Siemens F.R.S.* (Dresden, Commission der Schulbuchhandlung, 1873), speech of Dr G. Haseltine, member of the Preparatory Committee at 96.

12 UNITED KINGDOM, Parliamentary Papers, *Vienna Universal Exhibition, 1873; Report on the International Patent Congress by Thomas Webster, M.A., F.R.S., one of Her Majesty's Counsel* (March 1874), 376.

13 UNITED KINGDOM, *Parliamentary Papers* (1857–58) 235, vol II, 587.

14 See further, Davis, I.J.G., and Harrison, J., "Prelude to the United Kingdom's Accession to the Paris Convention, March 17, 1884" [1984] *Industrial Property* 395, 396–397.

In Chapter Three it was noted that one of the earliest verified statements in favour of some form of international patent treaty (or series of treaties) was made in a submission of the Chamber of Commerce of Huddersfield to the 1862–64 U.K. Select Committee on Patents.[15] Later, in the course of the 1871 and 1872 Select Committee Inquiries, a number of witnesses spoke in favour of international assimilation of patent laws, and the 1872 Report of the Select Committee endorsed the view that the U.K. Government should promote the international assimilation of patent laws.[16] Subsequently the U.K. Government had asked its representatives in the Colonies and foreign countries to provide information as to the patent laws operating in those territories, and whether assimilation was in any way feasible.[17] It was still receiving these reports at the time when the Vienna Congress was held in August 1873.

Apart from the contribution of the U.K. to the development of awareness about international patent rights, there were also a number of far-sighted German commentators who addressed the issue at an early date. These included C. Th. von Kleinschrod,[18] and R. Klostermann,[19] whose general contributions to the development of theories about patent protection were noted in the previous Chapter.

B The Importance of Bilateral Treaties

In his work on the origins of the *Berne Convention for the Protection of Literary and Artistic Works* 1886,[20] Professor Sam Ricketson argues that the

15 UNITED KINGDOM, Parliamentary Papers, *Report of the Commissioners appointed to Inquire into the Working of the Law Relating to Letters Patent for Inventions* (1864) 3419, vol XXIX, 321, 184.

16 See Chapter Three for more details on this point. UNITED KINGDOM, Parliamentary Papers, *Report from the Select Committee on Letters Patent; together with the Proceedings of the Committee, Minutes of Evidence, Appendix and Index* (1872) 193, vol XI, 395, v.

17 UNITED KINGDOM, Parliamentary Papers, *Reports by H.M. Secs of Embassy and Legation respecting Law and Practice in Foreign Countries with regard to Inventions* (1873) C. 741, vol LXVI, p483; UNITED KINGDOM, Parliamentary Papers, *Correspondence respecting International Arrangements for Assimilation in Law and Practice in regard to Letters Patent of Inventions* (1874) C. 999, vol LIV, 211.

18 von Kleinschrod, C. TH., *Die Internationale Patentgesetzgebung nach ihren Prinzipien nebst Vorschlägen für ein Künftiges Gemeines Deutsches Patentrecht* (Erlangen, Verlag von Ferdinand Enke, 1855).

19 Klostermann, R., *Das geistige Eigenthum an Schriften, Kunstwerken und Erfindungen nach Deutschem und internationalem Rechte* (Berlin, J. Guttentag, 1871).

20 Ricketson, S., *The Berne Convention for the protection of literary and artistic works: 1886–1986* (London, Centre for Commercial Law Studies, 1987).

development of bilateral treaties containing provisions relating to copyright was an important step which preceded the founding of the Berne Convention in 1886.[21] He states that the negotiation of bilateral treaties with precise terms under which protection was to be accorded, was considered preferable to the previous "haphazard" method of securing copyright protection on the basis of either substantive or formal reciprocity.[22] Upon the foundation of an extensive series of bilateral treaties, the Berne Convention was eventually established.

It is interesting to note that the Paris Convention of 1883 did not have the background of an extensive series of pre-existing bilateral patent treaties. As Pelletier and Vidal-Naquet state in their early, but comprehensive work on the Paris Convention,[23] before 1883, bilateral patent treaties were "*trés rares*"[24] and the only example known to the authors which specifically granted a right of "territoriality" or "national treatment" was the Austro-German treaty of 16 December 1878 (renewed in 1881 and 1891).[25] By the term "territoriality" was meant that a patent granted in one of the contracting States was only operative in that contracting State. However, the parties agreed to apply their domestic patent legislation equally to nationals and subjects of contracting States, amounting to what is now more commonly known as a right of "national treatment".[26]

It was more common for provisions relating to industrial property rights to be included in general commercial treaties, in what was known as "dispositions accessoires".[27] Yet only a few such treaties specifically referred to patents.[28]

---

21 *Ibid.* 25.

22 *Ibid.*

23 Pelletier, M., and Vidal-Naquet, E., *La Convention d'Union pour la Protection de la Propriété Industrielle du 20 mars 1883 et les Conférences de Revision Postérieures* (Paris, L. Larose, 1902).

24 Translation: "very rare". *Ibid* 4.

25 *Ibid.*

26 See further: *Ibid.* 4–5; Milhaud, L., *Des Brevets d'invention dans les Rapports Internationaux* (Paris, Larose et Forcel, 1892), 15–17.

27 Translation: "Accessory or additional provisions". Pelletier, M., and Vidal-Naquet, E., *op. cit.* 5.

28 Most commercial treaties which specifically included provisions relating to patents were negotiated at the instigation of the French Government. The most important were: Commercial Treaties between France and Italy of 1869 and 3 November 1881; Commercial Treaty between France, Prussia and the Zollverein of 2 August 1862; Commercial Treaty between France and Spain of 30 June 1876; Commercial Treaty between France and the U.S.A. of 10 April 1869; Commercial Treaty between France and the U.K. of 28 February 1882; Commercial Treaty between France and Austria of 7 November 1881. Source: Pelletier, M., and Vidal-Naquet, E., *op.cit.* 4–5; Plaisant, M., *Traité de Droit Conventionnel International concernant la Propriété Industrielle* (Paris, Sirey, 1949), 12–13.

Moreover, any reference to patent rights in commercial treaties was usually "bréve et précaire"[29] because "[p]ar suite de leur caractére secondaire, ces clauses son peu développées."[30] In most cases, the patent provisions in these bilateral treaties were based on principles of reciprocity,[31] which, combined with the constant succession of amendments to these treaties, led to much variation in the treatment of foreign nationals, and consequent uncertainty for inventors.[32]

It became increasingly clear that bilateral commercial treaties were not the most appropriate way to protect any form of industrial property right. As Pelletier and Vidal-Naquet state, "les traités de commerce sont, par leur nature, contractés pour un court laps de temps"[33] and were generally concerned to address a particular economic situation.[34] When this economic situation changed, the commercial treaty was denounced or replaced by another, which left the industrial property right holder in a difficult situation. In most cases, once the treaty had expired, the right holder was stripped of his or her rights, without access to compensation.[35]

Even in the case of trade marks and designs and models, the bilateral commercial treaty system did not offer many advantages. As with copyright, a significant number of commercial treaties included provisions relating to trade marks (and sometimes designs and models) either on the basis of "national treatment"[36] with or without the need for reciprocity,[37] or on the basis of the treatment of the "most favoured nation".[38] Before the Paris Convention of 1883, the countries which had negotiated the greatest network of commercial treaties containing provisions relating to trade marks (and sometimes also designs and models), were the United Kingdom,[39] France,[40] U.S.A.,[41] and Spain.[42]

29 Translation: "brief and uncertain".

30 Translation: "by reason of their secondary character, these clauses were little developed". Pelletier, M., and Vidal-Naquet, E., *op.cit.* 5.

31 Plaisant, M., *op.cit.* 13.

32 *Ibid.*

33 Translation: "commercial treaties are, by their nature, contracted for a short space of time".

34 Pelletier, M., and Vidal-Naquet, E., *op.cit.* 5.

35 Plaisant, M., *op.cit.* 13.

36 For example, the Treaty of Commerce between the U.K. and Austria-Hungary, dated 5 December 1876.

37 For example, the Treaty of Commerce between the U.K. and Belgium dated 23 July 1862.

38 For example the Declaration between the U.K. and Denmark of 28 November 1879.

39 See Appendix Three for details of these Treaties.

40 *Ibid.*

41 *Ibid.*

42 *Ibid.*

Bilateral commercial treaties containing provisions relating to trade marks and designs suffered the same disadvantages as those (relatively few) relating to patents, and prompted early proposals for a more unified approach. There was a growing conviction that industrial property rights were not appropriate subjects for inclusion in general commercial treaties. The Permanent Committee established by the 1878 Paris Conference[43] drafted a series of documents for submission to the French Government with the ultimate aim of establishing points of agreement to form the basis of an international treaty.[44] The second draft contained a general recommendation that "[i]l est á desirer que les stipulations de garantie réciproque de la propriété fassent l'object de conventions spéciales et indépendantes des traités de commerce."[45] The reason for this recommendation was that there were many types of commercial treaty, their duration was subject to fluctuations in political and economic circumstances, and they were liable to cease operation without warning.[46] However, it was the Committee's view that industrial property rights should be considered more permanent, they should have "une existence propre"[47] and should not be subject to sudden loss merely because a commercial treaty abruptly ceased, either through denunciation or expiration.[48] The only way this could be achieved was through "special conventions" dealing only with industrial property rights and providing some degree of uniformity and permanency.[49]

---

43 FRANCE, Ministére de L'agriculture et du Commerce, *Comptes rendus Sténographiques publiés sous les auspices du Comité Central des Congrés et Conférences et la direction de M. CH THIRION, Secrétaire du Comité, avec le concours des Bureaux des Congrés et des auteurs de Conférences: Congrés International de la Propriété Industrielle tenu á Paris du 5 au 17 Septembre 1878* (Paris 1879), 719. See Chapter Six for more details about this Conference and the work of the Permanent Committee.

44 *Ibid.* 719 "Project d'une Union Internationale pour la Protection de la Propriété Industrielle".

45 Translation: "It is to be desired that stipulations of reciprocal guarantee of industrial property are made the object of special conventions and are independent of commercial treaties." *Ibid.* 723. Note that this recommendation was consistent with the earlier Resolutions of the Paris Conference. (General Section, Resolution 3). See Appendix Five for the text of this Resolution.

46 *Ibid.*

47 Translation: "an independent existence/status" *Ibid.*

48 *Ibid.* 145. Le comte de Maillard de Marafy, President of the Consultative Committee on Foreign Legislation of the *Union des Fabricants* in Paris, noted at the 1878 Conference that since the recent denunciation of the Commercial Treaty between France and Russia, the rights of French trade mark holders in Russia had become entirely thrown into disorder.

49 *Ibid.* See also Vidal-Naquet, E., *Des Marques de Fabrique et de Commerce et du Nom Commercial en droit International* (Paris. L. Larose, 1898) Part Three.

C The Growth of the Spirit of Internationalism

During the 1850s to 1880s, there was a steady increase in what can generally be described as an awareness of potential benefits from closer international co-operation between States. Georges Maillard, a noted lawyer in Paris from 1882 and French delegate to the revision Conferences of the Paris Convention between 1911 and 1925, characterised this change in the following way:

> Dans la seconde moitié du dix-neuviéme siécle s'est manifestée entre les principaux gouvernements une tendance à substituer aux conventions particuliéres, pour le réglement des intérêts économiques dans les rapports internationaux, le systéme des conventions d'Union, c'est-à-dire des ententes liant par un même texte plusieurs nations, et pour le fonctionnement de ces ententes, des bureaux internationaux ... ont été créés.[50]

This desire to promote national interests through international conventions affected many areas of law, and was one of the major factors which lay behind the founding of the Paris Convention in 1883.

The spirit of internationalism which preceded the founding of the Paris Convention took two major paths. The first was the development of proposals for an international copyright treaty. The second was a more general interest in the law of nations which led to the establishment of treaties on various matters such as weights and measures and postal relations.

(1) *International Copyright*

Ricketson argues that as early as 1839 support can be found for a universal law of copyright.[51] In 1858 an International Congress on Literary and Artistic

50 Translation: "In the second half of the nineteenth century there was manifested between the principal governments a tendency to replace individual treaties for the regulation of economic interests in international relations, with what is known as understandings wherein many nations comply with the same text, and in relation to the functioning of such understandings, International Bureaus ... have been created." Maillard, G., *Le Bureau International de l'Union pour la Protection de la Propriété Industrielle* (undated extract from a journal entitled *Revue Internationale du Commerce, de l'industrie et de la Banque* held at W.I.P.O. Geneva), 145.

51 Ricketson, S., *The Berne Convention for the protection of literary and artistic works: 1886–1986* (London, Centre for Commercial Law Studies, 1987), 41.

Property was held in Brussels.[52] At that Congress, a number of Resolutions were passed which supported the notion of an "international recognition of property in works of literature and art".[53] The Congress also recommended that this principle ought to be admitted in all countries without the requirement of reciprocity,[54] and also favoured uniformity in the provisions of copyright legislation.[55]

It must be admitted, however, that support for an international copyright law did not necessarily translate into support for international treatment of any other area of intellectual property. In earlier Chapters, it has been shown that most patent abolitionists in the U.K. and France did not seek the repeal of copyright laws, and made a point of distinguishing between the theoretical bases of copyright and patent protection.[56] Robert Macfie, for example, wrote in 1863 that the "Copyright privilege is conceded in the absolute certainty that the grantee is their true and only originator, or first producer and creator ... To infringe copyright means to slavishly or meanly copy the work of another."[57] However, he added that "Patent-right, on the contrary, may be infringed where there is no exactness, and no copying whatever, but complete originality".[58] This amounted to a monopoly over ideas, which interfered with commercial activities.[59]

Despite his objections to the patent system, Macfie strongly supported proposals for international copyright. He was not alone in this opinion, particularly in the United Kingdom. The main reason why great support for international copyright developed in the U.K. was to allow U.K. authors access to foreign markets for their works. Macfie, for example, stated in 1869 that a system of international copyright should be established to enable U.K. authors protection for their works in the U.S. market. As Macfie explained, the "advantages to British authors and publishers of so large an extension of area is obvious. There are now in that country near forty millions of people much more

52 *Ibid.* See also Blaine, R., "On International Copyright Property in Works of Literature and the fine Arts" (1859) *Transactions of the National Association for the Promotion of Social Science* 272 (discussing the resolutions of the 1858 Brussels Conference).

53 Resolution 1 of the 1858 Brussels Congress. Blaine, R., *op.cit.* 272.

54 Resolution 2 of the 1858 Brussels Congress. Blaine, R., *op.cit.* 272.

55 Resolution 5 of the 1858 Brussels Congress. Blaine, R., *op.cit.* 272.

56 See further Chapters Three and Four.

57 Macfie, R.A., (ed), *Recent Discussions on the Abolition of Patents for Inventions in the United Kingdom, France, Germany, and the Netherlands: evidence, speeches and papers in its favour* (London, Longmans and Co, 1869), 241.

58 *Ibid.* 242.

59 *Ibid.*

able to read and to buy than our thirty millions."[60] As an American publishing house concluded in 1869, it was "high time for the passage of a well-considered International Copyright-Law, such as will wipe away from our country the reproach of what are known as 'pirated editions'."[61] The *Athenaeum* in 1869 described the American copyright legislation as amounting to " 'legalised robbery' of British copyright property in the United States"[62] and a writer in the *Law Magazine and Law Review* stated that it would be desirable to see "one law of international copyright obtaining in all civilized countries" ... but in particular it was of primary importance to "sham[e] the Americans into a copyright convention."[63]

Although the U.K. did not succeed in its attempts to negotiate a comprehensive copyright treaty with the U.S.A., disadvantage to U.K. authors in the U.S.A. focused public interest on proposals for international copyright. Ricketson states that between 1861 and 1877 there was no occasion upon which the question of copyright was raised in an international forum,[64] but this is not strictly correct. In fact, during 1873 and 1874 there were two meetings of international associations in which the question of international copyright was discussed. It is of particular note that many of the delegates to these conferences were also active participants in the discussion over national patent laws, and later helped to establish the Paris Convention.

During 1873 two Associations were formed which had a major interest in the promotion of international law. These were the Ghent Institute of International Law and the Association for the Reform and Codification of the Law of Nations.[65] Of these two Associations, it was the Association for the Reform and Codification of the Law of Nations which displayed an interest in international intellectual property protection.[66]

---

60 *Ibid.* 293.

61 Extract from the *Bookseller*, 1 May 1869. Quoted in *Ibid.* 308.

62 *Athenaeum*, 17 July 1869. Reproduced in Macfie, R.A., (ed), *op. cit.* 310.

63 "Anglo-American Copyright" (1868–9) 26 *The Law Magazine and Law Review* 49, 62. See further "International Copyright" (1872) 1 *The Law Magazine and Review* (*New Series*) 24.

64 Ricketson, S., *The Berne Convention for the protection of literary and artistic works: 1886–1986* (London, Centre for Commercial Law Studies, 1987), 45.

65 Webster, T., "Reform and Codification of the Law of Nations" (1874) 3 *The Law Magazine and Law Review* (New Series) 1016, 1017.

66 Webster explained the difference between the Ghent Institute and the Association as follows: The Ghent Institute was "limited to 50 members, men of eminence in special departments and well qualified to interpret the law; the Association assigns no limit to the number of its members; it consists of jurists, legislators and publicists, and others taking an interest in the Law of Nations, public and private." *Ibid.*

Although the Association for the Reform and Codification of the Law of Nations was a truly international body, its origins lay in the United Kingdom. At the Manchester Congress of the National Association for the Promotion of Social Science in 1866, a member, David Dudley Field, suggested the appointment of a Committee to "prepare a report on the outlines of an International Code with the view of having formed after careful revision and amendment, a complete code, to be presented to different Governments in the hope of its receiving their sanction".[67] Such a Committee was formed, and after seven years' work, "Draft Outlines of an International Code" were duly prepared and presented to the 1873 Norwich Social Science Congress.[68] It was these Outlines which gained international attention, and formed the basis of the work of the Association for the Reform and Codification of the Law of Nations which first met in Brussels in October 1873.[69]

Field, the main author of the Outlines explained the content of the work as follows:

> The work is divided into two books; one relating to peace, the other to war; or, to speak more accurately, the first treats of the relations of nations and of their members towards each other, except as they are modified by a state of war; the second treats of the modifications of those relations produced by a state of war. The first book is further subdivided into two portions, one containing the rules respecting the relations of nations to each other and to the members of other nations; the second respecting the relations of the members of each nation to the members of other nations; the first being that which is commonly known as public international law; the second, that which is known as private international law.[70]

Although the major portion of the Outlines was occupied with the essential rights of nations such as their "sovereignty, equality, perpetuity, territory, and property",[71] other provisions were inserted which impacted more clearly on the private interests of individuals.[72] Among these, "patents, trade marks,

67 Webster, T., *op.cit.* 1017.

68 Field, D., "On an International Code" (1874) 3 *The Law Magazine and Review* (New Series) 251.

69 Webster, T., *op.cit.* 1018. See further: "The Brussels Conference for the Reform and Codification of the Law of Nations" (1873) 2 *The Law Magazine and Review* (New Series) 1094.

70 Field, D., *op.cit.* 253–4.

71 *Ibid.*

72 *Ibid.*

copyrights" were mentioned as worthy of international protection. As Field explained, "[i]n respect to copyright, patent-right and trademarks, I would assert the right of the author, inventor, or first designer, as one to be held sacred and maintained in all countries."[73]

At the 1873 Brussels Conference, which was followed in August 1874 by a further Conference in Geneva, there was considerable support for the general principles contained in the Outlines. The 1873 Conference did not move beyond preliminary matters and a general espousal of the need for an International Code,[74] but it referred the questions of patents, trade marks and copyright to be dealt with at the 1874 Conference.[75] The 1874 Conference moved on to specifics, and more particularly, the proposals relating to international copyright. At the Geneva Conference, "communications were read, and discussions took place on the assimilation of Law and Procedure, and the extinction of the conflict of the Law of Nations in respect of property in intellectual labour ..." a subject which was described as being of "world-wide interest."[76] The British delegate Thomas Webster, who attended both the 1873 and 1874 Conferences, explained that the U.K. members pointed to the "noble example" of their own country, where copyright was granted to aliens without regard to nationality, provided there was first publication in some part of the United Kingdom.[77] He added that this point had been raised with the American delegates not only at the 1873 and 1874 Conferences, but also at the Vienna Patent Congress in 1873.[78] After discussions with the Americans, Webster reported that they "one and all declared that they hoped the anomaly as regard copyright to alien authors would cease ere long, and they pledged themselves to use their influence towards such an end."[79] He added that he left the 1874 Geneva Conference

73 *Ibid.*

74 Resolution 1 of the 1873 Conference stated as follows: "That an International Code, defining with all possible precision the rights and duties of nations and individuals is eminently desirable in the interests of peace, good relations, and common prosperity. Consequently, this Conference is of opinion that nothing must be neglected to arrive at the preparation and adoption of this Code. The Conference reserves the question how far the codification of the Law of Nations should be purely scientific, and how far it should be embodied in treaties or conventions formally accepted by sovereign states." "The Brussels Conference for the Reform and Codification of the Law of Nations" (1873) 2 *The Law Magazine and Review* (New Series) 1094, 1098.

75 *Ibid.* 1102.

76 Webster, T., "Reform and Codification of the Law of Nations" (1874) 3 *The Law Magazine and Law Review* (New Series) 1016, 1018.

77 *Ibid.* 1019.

78 *Ibid.* Many persons (such as Webster, and some of the Americans) apparently attended all three Conferences.

79 *Ibid.*

confident that there would be agreement for "a generous recognition of the claims and rights of all" in respect of copyright, and that the requirement of reciprocity would be "extinguished".[80]

From the above discussion, it can be seen that at an early stage, there was some overlap between the movement for international copyright and international industrial property protection. Not only did the Outlines refer to copyright, patents and trade marks, but the 1874 Conference referred to the general term "property in intellectual labour" which was a term of wider scope than merely copyright. In addition, many persons involved in the work of the 1873 and 1874 Conferences took an equal or greater interest in patent law. For example, Thomas Webster, Frédéric Passy, and Rolin Jaequemyns took an active part in the 1873 and 1874 Conferences, but they were also eminent specialists in the U.K., French and French/Belgian patent laws respectively. For these reasons, the movement towards international protection of industrial property rights should not be assessed only in the light of the international conferences of Vienna (1873), Paris (1878), Paris (1880) and Paris (1883).[81] Early theoretical discussion about copyright, the international copyright conferences, and, in addition the 1873 and 1874 meetings of the Association for the Reform and Codification of the Law of Nations, all focused attention on rights in "intellectual labour" and the need for international protection. It was clear that discussions over international copyright focused attention on international patents, and *vice versa*.

(2) *The Law of Nations*

It was not only the area of copyright and related industrial property issues which attracted calls for international protection. During the latter part of the nineteenth century there were established a number of other multilateral treaties which pre-dated the Paris Convention, but which demonstrated a growing interest in international regulation of legal issues. As Vidal-Naquet explained, the increasing development of communications technology, particularly by new means of transport and locomotion, permitted people separated by large distances to meet with relative ease.[82] Yet at the same time, this increasing internationalisation of business and communications resulted in greater legal difficulties, as the parties involved came into contact with the differing laws

80 *Ibid.*

81 Note that the Congress of Vienna (1873) was confined to patents, but the three later Paris Conferences concerned industrial property rights more generally.

82 Vidal-Naquet, E., *Des Marques de Fabrique et de Commerce et du Nom Commercial en droit International* (Paris, L. Larose, 1898), 196.

of several States. As Webster stated in 1874, "[r]ailways, steamers, telegraphs, postal arrangements, and free trade, are changing the conditions and relations of intercourse and enterprise throughout the whole world. Let law and procedure be adapted to the inevitable necessity ..."[83]

As early as 1865 a multilateral treaty was founded which attempted to deal with the legal problems which were consequent upon increased international communications. This was the International Telegraph Union (1865) which was followed by another multilateral treaty on communications in 1874, the Universal Postal Union.[84] As Roubier notes, the Universal Postal Union was strongly influential in some of the early discussions over the proposals for the Paris Convention.[85] The success of negotiations over the Postal Union appeared to engender a belief that there could be international uniformity in respect of any area of law, whether this be in relation to industrial property, undersea cables, international railways, weights and measures, monetary circulation, calculation of longitude, time, or quarantine.[86]

D More Immediate Factors: What Prompted the Vienna Congress of 1873?

The first international conference devoted primarily to the issue of patent law met in Vienna between 4 and 9 August 1873.[87] Prior to this time, patent law had been briefly considered at other international meetings such as those

---

83 Webster, T., "Reform and Codification of the Law of Nations" (1874) 3 *The Law Magazine and Review* (New Series) 1016, 1019.

84 Roubier, P., "Le droit unioniste de la propriété Industrielle" (1951) *Journal du Droit International* 676 (Part One); 1040 (Part two), 684; Pelletier, M., and Vidal-Naquet, E., *La Convention d'Union pour la Protection de la Propriété Industrielle du 20 mars 1883 et les Conférences de Revision Postérieures* (Paris, L. Larose, 1902), 7.

85 *Ibid.*

86 See further: Bouvier, H., *Essais sur la Recherche de Principes Géneraux Applicables aux unions internationales pour la protection de la propriété Industrielle* (Paris, Imprimerie Moquet, 1889), 8–19; Pelletier, M., and Vidal-Naquet, E., *op.cit.* 7; Field, D., "On an International Code" (1874) 3 *The Law Magazine and Review* (New Series), 251, 254.

87 The most complete record of the work of the Vienna Congress is contained in: Pieper, C., *Der Erfinderschutz und die Reform der Patentgesetze. Amtlicher Bericht über den Internationalen Patent-Congress zur Erörterung der Frage des Patentschutzes. Mit einer Einleitung von Dr. C.W. Siemens F.R.S.* (Dresden, Commission der Schulbuchhandlung, 1873). Other detailed commentaries on the Vienna Congress can be found in: Grothe, H., *Der Internationale Patent-Congress in Wien (4–9 August 1873)* (Berlin, Julius Springer, 1873); UNITED KINGDOM, Parliamentary Papers, *Vienna Universal Exhibition, 1873; Report on the International Patent Congress by Thomas Webster, M.A., F.R.S. one of Her Majesty's Counsel*

of the International Association for the Progress of Social Sciences and the Association for the Reform and Codification of the Law of Nations.[88] However, in none of these earlier meetings was the issue of international patent protection considered in any real detail. It is notable that patent issues were usually raised in these Associations by U.K. members, and, in the case of the International Association for the Progress of Social Science, the matter was discussed in the context of proposals to abolish the patent system. At the 1862 Brussels meeting of the Social Science Association, for example, Robert Macfie stated his objections to the patent system and proposed a scheme whereby patent protection should only be granted for a three year period, with a discretion to the State to grant a monetary sum or reward if it was shown that such a period was insufficient to recompense the inventor for his labour.[89] At the following meeting of the Social Science Association in Gand in 1863, William Armstrong proposed that patents be completely abolished, and replaced by a system of State rewards.[90] Neither of these proposals was seriously considered by the members of the Association, and there is no record that the Association ever considered the more general question of international patent rights.

What, then, were the immediate factors which prompted the Government of the Austro-Hungarian Empire to hold an International Patent Congress in Vienna in 1873? The Congress was primarily a reaction to concerns about inadequate industrial property laws expressed by U.S. inventors who were unwilling to exhibit their inventions at the 1873 Vienna International Exposition. This led the Government of Austria-Hungary to invite delegates from various countries to meet in Vienna to discuss the general question of international patent laws.

U.S. Concerns about Austro-Hungarian Patent Laws.

As Plasseraud and Savignon note,[91] the early 1870s saw the end of a difficult period in the political situation of the Austro-Hungarian Empire.[92] Both Prussian and Russian pretensions to parts of the Empire had finally been

(March 1874); and for a modern commentary see Ricketson, S., *The Paris Convention for the Protection of Industrial Property* (Oxford, Oxford University Press, 2015), 32–37.

88 The proceedings of this latter Association are discussed in Section C above.

89 ASSOCIATION INTERNATIONALE POUR LE PROGRES DES SCIENCES SOCIALES, *Annales de L'Association International pour le progrés des sciences sociales: Premiére Session (Bruxelles 1863)* (Paris, Guillaumin et Cie, 1863), 690–697.

90 Milhaud, L., *Des Brevets d'invention dans les Rapports Internationaux* (Paris, Larose et Forcel, 1892), 7.

91 Plasseraud, Y., and Savignon, F., *Paris 1883: Genése du droit Unioniste des Brevets* (Paris, Litec, 1983).

92 *Ibid.* 123.

deflected, and it was decided by the Government to hold an International Exposition as a point of focus for unity throughout the Empire, and to raise the international stature of the Empire.[93] As a result, a number of communications were made to various foreign governments to invite them to encourage their inventors to send inventions to the Exposition. On 13 January 1872, John Jay, of the American Legation in Vienna, reported to Washington that the Emperor Franz-Josef had personally met him to "express … his hope that the United States would be represented at the Grand Exhibition in Vienna, to be opened in 1873 …"[94]

Almost immediately after the plans for the Vienna Exposition were announced, U.S. inventors and manufacturers threatened that they would not send their inventions to Vienna unless the Austro-Hungarian Government afforded them sufficient legal protection. An article appeared in the *Scientific American*, dated 23 December 1871, in which it was stated that the Austrian Patent Law of 15 August 1852[95] provided most unsatisfactory protection to foreign patentees.[96] The complaint particularly related to the requirement that the manufacture of the patented article should commence in the Empire within one year from the grant of the patent, a condition with which it was often impossible for foreign inventors to comply. Even in one instance where an American patentee had been able to commence manufacturing in Vienna within the one year period, he had been threatened by Austrian officials that his proof of working was insufficient, and he was liable to lose his patent.[97] The *Scientific American* commented that:

> [Such] hindrance of the rights of foreigners gives rise to an uncomfortable suspicion that the value of Austrian patents issued to Americans and other foreigners can be easily escheated to the benefit of the Austrian

---

93 *Ibid.*

94 Jay added in his Report that "I am inclined to regard the project as one not only of importance to Austria-Hungary, in a political as well as an industrial point of view, but as one of no little interest to the United States in the opportunity it will afford, for the first time, of introducing American manufactures to the people of Eastern Europe and Western Asia, and of opening new markets which may prove of value." UNITED STATES OF AMERICA, Congressional Papers, *Papers Relating to the Foreign Relations of the United States – Message and Foreign Relations 1872*, 42nd Congress, 3rd Session, H. Ex Docs VI, part 1, 46.

95 In relation to Austrian patent laws see: Ratkowsky, M.G., *Zur Reform des Erfinder-Rechtes* (Wien, Alfred Hölder, 1870).

96 UNITED STATES OF AMERICA, Congressional Papers, *Papers Relating to the Foreign Relations of the United States – Message and Foreign Relations 1872*, 42nd Congress, 3rd Session, H. Ex Docs VI, part 1, 48.

97 *Ibid.* 49.

> public ... Under such laws it would be well for the Austrians to consider whether their invitation to the nations is not likely to be met with a contumelious refusal.[98]

The Austro-Hungarian Government seriously considered U.S. concerns about the inadequacy of its patent laws, and as a result Count Andrassy, Minister for Foreign Affairs, undertook an immediate study into the Law of 15 August 1852. He took particular note of the criticisms of the 1852 Law contained in the article in the *Scientific American,* and consulted with John Jay as to the differences between U.S. and Austro-Hungarian patent legislation.[99] Andrassy noted that "it was all-important that the genius of inventors should be encouraged and protected, and ... he ... pointed to the example of the United States as showing the wisdom of such a course, and its bearing upon the national wealth ..."[100] Jay explained in a note to Andrassy that the difficulties encountered by U.S. inventors in Austria stemmed from the "somewhat different patent policy" which had been adopted in Europe, as opposed to the U.S.[101] Although the U.S. considered the patentee to be a "public benefactor, who is to be tenderly and kindly treated",[102] in Europe, the laws of Germany, Austria and France had a different policy. In those latter countries, Jay said the patentee was viewed as a "monopolist who owes all his rights to exceptional law, and who must be jealously watched and severely restricted".[103] He argued that strict requirements as to working of patents, were a result of such policies.[104]

As a direct consequence of U.S. concerns, the Austro-Hungarian government enacted a special law "for the provisional protection of articles introduced at the Vienna Exposition."[105] This law was based on earlier laws passed by the

---

98 *Ibid.*

99 *Ibid.*

100 *Ibid.* Letter from John Jay to Washington, dated 7 March 1872.

101 Letter from John Jay to Count Andrassy, dated 17 March 1872. *Ibid.* 51.

102 *Ibid.*

103 *Ibid.* Jay's views were not correct. His assessment of the policy of the French patent system, for example, was clearly erroneous.

104 *Ibid.*

105 Appendix to letter of John Jay of the American Legation in Vienna in his Report to Washington dated 26 March 1872. UNITED STATES OF AMERICA, Congressional Papers, *Papers Relating to the Foreign Relations of the United States – Message and Foreign Relations 1872*, 42nd Congress, 3rd Session, H. Ex Docs VI, part 1, 52. The law did not come into force until 13 November 1872. The Official "Report of the Motives for the draught of the law" prepared by the Minister of Commerce, Dr Banhans, stated that the law was prompted by "anxiety" of exhibitors "in regard to possible imitation of their new inventions coming to the exposition ... and this anxiety in regard to the approaching Universal Exposition at Vienna, has already appeared in the foreign press, and especially in an article of the

United Kingdom and French governments in connection with International Expositions held in London in 1851 and 1862 and Paris in 1855 and 1867.[106] Yet, while the new Austro-Hungarian law might have afforded temporary protection to foreign exhibitors until 31 December 1873, it did not resolve the more general problem of the harsh treatment of foreign inventors under the Austro-Hungarian patent system. As Jay noted in his Report dated 21 August 1872, American exhibitors would "still be exposed to a loss of their future rights, unless they take out Austrian patents before [31 December 1873], and that this, … would involve time, trouble and expense, and that, as in many cases the inventors and manufacturers would not themselves accompany their goods, it would be for some almost an impossibility."[107] It was his view that only "mutual treaty stipulations" in respect of patent law could overcome these problems, and he considered it a "favourable moment" for the U.S. Government to enter into discussions with the Austro-Hungarian Government on the matter.[108]

As a result of Jay's Report, the U.S. Government made a "suggestion" to the Austro-Hungarian Government that the prospect of mutual treaty stipulations in connection with patent law should be studied.[109] Responding to the American "suggestion", the Austro-Hungarian Government proposed that the issue should be studied at an international congress united with the Vienna Exposition.[110] The Programme of the International Congress, prepared by Archduke Régnier, President of the Organising Commission of the Vienna Exposition and Baron de Schwarz-Senborn, Chief Manager of the Vienna Exposition, was sent to a wide range of potential participants in March 1873.[111]

New York journal, Scientific American, of the 23d December, 1871, which is of great circulation in industrial circles, wherein was expressed, in a marked manner, the want of a proper means of protection in the matter, and the danger arising thereby to foreign exhibitors." *Ibid.* 60.

106 Programme of the International Congress for the Consideration of the Question of Patent Protection. Reproduced in UNITED KINGDOM, Parliamentary Papers, *Vienna Universal Exhibition, 1873; Report on the International Patent Congress by Thomas Webster, M.A., F.R.S. one of Her Majesty's Counsel* (March 1874) 399, 401.

107 UNITED STATES OF AMERICA, Congressional Papers, *Papers Relating to the Foreign Relations of the United States – Message and Foreign Relations 1872*, 42nd Congress, 3rd Session, H. Ex Docs VI, part 1, 58.

108 *Ibid.*

109 Programme of the International Congress for the Consideration of the Question of Patent Protection. Reproduced in UNITED KINGDOM, Parliamentary Papers, *Vienna Universal Exhibition, 1873; Report on the International Patent Congress by Thomas Webster, M.A., F.R.S. one of Her Majesty's Counsel* (March 1874) 399, 401.

110 *Ibid.*

111 *Ibid.*

Not only were delegates of the governments of potential exhibitors invited, but the Organising Commission encouraged the attendance of other experts, including manufacturers, scientific artisans and political economists.[112]

The Programme of the Congress stated that the aim of the International Congress was to discuss the basic policy of patent right, bearing in mind the difference of views which had been expressed, both for and against patent protection in a number of States. Should the discussion lead to the likely conclusion that a patent system was desirable, it would then be necessary to consider the reformulation of the patent system, "corresponding to the altered international commercial relations".[113] It was further stated that "the solution of this question of reform should not be aimed separately as hitherto, by each State of the great international commercial area, but rather, that a complete solution common to all states should be accomplished by international agreement."[114] This was the most important aspect of the Vienna Congress, namely the search for fundamental principles for an international reform of patent legislation.[115]

E An Analysis of the Work of the Vienna Congress

In analysing the contribution of the Vienna Congress to the movement towards international protection of industrial property rights, there are two major issues to consider. The first is to examine the discussions and resolutions of the Congress to ascertain the attitude of the delegates towards international protection of patents. The second is to determine whether the Congress achieved its aim of promoting international assimilation of patent laws. If this aim was not achieved, were there other benefits which flowed from the work of the Congress, and which contributed to the development of the 1883 Paris Convention?

(1) *The Discussions and Resolutions of the Vienna Congress*

In examining the work of the Congress, it must be noted at the outset that it was of an unofficial nature. Although the Austro-Hungarian Government initially helped organise the Congress, wrote the Programme and advertised the meeting, the Congress itself had no official standing.[116] For this reason, there

112 *Ibid.* 401–402.
113 *Ibid.* 400.
114 *Ibid.*
115 *Ibid.* 401.
116 Penrose stated that the Congress was run under the "auspices" of the Austro-Hungarian Government. Penrose, E., *The Economics of the International Patent System* (Baltimore,

is no official report of the proceedings of the Congress. The most detailed report of its work was that provided by Carl Pieper, General Secretary of the Congress.[117] Other useful reports on the work of the Congress were provided by Thomas Webster,[118] a representative of the U.K.,[119] and Hermann Grothe, a member of the Preparatory Committee.[120]

John Hopkins Press, 1951), 45. Webster noted in his Report that there was some "misapprehension" concerning the character of the Congress, but that "accredited representatives" of various nations were present, although these were not official delegates. UNITED KINGDOM, Parliamentary Papers, *Vienna Universal Exhibition, 1873; Report on the International Patent Congress by Thomas Webster, M.A., F.R.S. one of Her Majesty's Counsel* (March 1874), 340.

117 Pieper, C., *Der Erfinderschutz und die Reform der Patentgesetze. Amtlicher Bericht über den Internationalen Patent-Congress zur Erörterung der Frage des Patentschutzes. Mit einer Einleitung von Dr. C. W. Siemens F.R.S.* (Dresden, Commission der Schulbuchhandlung, 1873).

118 UNITED KINGDOM, Parliamentary Papers, *Vienna Universal Exhibition, 1873; Report on the International Patent Congress by Thomas Webster, M.A., F.R.S. one of Her Majesty's Counsel* (March 1874).

119 Webster's Report implies that he was an accredited or "official" representative of the U.K. However, this is not strictly correct. He was authorised by the Patent Law Commission to attend the Vienna Congress and furnish a Report, but he was "not to consider himself as in any respect representing Her Majesty's Government." (*The Times*, 1 August 1873). However, on 5 August 1873 a report appeared in the "Continental Telegrams" which stated that on 4 August the Vienna Congress had opened and the "official representatives of the various Governments present were: England – Mr T. Webster." Robert Macfie enquired in the House of Commons as to whether the Under-Secretary of State for Foreign Affairs, Viscount Enfield, knew that Webster was misrepresenting his position in Vienna, and what steps would be taken to prevent further misrepresentation. Enfield stated that "he had no reason to believe that Mr Webster was officially authorized to represent the Patent Law Commission at the International Patent Law Congress at Vienna." However, further misapprehension would be avoided by Macfie calling attention to the subject in Parliament. (*The Times*, 6 August 1873).

120 Grothe, H., *Der Internationale Patent-Congress in Wien (4–9 August 1873)* (Berlin, Julius Springer, 1873). The work of the Vienna Congress is also mentioned in brief in a number of other general commentaries. These include: Pieper, C., and Schmid, P., *Geschichte der internationalen Union für den Schutz des gewerblichen Eigentums sammt Konvention und Staatsverträgen* (Berlin, Deutschen Vereins für den Schutz des gewerblichen Eigentums, 1894), 16–17; Akerman, C., *L'Obligation d'Exploiter et la Licence Obligatoire en Matiére de Brevets d'Invention* (Paris, Librairie du Recueil Sirey, 1936), 58–61; Milhaud, L., *Des Brevets d'invention dans les Rapports Internationaux* (Paris, Larose et Forcel, 1892), 8–9; Roubier, P., "Le droit unioniste de la propriété Industrielle" [1951] *Journal du Droit International* 676 (Part One), 1040 (Part Two), 728–729; Capuccio, M., "Le Convenzioni Internazionali per La Tutela della Proprietá Industriale" (1903) 3 *Rivista Tecnica* 1, 7–8; De Iturralde, T., *La Union Internacional para la proteccion de la Propriedad Industrial* (Paris, 1890), 2–3; Alexander-Katz, R., "Die Entstehung der Union und ihre Grundzüge" in Alexander-Katz, R., Lau, R., Osterrieth, A., and Wassermann, M., *Der Anschluss des Deutschen Reichs an die Internationale Union für gewerblichen Rechtsschutz* 39 (Berlin, Carl Heymann's

Apart from preliminary matters raised in the March 1873 Programme, the Austro-Hungarian Government did not have much influence in determining the content of the Congress. In fact, shortly after the Programme was circulated, the Austrian Minister of Commerce stated that he had received estimates of the cost of the Congress, and was not willing that the Government should bear the expense.[121] Consequently, all the work of practical organisation and financing of the Congress fell to private individuals, particularly those 26 who formed the Preparatory Committee.[122] Of these persons, it was reportedly Carl Pieper of Dresden, a founding member of the *Deutsche Patentschutz-Verein*,[123] who "saved" the Congress by selling subscriptions to it, particularly amongst his own countrymen.[124] This partly explains why Pieper, rather than any other person is remembered as the "founder" of the Congress,[125] and why there were so many Germans who attended. Of the 158 persons who were listed as having attended the Congress, 47 were Germans, 36 Americans, 35 Austrians, and 14

Verlag, 1902), 40–41; Osterrieth, A., and Axter, A., *Die Internationale Ubereinkunft zum Schutze des gewerblichen Eigentums vom 20 märz 1883 (Pariser Konvention) nebst den übrigen Verträgen des Deutschen Reichs über den gewerblichen Rechtsschutz* (Berlin, Carl Heymann's Verlag, 1903), 11; Beck Von Mannagetta, P., *Das Neue Osterreichische Patentrecht auf Grund des Patent-Gesetzes vom 11 Jänner 1897* (Wien, Alfred Hölder, 1897), 4; Einem Wiener Rechtsanwalte, *Zur Patent-Reform in Oesterreich: Vier Artikel der Wiener Allgemeinen Zeitung* (Wien, Alfred Hölder, 1881), 17–19; Pieper, C., *Gewerbe-und Industrieschutz: Ein Beitrag zu den Reformfragen betreffend den Patent-Muster-Marken- u. Handelsfirmen-Schutz und die Internationale Staaten-Convention* (Berlin, A. Haack, 1890), 1–4.

121 Grothe, H., *Der Internationale Patent-Congress in Wien (4–9 August 1873)* (Berlin, Julius Springer, 1873), 11.

122 UNITED KINGDOM, Parliamentary Papers, *Vienna Universal Exhibition, 1873; Report on the International Patent Congress by Thomas Webster, M.A., F.R.S. one of Her Majesty's Counsel* (March 1874), 403. Pieper also reports that J.M. Thacher of Washington served as a member of the Preparatory Committee, but Webster notes Thacher only as a "delegate" of the U.S.A. There is some discrepancy between the Pieper and Webster lists, possibly due to some members of the Preparatory Committee joining or leaving the Committee prior to the commencement of the Congress.

123 This Association operated in Germany between 1874 and 1877, seeking a uniform patent law for the whole of the German Reich. See further Chapter Four.

124 Grothe, H., *op.cit.* 11.

125 Hermann Grothe certainly states that Pieper's contribution to organising the Congress was indispensable. *Ibid.* The inaugural meeting of the International Association for the Protection of Industrial Property (A.I.P.P.I.) referred to the Vienna Congress as the initiative of Pieper. It also noted the contribution of Baron Schwarz (Vienna), Werner Siemens (Berlin), William Siemens (London), and Admiral Selwin (London). (Note that Selwin [actually Selwyn] does not appear on any list of Vienna Congress attendees!) *Annuaire de l'Association Internationale pour la Protection de la Propriété Industrielle* (Vienna, 1897), 20.

were from the United Kingdom.[126] While these were the largest contingents, there were also delegates from Hungary (6), Russia (4), Switzerland (3), France (3), Sweden (2), Italy (2), Belgium (1), Holland (1), Greece (1), Denmark (1), Canada (1), India (1), Brazil (1), and Japan (1).[127]

In furthering the objects set down in the Programme, the Preparatory Committee[128] "elaborated a series of questions", having reference to:

> the international rights of inventors – the boundaries of those rights, – whether such boundaries should be international or territorial – the granting, cost, lapsing, and duration of patents – the administration of the Patent Office, and the securing of international arrangements somewhat analogous to those existing in the case of copyright.[129]

These questions were sent in advance to registered participants, and their answers assisted the Preparatory Committee in formulating a series of Resolutions and reasons in support, which were presented for discussion at the Congress.[130]

The Congress met for five days between 4 and 8 August 1873, with a further meeting of the Executive Committee on Saturday 9 August.[131] The discussion centered upon the draft Resolutions which had been prepared by the Preparatory Committee. It soon became apparent that the majority of the delegates to the Congress, especially the Germans and Austrians, wholly accepted the opinions expressed in the draft Resolutions.

The first Resolution adopted by the Congress was that:

126 Pieper, C., *Der Erfinderschutz und die Reform der Patentgesetze. Amtlicher Bericht über den Internationalen Patent-Congress zur Erörterung der Frage des Patentschutzes. Mit einer Einleitung von Dr. C.W. Siemens F.R.S.* (Dresden, Commission der Schulbuchhandlung, 1873). Statistics derived from the list of attendees at 263–267.

127 *Ibid.*

128 For the composition of the Preparatory Committee see Appendix Four.

129 UNITED KINGDOM, Parliamentary Papers, *Vienna Universal Exhibition, 1873; Report on the International Patent Congress by Thomas Webster, M.A., F.R.S. one of Her Majesty's Counsel* (March 1874), 342.

130 *Ibid.* 342. This is similar to the approach still used today by organisations such as *The International Association for the Protection of Industrial Property* (A.I.P.P.I.).

131 Most of the places in the Executive Committee were given to members of the Preparatory Committee. As a mark of honour, Baron von Schwarz-Senborn, the Director-General of the Vienna Exposition, was made Honorary President of the Congress, and William Siemens was elected President. *Ibid.*

> The protection of inventions should be guaranteed by the laws of all civilised nations.[132]

There then followed a series of seven reasons justifying this statement. These justifications were as follows:

(a) The sense of right among civilised nations demands the legal protection of intellectual work.
(b) This protection affords, under the condition of a complete specification and publication of the invention, the only practical and effective means of introducing new technical methods without loss of time, and in a reliable manner, to the general knowledge of the public.
(c) The protection of invention renders the labour of the inventor remunerative, and induces thereby competent men to devote time and means to the introduction and practical application of new and useful technical methods and improvements, and attracts capital from abroad, which, in the absence of patent protection, will find means of secure investment elsewhere.
(d) By the obligatory complete publication of the patented invention, the great sacrifice of time and of money, which the technical application would otherwise impose upon the industry of all countries, will be considerably lessened.
(e) By the protection of inventions, secrecy of manufacture, which is one of the greatest enemies of industrial progress, will lose its chief support.
(f) Great injury will be inflicted upon countries which have no rational patent laws, by the native inventive talent emigrating to more congenial countries, where their labour is legally protected.
(g) Experience shows that the holder of a patent will make the most effectual exertions for a speedy introduction of his invention.[133]

These were not only instrumentalist justifications for the patent system, but also appeared to endorse the French concept of natural property rights in inventions.

To say that there was a "sense of right" that inventions should be legally protected, immediately raised for many delegates the notion of natural property

132 *Ibid.* 343.
133 *Ibid.* 343–344.

rights in inventions, and led to considerable debate. A small number (6 delegates)[134] were unwilling to accept the necessity for any patent system, and were particularly hostile to the concept of a natural property right in inventions. The four delegates who spoke at length against the patent system[135] argued that an invention should be considered as abandoned to the public once it was published, and that knowledge should be considered free for all to use. The only form of protection for inventions should be that of secrecy, and once secrecy was lost, there should be no further legal protection. Traun and Marchet also alleged that patents were in violation of the principles of free trade, and that as a monopoly, a patent right restrained freedom or liberty in lawful trades.[136]

Nevertheless, the great majority of the delegates supported the whole of the first Resolution, including the implication that inventions were entitled to protection as natural property rights. As has been discussed in earlier Chapters, the concept of natural property rights in inventions had never before received much support in either Germany or the United Kingdom. Yet, at the Vienna Congress, delegates such as Robert Collyer of the Inventor's Institute of London, George Haseltine, a patent agent in London,[137] and Dr Rosenthal, a representative of the *Vereins Deutscher Ingenieure,* were adamant than an invention represented a natural and absolute property right.[138] Collyer, for example, stated that "inventors have a natural right to demand protection of the production of their faculties".[139] Haseltine later added that he "believe[d] in the natural rights of invention and [thought] it a duty of every government to protect those rights aside from any question of state interests."[140] When Rosenthal referred to the concept of the "natürlichen Rechtes"[141] of inventors, his speech was received

---

134 Six delegates voted against the First Resolution. These were: Heinrich Traun, a manufacturer in Hamburg; C.O. Ohm, a trader in Pest; Joseph Görz, a civil engineer in Mainz; F.X. Neumann, Professor in Vienna; F.W. Exner, Professor in Mariabrunn and Gustav Marchet, Professor in Mariabrunn. However, 74 delegates supported the Resolution. Pieper, C., *Der Erfinderschutz und die Reform der Patentgesetze. Amtlicher Bericht über den Internationalen Patent-Congress zur Erörterung der Frage des Patentschutzes. Mit einer Einleitung von Dr. C.W. Siemens F.R.S.* (Dresden, Commission der Schulbuchhandlung, 1873), 107–108.

135 *Ibid.* Neumann (at 44 and 81); Marchet (at 50); Traun (at 65) and Görz (at 91).

136 *Ibid.*

137 Note that Haseltine was a U.S. citizen, who worked as a patent agent in London.

138 Pieper, C., *Der Erfinderschutz und die Reform der Patentgesetze. Amtlicher Bericht über den Internationalen Patent-Congress zur Erörterung der Frage des Patentschutzes. Mit einer Einleitung von Dr. C.W. Siemens F.R.S.* (Dresden, Commission der Schulbuchhandlung, 1873), 46 (Collyer); 94 (Rosenthal); 96 (Haseltine).

139 *Ibid.* 46.

140 *Ibid.* 97.

141 Translation: "natural rights". *Ibid.* 95.

with shouts of approval.[142] Many other speakers referred to the recognition of inventors' rights as a question of morality, which the State must protect.[143] As Webster notes in his Report, the majority view was that the "recognition of property in inventions was said to be analogous to the recognition of property in the first occupier or first finder …".[144]

In parallel with the natural property rights theory, the Congress also supported a number of the traditional instrumentalist justifications for the patent system. The second and fourth points of the first Resolution referred to usefulness of the patent specification as an effective means of introducing new technical methods to the general public. Upon these points there was little discussion, although the opportunity arose to condemn the delay of the U.S. Patent Office in publishing specifications.[145]

There was some discussion of the third point, namely that a patent rewards the inventor, acts as a stimulant to invention and induces capital investment in new technology. To support this point, a number of delegates referred to the "large proportion of capital embarked in the industrial arts in the United States" because of the security afforded by the patent system.[146] In addition, reference was made to the evidence which had been given before the 1871–1872 U.K. Select Committees on Patents that many foreigners were attracted to the U.S.A. and the U.K. because of their patent systems.[147] Particular reference was made to the case of William Siemens, the President of the Congress, who, with Bessemer, were examples of two Germans who had left their native country because of inadequate patent protection.[148] This argument was also reinforced by Point (f) of the first Resolution.

The fifth and seventh points of the first Resolution referred to secrecy as one of the greatest enemies of industrial progress. To a large degree, evidence

---

142 "(Bravo! Bravo!)" appears in the records. *Ibid.*

143 See for example, *Ibid.* 84 (Franz von Rosas of Vienna); 55 (Alexander Friedmann, engineer in Vienna); 69 (Eduard Könyei, advocate in Pest); 75 (Professor Klostermann of Bonn); 57 (Dr Jannasch of Proskau); 64 (Dr Ratkowsky of Vienna).

144 UNITED KINGDOM, Parliamentary Papers, *Vienna Universal Exhibition, 1873; Report on the International Patent Congress by Thomas Webster, M.A., F.R.S. one of Her Majesty's Counsel* (March 1874), 344.

145 *Ibid.* 346.

146 *Ibid.* 347. See for particular examples: Pieper, C., *Der Erfinderschutz und die Reform der Patentgesetze. Amtlicher Bericht über den Internationalen Patent-Congress zur Erörterung der Frage des Patentschutzes. Mit einer Einleitung von Dr. C.W. Siemens F.R.S.* (Dresden, Commission der Schulbuchhandlung, 1873), 80 (Max Hoffmann-Linke, manufacturer in Leipzig).

147 *Ibid.* 96–98 (Haseltine).

148 *Ibid.*

in support of this was again provided by the reports of the 1871 and 1872 U.K. Select Committees on Patents. As Webster explains, the Congress referred to the "consequences of secret manufacture in retarding progress, and in maintaining prices, as contrasted with the effect of open manufacture under a patent system."[149] The Congress resolved that where a patent system operates, an inventor is induced to make the most effectual exertions for a speedy introduction of the invention.[150]

While the first Resolution concerned the theoretical justifications for a patent system, the second Resolution dealt with the principles upon which an "effective and useful patent law should be based". The text finally adopted by the Congress was as follows:

(a) Only the inventor himself, or his legal representative, should be entitled to a patent.
(b) A patent should not be refused to a foreigner.
(c) It is advisable, in carrying out these principles, to introduce a system of preliminary examination.
(d) A patent should be granted either for a term of fifteen years or be permitted to be extended to such a term.
(e) Simultaneously with the issue of a patent a complete publication of the same should take place, rendering the technical application of the invention possible.
(f) The expense of obtaining a patent should be moderate, but in the interest of the inventor a progressive scale of fees should be established, enabling him to abandon when convenient, a useless patent.
(g) Facilities should be given by a well-organized patent office to obtain in an easy manner the specification of a patent, as well as to ascertain what patents are still in force.
(h) It is advisable to establish legal rules, according to which the patentee should be induced, in cases in which the public interest may require it, to allow the use of his invention to all suitable applicants for an adequate compensation.
(i) The non-application of an invention in one country shall not involve the forfeiture of the patent if the patented invention has been carried into practice at all, and if it has been possible for the inhabitants of such country to purchase and make use of the invention.

---

149 UNITED KINGDOM, Parliamentary Papers, *Vienna Universal Exhibition, 1873; Report on the International Patent Congress by Thomas Webster, M.A., F.R.S. one of Her Majesty's Counsel* (March 1874), 347.

150 *Ibid.* 349.

(j) In all other respects, and particularly as regards the proceedings in the granting of patents, the congress refers to the English, American and Belgian patent laws, and to the draft of a patent law prepared for Germany by the society of German engineers.[151]

Of these ten points, numbers (a), (b), (h) and (i) were particularly relevant to the question of international patent protection.

In stating that only the true inventor or his legal representative should be entitled to a patent, the Congress was referring to the historic practice in countries such as the U.K. where patents were still granted to importers of inventions, whether or not those persons were the original inventors.[152] Since Germans and Austrians formed over one-half of the delegates to the Congress, it is unsurprising that the U.K. system of patents of importation should have been severely criticised. Both Germany and Austria required universal novelty in any patented invention, and would not have registered a patent for an invention merely imported from another country. The Congress was pleased to note that the 1871–1872 U.K. Select Committees on Patents had recommended the abolition of patents of importation,[153] and thought that other countries should be encouraged to abolish this category of patent. As Webster notes, granting patents only to the first and true inventor was a matter which should become "the law and practice in all countries ... and is, in fact, essential to the establishment of any system deserving the name of international."[154] J.M. Thacher, Assistant-Commissioner of Patents in Washington, argued that the "natural right belongs to the inventor only, and if he neglects to secure it for any reason whatever, it reverts to the public, and should become a part of the public domain."[155]

---

151 Translation derived from: UNITED STATES OF AMERICA, Congressional Papers, *Report of the Commissioners appointed to Revise the Statutes relating to Patents, Trade and other Marks, and Trade and Commercial Names under Act of Congress approved June 4, 1898* (1900) 56th Congress, 2nd Session, Senate document 20, 224.

152 UNITED KINGDOM, Parliamentary Papers, *Vienna Universal Exhibition, 1873; Report on the International Patent Congress by Thomas Webster, M.A., F.R.S. one of Her Majesty's Counsel* (March 1874), 350–351.

153 Grothe, H., *Der Internationale Patent-Congress in Wien (4–9 August 1873)* (Berlin, Julius Springer, 1873), 49.

154 UNITED KINGDOM, Parliamentary Papers, *Vienna Universal Exhibition, 1873; Report on the International Patent Congress by Thomas Webster, M.A., F.R.S. one of Her Majesty's Counsel* (March 1874), 351.

155 Pieper, C., *Der Erfinderschutz und die Reform der Patentgesetze. Amtlicher Bericht über den Internationalen Patent-Congress zur Erörterung der Frage des Patentschutzes. Mit einer*

There was also little debate over the proposal that patents should be granted to foreigners as well as nationals. By 1873, most of the major nations such as the U.K., France, the U.S.A., Prussia, Belgium and Austria-Hungary, granted patents to foreigners, but this was not the case in some less-developed countries. Webster, for example, refers to the smaller German States of Saxony, Bavaria and Wurtemburg as requiring all patentees to be nationals.[156]

Probably the most controversial resolution of the Congress was that which allowed patented inventions to be used by "all suitable applicants for an adequate compensation". This was effectively an approval of schemes of compulsory licensing. Penrose later commented that:

> [This] principle was not again to be accepted by an international conference for 50 years but the anti-patent movement in the 19th century had created such an awareness of the possible monopolistic and restrictive effects of the patent system that some limitation of the patent monopoly had to be conceded by the patent advocates.[157]

The main reason why the proposals relating to compulsory licensing were adopted by a large majority at the Vienna Congress,[158] (but not at the later Paris Conferences), was undoubtedly the strong influence of the German delegates in Vienna. Klostermann noted that the proposals relating to compulsory licensing were primarily suggested in order to gain more acceptance for the patent system in Germany,[159] (which would have thwarted von Bismarck's policies of abolition and promoted the interests of the *Deutsche Patentschutz Verein*). Klostermann realised that the proposals would be unacceptable to most of the U.S. delegates, but urged them to support the proposals for the sake of the future of the German patent system. He explained that:

> We Germans do not see any other way to carry out our intentions in Germany, but by accepting the principle of granting licences in some way.

Einleitung von Dr. C.W. Siemens F.R.S. (Dresden, Commission der Schulbuchhandlung, 1873), 190–191.

156 UNITED KINGDOM, Parliamentary Papers, *Vienna Universal Exhibition, 1873; Report on the International Patent Congress by Thomas Webster, M.A., F.R.S. one of Her Majesty's Counsel* (March 1874), 352.

157 Penrose, E., *The Economics of the International Patent System* (Baltimore, John Hopkins Press, 1951), 47.

158 The proposal was adopted with 42 votes in favour, and 17 against. Pieper, C., *Der Erfinderschutz und die Reform der Patentgesetze etc.*, at 211.

159 *Ibid.* 165 (Klostermann).

> We do not think that it is indispensable to accept the same principle in every other country as a home rule. But as for the international character, which we want to give to the patent system, and in the special interests of Germany this amendment, in our opinion, is necessary.[160]

Other Germans such as André,[161] Werner Siemens,[162] Hoffmann,[163] and Marchet,[164] agreed with Klostermann that compulsory licensing was essential. In particular, Marchet, an opponent of the patent system, raised an argument common in Germany that patents were an unjust monopoly, and were obstructive of industrial progress, but that a system of compulsory licensing could go some way towards lessening the evil.[165]

The Congress was also influenced by the evidence presented concerning the attitude of U.K. patent abolitionists towards compulsory licensing. A letter was read to the Congress from Robert Macfie, who stated that he firmly supported compulsory licensing because it resulted in the "abolition of the monopoly element in grants of patents."[166] Webster told the Congress that:

> [The] principle of compulsory license had been accepted by Sir W. Armstrong and Mr Macfie as going a long way to mitigate their objections to patents and he thought it would be expedient to close with this concession, which would do away with the objection urged against patents as an obstruction.[167]

He added that compulsory licensing would not harm inventors, but only "capitalists". This was because most cases of obstruction were caused by "capitalists" who bought up patents to prevent the invention being worked.[168] Webster acknowledged that this did not seem to be a problem in the U.S.A. Therefore, he suggested that the U.S. delegates, "having little or no experience of the evil, did not appreciate the importance of the remedy."[169]

---

160 *Ibid.*
161 *Ibid.* 148.
162 *Ibid.* 153, 200.
163 *Ibid.* 179.
164 *Ibid.* 182.
165 *Ibid.*
166 *Ibid.* 158.
167 *Ibid.* 167.
168 *Ibid.*
169 *Ibid.*

While Webster's report notes that the proposal for compulsory licensing "was opposed by a considerable section of the representatives from the United States",[170] not every American was of this view. Professor Blake of Yale stated that:

> Although all legislations ought always rather to protect the inventor instead of limiting his right, it is expedient to adopt measures, by which the patentee must in the public interest permit suitable persons the use of his invention for an adequate consideration, but not before the expiration of the first three years of the patent.[171]

The major difference between Blake's opinion, and that of most other U.S. delegates at the Congress, was that he did not see that the grant of compulsory licences in any way interfered with the ability of the patentee to exploit his invention.[172] Hall, of Cincinatti, also supported compulsory licensing, but on the grounds that patents were too obstructive.[173] He mentioned that he knew of a case where a patent was held with such "strict exclusiveness" that 100 inventors were refused a licence to work it, and consequently the progress of manufacture had been retarded.[174]

The majority view of the Americans, however, was that the inventor had "natural rights", and these rights were the same as "property in land or houses".[175] They argued that the proposals relating to compulsory licensing were "inconsistent with what the Congress had already decided in and by the first resolution; that to give a patent and then compulsorily to abstract a part was inconsistent and unjust".[176] Professor Wheeler, of Chicago, for example, in rejecting the proposal, stated that "the property of an inventor should be recognised as any other property, as any other right".[177] This view was also supported by Dr Raymond of New York,[178] and Albin Warth of

---

170 UNITED KINGDOM, Parliamentary Papers, *Vienna Universal Exhibition, 1873; Report on the International Patent Congress by Thomas Webster, M.A., F.R.S. one of Her Majesty's Counsel* (March 1874), 358.

171 Pieper, C., *Der Erfinderschutz und die Reform der Patentgesetze etc.*, at 166.

172 *Ibid.*

173 *Ibid.* 202. Only Hall's surname is provided in Pieper's records.

174 *Ibid.*

175 UNITED KINGDOM, Parliamentary Papers, *Vienna Universal Exhibition, 1873; Report on the International Patent Congress by Thomas Webster, M.A., F.R.S. one of Her Majesty's Counsel* (March 1874), 358.

176 *Ibid.*

177 This statement was received with "Cheers". Pieper, C., *Der Erfinderschutz und die Reform der Patentgesetze etc.*, at 151.

178 *Ibid.* 203.

Stapleton.[179]

The American view received some support from other delegates. A U.K. delegate, Robert Collyer, opposed his compatriot Webster in speaking strongly against the compulsory licensing proposal. Collyer, the "honorary Commissioner of the Inventors Institute of Great Britain",[180] said that if "any proposition is well calculated to undermine, to destroy the ambition and the perseverance of the inventor, it is that of the knowledge, that he is labouring to benefit those, who would take the results of his exertions for the payment of some paltry remuneration."[181] He further argued that compulsory licenses meant that the inventor would be at the mercy of "those who can ruin him", and it would be "moral suicide" to adopt such a provision in a patent system.[182] Not only was such a proposal morally unjust. It also lacked practical usefulness. Even though some alleged that compulsory licensing would appease the opponents of the patent system, Collyer argued that it was of doubtful practicality because of the need to permit the inventor at least five years to practise and perfect the invention before any compulsory licence could be granted.[183] It was also unsurprising that the sole Belgian delegate, Gustav Grave of Brussels, should have joined the Americans in rejecting the compulsory licensing proposal in strongly worded terms.[184] This was because the Belgian Patent Law of 24 May 1854 had been heavily influenced by French theories of natural property rights in inventions, and such theories did not allow for compulsory licensing.[185]

In comparison with the issue of compulsory licensing, there was little debate on the proposal that the non-working of an invention in one country should not automatically cause the forfeiture of the patent. The Congress resolved that forfeiture should not occur if the patented invention had been worked in one country, and goods made under the patent were exported to other countries to satisfy the needs of the inhabitants. Forfeiture for non-working was a feature of most patent systems other than the U.K. or the U.S.A., and it caused much disaffection amongst inventors.[186] Webster notes in his Report that:

179 *Ibid.* 145, 176.

180 *Ibid.* 173.

181 *Ibid.* 172.

182 *Ibid.*

183 *Ibid.*

184 *Ibid.* 179. The Americans also received the support of two Austrians of lesser note, the engineer Alexander Friedmann of Vienna and Baron von Gilgenheimb of Weidenau. *Ibid.* 144, 146.

185 See Chapter One, Section C, for further details about the enactment of this law.

186 For example, U.S. inventors had earlier criticised such a provision in the Austrian patent legislation. This had been one of the factors leading to the Vienna Congress in 1873.

> "[T]he dissatisfaction as to the operation of this condition of forfeiture was universal; no one was found to approve or support it, its abandonment would be necessary if the establishment of any international system of patents is to be agreed upon ... [Amongst the members of the Congress, the] opinion as to the inefficacy of such a condition to secure the establishment of manufactures in any country was equally unanimous."[187]

The third, and final, Resolution of the Congress was as follows:

> Considering the great differences in present patent administration and considering the altered international commercial relations, the necessity of reform is evident, and it is of pressing moment that Governments should endeavour to bring about an international understanding upon patent protection as soon as possible.[188]

Although the original intention of the members of the Preparatory Committee was to promote international unification of patent laws, the debates which took place at the Congress made it apparent that such unification would be almost impossible to achieve. The question of compulsory licensing illustrated a lack of agreement in at least one important area, and it was considered that an international patent law would be even more difficult to achieve than an international copyright law.[189] For this reason, the Congress decided that the more achievable plan was "to assimilate as closely as possible the law, practice and procedure of countries by a system founded on the principles indicated in the resolutions of the Congress".[190] As J.M. Thatcher, Assistant-Commissioner of Patents in Washington explained, it would be inadvisable and impractical

187 UNITED KINGDOM, Parliamentary Papers, *Vienna Universal Exhibition, 1873; Report on the International Patent Congress by Thomas Webster, M.A., F.R.S. one of Her Majesty's Counsel* (March 1874), 361.

188 English translation in UNITED STATES OF AMERICA, Congressional Papers, *Report of the Commissioners appointed to Revise the Statutes relating to Patents, Trade and other Marks, and Trade and Commercial Names under Act of Congress approved June 4, 1898* (1900) 56th Congress, 2nd Session, Senate document 20, 225.

189 UNITED KINGDOM, Parliamentary Papers, *Vienna Universal Exhibition, 1873; Report on the International Patent Congress by Thomas Webster, M.A., F.R.S. one of Her Majesty's Counsel* (March 1874), 376. See also Pieper, C., *Der Erfinderschutz und die Reform der Patentgesetze etc.*, von Baumhauer at 234; Werner Siemens at 234; Friedmann at 235; Pieper at 237, 241; and Hartig at 241.

190 UNITED KINGDOM, Parliamentary Papers, *Vienna Universal Exhibition, 1873; Report on the International Patent Congress by Thomas Webster, M.A., F.R.S. one of Her Majesty's Counsel* (March 1874), 376.

to take the principles of one particular patent system, and attempt to engraft them onto the systems of other countries.[191] However, it was thought that if the Congress was to recommend a few "principles as the proper basis for patent legislation", then these principles "sent forth to the world with the endorsement of [the] Congress" could eventually lead to important reforms.[192] Thus, the Congress aimed for the harmonisation of important, general principles of patent law, but considered that how this was actually achieved in practice "should be left to the different countries to work out for themselves."[193] The Congress did not envisage the introduction of any form of multilateral treaty on the subject of patent law.

The final task of the Congress was to establish a Permanent Executive Committee to continue its work and ensure that the Resolutions of the Congress were made known as widely as possible.[194] The Permanent Executive Committee was also to appoint the time and place of the next meeting of the International Congress, which was agreed would be held in Philadelphia at the time of the 1876 Centennial Exhibition.[195]

(2) *The Consequences of the Work of the Vienna Congress*

What were the consequences of the Vienna Congress? Was the work of the Congress accepted by a wider audience and did it promote the harmonisation of domestic patent laws? In answering these questions, it should be noted that the reaction to the Congress varied from one country to another. In Germany, the U.K. and the U.S.A., the Congress had some influence upon domestic patent law reform, but there was certainly no evidence of harmonisation. The Congress had no effect in France. Of more significance was the fact that in Germany and the U.K., the Congress largely put an end to the patent abolition movements. In this way, it removed a major obstacle to an international patent treaty.

---

191 Pieper, C., *Der Erfinderschutz und die Reform der Patentgesetze etc.*, at 197.

192 *Ibid.*

193 *Ibid.* (Thacher) This statement was met with "cheers".

194 The members of the Preparatory Committee formed the Permanent Executive Committee. UNITED KINGDOM, Parliamentary Papers, *Vienna Universal Exhibition, 1873; Report on the International Patent Congress by Thomas Webster, M.A., F.R.S. one of Her Majesty's Counsel* (March 1874), 377.

195 Pieper, C., *Der Erfinderschutz und die Reform der Patentgesetze etc.*, at 253.

(i) France

There is no evidence that the work of the Vienna Congress had any influence in France. As noted above, there were only 3 delegates at the Congress who gave their address as being in France, namely Francis Hoffmann, an engineer in Plancher-les Mines,[196] B.B. Hotchkiss, a factory owner in Paris,[197] and de Walcher-Moltheim, Austro-Hungarian Consul-General in Paris.[198] As Akerman commented, the French were "trés faiblement représenté"[199] at the Congress, a point also made by Franz Edlen von Rosas of the Austrian Finance Ministry.[200] However, very little explanation is ever given as to why no influential French person took part.

It is known that Louis Wolowski was invited to the Congress, but due to other pressing engagements he sent a letter stating his inability to attend.[201] Plasseraud and Savignon suggest that there may have been political tensions which prevented the French from taking part in the Congress, particularly because, as was noted above, the Congress was effectively a German project, run from Berlin, and only physically located in Vienna.[202] Combaldieu, also agrees with Plasseraud and Savignon, stating that after France's military defeat by Prussia in the Franco-Prussian War of 1870–71, "latent nationalist fever continued to mount under cover and broke out on the surface each time it was thought that 'the hand of Germany' was to be seen in some matter of an international nature."[203] Writing in 1877, Charles Letort noted that the relationship between Germany and France had never been good, and that the two countries habitually disagreed on most matters.[204] Yet he was ignorant of the reasons why France had not been represented at the Congress, and had no

196 Hoffmann's name suggests he was originally of Germanic origin.

197 Hotchkiss is also not a typical French name.

198 De Walcher-Moltheim was not French. He was a diplomat of the Austro-Hungarian government, stationed in Paris, possibly on leave in Vienna at the time of the Congress.

199 Translation: "very feebly represented". Akerman, C., *L'Obligation d'Exploiter et la Licence Obligatoire en Matiére de Brevets d'Invention* (Paris, Librairie du Recueil Sirey, 1936), 58.

200 Von Rosas, F.E., *Das Industrielle Eigenthum (Privilegien-, Marken- und Musterschutz). Bericht uber die Verhandlungen des Internationalen Congresses zu Paris 1878* (Wien, Verlag der Handels-und Gewerbekammer, 1878), 1.

201 Pieper, C., *Der Erfinderschutz und die Reform der Patentgesetze etc.,* at 20. Wolowski is called "Wolowsky" in the Records.

202 Plasseraud, Y., and Savignon, F., *Paris 1883: Genése du droit Unioniste des Brevets* (Paris, Litec, 1983), 143.

203 Combaldieu, J.C., "The Ratification of the Paris Convention by France and the Reactions Thereto" [1984] *Industrial Property* 374, 375.

204 Letort, C., "Une Législation Internationale sur les Brevets d'invention" *L'économiste Français,* 29 September 1877, 389.

evidence to prove that hostility towards Germans was the cause.[205] He added that the work of the Congress remained unknown in France until Charles Thirion[206] published a translation of Webster's Report shortly before the 1878 Paris Conference.[207] Leaving aside the reasons for France's non-attendance at the Vienna Congress, it cannot be said that the Congress had any direct effect in France.

(ii) The United Kingdom

Unlike France, the U.K. was relatively well represented at the Vienna Congress, with 14 delegates. However, a number of persons who had been active in the cause of patent law reform did not attend. The patent abolitionist Robert Macfie, for example, was invited by the Congress organisers,[208] but he excused himself on the grounds of so-called "decisive" engagements.[209] It is likely that Macfie did not attend because the U.K. Government would not authorise him as one of its representatives. His early interest in the Congress was great. In April 1873 he asked the Under-Secretary of State for Foreign Affairs "whether Her Majesty's Government would be represented at that conference",[210] which suggested that he was putting himself forward for the position. When Webster was chosen to represent the U.K. instead of him, it explains his later outburst against Webster's conduct at the Congress, and also why he refused to attend the Congress as a private delegate.[211] Sir William Armstrong, another strong critic of the patent system, also failed to attend.

The Vienna Congress had a significant influence upon proposals for patent law reform in the United Kingdom. Davis and Harrison have noted how the Vienna Congress "was regarded with enthusiasm by some members of the U.K. patent reform groups."[212] This was shown in a series of articles written at the time in the weekly publication, *Engineering*.[213] An extract from one of the articles stated that:

---

205 *Ibid.*

206 Thirion was a civil engineer in Paris, a patent attorney and later became Secretary of the Central Committee organising the Paris Universal Exposition in 1878.

207 Letort, C., *op.cit.* 389.

208 UNITED KINGDOM, Parliamentary Papers, *Vienna Universal Exhibition, 1873; Report on the International Patent Congress by Thomas Webster, M.A., F.R.S. one of Her Majesty's Counsel* (March 1874), 340.

209 Pieper, C., *Der Erfinderschutz und die Reform der Patentgesetze etc.*, at 156.

210 *The Times,* 8 April 1873.

211 *The Times,* 6 August 1873.

212 Davis, I.J.G., and Harrison, J., "Prelude to the United Kingdom's Accession to the Paris Convention, March 17, 1884" [1984] *Industrial Property* 395, 397.

213 *Ibid.*

> [T]he protection of the rights of inventors need new forms corresponding to altered commercial relations, and that the solution of this question of reform should not be aimed at separately, as hitherto, by each unit of the great commercial community, but rather that a complete solution, common to all countries, should be accomplished by international agreement.[214]

The article then went on to praise the ability of the persons who served as delegates to the Congress, stating they were "all men of high standing and reputation in their respective spheres of life, from various countries".[215]

Although the U.K. delegates were clearly outnumbered by the German-speaking group, Webster, Collyer and Haseltine made a large contribution to the work of the Congress. Overall, Webster's Report suggests that the U.K. delegates were happy with the outcome, and that the Resolutions adopted generally corresponded with the U.K. position. While there was little discussion of the Congress in the mainstream press, the U.K. Government used the Recommendations of the 1872 Select Committee on Patents, combined with the Resolutions of the Vienna Congress, to form the basis of a patent law reform Bill which was introduced into the House of Lords in February 1875. As the Lord Chancellor, Lord Cairns, explained, when introducing the Bill, the Government was of the view that the Resolutions of the Congress contained "the great landmarks as to the direction in which any alteration of the laws as to patents ought to proceed."[216] The Government had therefore decided that "some response should be given" and a Bill was formed which included important provisions accepted at the Congress, such as preliminary examinations and compulsory licensing.[217] In response to the wider question of whether there should be some "international system of patent rights", the Lord Chancellor said that the Government did not understand what was meant by this.[218] If an international system included "an international patent" recognised in all member States, this would be an impossible goal.[219] In essence, the patentee would

---

214 *Ibid.*

215 *Ibid.*

216 *The Times*, 13 February 1875. See also UNITED KINGDOM, Parliamentary Papers, *Bill, intituled, Act for consolidating Acts relating to Letters Patent for Inventions* (1875) 133, vol IV, 491.

217 *Ibid.*

218 *Ibid.*

219 *Ibid.* The *European Patent Convention* of 1973 and the *Patent Cooperation Treaty* of 1970 (as amended) establish the ability to make an international application for a series of patents throughout the member States, but these are not truly "international" patents, because the separate requirements of patentability in each country must still be satisfied. Only the *Community Patent Convention* of 1975 establishes an "international" patent within the

have to prove that the invention was absolutely novel in all parts of the world in order to gain such a patent, which the Lord Chancellor thought "would be impossible for any one to do".[220]

The 1875 Bill was never passed, largely because of deep division over the issue of examination. As Davis and Harrison note, there "was strong feeling – based in part on the experience of British inventors in Prussia and the U.S.A. – against what were referred to as 'irresponsible examiners' ".[221] Nevertheless, the desire for patent reform remained strong, and a further series of Bills were introduced,[222] which after long discussion, culminated in the passage of the *Patents, Designs and Trade Marks Act* 1883 (U.K.). The Vienna Congress was partly responsible for this outcome, as it was one of the factors which encouraged the U.K. Government to pursue patent law reform, despite the difficulties this entailed.

The Vienna Congress also contributed to the demise of the patent abolition movement in the United Kingdom. It was noted in Chapter Three that by 1872–3 this movement was already in severe decline in the U.K., but the Congress signalled its end. As C.E. Brunskill Cooke wrote in *The Law Magazine and Review* in 1876, the patent abolitionists were generally pleased with the Vienna Congress Resolution in favour of compulsory licensing, and believed that the implementation of such schemes would go a long way towards redressing their concerns about the patent system.[223] Abolitionists had earlier supported compulsory licensing before the 1871–1872 Select Committees on Patents, and had suggested that their concerns could be overcome by the introduction of some

---

territory of the European Community, but the Community Patent is still not operational at the date of writing. The Lord Chancellor was therefore correct to have stated in 1875 that an international patent is an [almost] impossible goal.

220 *Ibid.*

221 Davis, I.J.G., and Harrison, J., "Prelude to the United Kingdom's Accession to the Paris Convention, March 17, 1884" [1984] *Industrial Property* 395, 398. See also "Patents, Designs and Trade Marks" (1883) 27 *The Solicitors' Journal* 735.

222 UNITED KINGDOM, Parliamentary Papers, *Bill, intituled Act for consolidating Acts relating to Letters Patent for Inventions* (1876) 137, vol V, 461; UNITED KINGDOM, Parliamentary Papers, *Bill for consolidating Act relating to Letters Patent for Inventions* (1877) 64, vol IV, 359; UNITED KINGDOM, Parliamentary Papers, *Bill for Amendment of Patent Laws* (1878) 127, vol V, 387; UNITED KINGDOM, Parliamentary Papers, *Bill to amend Patents for Inventions Laws* (1878–9) 55, vol V, 71; UNITED KINGDOM, Parliamentary Papers, *Bill to consolidate, with Amendments, Act relating to Letters Patent for Inventions* (1878–9) 77, vol V, 75; UNITED KINGDOM, Parliamentary Papers, *Bill to amend and consolidate Law relating to Patents for Inventions, Trade Marks and Registration of Designs* (1883) 3, vol VIII, 301.

223 Cooke, C.E.B., "Patent Law Amendment" (1876–7) 2 *The Law Magazine and Review* (4th Series) 209, 210.

form of international protection of patent rights.[224] The Vienna Congress showed that some progress was being made towards this goal.

(iii) U.S.A.

In 1947 Kronstein and Till wrote that the "very fact of American parentage elevated the prestige of the conference".[225] They added that the Vienna Congress would not have been successful if it had been viewed only as an initiative of "the semi-feudal country of Austria, conspicuously lacking in industrial development".[226] They also alleged that the U.S.A., "already at the forefront industrially and with the strongest patent system in the world", came from the Vienna Congress with an "outstanding ... victory, won by a purposeful policy."[227]

While it has already been demonstrated that the Congress was primarily a U.S. initiative, it is hardly accurate to describe the outcome of the Congress as a U.S. victory.[228] In fact, the U.S. delegates to the Congress were generally unheard, understood little of the discussion which was mostly conducted in German, and suffered a crushing defeat on the question of compulsory licensing. Nevertheless, the Congress did have a lasting effect in the U.S.A. because it inspired great interest in international patent issues, and led to the formation of the U.S. Patent Association.

As the Commissioners appointed to revise the U.S. patent laws wrote in their Report to Congress in 1900, their opinion about the Vienna Congress was that "the German element, as would naturally be expected from the locality in which the Congress was held, [was] largely predominant."[229] This was an understatement. Reports published in the *New York Times* by delegates to the Congress show that the Americans felt overwhelmed by the German presence, and were bitterly disappointed at the outcome.

One of the major U.S. objections to the Congress was its unofficial character. In a letter dated from Vienna on 6 August 1873, the *New York Times'* correspondent to the Congress noted with bitterness that the Congress had "turned

224 See Chapter Three for further details.

225 Kronstein, H., and Till, I., "A re-evaluation of the International Patent Convention" (1947) 12 *Law and Contemporary Problems* 765, 767.

226 *Ibid.*

227 *Ibid.* 767, 770.

228 Penrose also dismisses Kronstein and Till on this point. Penrose, E., *The Economics of the International Patent System* (Baltimore, John Hopkins Press, 1951), 46.

229 UNITED STATES OF AMERICA, Congressional Papers, *Report of the Commissioners appointed to Revise the Statutes relating to Patents, Trade and other Marks, and Trade and Commercial Names under Act of Congress approved June 4, 1898* (1900) 56th Congress, 2nd Session, Senate document 20, 7.

out a fiasco".[230] He explained that, having "no official character, no official dignity to maintain, the delegates run riot in all sorts of schemes".[231] There were men with " 'axes to grind', who will bring in their private affairs", and what was worse, all this was carried out in German, "a language which very few of [the U.S.] members understand".[232] The correspondent noted that the position of Thatcher, the U.S. Assistant Commissioner of Patents, was unclear, and an embarrassment. Thatcher had been sent to the Congress as an official representative of the U.S. Government, and he was the only person who attended in any official capacity.[233] In the circumstances, Thatcher's position became the "laughing stock in the Diplomatic Corps", he refused to present his credentials to the Congress and felt that his dignity required that he abstain from the debates.[234] It was only at the seventh meeting on the afternoon of 7 August that he finally broke his silence, and this was only upon the urging of Jay.[235] Even so, it was reported that Thatcher's speech did not receive the attention it deserved. Being delivered in English, the speech was understood only by a minority, the "Germans grew impatient before he closed, and he was forced to wind up abruptly, leaving unsaid the more important things he had reserved for his peroration."[236]

The use of the German language throughout the Congress clearly disadvantaged the English speakers such as the U.S. and U.K. delegates. Most were not fluent in German, and equally, their views could not be understood by the majority of German speakers. It was reported that at the very outset a U.S. delegate "made a very violent attack upon the meeting because the proceedings were conducted in German".[237] He admitted that he "did not comprehend a word of what had been said, and that was a great injustice to him."[238] Although German was voted the official language of the Congress, as time went on it was

230 *New York Times*, 24 August 1873.
231 *Ibid.*
232 *Ibid.*
233 *Ibid.* Note that Thatcher is called "Thacher" throughout Pieper's Report. Although it is alleged that the U.S. diplomatic representative in Vienna, John Jay, had originally been advised by Count Andrassy that the Austrian Government favoured an official Congress, Andrassy later announced that the "Congress was purely academic, and did not have the official sanction of the Austrian Government." In the interim, Thatcher had been appointed official U.S. representative, but Andrassy's subsequent statements prevented other countries from sending official delegates.
234 *Ibid.*
235 *New York Times*, 26 August 1873.
236 *Ibid.*
237 *New York Times*, 28 August 1873.
238 *Ibid.*

alleged that the Americans became so frustrated that they demanded to talk in English, "and English was heard as much as any other language".[239] These speeches were generally not reported by Pieper in his quasi-official Report, which suggests that the English speakers were marginalised by the Germans and Austro-Hungarians.

Another point to note is the allegation made concerning the composition of the U.S. delegation. The *New York Times* correspondent noted that the American delegates were largely inventors,[240] whose main interest was to see reform in the Austrian patent legislation "for the sake of their own pockets".[241] With one or two exceptions, it was argued that most of the U.S. delegates "did not appear to be men whose names would carry any great weight when it comes to getting their ideas adopted."[242] Perhaps this mediocrity and self-interest was apparent to the delegates from other countries at the Congress, and explains why the U.S. proposals (particularly those rejecting any form of compulsory licensing) were not accepted.

The overall opinion in America was that the Vienna Congress was a success for the Germans, but otherwise only "a partial understanding" had resulted.[243] Nevertheless, the Vienna Congress spurred American interest in patent law reform, associations were formed and meetings held. On 16 December 1873, for example, a meeting of the New England patentees and owners of patents was held for the purpose of forming an association "to promote uniformity of action" in connection with patent law reform.[244] On 15 January 1874 "a large and respectable meeting of gentlemen" met in Washington in accordance with the proposal of Thatcher to form a U.S. Patent Association, with the aim of generally adopting "measures in aid of the movement for patent protection inaugurated [in Vienna]".[245] At that meeting, not only was the Association formed, but the members agreed with the suggestion made by Professor Blake in Vienna that the next International Patent Congress should be held in Philadelphia to coincide with the 1876 Centennial Exhibition.[246] It was hoped that such a meeting would build upon the [meagre] foundations of the Vienna Congress, and create a "favourable influence" … "in promoting a greater uniformity among the

239 *Ibid.*
240 Presumably most had attended the Vienna Exhibition with their inventions.
241 *New York Times*, 26 August 1873.
242 *Ibid.*
243 *New York Times*, 28 August 1873.
244 *New York Times*, 17 December 1873.
245 *New York Times*, 25 December 1873, 8 January 1874, 12 January 1874, 26 January 1874.
246 *New York Times*, 26 January 1874.

now discordant systems of the world".[247] This meeting never occurred, again showing that Europeans dismissed or lightly valued the contribution which the U.S. could make towards international patent law reform.

(iv) Germany

Which national group really won greatest benefits from the Congress? The answer to this question is clearly the German delegates. It has already been noted that influential German members of the *Deutsche Patentschutz-Verein,* such as Pieper, Werner Siemens and André took major roles in organising the Congress after it was effectively "abandoned" by the Austrian Government, and that large numbers of Germans travelled to Vienna to take part. It has also been shown how the Germans, particularly Klostermann, told the Congress that certain of the draft Resolutions[248] were particularly directed towards facilitating patent law reform in Germany, and overcoming the objections of the anti-patent movement. For these reasons, it is not unreasonable that U.S. delegates should have seen the Congress as having been hijacked by the Germans for their own self-interested, political motives. Indeed, the German delegation succeeded in arranging the adoption of a Resolution which approved "the draft of a patent law prepared for Germany by the society of German Engineers."[249] This was a blatantly political move on the part of the German delegates, since it made it harder for von Bismarck and other patent abolitionists to continue their opposition to the patent system. Some time after the Congress, Thatcher received a communication from Pieper stating that the Congress had been a great success from the point of view of his task to reform and strengthen the patent system in Germany.[250] Pieper reported that he was "now hard at work as a 'missionary,' as he terms it, in his own country, organising associations everywhere and endeavouring to secure the election of such men to their next legislative body as will favor a careful revision of the patent system of Germany."[251] Pieper and the other members of the *Deutsche Patentschutz-Verein* succeeded in this mission with the adoption of the German Patent Law of 1877. Although the German patent abolition movement would probably have failed

247 *Ibid.*

248 Such as that relating to compulsory licensing.

249 Extract from Resolution II(j).

250 UNITED STATES OF AMERICA, Congressional Papers, *Report of the Commissioners appointed to Revise the Statutes relating to Patents, Trade and other Marks, and Trade and Commercial Names under Act of Congress approved June 4, 1898* (1900) 56th Congress, 2nd Session, Senate document 20, 7.

251 *Ibid.*

irrespective of the influence of the Vienna Congress,[252] the Congress hastened this process.

This Chapter has set out the various factors which prompted many persons to give serious consideration to international reform of the patent system in the period leading up to and including the Vienna Congress in 1873. Although it cannot be denied that the Congress was exploited by the German delegates as a means by which they could increase support for their own national patent policies, the Congress did make a useful start towards its goal of harmonisation of general principles of patent law. This was achieved in two ways. First, it drew attention to the concept of international patent protection and provided a basis upon which further discussions could ensue. This led to the more influential Paris Conferences of 1878, 1880 and 1883. Second, it contributed to the collapse of the patent abolition movements in the U.K. and Germany, which was a necessary precondition to any plan for international patent protection.

252 See Chapter Four for further details of the course of this movement.

CHAPTER 6

Springtime in Paris

The Paris Conference 1878

> Le droit des inventeurs et des auteurs industriels sur leurs oeuvres ou des fabricants et négociants sur leurs marques est un droit de propriété. La loi civile ne le crée pas; elle ne fait que le réglementer.[1]
>
> Un des buts de la Commission permanente créée par l'initiative privée sera d'obtenir de l'un des Gouvernements la réunion d'une Conférence internationale officielle á l'effet de determiner les bases d'une législation uniforme.[2]
>
> Paris Resolutions 1878

∴

Chapter Five has discussed the factors which led to a growing interest in international patent protection in the early 1870s. This international focus was particularly evident in the Resolutions favouring international harmonisation of patent laws at the Vienna Patent Congress in 1873. At the subsequent international industrial property conferences in Paris in 1878, 1880 and 1883, the most difficult task was to determine to what extent international harmonisation of industrial property legislation could be achieved.

This Chapter examines the work of the unofficial 1878 Paris Conference and the manner in which this work was used as a basis for the drafting of a

1 Translation: "The right of inventors and industrial originators in their works or manufacturers and traders in their marks is a right of property. The civil law does not create it; it only regulates it." General Question Section, Resolution 1, Paris Conference 1878. FRANCE, Ministére de L' agriculture et du Commerce, *Comptes rendus Sténographiques publiés sous les auspices du Comité Central des Congrés et Conférences et la direction de M. CH THIRION, Secrétaire du Comité, avec le concours des Bureaux des Congrés et des auteurs de Conférences: Congrés International de la Propriété Industrielle tenu á Paris du 5 au 17 Septembre 1878* (Paris 1879), 427.

2 Translation: "One of the aims of the Permanent Committee created by private initiative will be to organise with one of the Governments an official meeting of an international Conference with the task of determining the bases of uniform legislation." Section on the Permanent Committee, Paris Conference, 1878. *Ibid.* 435.

 | DOI:10.1163/9789004470125_008

series of proposed multilateral industrial property treaties between the ending of that Conference in September 1878 and the first session of the diplomatic Conference in November 1880. Although the 1883 Convention was largely based upon another, independent draft presented to the 1880 diplomatic Conference by the French Government, nevertheless, the 1878 Conference did have significant influence at a more general level. In particular, the 1878 Conference strongly supported uniform industrial property legislation, and the implementation of the 1883 Convention was a first step towards this goal.

A The Paris Conference of 1878

(a) *Reasons for the 1878 Paris Conference, Explanation of the Role of the French Government and Composition of the Delegates*

There were a number of factors which led to the convening of an international conference on industrial property rights in Paris between 5–17 September 1878.[3] These included:

3 In addition to the commentaries discussed below, there are a number of works which contain brief reference to the 1878 Paris Conference. These include: Plaisant, M., *Traité de Droit Conventionnel International concernant la Propriété Industrielle* (Paris, Sirey, 1949), 14; Pieper, C., and Schmid, P., *Geschichte der internationalen Union für den Schutz des gewerblichen Eigentums sammt Konvention und Staatsverträgen* (Berlin, Deutschen Vereins für den Schutz des gewerblichen Eigentums, 1894), 17–23; Milhaud, L., *Des Brevets d'invention dans les Rapports Internationaux* (Paris, Larose et Forcel, 1892), 10; Drouets, C., "La Convention d'Union de la Propriété Industrielle: L'oeuvre de la Conférence de Revision de Londres de 1934" (1935) 134 *Bulletin de la Société d'Encouragement pour L'Industrie Nationale* 376–377; COMITE CENTRAL DES CHAMBRES SYNDICALES, *Protection Internationale de la Propriété Industrielle: Rapport presenté au nom de la Commission, par M. Crinon* (Paris, 1897), 1–2; France, CONSEIL GENERAL DE LA DORDOGNE, *Rapport sur la Convention du 20 mars 1883 relative a L'Union de la propriété industrielle présenté au nom de la Commission des Objects divers* (1888), 6–7; Capuccio, M., "Le Convenzioni Internazionali per La Tutela della Proprietá Industriale" (1903) 3 *Rivista Tecnica* 1, 8; De Iturralde, T., *La Union Internacional para la proteccion de la Propriedad Industrial* (Paris, 1890), 3–4; Alexander-Katz, R., "Die Entstehung der Union und ihre Grundzüge" in Alexander-Katz, R., Lau, R., Osterrieth, A., and Wassermann, M., *Der Anschluss des Deutschen Reichs an die Internationale Union für gewerblichen Rechtsschutz* 39 (Berlin, Carl Heymann's Verlag, 1902), 40–41; Osterrieth, A., and Axter, A., *Die Internationale Ubereinkunft zum Schutze des gewerblichen Eigentums vom 20 märz 1883* (*Pariser Konvention*) *nebst den übrigen Verträgen des Deutschen Reichs über den gewerblichen Rechtsschutz* (Berlin, Carl Heymann's Verlag, 1903), 11–12; Beck Von Mannagetta, P., *Die Internationale Union zum Schutze des gewerblichen Eigentumes und ihre Bedeutung für Osterreichs Handel und Industrie* (Vienna, Niederösterreichischen Gewerbevereines, 1903), 4–5.

(1) The U.K. Government's emerging interest in international assimilation of patent laws;
(2) The work of the Association for the Reform and Codification of the Law of Nations;
(3) The work of Carl Pieper of Germany; and
(4) The Paris Universal Exposition of 1878.

Although it was noted in the previous Chapter that the 1873 Vienna Congress had resolved that the next international patent conference should be held in Philadelphia in 1876 to coincide with the Centennial Exhibition,[4] this did not occur. It is unclear why the U.S. Patent Association did not succeed in obtaining Government support for a Philadelphia patent conference, but U.S. Congressional papers note that visitors to the Centennial Exhibition from the "Old World" were "few".[5] Perhaps it was thought that few Europeans would wish to attend a patent conference held so far away as Philadelphia. A Committee which reported to the 1876 Bremen meeting of the Association for the Reform and Codification of the Law of Nations stated that there had been little progress in implementing the Vienna resolutions. The report noted that as "far as we are aware, the only bodies which are doing anything to carry out the resolutions of the Vienna Congress are the committee in Germany which prepared the draft Law,[6] and a Committee in London of which Dr. C.W. Siemens, FRS is chairman."[7] These proposed reforms were concerned chiefly with national patent systems, and regard for any more general assimilation or harmonisation at the international level was a secondary consideration.

However, since 1872, the U.K. Government had been considering the manner in which some form of international assimilation of patent law and practice could be achieved. This interest was prompted by the recommendations of the 1872 Select Committee on Patents, and later, the work of the Vienna Congress.[8]

---

4 This was an exhibition to commemorate the signing of the Declaration of Independence on 4 July 1776.

5 UNITED STATES OF AMERICA, Congressional Papers, *Arguments before the Committee on Patents of the Senate and House of Representatives, in support of, and suggesting amendments to, the Bills, (S. No. 300 and H.R. 1612) to amend the Statutes in relation to Patents, and for other purposes* (1878) 45th Congress, 2nd Session, Senate 1788, Misc Docs 50, 448.

6 By the term "draft Law", was meant the draft law which eventually became the German Patent Law of 1877.

7 Davis, I.J.G., and Harrison, J., "Prelude to the United Kingdom's Accession to the Paris Convention, March 17, 1884" [1984] *Industrial Property* 395, 398. Note that Siemens' work in the United Kingdom was mainly concerned with reform of U.K. patent legislation, not questions of international law reform.

8 The Select Committee had reported that there should be an assimilation of law and practice in regard to inventions in all civilised countries, and recommended that the Government

As a preliminary matter, the Secretary of State for the Colonies, Earl Kimberley, sent a despatch to the Governors of all colonies, asking them to report "how far the Colonial Governments are ready to concur in international arrangements for an assimilation in the law and practice in regard to inventions."[9] The answers were received in the course of the next two years. Overall, most of the colonial governments thought of "international assimilation" in the context of assimilation of United Kingdom and colonial patent systems. Very few considered a wider assimilation of patent law throughout the world. One exception was the opinion of the Attorney-General of New Zealand, James Prendergast, who reported that:

> [If] the countries of Europe, America, and Australasia were agreed as to the question whether the protection of a patent ought in all or in what cases to be given, I apprehend there would not be much difficulty in agreeing that the mode of procedure in obtaining the patent, and the effect when obtained, should be the same in all countries.[10]

There is no doubt that the recommendations of the 1872 U.K. Select Committee also had influence outside the U.K. and its colonies. The Association for the Reform and Codification of the Law of Nations, which had a strong U.K. background and membership, had been interested in international industrial property law and copyright since its inception in 1873.[11] The Association's interest in industrial property and copyright law was advanced largely by the contribution of the U.K. members, many of whom had given evidence to the 1871 and 1872 U.K. Select Committees and were doubtless aware of the recommendations. However, after 1876, many non-U.K. members of the Association, particularly French nationals, promoted the cause of international patent protection.

In 1877, the Association met in Anvers, and adopted a Resolution stating that it was desirable to assimilate, as far as possible, the patent laws of the

---

should undertake enquiries of foreign and colonial governments, how far they would be ready to concur in such international arrangements. UNITED KINGDOM, Parliamentary Papers, *Report from the Select Committee on Letters Patent; together with the Proceedings of the Committee, Minutes of Evidence, Appendix and Index* (1872) 193, vol XI, 395, v.

9 UNITED KINGDOM, Parliamentary Papers, *Correspondence respecting International Arrangements for Assimilation in Law and Practice in regard to Letters Patent of Inventions* (1874) C.999, vol LIV, 211, A2.

10 *Ibid.* See letter from the Attorney-General of New Zealand, James Prendergast, dated 6 February 1873.

11 In relation to the work of this Association before 1875, see Chapter Five.

various nations.[12] It also supported in principle, the notion that the law should more readily facilitate the lodging of simultaneous applications for patents in several countries. It proposed that the filing of a patent application (and possibly also a trade mark or design application) should be effected simultaneously through deposit at foreign consulates. However, as the International Bureau later noted in 1886, this solution would not have alleviated the problems of expense and inconvenience associated with making patent applications in various countries, given the difficulty of gaining access to all the required foreign consulates in one day.[13]

Of great interest is the fact that many of the more influential delegates to the 1878 Paris Conference also attended the 1877 Anvers meeting. In particular, Bozérian, Charles Lyon-Caen, Pataille, Huard and Pouillet were members of the French Committee at the 1877 meeting and 1878 Conference; Alexander, Bailey, Carmichael, Jencken, Selwyn and Wise were U.K. delegates at both conferences; and Pieper and Kaupé represented Germany and Russia respectively on both occasions.[14] This 1877 meeting was a strong influence upon the French Government's support for the holding of the Paris Conference in 1878.

References to the 1877 meeting of the Association appear frequently in the records of the 1878 Paris Conference. For example, it was from the Association that the 1878 Conference adopted the concept of simultaneous lodging of industrial property applications at foreign consulates. The 1878 Conference also made reference to the work of the Association, and included some of the Association's reports as Annexes to the report of its proceedings.[15]

Another factor which undoubtedly influenced the French Government's decision to support the holding of the Paris Conference was the work of Carl Pieper. In his commentary on the early history of the Paris Convention, Pieper claims to have written to the French Minister of Commerce in 1876, suggesting

---

12 FRANCE, Ministére de L' agriculture et du Commerce, *Comptes rendus Sténographiques publiés sous les auspices du Comité Central des Congrés et Conférences et la direction de M. CH THIRION, Secrétaire du Comité, avec le concours des Bureaux des Congrés et des auteurs de Conférences: Congrés International de la Propriété Industrielle tenu á Paris du 5 au 17 Septembre 1878* (Paris 1879) Annexe 11, 498–501.

13 BUREAU INTERNATIONAL DE LA PROPRIETE INDUSTRIELLE, "l'Article 4 de la Convention" (1886) 2 *La Propriété Industrielle* 17, 18.

14 FRANCE, Ministére de L' agriculture et du Commerce, *Comptes rendus Sténographiques publiés sous les auspices du Comité Central des Congrés et Conférences et la direction de M. CH THIRION, Secrétaire du Comité, avec le concours des Bureaux des Congrés et des auteurs de Conférences: Congrés International de la Propriété Industrielle tenu á Paris du 5 au 17 Septembre 1878* (Paris 1879), 13–15, Annexe 14.

15 FRANCE, Ministére de L' agriculture et du Commerce, *Comptes rendus Sténographiques etc.* at Annexes 11 and 14.

that the Permanent Committee established by resolution of the 1873 Vienna Congress should meet in a general Conference to be held at the time of the Paris Exhibition in 1878.[16] It is unsurprising that Pieper should have made this suggestion, since at the time he was occupied with questions of patent law reform in Germany. He may have thought that another international meeting could provide further impetus for the V.D.I.'s demands.[17] In addition, Pieper, as one of the leaders of the Vienna Congress, must have been concerned that little further work had been done by the Permanent Committee since 1873.

The French Government attributed its decision to hold the 1878 Paris Conference to its support for international social and economic development, as exemplified by the Paris Universal Exposition. The Exposition was announced by Presidential Decrees dated 4 and 13 April 1876, and was intended to promote and display "works of art and industry of all nations".[18] However, the organisers of the Exposition were not concerned merely to facilitate a great display of new inventions. They also wanted to promote social progress. For this reason, the Consultative Committee of the Exposition encouraged the holding of international conferences on a diverse range of subjects. There were 32 international conferences held in Paris in 1878 in conjunction with the Exposition. One of those related to legal protection for industrial property rights.[19]

In welcoming the delegates to the Paris Conference, Charles Thirion, Secretary of the Organising Committee of the Paris Universal Exposition,

---

16 Pieper, C., and Schmid, P., *Geschichte der internationalen Union für den Schutz des gewerblichen Eigentums sammt Konvention und Staatsverträgen* (Berlin, Deutschen Vereins für den Schutz des gewerblichen Eigentums, 1894), 7. See also Plasseraud, Y., and Savignon, F., *Paris 1883: Genése du droit Unioniste des Brevets* (Paris, Litec, 1983), 157.

17 See Chapter Five for further details on this point.

18 UNITED KINGDOM, Parliamentary Papers, *Report of Her Majesty's Commissioners for the Paris Universal Exhibition of 1878* (1878) vol 1, (C 2588) XXXII, 1 at 9.

19 The wide range of subjects covered by the Paris Conferences indicates that this was an era of internationalism. Besides industrial property, the Conferences covered the following subjects: protection of literary property, agriculture, unification and numbering of threads, Provident Institutions, demography, ethnographic sciences, geometry, statistics, improvement of the means of transportation, prevention of cruelty to animals, architecture, hygiene, mental medicine, civil engineers, monetary conferences, homeopathy, military ambulance services, legal medicine, alcoholism, anthropological sciences, commerce and industry, botany and horticulture, meteorology, geology, unification of weights, measures and coins, silk culture, relief to released prisoners, protection of artistic property, commercial geography, improvement of the conditions of the blind and deaf-mutes and Friends of Peace. UNITED STATES OF AMERICA, Congressional Papers, *Paris Universal Exposition of 1878* (1878) 46th Congress, 3rd Session, H. Ex Docs vol 20, No 42, Pt 1, 455 (Appendix N).

stated that the idea for the industrial property Conference had emanated from the Section of Industrial and Artistic Property of the Consultative Committee of the Universal Exposition.[20] The suggestion had been directed to the French Minister of Agriculture and Commerce, Teisserenc de Bort, who had agreed that an industrial property Conference should be held in conjunction with the Universal Exposition.[21] Teisserenc de Bort considered that such a Conference would be a tribute to the "grand movement intellectuel"[22] which was apparent at the time, and gave directions that the Organising Committee of the Exposition should make the necessary arrangements. Consequently, the Organising Committee recruited 50 influential Frenchmen to form a Preparatory Committee for the Industrial Property Conference, with the main task of establishing its programme. Amongst the members of the Preparatory Committee were many industrial property lawyers, manufacturers, and representatives of non-governmental associations interested in industrial property issues.

Of particular note were the members of the Executive Committee: Bozérian (attorney and member of the French Senate); Christofle (manufacturer in the gold and silver trade); Clunet (attorney and editor of the *Journal du droit international privé*); Dumoustier de Frédilly (head of the Office of Industry in the Ministry of Agriculture and Commerce); Houette (President of the Chamber of Commerce of Paris); Huard (attorney and Vice-President of the Society of Inventors and Industrial Artists); Charles Lyon-Caen (Professor of the Faculty of Law in Paris); Maillard de Marafy (President of the Consultative Committee on Foreign Legislation of the Union of Manufacturers); Renouard (member of the French Senate, formerly of the Court of Cassation); Tranchant (of the Privy Council); and Thirion.[23]

The 50 members of the Preparatory Committee were responsible for final decisions concerning the subject-matter of the Conference, and it was they who determined that the Conference should discuss all aspects of industrial property rights, and not follow the lead of the Vienna Congress in confining

20 FRANCE, Ministére de L' agriculture et du Commerce, *Comptes rendus Sténographiques publiés sous les auspices du Comité Central des Congrés et Conférences et la direction de M. CH THIRION, Secrétaire du Comité, avec le concours des Bureaux des Congrés et des auteurs de Conférences: Congrés International de la Propriété Industrielle tenu á Paris du 5 au 17 Septembre 1878* (Paris 1879) (Thirion at 36).

21 *Ibid.*

22 Translation: "Major intellectual movement". *Ibid.*

23 FRANCE, Ministére de L' agriculture et du Commerce, *Comptes rendus Sténographiques etc.* at 2–3.

the Programme to patents.[24] The Committee established three sections: the Patent Section, the Trade Mark Section, and the Industrial Designs and Models Section, each having a separate special programme. Once these Sections had been established, and the Provisional Programme drawn up, the Preparatory Committee sought views from interested parties regarding the general issues to be raised at the Conference.[25] The types of interested parties canvassed by the Committee included "[p]lusiers gouvernements, des chambres de commerce de villes importantes, des sociétés savants et industrielles".[26]

Responses to the Provisional Programme

The Preparatory Committee received an overwhelming response to its request for views about how industrial property protection could be improved. These views were diverse, although French responses predominated. The following discussion shows that the nationality of the correspondent was less important than that person's occupational group. Attitudes to industrial property rights were clearly defined by occupation.

(1) *Legal Professionals and Patent Agents*

A number of lawyers, patent agents and counsel operating in the field of industrial property law responded to the Committee's circulars. In general, French lawyers and patent agents appeared to support the view that the right in an invention was a *sui generis* property right, which was not perpetual, but was subject to limitations imposed by reference to wider social interests.[27] They generally accepted that an invention gave rise to a natural property right, but once disclosed to the public and patented, its terms of protection were subject to more instrumentalist considerations. Logically following on from the above concept, they did not support preliminary examination of patent applications, as the State only protected pre-existing rights, and should not have the power to control the grant of such rights. Instead of preliminary examination, they supported progressive taxation through patent fees, encouraging forfeiture for non-payment.[28] In comparison, patent agents and lawyers of

24 *Ibid.* 36 (Thirion).
25 *Ibid.* 36–37 (Thirion).
26 Translation: "many governments, chambers of commerce of important towns, industrial and learned societies". *Ibid.*
27 Emile Barrault, engineer and patent counsellor in Paris, *Ibid.* 57–58, 529–540; C. Couhin, lawyer of Paris, also argued that trade marks were inherently a right of property. *Ibid.* 107, 612–617; Champetier de Ribes, lawyer of Paris. *Ibid.* 69–72, 568–578.
28 M. Méneau, lawyer of Paris. *Ibid.* 107, 600–611; Emile Barrault, engineer and patent counsellor in Paris, *Ibid.* 57–58, 529–540.

Belgium[29] and the United Kingdom[30] were less concerned with theoretical questions, and were more interested in the abolition or strict regulation of any laws providing for forfeiture of patents for non-working.

(2) *Manufacturers and Traders*

Manufacturers and traders raised similar concerns to lawyers and patent agents. They were not as interested in theoretical questions as legal professionals and patent agents, although there was some difference of opinion on this matter. Some French manufacturers argued that an inventor had a right of property in his invention, and the law should enshrine this right.[31] Others rejected the belief that the invention gave rise to a natural right of property, stating that such rights were traditionally viewed as having a contractual basis in the relationship between the inventor and the State.[32] Manufacturers and traders were more likely to support natural property rights in trade marks or designs, rather than inventions.[33]

Manufacturers and traders had a particular interest in practical issues, especially legal provisions which allowed forfeiture of patents. They had great hostility to the French law which ordered the forfeiture of patents for importation of goods made under a patent.[34] Most believed that some form of international agreement in connection with industrial property rights could be of great practical benefit to their industries.[35]

29 Gustave Biebuyck, lawyer of Brussels. *Ibid.* 50, 450–453.

30 M.H. Murdoch, patent lawyer in London. *Ibid.* 50, 454; Lloyd Wise, patent agent in London. *Ibid.* 63, 557, 562.

31 A. Poirrier, manufacturer of chemical products in Paris, *Ibid.* 52, 471; G. Leboyer, President of the Commercial Tribunal of Riom, *Ibid.* 61–62, 546–551.

32 Commercial Tribunal of Saint-Etienne, *Ibid.* 55, 516–520; Chamber of the Fabric Traders of Saint-Etienne, *Ibid.* 56, 525–528.

33 Board of Arbitration of Elbeuf. *Ibid.* 584–588; Chamber of Commerce of Lille, *Ibid.* 589–591; Chamber of the Fabric Traders of Saint-Etienne, *Ibid.* 56, 525–528.

34 T. Givry, a trader of Paris. *Ibid.* 50, 455–460; A. Poirrier, manufacturer of chemical products in Paris, *Ibid.* 52, 471.

35 Consultative Chamber of Arts and Manufacturers of Rethel (Ardennes). *Ibid.* 56–57, 521–522; Chamber of the Fabric Traders of Saint-Etienne. *Ibid.* 56, 525–528; Chamber of First-Class Pharmacists of the Region of the Seine. *Ibid.* 625–627; A. Poirrier, *Ibid.* 52, 471. Support for an international understanding was also clear in the correspondence of Robert Macfie, who had modified his abolitionist stance, but still considered that inventions were not a right of property. *Ibid.* 514–515.

(3) *Inventors and Engineers*

Inventors and engineers were mainly concerned to promote the benefits of the patent system, and to ensure that they could obtain legal protection for their inventions throughout the world. Most did not dispute the assumption that an invention gave rise to a property right, and they supported international protection.[36] However, there was some difference between the proposals of French inventors and engineers, and those from Austria. Most French inventors and engineers argued that international protection should only be granted to foreigners upon the basis of reciprocity.[37] This comment was motivated by a concern to protect French industry, as was the argument by one civil engineer that forfeiture of patents for non-working was a useful policy.[38]

In contrast, the Austrian inventors and engineering associations which replied to the Committee's request rejected the requirement of reciprocity, and wanted to abolish forfeiture for non-working. These recommendations were included in a Report of the Viennese section of the *Austrian Society of Engineers and Architects,* which had passed a number of Resolutions concerning the operation of the patent system, and whose Resolutions received the support of several other Austrian societies.[39] The Society argued that the protection of inventions should be guaranteed by all civilised nations, but proposed that the best approach was to uniformly adopt a system like that in Austria.[40] This system had no concept of forfeiture for non-working, but the duration of the exclusive rights of the patent was only for 10 years, after which time the invention was open to public exploitation, subject to continued payment of a royalty to the inventor. A similar point was made by the *United Industrial Societies of North-West Bohemia,* headed by Carl Pieper.[41] It also rejected forfeiture of patents for non-working, and compulsory licenses. One of the most interesting aspects of the recommendations of this Society was its rejection of compulsory licenses, because this was directly opposed to the Vienna Congress Resolutions earlier supported by Pieper.

---

36 Duroy de Bruignac, civil engineer of Versailles, *Ibid.* 58–59, 541–545; D.-A. Casalonga, civil engineer of Paris. *Ibid.* 63, 552–556.

37 *Ibid.*

38 Duroy de Bruignac, *Ibid.* 58–59, 541–545.

39 For example, the Industrial Society of Korneuburg, the Industrial Society of Brünn, the Society for the Encouragement of Industry in Bohemia, the German Polytechnical Society in Bohemia, the Administrative Council of the Society of Architects and Engineers of Bohemia, and the Polytechnical Club of Graz. *Ibid.* 493–495.

40 *Ibid.* 53, 487–493.

41 *Ibid.* 55, 496–497.

These Memoranda were studied by the members of each of the three Sections of the Preparatory Committee, and three Reports were prepared incorporating the comments, which were then submitted to the delegates for consideration at the first general session of the Paris Conference on 5 September 1878.[42]

Was the 1878 Conference Truly International?

It seems to be assumed by some commentators that the 1878 Conference was dominated by French interests. This opinion has been propounded by modern commentators such as Edith Penrose, as well as historical figures, (such as the Parisian lawyer Louis Donzel), who were present at the Conference in 1878. If the 1878 Conference was dominated by French interests, then it was not a truly "international" industrial property conference.

Many claims have been made about the overbearing attitude of the French delegates at the 1878 Conference. Penrose wrote that "the French point of view completely dominated the conference".[43] A similar argument was advanced by Donzel, a strident French critic of the Paris Convention, who from 1885 sought France's denunciation of the Convention.[44]

Donzel's allegations bear more weight than those of Penrose, since he had been present at the 1878 Conference. He alleged that the Conference was dominated by French lawyers and patent agents, who acted to secure their own interests, rather than the larger interests of France.[45] In this regard, he made

---

42 The Reports were as follows: (1) "*Rapport présenté au nom de la section des Brevets d'Invention par M. Charles Lyon-Caen*". (2) "*Rapport présenté au nom de la section des Dessins et Modéles de Fabrique, par M. J. Bozérian*". (3) "*Rapport présenté au nom de la section des Marques de Fabrique et de Commerce, par M. le Comte de Maillard de Marafy*" *Ibid.* 48–110.

43 Penrose, E., *The Economics of the International Patent System* (Baltimore, John Hopkins Press, 1951), 48.

44 BUREAU INTERNATIONAL DE L'UNION POUR LA PROTECTION DE LA PROPRIETE INDUSTRIELLE, "l'Article 5 de la Convention" (1886) 2 *La Propriété Industrielle* 1, 2; BUREAU INTERNATIONAL DE L'UNION POUR LA PROTECTION DE LA PROPRIETE INDUSTRIELLE, "l'Article 4 de la Convention" (1886) 2 *La Propriété Industrielle* 17, 18.

45 Donzel later argued that the creation of the *International Association for the Protection of Industrial Property* in 1897 was an acknowledgement of the dominant position of the patent lawyers and agents in shaping the evolution of the Paris Convention. See for example, Donzel, L., *M. Eugéne Pouillet au Congrés International pour la protection de la Propriété Industrielle tenu á Londres, les 1er, 2 et 3 Juin 1898* (Paris, Imprimerie Jean Gainche, 1898); Donzel, L., *Rapport adressé sur sa demand a Monsieur le Ministre des Affaires étrangéres sur la Législation internationale de la Propriété Industrielle au point de vue de la Conférence internationale qui aura lieu á Madrid le 1er avril 1890* (Paris, Marchel et Billard, 1890); Donzel, L., "Commentaire de la Convention Internationale signée á Paris le 20 mars 1883 pour la protection de la Propriété Industrielle" (1891) *Journal des Procés en Contrefaçon* 1; Further extracts from Donzel's writings are contained in: Cahen, A., and Lyon-Caen, L., "De la Convention conclue á Paris entre divers états le 20 Mars 1883 pour la protection de

particular reference to the activities of Senator Bozérian and Eugéne Pouillet, both of whom had been members of the Preparatory Committee for the 1878 Conference, and who he alleged had led the patent lawyer/agent/engineer sectional group to a position of dominance.[46] He also alleged that most of the delegates were incompetent and lacked the ability to understand the significance of their decisions.[47]

If Donzel's allegations are true, they seriously compromise the work of the Conference and lessen its international significance. There seem to be two related allegations: (1) that French delegates dominated the Conference and (2) that these persons were biased and/or incompetent. Both of these allegations are not founded in fact.

Although the 50 eminent persons who constituted the Preparatory Committee were all French nationals, the general delegates who attended the Conference were from a wide range of countries. In addition, it has already been noted that many non-French correspondents provided detailed written responses to the Committee's preliminary Circular.

Of the 484 delegates who attended the Conference, 94 were not French nationals.[48] In particular, as the Conference had received the "patronage" of the French Government,[49] a number of countries sent official representatives. These countries were Germany,[50] Spain,[51] U.S.A.,[52] Hungary,[53]

---

la propriété industrielle et des Modifications urgentes á apporter á la loi du 5 Juillet 1844" *Report presented to the Association des Inventeurs et Artistes Industriels* (Paris, 1885), 3.

46 Donzel, L., *M. Eugéne Pouillet au Congrés International pour la protection de la Propriété Industrielle tenu á Londres, les 1er, 2 et 3 Juin 1898* (Paris, Imprimerie Jean Gainche, 1898), 2.

47 Extracts of Donzel's writings contained in Cahen, A., and Lyon-Caen, L., "De la Convention conclue á Paris entre divers états le 20 Mars 1883 pour la protection de la propriété industrielle et des Modifications urgentes á apporter á la loi du 5 Juillet 1844" *Report presented to the Association des Inventeurs et Artistes Industriels* (Paris, 1885), 3.

48 Statistics derived from the list of participants at the Conference. FRANCE, Ministére de L' agriculture et du Commerce, *Comptes rendus Sténographiques publiés sous les auspices du Comité Central des Congrés et Conférences et la direction de M. CH THIRION, Secrétaire du Comité, avec le concours des Bureaux des Congrés et des auteurs de Conférences: Congrés International de la Propriété Industrielle tenu á Paris du 5 au 17 Septembre 1878* (Paris 1879), 15–28. See also Bozerian, M.J. *La Convention Internationale du 20 Mars 1883 pour la Protection de la Propriété Industrielle* (Paris, Imprimerie C. Pariset, 1885), 6.

49 *Ibid.* 29 (Opening speech of the French Minister of Agriculture and Commerce, Teisserenc de Bort).

50 Represented by Professor Reuleaux, member of the Patent Office in Berlin.

51 Represented by E. de Santos, Spanish Commissioner to the Universal Exposition.

52 Represented by Pollok, (an engineer), Lincoln (a lawyer), and Blake (a member of the international jury of the Exposition).

53 Represented by Hegedüs, member of the Hungarian Parliament.

Italy,[54] Luxembourg,[55] Norway,[56] Russia,[57] Sweden,[58] and Switzerland.[59] Amongst the delegates there were also representatives of various associations which were not primarily of French origin, including delegates from the Association for the Reform and Codification of the Law of Nations, the U.K. Society of Arts, the Union Syndicale of Brussels, the Austrian Society of Engineers and Architects, the Viennese section of the Chamber of Commerce and Industry of Austria, the German Society of Patent Agents, the Union of Industrial Societies of Bohemia, the Industrial Society of North-West Bohemia, the U.K. Inventors' Institute, and the Frankfurt Chamber of Commerce.[60] Even among the general members of the Conference, there were representatives from a large number of countries, including Germany (19), United Kingdom (15), Belgium (11), Austria (10), U.S.A. (7), Switzerland (5), Italy (5), Greece (4), Russia (4), Spain (3), Sweden (2), Hungary (2), Denmark (2), Luxembourg (1), Portugal (1), Norway (1), Egypt (1), and the Netherlands (1).[61] Sixteen of these delegates had previously attended the 1873 Vienna Patent Congress.[62]

There is another reason why it is incorrect to state that the "French point of view"[63] dominated the Conference. This was because there was no consistent

---

54 Represented by Torrigiani (of the Italian Parliament), and Romanelli (Director of Commerce and Industry at the Ministry of Agriculture, Industry and Commerce in Rome.)

55 Represented by Müllendorff, member of the Government.

56 Represented by Dr Stoltz, civil engineer.

57 Represented by A. de Nebolsine, Counsel of State in St Petersburg.

58 Represented by L. Groth, (civil engineer) and C. Lundström (factory owner).

59 Represented by Bodenheimer, (member of the Government), Imer-Schneider (civil engineer), and Schreyer (Professor of Law in Geneva).

60 FRANCE, Ministére de L' agriculture et du Commerce, *Comptes rendus Sténographiques publiés sous les auspices du Comité Central des Congrés et Conférences et la direction de M. CH THIRION, Secrétaire du Comité, avec le concours des Bureaux des Congrés et des auteurs de Conférences: Congrés International de la Propriété Industrielle tenu á Paris du 5 au 17 Septembre 1878* (Paris 1879), 13–15.

61 Statistics derived from an analysis of the list of participating delegates. *Ibid.* 15–28.

62 The following delegates attended both the 1873 and 1878 conferences: W. Blake, (U.S.A.), A. Friedmann (Austria), R. Gottheil (Germany), L. Groth (Sweden), Prof. Hartig (Germany), B. Hotchkiss (France), A. Joy (U.S.A.), F. Kaupe (Russia), Prof. Klostermann (Germany), C. Pieper (Germany), Prof. Reuleaux (Germany), F. de Rosas (Austria), William Siemens (U.K.), A. Steenberg (Denmark), F. Wirth (Germany) and J. Zimmermann (Germany). Derived from an examination of the lists of delegates to the 1873 Vienna Congress and 1878 Paris Conference. *Ibid.* Pieper, C., *Der Erfinderschutz und die Reform der Patentgesetze. Amtlicher Bericht über den Internationalen Patent-Congress zur Erörterung der Frage des Patentschutzes. Mit einer Einleitung von Dr. C.W. Siemens F.R.S.* (Dresden, Commission der Schulbuchhandlung, 1873), 263–267.

63 Penrose, E., *The Economics of the International Patent System* (Baltimore, John Hopkins Press, 1951), 48.

"French view" about any area of industrial property law. Many views were expressed on various subjects, and opinions were more clearly grouped along occupational rather than national lines. This was apparent in the preliminary correspondence analysed above, as well as in the work of the Conference.

Donzel's allegations concerning the motives of many of the Conference delegates are also not borne out by the facts. As Bozérian later argued in response to Donzel's criticisms, the delegates were not only professional persons with occupations closely connected to the promotion of the patent system.[64] Of the 484 delegates, there were only 73 who were patent agents or engineers.[65] In contrast, there were 107 in the more general class of lawyers, economists and journalists, and 304 traders and manufacturers.[66] Fifty-eight of these delegates were also representatives of important associations such as Chambers of Commerce, trade unions, and industrial and intellectual societies.[67] It is impossible to find evidence to sustain the argument that such a diverse gathering of persons was incompetent or unfit to make decisions about future protection of industrial property rights, or, more seriously, that they were unduly influenced by a minority interest group of patent professionals.[68]

(b) *The Work of the 1878 Paris Conference*

In his commentary upon the Paris Convention of 1883, Examiner F.A. Seeley of the U.S. Patent Office remarked that the 1878 Conference did not actually achieve anything of substance.[69] Instead, it was marked by "an elaborate programme, largely of papers on theoretical subjects", and the plan or general

64 Bozerian, M.J., *La Convention Internationale du 20 mars 1883 pour la Protection de la Propriété Industrielle* (Paris, Imprimerie C. Pariset, 1885), 6.

65 *Ibid.*

66 *Ibid.*

67 *Ibid.*

68 Léon Lyon-Caen, in his co-authored work with Albert Cahen, branded Donzel and his supporting Chambers of Commerce as protectionists, and denied that the Paris Convention of 1883 was the progeny of sectional interest groups such as patent agents. Franz Edlen von Rosas, an influential Austrian representing many commercial associations, who was voted a member of the Bureau of the 1878 Conference, made a similar point. Cahen, A., and Lyon-Caen, L., "De la Convention conclue á Paris entre divers états le 20 Mars 1883 pour la protection de la propriété industrielle et des Modifications urgentes á apporter á la loi du 5 Juillet 1844" *Report presented to the Association des Inventeurs et Artistes Industriels* (Paris, 1885), 3–4. Von Rosas, F.E., *Das Industrielle Eigenthum (Privilegien-, Marken- und Musterschutz). Bericht uber die Verhandlungen des Internationalen Congresses zu Paris 1878* (Wien, Verlag der Handels- und Gewerbekammer, 1878), 1.

69 Seeley, F.A., *The International Union for the Protection of Industrial Property* (prepared under the direction of the Commissioner of Patents, Washington, 1 September 1887), 1.

idea of "a permanent international union for the protection of industrial property" was more important to the Conference participants than the substantive points of discussion.[70] In 1886, Anthony Pollok, an official U.S. representative at the 1878 Conference, told the U.S. Senate that the Conference had been of limited value because of the large amount of time devoted to discussion of abstract subjects.[71] Like Seeley, Pollok considered that the real benefit of the 1878 Conference was that it prepared the way for later diplomatic negotiations which led to the signing of the Paris Convention in 1883.[72]

To a certain degree, the views of Seeley and Pollok were correct. The 1878 Conference spent much time discussing abstract subjects, particularly the theoretical basis of the patent system, and the desirability of uniform industrial property laws. To focus on theoretical issues in such a forum would always be difficult, but the work of the Conference was made even harder to fully comprehend because there was no real direction to the discussion. Many of the delegates spoke in a general and rambling fashion, and it was difficult to fully understand the points they were making. A principal reason for this was the lack of structure in the Programme of the Conference. It jumped from one subject to another, and some important matters were overlooked or dealt with in a cursory fashion.

Although the Conference did have a "Programme", this was essentially the series of questions drawn up by the Preparatory Committee and submitted to interested parties for their comment before the Conference began.[73] In addition, there were three Reports based on the responses to the Programme, which were submitted to the delegates for consideration at the first general session on 5 September 1878.[74] However, these documents were of a very general character. Being in the form of questions, the Programme did not provide much subsequent guidance for the work of the Conference. While the Reports

---

70 *Ibid.*

71 Sautter, M., *La Convention Internationale pour la Protection de la Propriété Industrielle aux états-Unis: Argumentation de M. A. Pollok, de Washington, devant le Sénat Fédéral* (Paris, 1886), 2.

72 *Ibid.* For a modern commentary on the work of the 1878 Conference see Ricketson, S., *The Paris Convention for the Protection of Industrial Property* (Oxford, Oxford University Press, 2015), 37- 49.

73 FRANCE, Ministére de L' agriculture et du Commerce, *Comptes rendus Sténographiques publiés sous les auspices du Comité Central des Congrés et Conférences et la direction de M. CH THIRION, Secrétaire du Comité, avec le concours des Bureaux des Congrés et des auteurs de Conférences: Congrés International de la Propriété Industrielle tenu á Paris du 5 au 17 Septembre 1878* (Paris 1879), 4–8.

74 *Ibid.* 48–110.

highlighted problems, and discussed different legal approaches in various countries, they did not propose any solutions.

When the delegates arrived at the Conference they had no firm idea of what would be discussed. There was certainly no draft text of resolutions. Subsequently, it was decided to hold a "Preparatory Session" before each daily general meeting. In this Preparatory Session, individual delegates or groups of delegates put forward draft propositions or resolutions, for later discussion at the afternoon meeting. These draft propositions usually related to many different issues. For example, in the first Preparatory Session, propositions were put forward relating to:

(1) The philosophical basis of patent protection;
(2) Rights of foreigners in relation to making applications for industrial property rights;
(3) The need to ensure that industrial property rights were protected independently of general commercial treaties;
(4) The creation of a central office of industrial property in each country;
(5) Protection of industrial property rights in inventions exhibited in international expositions;
(6) Codification of industrial property laws; and
(7) The need for comprehensive and consistent industrial property laws in countries with a colonial empire.[75]

Naturally, not all these propositions were discussed in one afternoon session, and the result was that delegates often jumped from one proposition to another, spending a minimum of time on each. This piecemeal approach also meant that dissenting opinions were given little prominence. As soon as the President (Bozérian) believed that he had "sensed" agreement on a matter, it was adopted and formed one of the official Resolutions of the Conference. Since the Conference rarely voted on any issue, Bozérian apparently "sensed" agreement by noting the amount of cheering or applause for any particular proposition.[76] As soon as the cheering or applause reached a certain level, the proposition was adopted. This occurred even in relation to difficult questions such as forfeiture of patents for non-working. It can thus be seen that many of the resolutions of the Conference were adopted without a great deal of thought, and their implications were not clear. It is unsurprising that in the following examination of the work of the Conference, the reader will find confusion and lack of clarity.[77]

---

75 *Ibid.* 112.

76 This conclusion is reached from studying the Records of the 1878 Conference. *Ibid.*

77 For the text of some of the more important Resolutions of the 1878 Conference, see Appendix Five.

Nevertheless, two main themes ran through the work of the Conference:
(a) The recognition by delegates of natural property rights in industrial property, particularly patented inventions; and
(b) The need for uniform industrial property legislation at the international level.

(1) *Natural Property Rights*

At a theoretical level, one of the main Resolutions of the 1878 Conference was the statement that:

> Le droit des inventeurs et des auteurs industriels sur leurs oeuvres ou des fabricants et négociants sur leurs marques est un droit de propriété. La loi civile ne le crée pas; elle ne fait que le réglementer.[78]

This Resolution had its foundation in the Programme of the Conference which was circulated by the Preparatory Committee some months before the Conference began. In the Programme, several of the questions raised by the Preparatory Committee related to the theoretical basis of industrial property rights. Thus, comments were sought as to "the nature of the right of the inventor", including questions of legitimacy and utility,[79] "the nature of the right of authors in their designs and models" and the "right of property in a trade mark".[80] The Committee asked generally, "Was this a right of property?", and if so, what kind of property was it?[81] In response to the questions asked in the Programme, many individuals and organisations wrote to the Preparatory Committee with decided views that there were natural property rights in inventions, trade marks and designs. Persons or organisations communicating such views included Claude Couhin, Emile Barrault, A. Poirrier, G. Leboyer, Duroy de Bruignac, the Commercial Tribunal of Saint-Etienne and the Board of Arbitration of Elbeuf.[82]

---

78 Translation: "the right of inventors and industrial originators in their works of manufacture and traders in their marks is a right of property. The civil law does not create it; it only regulates it." (General Section, Resolution 1). FRANCE, Ministére de L' agriculture et du Commerce, *Comptes rendus Sténographiques etc.* Resolutions at 427–435.

79 "Programme due Congrés", Question 1. FRANCE, Ministére de L' agriculture et du Commerce, *Comptes rendus Sténographiques etc.* at 4–10.

80 *Ibid.*

81 *Ibid.*

82 For further details on these submissions see previous discussion under the heading Responses to the Provisional Programme above.

The issue of whether or not inventors, industrial creators and trade mark owners had a right of property in their creations was the first matter to be considered by the Conference after the opening meeting on 5 September 1878. The fact that this matter was dealt with first suggests that it was considered to be of great importance, and that agreement on this matter needed to be reached before the Conference could turn to more specific, practical issues.

In their discussions regarding the theoretical basis of industrial property protection, the delegates were presented with three alternatives. The original proposal was that of Pouillet[83] and Droz,[84] whose draft Resolution was the same as that eventually adopted, except that there was in addition an explicit statement that the property right was founded in natural law.[85] In contrast, a draft Resolution was proposed by an official representative of the Swiss Government, Professor Schreyer, who urged the Conference to accept the following:

> Il est juste d'accorder aux inventeurs et aux auteurs industriels, dans leur intérêt comme dans celui de l'industrie, un droit exclusif temporaire, d'une durée suffisante pour leur assurer la rémunération de leurs travaux et de leurs dépenses.[86]

Schreyer's proposal was clearly an instrumentalist approach, aimed at appeasing those who did not share the view that inventions gave rise to inherent property rights. There was also a proposal of Emile Barrault, a Parisian engineer and patent agent,[87] that the Pouillet and Droz proposal should be adopted without specific reference to natural law.[88]

Although the Barrault proposal was eventually adopted by the Conference, the discussion made no clear distinction between that proposal, and the original one of Pouillet and Droz. On the other hand, the Schreyer proposal was rejected by a majority of the delegates. Although the majority in favour of the

83 Pouillet was Parisian lawyer and the author of works on patent and trade mark law. He was one of the founders of AIPPI in 1897.

84 Droz was a Parisian lawyer.

85 FRANCE, Ministére de L' agriculture et du Commerce, *Comptes rendus Sténographiques etc.* Resolutions at 127.

86 Translation: "It is just to accord to inventors and industrial authors, in their interest as in that of industry, an exclusive temporary right for a duration sufficient to assure to them remuneration for their work and their expenses." *Ibid.* 129.

87 Barrault was also active in the Association for the Reform and Codification of the Law of Nations. *Ibid.* 13, 16, 127.

88 *Ibid.* 127.

Barrault proposal is unspecified, it was clearly large because those speaking in its favour received shouts of "Trés Bien! Trés bien! et applaudissements",[89] whereas those speaking in favour of the Schreyer proposal were met with "rumeurs diverses".[90]

Representative of the majority was Dupray de Lamahérie, a lawyer from Caen, who stated that in looking at the history of legal protection of inventions and industrial arts, as well as theoretical concerns, it was clear that such rights must be considered property.[91] As a matter of history, he asked whether anyone could overlook the fact that the French Ordinances of the 17th and 18th centuries dealing with the rights of inventors, were clearly based on the proposition that such legislation conferred a "Privilége fondé en justice".[92] Furthermore, one could not ignore the statement of Mirabeau that "[l]e droit de l'inventeur est un droit de propriété",[93] or the Preamble to the French Law of 7 January 1791 which enshrined the property right of the inventor in his invention.[94] In de Lamahérie's opinion, this concept lay at the heart of the French laws concerning all forms of industrial "property", including the later patent law of 5 July 1844, even though many had previously argued that the 1844 law was based upon contractual or instrumentalist theory rather than that of the property right of inventors.[95] However, he stated that the law of 1844 recognised the pre-existing proprietary interest of the inventor, and merely attempted to more closely regulate the conditions under which this right was exercised.[96] Thus, he argued, both historically and theoretically, there was a clear and unwavering perception of inventions and allied rights as industrial property.[97]

The arguments of Dupray de Lamahérie were supported by many delegates. Droz's speech in support of his joint proposal with Pouillet made many similar points, in particular that the inventor's right was not a "gracious concession" granted by law, but was rather a right which attached to the inventor automatically.[98] He added that the limited term of the patent was not a justifiable basis upon which to attack property rights in inventions, because not all property

89 Translation: "Very good! Very good! and applause". *Ibid.* 118.
90 Translation: "Various murmurs" (of discontent). *Ibid.* 129.
91 *Ibid.* 114–119.
92 Translation: "Privilege founded in justice". *Ibid.* 115.
93 Translation: "the right of an inventor is a right of property". *Ibid.*
94 *Ibid.*
95 *Ibid.* 117. For further details of this law see Chapter One.
96 *Ibid.*
97 *Ibid.*
98 *Ibid.* 123.

rights were absolute or perpetual.[99] He characterised industrial property as "une propriété d'une nature spéciale",[100] and also described it as "*sui generis*".[101] After this speech, there were many calls for the closing of the debate on this question, as the majority appeared to be fully in support of Droz.[102] Others speaking in favour of industrial property rights as automatically attaching to the work of creators included Jaubert,[103] Limousin,[104] Turquetil,[105] Pouillet,[106] and Selwyn.[107]

It must be noted, however, that not all delegates supported the Pouillet/Droz and Barrault proposals. Lloyd Wise, an engineer, and representative of the Society of Arts, found himself unable to accept the concept of one person having property rights in an idea which could be equally shared by many others.[108] He warned that the Resolutions of the Conference would not readily be accepted in the United Kingdom if either of the proposals were adopted.[109] Claude Couhin, a Parisian lawyer, also rejected the concept of industrial property rights in inventions, although he supported such rights in respect of trade marks.[110] He considered that the French law of 5 July 1844 was correct in eliminating any reference to property rights in inventions, and stated that, while an idea could give rise to a right of property, its physical embodiment, the published invention, could not.[111] Once the invention was revealed to the world, all persons could use it, and thus it could not qualify as the property of an individual.[112] He also argued that if an invention gave rise to a right of property, it should be perpetual, but as few were prepared to support perpetual patents, this proved there was no property interest in an invention.[113]

---

99 *Ibid.* He referred particularly to laws of succession which forced persons to leave a certain part of their fortune to their relatives.

100 Translation: "property of a special character". *Ibid.*

101 *Ibid.*

102 *Ibid.* 124.

103 Léon Jaubert was a Parisian maker of optical instruments. *Ibid.* 126.

104 Charles Limousin, the noted French economist, considered that the Conference should make a firm statement supporting industrial property rights in order to combat the adversaries of the concept, particularly Michel Chevalier. *Ibid.*

105 Turquetil was a Parisian manufacturer of coloured paper. *Ibid.* 127.

106 *Ibid.* 128.

107 Selwyn was a U.K. delegate and representative of the Inventors' Institute. *Ibid.* 121.

108 *Ibid.* 119.

109 *Ibid.*

110 *Ibid.*

111 *Ibid.* 120.

112 *Ibid.*

113 *Ibid.* 121.

Schreyer's proposal, which appeared to be based upon the notion that an inventor or other industrial creator entered into a contract with the State, was suggested in a spirit of compromise. He noted that whether or not industrial property rights existed was a divisive matter, and that it was better avoided by the Conference.[114] Since "[t]outes les lois modernes ont supprimé le mot de propriété",[115] largely because of the metaphysical nature of the issue, it was not advisable for the Conference to direct its energies to this matter.[116] Both Lyon-Caen and Demeur agreed. Demeur, a Belgian lawyer, and representative of the Union Syndicale of Brussels, argued that the Conference should not try to resolve this difficult issue,[117] but his speech was received with "rumeurs diverses".[118] Lyon-Caen, a Professor of Law in Paris who had written extensively in the area of patent law, agreed with the Schreyer proposal because the Pouillet/Droz and Barrault proposals were too divisive and he knew that they would never receive universal support outside the Conference.[119] He thought that the Resolutions of the Conference could have a positive influence upon future legislation, but it would not be so if the Conference concentrated its efforts upon abstract issues of little practical importance.[120]

Despite the warnings of Wise, Schreyer, Cohin, Lyon-Caen and Demeur, the Conference voted to adopt the Barrault resolution recognising industrial property rights, regulated, but not created, by civil law.[121] Acceptance of the concept of industrial property rights had a significant influence upon many of the later Resolutions of the Conference. It was particularly influential in connection with the debates on the following matters: (a) the right of foreigners to be treated as nationals; (b) compulsory licensing; (c) forfeiture of patents for non-working; and (d) the type of inventions which should be patentable.

(i) The Right of Foreigners to Be Treated as Nationals

The fact that the Conference had voted to accept industrial property rights meant that it was only a short step to the Resolution that "[l]es étrangers doivent être assimilés aux nationaux".[122] If the inventor or industrial creator

114 *Ibid.* 124.
115 Translation: "all the modern laws have removed the word property". *Ibid.* 124.
116 *Ibid.*
117 *Ibid.* 129.
118 Translation: "various murmurs" (of discontent). *Ibid.*
119 *Ibid.* 128.
120 *Ibid.*
121 *Ibid.* 130. For further general commentary see also: "Le Congrés International de la Propriété Industrielle tenu á Paris en Septembre 1878" (1878) *Journal des économistes* (4th Series) 87, 89.
122 Translation: "foreigners must be treated as nationals". *Ibid.* 130.

had a property right that was of an intrinsic nature, and not reliant upon domestic law for its creation, then it followed that this property right must be protected without regard to national boundaries. Foreigners should be treated as nationals.

In debating this Resolution, a number of interesting points were raised. In particular, not one delegate spoke against the proposal that foreign inventors should be treated as nationals when seeking a patent. However, a counter-proposal by Pouillet, Lyon-Caen, Armengaud, Droz, Sautter and Depoully, proposed that foreign owners of trade marks and industrial designs should only be granted protection upon conditions of reciprocity.[123] Lyon-Caen explained that there were clear reasons why inventions should be treated differently from trade marks and designs in this respect. The first reason was that it had become customary State practice for foreign inventors to be treated as nationals when applying for patents, and reciprocity was not generally required.[124] However, for trade marks and designs, there was no such customary State practice, and for example, in France, reciprocity was still required.[125] The second reason was that most countries considered it was in the interest of national industry to grant patents as widely as possible, to both nationals and foreigners, in order to have timely access to new inventions.[126] However, there was no such national imperative in relation to trade marks and designs, as the main beneficiary of such legal protection was the manufacturer, and the community's interest was limited.[127]

The counter-proposal was vigorously combated by several delegates, particularly Clunet, a Parisian lawyer, and editor-in-chief of the *Journal du droit international privé*. He argued that no distinction should be made between patents, trade marks and designs, and that all should be subject to the same legal treatment.[128] This was particularly the case since the Conference had just resolved that these were all rights of industrial property. As to the argument based on the different State practices concerning patents, trade marks and designs, Clunet said that the aim of the Conference was to arrive at a "législation universelle",[129] and it should not be overly concerned with current State practice. He also rejected the notion that the community did not benefit from

123 *Ibid.* 130.
124 *Ibid.* 134.
125 *Ibid.* 135.
126 *Ibid.*
127 *Ibid.*
128 *Ibid.* 136.
129 Translation: "universal law" or "universal legislation". *Ibid.*

protection of foreign trade marks, stating that the consumer had every right to know the truth about the origin of goods.[130] Clunet's remarks were met with "Vive approbation" and "Applaudissements",[131] as were those of Séve, Belgian Consul-General to Chile, and representative of the Union of Manufacturers. Like Clunet, Séve stated that once the Conference had resolved that patents, trade marks and designs were industrial property rights, they must all be respected without regard to national boundaries or requirements of reciprocity.[132] This was a view of the majority at the Conference, since the original proposal was adopted.[133]

(ii) Compulsory Licensing

Although the 1873 Vienna Congress had endorsed compulsory licensing "in cases in which the public interest may require it",[134] the 1878 Conference rejected this concept. After some debate, the Conference resolved that:

> Les brevets doivent assurer, pendant toute leur durée, aux inventeurs ou á leurs ayants cause, le droit exclusif d'exploiter l'invention et non un simple droit á une redevance qui leur serait payée par les tiers exploitants.[135]

Most of the delegates at the 1878 Conference appeared hostile to any form of compulsory licensing. Charles Lyon-Caen was one of those who represented the position of the majority.[136] He noted that in Germany and Austria there were systems in operation for the grant of compulsory licenses, but stated that these schemes did not accord with the notion of the patented invention as representing an exclusive property right.[137] In Germany, the system of *Licenzwang* granted a patent to the inventor, but also allowed any other person to make

130 *Ibid.*
131 Translation: "Lively approval" and "Applause". *Ibid.* 136–137.
132 *Ibid.* 137.
133 The record of the Conference does not specify the size of the majority in favour of the Resolution. *Ibid.*
134 See further discussion of this point in Chapter Five.
135 Translation: "Patents must afford, during their period of validity, to inventors or to their third party successors, the exclusive right to exploit the invention and not simply a right to remuneration paid by third party exploiters." (Patents Section, Resolution 2). FRANCE, Ministére de L' agriculture et du Commerce, *Comptes rendus Sténographiques etc.* at 259.
136 Other delegates who subscribed their names to the proposal rejecting compulsory licensing were: Pouillet, Couhin, Dumoustier de Frédilly, Pataille, L. Lyon-Caen, Barrault, and Huard. *Ibid.* 230.
137 *Ibid.* 248–249.

use of the invention on payment of a license fee.[138] In Austria, the patentee received an exclusive right for the initial part of the patented period, but at a later stage the Austrian patent lost its exclusivity, and licenses were granted on a basis similar to that in Germany.[139] Lyon-Caen considered that such systems were inconsistent with the earlier Resolution of the Conference that an invention gave rise to industrial property rights.[140] He argued that if a person had a property interest, then it must amount to more than merely a right to receive license fees.[141] To allow compulsory licensing would amount to saying to an owner of a house that he was not permitted sole occupation, but must open it to all who wished to live there, provided they pay a fee.[142] He also argued that compulsory licenses allowed no protection to the inventor against the actions of competitors, and licensing schemes were too difficult to formulate and administer.[143] Lyon-Caen's speech received "Bravos et vifs applaudissements".[144] Selwyn also spoke in the same terms, and severely criticised any attempt to limit the exclusivity of the patent.[145] Even Max Wirth of Germany supported Lyon-Caen, stating that he found it impossible to fix an adequate fee for compulsory licensing, and severely criticising the recommendation of the Vienna Congress on this point.[146]

Although the Conference endorsed Lyon-Caen's view on compulsory licensing, some delegates were of a different opinion. Two counter-proposals were presented. The first was that of two prominent Austrians, Earnest Gaertner and Franz de Rosas,[147] who proposed the adoption of the Austrian system, with its combination of limited exclusive right, followed by a later right to receive remuneration only.[148] The second counter-proposal was that of Poirrier, Torrigiani,[149] and Limousin,[150] who argued that, in order to reconcile the interests of the public and the inventor, it was necessary for compulsory

138 *Ibid.*
139 *Ibid.*
140 *Ibid.*
141 *Ibid.*
142 *Ibid.*
143 *Ibid.*
144 Translation: "Bravos and lively applause". *Ibid.* 250.
145 *Ibid.* 256–257.
146 *Ibid.* 258–259.
147 Both Gaertner and de Rosas were representatives of the Austrian Society of Engineers and Architects. *Ibid.* 14–15.
148 *Ibid.* 230.
149 Torrigiani was one of the representatives of the Italian Government. He was a member of Parliament. *Ibid.* 12.
150 Charles Limousin, the French economist. *Ibid.* 23.

licenses to be granted at any time during the term of the patent.[151] Poirrier, a manufacturer of chemical products, was the strongest advocate of compulsory licensing. He stated that such a system was necessary to overcome the intrinsic problems of granting a monopoly right to inventors, which was contrary to the public interest, and particularly to the interests of industry.[152] Limousin agreed that the granting of compulsory licenses did not necessarily cause harm to the interests of the inventor.[153] However, in the face of the strong opposition to the counter-proposal, he suggested merely that the matter should be adjourned to the next Conference.[154] This suggestion was rejected, and the Conference resolved to support Lyon-Caen's position against compulsory licensing.[155]

It has previously been noted that one of the main shortcomings of the Conference was its lack of structure, and the tendency to try to deal with many unrelated issues in one session. The debate over compulsory licensing, and the closely related subject of expropriation of patents for reasons of public utility, suffered from this problem. For example, it is obvious from reading the records of the Conference that as soon as Charles Lyon-Caen gave his speech rejecting compulsory licensing, many delegates considered that this should be the end of the matter, and they were unwilling to listen to any opposing speeches. Thus, the speeches of supporters of compulsory licensing were cut as short as possible, and were received with impatience. Due to the short discussion of most issues, it is often difficult to ascertain exactly what the delegates meant when they adopted a particular Resolution.

This lack of clarity in the work of the Conference is particularly apparent in the case of the related question of the expropriation of patents for reasons of public utility. Eventually, after a series of short debates over a number of sessions, the Conference agreed that "[l]e principe de l'expropriation pour cause d'utilité publique est applicable aux brevets d'invention."[156] It is obviously quite strange that the Conference rejected compulsory licensing, yet supported expropriation in the public interest. However, the two Resolutions can be reconciled if it is noted that the Conference appeared to restrict expropriation to circumstances in which the government needed to make use of an invention to promote public purposes. Particular reference was made to the

151 *Ibid.* 230.
152 *Ibid.* 250.
153 *Ibid.* 258.
154 *Ibid.* 257.
155 *Ibid.* 259.
156 Translation: "the principle of expropriation for reasons of public utility is applicable to patents." *Ibid.* 428.

need to ensure inventions could be utilised by government in time of war.[157] In contrast, the type of compulsory licensing discussed by the Conference would not be restricted to government utilisation of inventions.

Another reason why the Conference supported expropriation but not compulsory licensing related to the acceptance of natural property rights in inventions. In the words of Limousin, expropriation did not constitute a violation of property rights.[158] As Pouillet stated, the concept had been in existence in all jurisdictions for a long time, and was considered a sound policy.[159] These brief speeches appeared to reflect the opinion of the majority, since the Resolution was adopted with little further discussion or explanation. The only delegates to speak in opposition were Count de Douhet, (a French Senator), Léon Lyon-Caen, (a Parisian lawyer), Torrigiani, (a member of the Italian legislature), and Selwyn. These delegates argued that there was no real theoretical difference between compulsory licensing and expropriation, as both caused the limitation or loss of the patentee's exclusive rights.[160] They argued that the exclusive property right arising from the contract between the inventor and the public should not be breached by any form of public expropriation, as this would be contrary to principles of justice or equity.[161] These arguments were clearly important, and needed to be considered, but the majority of the delegates were unwilling to debate the matter in any detail.

(iii) Forfeiture of Patents for Non-working

Just as the Conference had considered it consistent with industrial property rights to permit expropriation of patents in the public interest, it also supported forfeiture of patents for non-working.[162] A Resolution was passed which stated that:

> Il y a lieu d'admettre déchéance pour défaut d'exploitation. Cette déchéance devra être prononcée par la juridiction compétente.[163]

157 *Ibid.* 409.

158 *Ibid.* 320.

159 *Ibid.* 312–314.

160 *Ibid.* 287, 411.

161 *Ibid.* See also 318–319. Torrigiani's support for compulsory licensing, but rejection of expropriation is interesting, but can perhaps be explained by his hostility towards the German patent system, which was used as an example of a system where expropriation of patents for public utility often occurred.

162 *Ibid.* 286.

163 Translation: "It is acceptable to allow forfeiture for non-working. Such forfeiture must be pronounced by a competent judicial authority." (Patents Section, Resolution 10) *Ibid.* 429.

It might seem strange that the Conference should do this, giving support, in effect, for the complete loss of property rights instead of a partial restriction, as in the case of compulsory licensing. However, the majority did not see this contradiction. Pouillet, who proposed the forfeiture resolution, justified it on the basis that such provisions existed in many patent systems, such as those of France, Italy and Germany[164] and were intended to protect the public interest.[165] He added that patents were granted in order to secure to the public the use of new inventions, but if the patentee did not work the invention, he did not keep his side of the bargain, and the loss of the patent was justified.[166]

In vain did delegates such as Selwyn, von Rosas, and Charles Assi attempt to illustrate the threats to property rights which flowed from such theorising. Selwyn argued that forfeiture for non-working was as bad as or worse than compulsory licensing.[167] He questioned whether a patentee should lose his property interest merely for non-working, particularly when it might have been the case that the non-working was the result of circumstances over which he had no control.[168] Assi, a Parisian civil engineer, argued that important countries such as the U.K. or U.S.A. did not have such provisions in their patent systems,[169] and that such obligations never produced any useful results.[170] This was also a position taken by de Rosas, who said that forfeiture for non-working was impossible to administer in practice.[171] Nevertheless, and after a very short debate, the Conference did accept forfeiture of patents for non-working.[172] The haste in which the Resolution was adopted shows that the advocates of natural property rights theories were in the overwhelming majority at the Conference. Such delegates accepted either total recognition or total loss of a right, and not its partial limitation. In contrast, the minority who supported a more practical, instrumentalist approach, (such as Selwyn, de Rosas and Assi), argued that partial loss of rights was better than total loss. This result shows how far the Conference was guided by theoretical, rather than practical, considerations. If

164 *Ibid.* 285.
165 *Ibid.* 282.
166 *Ibid.*
167 *Ibid.* 282.
168 *Ibid.*
169 Although in the U.S.A., foreign patentees (but not nationals) were subject to working requirements. *Ibid.* 284.
170 *Ibid.* 283.
171 *Ibid.*
172 *Ibid* 285. See further on this point: Akerman, C., *L'Obligation d'Exploiter et la Licence Obligatoire en Matiére de Brevets d'Invention* (Paris, Librairie du Recueil Sirey, 1936), 58–61.

an inventor was asked to choose between total and partial loss of patent rights, it is unlikely that he or she would choose the former option.

On the other hand, the Conference did not accept forfeiture of patents for importation of patented products from abroad. Such a provision was enshrined in Article 33 of the French law of 5 July 1844, and had given rise to considerable criticism by foreign patentees. For example, in a letter dated 19 January 1878, K. B. Murray, Honorary Secretary of the British Chamber of Commerce had written to the Earl of Derby that:

> British inventors and merchants have just cause of complaint respecting the want of reciprocity enjoyed by them under French patent law.
>
> Dating as far back as 1844, the existing legislation in France is not only contrary to the friendly international relations introduced by the Anglo-French commercial treaty of 1860, but is even diametrically in opposition to the spirit of that Treaty, inasmuch as it enforces the manufacture in France of the patented article, whatever it may be, and however costly the plant, machinery or materials necessary for its production.
>
> According to this law the patented article cannot be made in the United Kingdom and thence shipped to France; No! although French patentees are permitted by British law to produce their ... [products] in *their* own country, and thence sell them to us, under the same protection as that enjoyed by Her Majesty's subjects, the British inventor, to obtain protection in France, must *manufacture in that country* under pain of forfeiting his rights, and of seeing his article copied and made by a French merchant, without the possibility of preventing this moral fraud.[173]

Although Article 27 of the French Law of 5 July 1844 stated that "the patent, which is the just reward of invention, is therefore granted without distinction of nationality, and even when the foreigner's country does not admit reciprocity",[174] Murray argued that the effectiveness of this provision was reduced by the operation of Article 33. Article 33 stated that "the interest of the State requires, that, in exchange for the monopoly which is granted him, the patentee shall cause the national labour to enjoy the handiwork resulting from the exercise of his trade; were it otherwise, a patent would amount to a premium accorded to foreign labour. Consequently the patentee who shall introduce

173 UNITED KINGDOM, Parliamentary Papers, *Report of Her Majesty's Commissioners for the Paris Universal Exhibition of 1878* (1878) vol 1, (C 2588), XXXII, 1, 110–111.

174 *Ibid.*

into France articles manufactured abroad similar to those guaranteed by his patent, shall lose his rights."[175]

At the 1878 Conference, the only delegate who spoke in favour of forfeiture for importation was Pataille, who argued that such provisions remained necessary to protect national industry from competition.[176] He referred particularly to the threat to French industry posed by U.S. and U.K. producers, who sought to flood the French market with imported goods.[177] He was, however, in the minority, as the Conference voted to support the proposal of Barrault, Knoop,[178] and Pieper, that "[l]'introduction dans le pays ou le brevet a été délivré de la part du breveté, d'objets fabriqués á l'étranger, ne droit pas être interdite par la loi."[179] As Droz, speaking on behalf of the [unspecified] majority stated, the views of Pataille were "gothic" and "superannuated".[180] Not only were Pataille's arguments in contradiction with the earlier Resolution of the Conference that foreigners and nationals should be treated equally, but markets were increasingly international, and the law should accommodate these developments.[181]

(iv) Types of Patentable Inventions

An anonymous delegate to the 1878 Conference wrote that one of the most "trés-chaudes"[182] battles of the Conference concerned the issue of whether chemical and pharmaceutical products should be afforded protection.[183] By an unspecified majority, the Conference finally decided that chemical products and foodstuffs were patentable, and by a majority of 46 to 38 it was decided that pharmaceuticals were also patentable.[184]

The Resolution which was adopted by the Conference stated as follows:

175 *Ibid.* 112.

176 FRANCE, Ministére de L' agriculture et du Commerce, *Comptes rendus Sténographiques etc.* at 280.

177 *Ibid.*

178 Knoop was a patent agent in Berlin and Dresden, and represented the German Society of Patent Agents. *Ibid.* 14.

179 Translation: "the importation into the country where the patent has been granted, by the patentee, of foreign-made objects, must not be forbidden by law." *Ibid.* 280.

180 *Ibid.* 280.

181 *Ibid.*

182 Translation: "very hot".

183 Note, 'Le Congrés International de La Propriété Industrielle tenu á Paris en Septembre 1878' (1878) *Journal des économistes* (4th series) 87, 91.

184 FRANCE, Ministére de L' agriculture et du Commerce, *Comptes rendus Sténographiques etc.* at 182, 185.

> En dehors des combinaisons et plans de finances et de crédit, et des inventions contraires á l'ordre public et aux bonnes moeurs, toutes les inventions industrielles seront brevetables. Des brevets doivent être accordés aux inventeurs de produits chimiques, alimentaires et pharmaceutiques.[185]

This Resolution stemmed from a proposal initially put forward by Pouillet and Casalonga.[186] The Conference debate fell into two parts: the first dealing with chemical products and foodstuffs, and the second with pharmaceuticals.

One of the reasons why the delegates were so interested in the patentability of chemical products was because under the prevailing French and German patent laws of the time, only chemical processes, and not products, were patentable.[187] The reason for this limitation was that it was thought right to recognise the fact that more than one inventor could discover the same chemical product, but by using different processes.[188] If a patent had been granted in relation to the product, it would prevent the exploitation of other inventions which attained the same aim, but perhaps by a more economical process.[189] The policy was that competition to discover the most economical process was advantageous to national industry.[190] However, many had begun to question whether this policy was correct. Poirrier, for example, who spoke in favour of the patentability of chemical products, said that the invention of chemical products, like all inventions, required intellectual effort, work, expense, long and difficult scientific study and sometimes involved danger.[191] Similar points were made by other French delegates such as Limousin,[192] Pouillet,[193] and Meissonier,[194] supported by the U.S. delegate Pollok.[195] These delegates

185 Translation: "Apart from financial and credit schemes and plans, and inventions contrary to public order and morality, all industrial inventions should be patentable. Patents should be accorded to inventions of chemical, food, and pharmaceutical products". *Ibid.* 428.

186 D.-A. Casalonga was a patent agent, civil engineer, and member of the Society of Engineers in Paris. He also owned a journal called *La Chronique Industrielle. Ibid.* 17.

187 *Ibid.* 174. See also Note, "Le Congrés International de La Propriété Industrielle tenu á Paris en Septembre 1878" (1878) *Journal des économistes* (4th series) 87, 91.

188 For further details see: (1885) 1 *La Propriété Industrielle* 49.

189 *Ibid.*

190 *Ibid.*

191 FRANCE, Ministére de L' agriculture et du Commerce, *Comptes rendus Sténographiques etc.* at 174.

192 *Ibid.* 180.

193 *Ibid.*

194 *Ibid.* 181. Charles Meissonier was a trader and manufacturer in Paris.

195 *Ibid.* 179.

were most concerned by the fact that excluding chemical products from patentability meant that there was nothing to prevent a person from stepping in and manufacturing the product in competition with the original inventor, thus depriving the inventor of the fruits of his labour. They also thought that there was currently little to encourage inventors to discover new chemical products, since they faced the constant danger of others inventing around their patent.

The contrasting argument was propounded by the Swiss delegate, Schreyer, who warned that if the French Government permitted the patenting of chemical products, many French manufacturers of such products would leave the country, and transfer to Switzerland or Germany.[196] There was evidently a large number of French manufacturers who took the trouble to invent around process patents to arrive at the same chemical product. If this action suddenly was considered an infringement, then it is possible to understand why Schreyer would warn of an exodus. He considered that any manufacturer should be free to make and sell a chemical product, and that the law should encourage the discovery of more efficient and cheaper ways to create certain products.[197] Nevertheless, his views were not persuasive, and the Conference resolved that chemical products should be patentable.

In relation to pharmaceuticals, the opinion of the majority was reflected in the words of Léon Lyon-Caen, who stated that there was no longer any logical reason why inventors of pharmaceuticals should not benefit from the patent system.[198] He noted that in countries such as France there was a long history of excluding pharmaceuticals from patentability. The justification put forward for this exclusion was that in order to protect public health, it was thought best not to encourage charlatans selling patented medicines as the term "patented" might have implied some endorsement of quality by the State.[199] There was also a subsidiary issue that patenting pharmaceuticals might have restricted their general availability to the community.[200]

Most delegates who spoke on the issue supported Lyon-Caen. For example, Georges Lecocq, a lawyer from Amiens, considered that inventors of pharmaceuticals should be treated the same as any other inventor, and that patenting pharmaceuticals could lead to a faster pace of development in this area.[201] A similar view was stated by Barault.[202] In contrast, Emile Genevoix,

196 *Ibid.* 175.
197 *Ibid.*
198 *Ibid.* 178.
199 *Ibid.* 175–176.
200 *Ibid.*
201 *Ibid.* 182–183.
202 *Ibid.* 184.

a pharmacist, and member of the Union of Manufacturers, stated that pharmacists already had quasi-monopoly rights granted by the State through a system of Ordinances, Codes and the need to obtain approval from the Academy of Medicine.[203] He feared that granting patents for pharmaceutical products would encourage charlatanism and urged the Conference not to support the proposal.[204] His basic point was that, in the hands of charlatans, a patent is a means of inducing members of the public to buy products of questionable value, at inflated prices. With similar concerns in mind, Pataille said the matter required further investigation, and noted that in systems where no substantive examination of patents was practised, a patent could be granted for a useless, or even harmful medicine.[205] He considered that this would clearly be against the public interest. However, the majority opinion prevailed that inventors of pharmaceutical products were creators of industrial property, and should not suffer discrimination. Consequently, pharmaceuticals should be patentable. The adoption of the Resolution endorsing the granting of patents for most kinds of inventions was a reaffirmation of the concept of the patent as a natural property right. It signified the Conference's view that the inventor's property right should prevail over any opposing social or utilitarian concerns.

(2) *The Debate over Future Uniform Industrial Property Legislation*

The most momentous and enduring act of the 1878 Conference was the Resolution that:

> Un des buts de la Commission permanente créée par l'initiative privée, sera d'obtenir de l'un des Gouvernements la réunion d'une Conférence internationale officielle, á l'effet de déterminer les bases d'une législation uniform.[206]

This Resolution demonstrated the delegates' commitment to inspiring official interest in uniform industrial property legislation. It was a substantial link between the work of the 1878 Conference, the Diplomatic Conferences of 1880 and 1883, and the Paris Convention.

---

203 *Ibid.* 183–184.

204 *Ibid.*

205 *Ibid.* 185.

206 Translation: "One of the aims of the Permanent Committee created by this private initiative is to obtain from one of the Governments a meeting of an official international Conference to determine the bases of uniform legislation." *Ibid.* 242. In relation to the work of this Permanent Committee, see section B below.

There was, however, a major problem with the Resolution. In essence, it is unclear what the Conference meant by the term "les bases d'une législation uniform". There are several different alternatives which could be used to achieve this aim. Two major ones are: (1) encouraging States to enter into an international treaty devoted to the regulation of industrial property law, or (2) encouraging States individually to adopt certain uniform principles in their domestic legislation, without the need for a specific international treaty. Apart from these two alternatives, there are also questions as to the degree of uniformity sought. The plan could be to seek uniformity in every aspect of industrial property law and procedure, or to recognise that this would be impossible, and to seek uniformity only in respect of certain important matters. These are the sort of issues that arise in implementing the above Resolution. Yet, the 1878 Conference sidestepped these weighty questions, and too readily delegated the task of implementation to the Permanent Committee which it set up.[207]

It is interesting to contrast the words of Teisserenc de Bort, French Minister of Agriculture and Commerce, in his opening address to the 1878 Conference, with the speech of Bozérian at the final session. They had two quite different ideas of the task of the Conference. De Bort stated that the major aim of the Conference was to "comparer les mérites de ces legislations et de préparer une entente destinée á les rendre uniformes, est donc non seulement opportune, mais d'une pressante nécessité."[208] Thus, he appeared to believe that the Conference should draw up some form of international understanding or agreement, which would promote uniformity. In contrast, Bozérian, attorney and member of the French Senate, stated that it would be up to the Permanent Committee and the governments to advance the matters agreed at the Conference from the domain of theory to that of international practice.[209] Thus, Bozérian was admitting that the Conference should not attempt to suggest how uniformity would be achieved. His opinion was typical of the majority of the delegates who thought that the theory or general idea of "uniformity" was good, but did not go any further in thinking about what "uniformity" really entailed.

One reason why many delegates were satisfied to support the bare goal of uniformity, without thinking any further about its implications, was that in 1878, international uniformity in any area of law was exceptional. In the previous

207 For further details about the work of this Committee, see section B below.

208 Translation: "compare the merits of these laws and prepare an understanding destined to render them uniform; this is not only opportune, but of pressing necessity." FRANCE, Ministére de L' agriculture et du Commerce, *Comptes rendus Sténographiques etc.* at 31–32.

209 *Ibid.* 420.

Chapter, it was shown that the "spirit of internationalism" was something quite new in the 1870s and, therefore, the delegates had little guidance from other international conventions. To strive for international uniformity in any area of law was a largely uncharted path. It is therefore unsurprising that the work of the Conference lacked direction on this issue. Before the Conference, commentators had spoken of international uniformity in industrial property legislation, but they did not specify how this should be achieved. For example, in September 1877, Charles Letort wrote in the *L'économiste Français* that uniform patent legislation, which he termed "an international code" was a clear goal, yet he did not address the practical issues associated with its implementation.[210] Many of those who responded to the circular of the 1878 Preparatory Committee also mentioned the need for greater international protection of industrial property rights, particularly patents, but there was no clear consensus on how this goal should be achieved.[211] Therefore, the work of the 1878 Conference on the question of uniformity was no more or less exhaustive than other contemporaneous discussions.[212] For this reason, it is necessary to moderate criticism of the work of the Conference on this point, despite the fact that from an objective view, it was of limited value merely to advocate international uniformity, and leave it to the Permanent Committee and the governments to struggle with the practical application of this recommendation.

The 1878 Conference initially discussed the feasibility of persuading all governments to adopt a uniform industrial property code. At this early stage, there was no serious discussion of an international Treaty. The tenor of the discussion appeared to be in favour of leaving to each government

---

210 Letort, C., 'Une Législation Internationale sur les Brevets d'invention', *L'économiste Français,* 29 September 1877, 390.

211 See for example, the submissions of Robert Macfie, Duroy de Bruignac, D.-A. Casalonga, the Consultative Chamber of Arts and Manufactures of Rethel (Ardennes), the Chamber of the Fabric Traders of Saint-Etienne, and the Chamber of First-Class Pharmacists of the Region of the Seine.

212 Note the harsh criticism of the work of the Conference by Edmond Vidal-Naquet, a Parisian lawyer who had not been present in 1878. He later commented that the fact that the Conference had even for a moment considered the feasibility of an international code on industrial property law showed that the delegates were ignorant of the profound differences which existed in the various legal systems. Vidal-Naquet, E., *Des Marques de Fabrique et de Commerce et du Nom Commercial en droit International* (Paris, L. Larose, 1898), 200–201. Louis Donzel alleged that the 1878 Conference was nothing more than a reflection of excessive "international lyricism" and that even in its amended goal of a "minimum of unification" its work was "impossible and impracticable." Donzel, L., "Commentaire de la Convention Internationale signée á Paris le 20 mars 1883 pour la protection de la Propriété Industrielle" (1891) *Journal des Procés en Contrefaçon* 1, 125–133.

the task of voluntarily adopting common legislation in its own time. A proposal to this effect was made by several influential French delegates, namely Albert Grodet,[213] Count de Maillard de Marafy, Georges Lecocq, F. Tacon,[214] C. Meissonier and L. Jaubert, which sought the "codification des lois sur la propriété industrielle".[215] This proposal was discussed on several occasions during the Conference. It apparently received the support of many delegates, who did not stop to consider how difficult it would be to achieve any degree of international uniformity in industrial property legislation. For example, at the sixth session on 11 September 1878, when the question of an international agreement was discussed at length, some influential members continued to refer to the ultimate goal of a uniform code.[216] A proposed Resolution was suggested by Schreyer, Pieper, de Rosas, Thirion and Clunet that:

> Le Congrés êmet le voeu que l'un des Gouvernements provoque la réunion d'une Conférence international *officielle*, á l'effet de jeter les bases d'une législation uniform.[217]

It is quite remarkable that delegates of such experience and reputation should have believed it possible that the governments could reach such an agreement, especially considering the lack of any useful precedent.

The Conference did finally resolve that "uniform legislation" was necessary, but left it to the Permanent Committee to develop the matter further. Nonetheless, some further guidance as to what was meant by "uniform legislation" can be gleaned from the records of the Conference.

Thus, it is clear that the majority of delegates in favour of "uniform legislation" thought only of a "minimum of uniformity". The meaning of this term varied widely from one person to another, but a few points can be made. De Rosas, for example, appeared to represent a majority view when he said that the "minimum of understanding" meant ensuring foreigners had the ability to apply for patents in countries other than their own.[218] J. Armengaud stated

---

213 Grodet was Secretary of the Industrial Property Section of the Legal Committee of the Paris Exhibition, and a member of the Bureau of the 1878 Conference. FRANCE, Ministére de L' agriculture et du Commerce, *Comptes rendus Sténographiques etc.* at 11.

214 Tacon was an owner of lead-works in Paris. *Ibid.* 27.

215 Translation: "codification of industrial property laws". *Ibid.* 112.

216 *Ibid.* 234.

217 Translation: "The Congress is of the view that one of the Governments should arrange a reunion of an official international Conference, with the purpose of laying down the bases of uniform legislation." *Ibid.* 234.

218 *Ibid.* 239.

that there should be uniformity in relation to such things as the duration of protection, the grant of a priority right for filing patent applications, the requirements for working of patents and the transfer of patent rights.[219] At the same session, the Conference resolved that applicants for patents, designs, models and trade marks should be able to lodge their applications at foreign consulates in their country of residence.[220] On a later occasion, at the session of 14 September, the Conference resolved that any trade mark filed in one country should be equally admitted for filing "as is" in any other contracting State.[221] These were the types of issues that would be the focus of the "minimum of uniformity". Therefore, what the Conference was really saying was that uniform industrial property legislation was a general goal, but at the same time most delegates recognised that uniformity could only initially be achieved in a very restricted sense. It was the task of the Permanent Committee to persuade the governments to agree on uniform legislation on as many issues as possible, but it was noted that this agreement might initially relate only to a small number or "minimum" of issues. However, it is impossible to ascertain from the records of the Conference whether the majority of delegates eventually ended up in supporting an international Treaty, or merely a voluntary text to be individually implemented in each State. The reason for this uncertainty is that, as Bozérian stated, the Conference resolved that all such practical matters would be left to the Permanent Committee.

Despite this Resolution, there were still delegates who thought any unification or codification of industrial property laws was impossible, and who saw the adoption of a limited international treaty as the only realistic solution. Charles Lyon-Caen supported this more practical approach when he argued that it was utopian to suggest that there could be one common industrial property law operating in all countries.[222] He believed that the most the Conference could do was to determine the principal points on which there could be some later international agreement in the form of an international treaty. This treaty would contain a limited number of points on which there could be a common view. He added that it was impossible to arrive at international uniformity of industrial property laws when international relations were based on national treatment, rather than reciprocity.[223] If requirements of reciprocity had been adopted, then Lyon-Caen believed that it would have been easier to

219 *Ibid.* 241–242.
220 *Ibid.* 248.
221 *Ibid.* 333.
222 *Ibid.* 139.
223 *Ibid.* 138.

arrive at international uniformity. Nevertheless the task would still have been extremely difficult.

A similar point was made by Edmond Imer-Schneider, a civil engineer from Berne, and one of the official Swiss delegates. He argued that any proposed international code was impractical, in view of the large differences in the operation of the patent systems in the various States.[224] Although he believed that international uniformity in trade mark legislation might be achieved, it could never be the case for patents so long as some countries practised substantive examination of applications, and others did not.[225] For these reasons, both Lyon-Caen and Imer-Schneider referred the Conference to the recent work of the Viennese section of the Austrian Society of Engineers and Architects, which had adopted certain resolutions calling for an international treaty in the area of industrial property law. One Resolution in particular stated:

> Vu la grande inégalité des lois de brevets d'invention présentes et le changement des relations commerciales internationales actuelles, il est d'une importance urgente que les Gouvernements cherchent, le plus tôt possible, á amener un accord international sur la protection de la propriété industrielle.[226]

The Swiss delegate, Bodenheimer, and the Austrian, Gaetner, also preferred this text,[227] and they were supported by the U.S. delegate Pollok, the French delegates Barrault and d'Oliveira, and the Belgian delegate, Demeur, who believed it impractical to refer directly to the goal of "uniform legislation".[228] Although these views remained in the minority at the Conference, they did appear to have some little influence, especially upon the subsequent work of the Permanent Committee. For example, in 1885 Bozérian wrote that although the original 1878 proposals sought a comprehensive international code, after

224 *Ibid.*

225 *Ibid.*

226 Translation: "In view of the large inequality of current patent laws and the changing international commercial relations, it is of urgent importance that the Governments seek, as soon as possible, to reach an international understanding concerning the protection of industrial property." *Ibid.* 490. The Resolutions had received the support of other Austrian societies, particularly the Industrial Society of Korneuburg, the Industrial Society of Brünn, the Society for the Encouragement of Industry in Bohemia, the German Polytechnical Society in Bohemia, the Administrative Council of the Society of Architects and Engineers of Bohemia, and the Polytechnical Club of Graz. *Ibid.* 493–495.

227 *Ibid.* 234.

228 *Ibid.*

Lyon-Caen's speech there was a realisation that the original goal was too difficult and only a minimum of uniformity was sought.[229] Subsequently, the Permanent Committee tasked to continue the work of the Conference ultimately favoured implementation of the goals of the Conference by way of an international treaty.[230]

Conclusion

Overall, it is possible to see how the 1878 Conference laid the foundations for the eventual adoption of the Paris Convention in 1883. Despite the loose talk of "uniformity" and "international codes", the 1878 Conference was a significant step towards the international recognition of industrial property rights. This was its major achievement, together with its discussion and examination of the theoretical basis of the patent system and industrial property rights generally. Its one major failing was the lack of a more detailed examination of the implications of its support for "uniform legislation". It was unsatisfactory merely to leave this to the Permanent Committee and subsequent international Conferences.

B The Work of the Permanent Committee

The Link between the Unofficial 1878 Conference and the Later Diplomatic Conferences

Introduction

As a result of the work of the 1878 Paris Conference, interest in industrial property rights was no longer confined to the national level; it had become a subject of international concern. In addition, the benefits of the patent system seemed to be even more widely accepted than before. For example, after the Conference ended, an editorial in *The Times* newspaper asserted that the rights of the patentee were "at present in the ascendant", and added that "the principle of patents appears to be admitted too universally to leave its equity a subject for practical discussion."[231]

It is important to explain how the comprehensive Resolutions of the 1878 Conference eventually gave rise, five years later, to the Paris Convention, the major features of which were simply: the establishment of a right of national

229 Bozerian, M.J., *La Convention Internationale du 20 Mars 1883 pour la Protection de la Propriété Industrielle* (Paris, Imprimerie C. Pariset, 1885), 7–8.

230 *Ibid.*

231 *The Times,* 26 September 1878.

treatment, and the inauguration of priority periods for filing patent, design and trade mark applications. The Paris Convention did not establish uniform industrial property legislation, and thus did not achieve the main objective of the 1878 Paris Conference. Why was there such a gulf between the aspirations of 1878 and the achievements of 1883? In essence, while the majority of the delegates to the 1878 Conference had been interested in what the law *should* be, proposals for a diplomatic treaty were only concerned with what *could* realistically be achieved at that time.

(a) *The First Draft Treaty*

One of the Resolutions of the 1878 Conference had proposed that a Permanent Committee should be established "to give effect to the propositions adopted by the Congress of Industrial Property".[232] This proposal for a Permanent Committee had been made by one of the official Italian delegates, Romanelli, who was Director of Commerce and Industry at the Ministry of Agriculture, Industry and Commerce in Rome.[233] The main reason for his proposal was his view that, while uniform industrial property legislation might be the ultimate goal, there were clearly many opinions as to exactly what this entailed and how it should be achieved.[234] The 1878 Conference appeared incapable of finally determining the matter, and it would have to be referred to another body for a longer and more detailed study. The other delegates quickly agreed with this proposal, and the Permanent Committee was established. The Committee, in carrying out its duties, was divided into National Sections, of which the French Section was the largest numerically.[235] A number of influential persons were nominated as members,[236] most of whom had been present at the 1878 Conference. However, only four of these persons, Imer-Schneider (Switzerland), de Nebolsine (Russia), Bozérian and A. Dumoustier de Frédilly

232 FRANCE, Ministére de L' agriculture et du Commerce, *Comptes rendus Sténographiques etc.* at 236.

233 *Ibid.* 12.

234 *Ibid.* 235.

235 *Ibid.* 421. Clunet made the proposal to divide the work of the Committee into "National Sections".

236 Bozérian (France) was elected President of the Permanent Committee. Other members were FRANCE Tranchant, Dumoustier de Frédilly, Meurand, Thirion, Clunet, Grodet, Rendu, Barrault, Charles Lyon-Caen, Barbedienne, Maillard de Marafy, Christofle and Fumouze; RUSSIA: de Nebolsine and Kaupé; U.S.A.: Pollok, Lincoln and Blaze; SWITZERLAND: Bodenheimer and Imer-Schneider; HUNGARY: Hegedüs; GERMANY: Klostermann, Reuleaux and Pieper; LUXEMBOURG: Mullendorff; AUSTRIA: de Rosas and Schmidt; U.K.: Selwyn; NORWAY: Stoltz; ITALY: Torrigiani and Romanelli; BELGIUM: Biebuyck; SWEDEN: Groth. *Ibid.* 420–421.

(France), later went on to represent their countries at the 1880 Conference. Membership of the Committee was entirely voluntary. In addition, the Conference made no special provision for the payment of the expenses of the Committee, or for administrative support. It was unsurprising, therefore, that the issue of funding was raised at the first session of the Committee when Pieper and Grodet requested to know what provision had been made for funding its work.[237] Bozérian replied that there were some funds left over from the Conference, and in addition, the Committee had been promised financial aid from the French Minister of Agriculture and Commerce, Teisserenc de Bort.[238]

The Permanent Committee's main task was to give effect to the Conference's Resolution in favour of uniform industrial property legislation. The work of the Conference assisted the Committee to a certain degree, because the Conference had developed a very comprehensive set of Resolutions which represented optimum legal protection of industrial property rights. However, the Conference had given no indication of whether the Committee should seek immediate implementation of all of the Resolutions, or only some of them. If only some, then there was no indication as to which were the most important. The Committee also had to determine the means of implementation, whether by multilateral treaty, exhortation to universal legislative measures, or something else.

For two days after the 1878 Conference ended, on 18 and 19 September 1878, the Permanent Committee met and considered these questions. There was initially some dispute about the mandate of the Committee, and particularly whether it could discuss matters outside the Resolutions voted by the Conference.[239] Hence it was argued by the Hungarian member, Hegedüs, that the Committee could not draw up a draft for an International Treaty, since this had not been the subject of a specific Resolution of the Conference.[240] However, this view was not widely supported, and the members of the Committee studied with great interest an "Avant-Projet d'un Traité concernant la Création de l'Union Générale pour la Protection de la Propriété Industrielle".[241] This was an extremely detailed and comprehensive draft Treaty, largely based on the work of the Swiss member, Bodenheimer,[242] and included all the matters dealt with at the 1878 Conference. Bodenheimer's idea to incorporate the Resolutions of

237 *Ibid.* 694.
238 *Ibid.*
239 See, for example, the arguments of Tranchant at *Ibid.* 702.
240 *Ibid.* 698.
241 For the text of this draft see: *Ibid.* 712–718.
242 *Ibid.* 696.

the 1878 Conference into a draft Treaty had been inspired by the success of previous multilateral treaties, such as those concerning posts and telegraphs.[243] He had also obviously been influenced by the opinions of Charles Lyon-Caen and Imer-Schneider, who had spoken forcefully in favour of an international Treaty during the Conference.

Bodenheimer's proposed Treaty was well received by the Committee. During this first session, it seemed that the Committee believed that a comprehensive international industrial property Treaty was quite feasible. At the same time, the Committee did not think that complete uniformity in all areas of industrial property law could be achieved immediately. Maillard de Marafy stated, for example, that the aim of the international agreement at this stage was a "minimum d'unification",[244] but cautioned that such unification would have to be compatible with existing domestic legislation.[245] Bozérian agreed that the task of the Committee was to ascertain "le minimum réalisable dans chaque branche de la propriété industrielle",[246] although Reuleaux spoke more generally of "une législation uniforme".[247]

The Bodenheimer draft Treaty was adopted by the Committee with little amendment. The subject-matter of the Treaty was very comprehensive and, if implemented in its original form, would have amounted to more than a minimum of uniformity. Overall, looking at the work of the Committee, it would have to be concluded that the members took the option which made their work easy. All they really did was put the Resolutions of the Conference into a document, and call this an international Treaty. This first draft went beyond the minimum of uniformity which could realistically be achieved, and it was far too detailed for an international instrument.

(b) *The Second Draft Treaty*

It was when the French Section of the Permanent Committee submitted the draft treaty to the French Government, that the conflict between official and private objectives became readily apparent. As Max Outrey, of the French Legation in Washington wrote to William Evarts, U.S. Secretary of State on 9 January 1880:

243 *Ibid.* 698.
244 Translation: "minimum of unification". *Ibid.* 695.
245 *Ibid.*
246 Translation: "the minimum realisable in each branch of industrial property law". *Ibid.* 702.
247 Translation: "a uniform law/legislation". *Ibid.*

> This draft treaty was transmitted by the executive committee to the minister of agriculture and commerce, [Teisserenc de Bort] with a request that he would take the necessary steps to induce the Government of the Republic to take the initiative in bringing about the assembling of an international conference to carry out the work undertaken by the congress. Mr Teisserenc de Bort thought that it was proper to submit at first to the deliberations of an international conference only drafts of resolutions rather of an executive (administrative) than of a legislative character, easy of application, and whose adoption would not require serious modifications of the laws, which are based in various countries on different principles. He consequently requested the French section, acting as an executive committee and representing the commission of the congress, to extract from the draft of the treaty to be recommended to the governments for their adhesion those provisions which seemed to it to enter more particularly into this order of ideas.[248]

Bozérian also expressed a similar view about the attitude of the French Government and the reasons why the first draft was rejected. He stated that the Government received the first draft "with beneficence", but believed that it was necessary to take more account of the divergent legislation of the various States.[249] Consequently, the French Section had to extract from the draft Treaty the articles that could be put into operation without requiring major modifications to domestic laws.[250] In doing so, the French Section adopted a second draft treaty, divided into parts A and B. Under Section A, were provisions which the Section believed would be possible to incorporate immediately into an international Treaty, and under Section B were simple recommendations suggesting the direction in which national laws should in future be modified.[251]

---

248 UNITED STATES OF AMERICA, Congressional Papers, *Report of the Commissioners appointed to Revise the Statutes relating to Patents, Trade and other Marks, and Trade and Commercial Names under Act of Congress approved June 4, 1898* (1900) 56th Congress, 2nd Session, Senate document 20, 231.

249 FRANCE, Ministére des Affaires étrangéres, *Conférence Internationale pour la protection de la propriété Industrielle* (Paris 1880), 20. See also Drouets, C., "La Convention d' Union de la Propriété Industrielle: L' oeuvre de la Conférence de Revision de Londres de 1934" (1935) 134 *Bulletin de la Société d'Encouragement pour L'Industrie Nationale* 376–377; Pelletier, M., and Vidal-Naquet, E., *La Convention d'Union pour la Protection de la Propriété Industrielle du 20 mars 1883 et les Conférences de Revision Postérieures* (Paris, L. Larose, 1902), 10–11.

250 *Ibid.*

251 FRANCE, Ministére de L' agriculture et du Commerce, *Comptes rendus Sténographiques etc.* at 721. For the text of the Second draft Treaty see 721–732. See also Appendix Six.

The second draft treaty contained few substantive provisions. In particular, there was no reference to the theoretical basis of industrial property rights. Perhaps the French Government was too cautious over this issue. It ignored the fact that the 1878 Conference delegates had considered theoretical matters of great importance. Without submitting the issue to official international scrutiny, the French Government appeared to think that theoretical issues were just too difficult to be dealt with at that time.[252]

In consequence, the second draft Treaty contained little of the work of the 1878 Conference. Its major proposal was to accept the principle of national treatment in relation to patents, designs and models, trade marks and commercial names. This had been proposed by the 1878 Conference[253] and was based on the provisions of many earlier bilateral treaties, particularly those containing provisions relating to trade marks.[254] However, for the first time, the second draft treaty provided for rights of priority for the filing of patents, designs and trade marks.[255] This was a departure from the earlier resolution of the 1878 Conference, which had favoured simultaneous deposit in foreign consulates.

It is unsurprising that the amendment favouring the introduction of priority rights should have been included in the second draft Treaty. It is clear that the Resolution relating to deposit at foreign consulates was only adopted by the 1878 Conference because of the strong influence of the work of the Anvers meeting of the Association for the Reform and Codification of the Law of Nations. Bozérian, (together with Pieper, Lyon-Caen, Pouillet, Klostermann and Dumoustier de Frédilly), was one of the proposers of the "foreign consulates" approach who managed to silence opposing opinions by referring to the considerable work done on this issue at the Anvers meeting.[256] However,

252 It also must be acknowledged that statements of a theoretical or philosophical nature are not generally included in international treaties.

253 General Section, Resolution 2, 1878 Paris Conference. See Appendix Five for the text of the Resolution.

254 See, for example, the Commercial Treaties between the U.K. and Austria dated 16 December 1865; the U.K. and Colombia dated 16 February 1866; the U.K. and France dated 23 January 1860; and the U.K. and the Zollverein dated 30 May 1865. These all contained provisions according national treatment. UNITED KINGDOM, Parliamentary Papers, *Extracts from Treaties and Declarations now in force between Great Britain and Foreign Powers relating to Trade Marks, Designs, and Industrial Property, August 1888* (1888) vol XCVIII, C. 5554, 745.

255 See for example, Patents Section, Article 1 of the (second) draft treaty. See Appendix Six for the text of the draft Treaty.

256 FRANCE, Ministére de L' agriculture et du Commerce, *Comptes rendus Sténographiques etc.* at 245.

even during the 1878 Conference there was an outspoken minority which favoured the implementation of priority rights, and it was this view which eventually prevailed in the second draft. Barrault, for example, argued at the 1878 Conference that a 12 month priority period should be granted to inventors to allow them time to file their applications in foreign countries.[257] He stated that the proposal relating to simultaneous filing in foreign consulates would be useless in practice.[258] Similar points were made by Pollok and Colfavru.[259] As Barrault and Pollok were influential members of the Permanent Committee, it was to be expected that their strong views on the matter would eventually prevail. In addition, as time passed, and the influence of the Anvers meeting decreased, it was increasingly apparent that the priority rights approach would be more practical than that of deposit at foreign consulates.[260]

In relation to patents, the only other substantive provision in the second draft was the statement that subsequent patents granted in contracting States in relation to an invention should be granted for a duration of time independent of the original patent in the country of origin.[261] This provision was apparently not based on any pre-existing State practice in commercial treaties, but evolved from a resolution of the 1878 Conference.[262] The Resolution had been a joint proposal of the French delegates Barrault, Pouillet, Charles Lyon-Caen, Dumoustier de Frédilly, Armengaud, Couhin, Grodet, and d'Oliveira, the U.K. delegates Alexander and Wise, and the U.S. delegate Pollok.[263] It was adopted by the 1878 Conference after a brief discussion, and without dissent.[264] There were also general provisions in the second draft treaty relating to the provisional protection of inventions, designs and models, and trade marks displayed at international exhibitions. These provisions were basically in accord with the resolutions of the 1878 Conference.

257 *Ibid.*

258 *Ibid.*

259 *Ibid.* 245–247.

260 *Ibid.* 724.

261 Patents Section, Article 2 of the (second) draft treaty. See Appendix Six for the text of the draft Treaty.

262 Patents Section, Resolution 11 of the 1878 Conference. See Appendix Five for the text of the Resolution. See further: BUREAU INTERNATIONAL DE L'UNION POUR LA PROTECTION DE LA PROPRIETE INDUSTRIELLE, "L'Article 4 de la Convention et les Brevets d'importation" [1886] 2 *La Propriété Industrielle* 27.

263 FRANCE, Ministére de L' agriculture et du Commerce, *Comptes rendus Sténographiques etc.* at 418–419.

264 *Ibid.*

As noted above, the second draft Treaty also contained a series of non-binding Recommendations attached in Section B. Here there was an oblique reference to the importance of industrial property rights. This was expressed in terms of the need for the contracting States to take effective measures to ensure the protection of the rights of inventors, industrial creators, traders and manufacturers.[265] Infringement of such rights should be considered as an offence under the penal law, and not merely give rise to a civil action in damages.[266] Another notable point was that the 1878 Conference Resolution outlawing forfeiture of patents for importation of patented goods was also relegated to the Recommendation Section in Section B.[267] Since this provision was contrary to the French patent law of 5 July 1844, the French Government must have suggested that this form the basis of a Recommendation only. Other Recommendations suggested that the term "design" should be defined in domestic legislation, and that the duration of protection of designs and models should be the same.[268] The French Section also drew up an extensive definition of "trade mark" which it recommended to all contracting States to adopt.[269] It further suggested that purchasers of goods who were misled by false trade marks should have the same legal rights as the owners of the mark.[270] It was also recommended that trade marks and commercial names should be regulated under the same law.[271]

(c) *The Third Draft Treaty*

Despite the fact that the second draft Treaty was a substantially truncated version of the first, it still did not meet with the approval of the French Government. As Bozérian told the 1880 Paris Conference, the second draft was still considered too ambitious, and a third draft was requested.[272] It was this third draft which in August 1880 was submitted to foreign governments who

265 General Section, Section B, Recommendation 1 of the second draft Treaty. See Appendix Six for the text of the draft Treaty.

266 General Section, Section B, Recommendation 2 of the second draft Treaty. See Appendix Six for the text of the draft Treaty.

267 Patents Section, Section B, Recommendation 1 of the second draft Treaty. See Appendix Six for the text of the draft Treaty.

268 Designs and Industrial Models Section, Section B, Recommendations 1 and 2 of the second draft Treaty.

269 Trade Marks Section, Section B, Recommendation 1 of the second draft Treaty.

270 Trade Marks Section, Section B, Recommendation 3 of the second draft Treaty.

271 Commercial Names Section, Section B, Recommendation 1 of the second draft Treaty.

272 FRANCE, Ministére des Affaires étrangéres, *Conférence Internationale pour la protection de la propriété Industrielle* (Paris 1880), 20. See Appendix Seven for the test of the third draft Treaty.

had "made known their assent to the project of meeting and have announced their intention to be represented thereat."[273] The third draft treaty took the form of eleven Articles, divided into five sections: General Questions, Patents of Invention, Designs and Industrial Models, Trade Marks, and Commercial Names.[274] The major point of difference between the second and third draft treaties was that the third only contained substantive provisions, and did not include any additional and non-binding Recommendations. The substance of the provisions was largely the same, but there were some points of difference. In particular, the third draft treaty removed any reference to the need to recognise the independence of patents, designs and models, where such rights were registered in more than one country. Instead, there was a provision which outlawed forfeiture of patents where there had been importation of patented goods,[275] a matter which had only been dealt with by Recommendation in the second draft. The reason for this change is unclear, but it could probably be due to the fact that the question of forfeiture for importation was considered less controversial than independence of industrial property rights.[276] In the later history of the Paris Convention, when the independence of patents was debated, this proved to be a controversial topic and a corresponding article was not included in the Convention until 1900.[277] Other changes significantly

273 In August 1880, those countries which had informed the French Government of their intention to send representatives to the Conference included the U.S.A., United Kingdom, Austria-Hungary, Belgium, Italy, Russia and Switzerland. UNITED STATES OF AMERICA, Congressional Papers, *Report of the Commissioners appointed to Revise the Statutes relating to Patents, Trade and other Marks, and Trade and Commercial Names under Act of Congress approved June 4, 1898* (1900) 56th Congress, 2nd Session, Senate document 20, 233.

274 *Ibid.*

275 Article 6 of the third draft Treaty. See Appendix Seven for the text of the draft Treaty.

276 In France, for example, Art 29 of the law of 5 July 1844 provided that an inventor who had already obtained a patent in a foreign country, could only obtain a patent in France for the same duration as that foreign patent. It had also been held by French courts that if the patent in the foreign country was forfeited, then the French patent would also be forfeited. The patents were said to be "dependent" upon each other. Thaller, E., "Dépendance ou indépendance de Brevets pris pour une même invention dans divers états" (1908) *Revue de droit international privé* 5.

277 The independence of patents was raised again at the Rome Revision Conference in 1886, and was finally inserted in the Paris Convention as Article 4*bis in the Act of Brussels,* 1900. See the Debate over this matter in the records of the 1897 and 1900 Revision Conferences. BUREAU INTERNATIONAL DE L' UNION POUR LA PROTECTION DE LA PROPRIETE INDUSTRIELLE, *Conférence de Bruxelles: Decémbre 1897 et Décembre 1900* (Berne 1901); BUREAU INTERNATIONAL DE L' UNION POUR LA PROTECTION DE LA PROPRIETE INDUSTRIELLE, "La Solidarité des Brevets" (1893) 9 *La Propriété Industrielle* 107. Even after Article 4*bis* had been inserted into the Paris Convention, there remained a significant national practice in countries such as Belgium and France which linked the duration

reduced the impact of the substantive provisions relating to trade marks and designs.[278]

The 1878 Paris Conference strongly supported comprehensive international industrial property protection, with at least a minimum of uniformity, and based upon the notion of inherent property rights in products of intellectual labour. These were lofty ambitions, and the Conference did not avoid tackling the hard issues, such as clarifying the theoretical basis of patent protection. Throughout this book it has been shown that the stability and wide acceptability of the patent system has historically depended upon an understanding of its theoretical basis. Theoretical issues have been at the forefront of debates over the patent system, whether at the time of the passage of the French patent law of 1791, or the abolition controversies of the 1860s to 1870s. The delegates to the 1878 Conference were skilled in patent law and understood this point very well. However, they failed to consider how their proposals could be achieved, and this made the task of the Permanent Committee and French Government more difficult.

It is clear that the French Government took a narrow view of the international industrial property agreement which it had undertaken to promote. It imposed upon the draft its own (realistic but cautious) opinion of what other governments would accept in a multilateral Treaty. Perhaps it would have been better if the French Government had consulted more widely with other governments before finalising the Programme for the 1880 Conference. This contrasts with the approach later taken by the Italian Government in 1886 and subsequent governments which have had the task of organising the Paris Convention revision conferences. After 1886, it became customary for the host government and/or the International Bureau to advise member States of a forthcoming revision Conference and ask them to forward their proposals for revision of the text of the Convention. These proposals have then been forwarded to all member States prior to the Conference, and further comments in reply received and distributed. In this way, all member States have had the opportunity to influence the preparation of the Conference Programme. However, as there was no precedent for the negotiation of such a Treaty in 1880, we should not use the benefit of hindsight to judge the actions of the French Government too harshly.

---

of subsequent patents to that of the original. Note, "De l' indépendance réciproque des Brevets d'aprés l'Article 4*bis* de la Convention d' Union Revisée" (1903) 19 *La Propriété Industrielle* 97.

278 Articles 7–11 of the third draft Treaty.

CHAPTER 7

The Logical Conclusion

A Diplomatic Treaty

> Est-ce á dire que nous vous proposions de préparer, dans cette premiére Conférence, un traité international complet sur la propriété industrielle? Evidemment non: nous comprenons trop bien les difficultés que pourrait présenter l'unification immédiate des legislations de chacun des Etats contractants.[1]
>
> French Minister TIRARD, Paris 1880

The 1880 Paris Conference was the first diplomatic conference concerned solely with the question of international legal protection of industrial property rights. At this Conference, and at the later Paris Conference of 1883, the government representatives faced the difficult task of transforming the aspirations of private individuals and groups into a diplomatic treaty.[2] In many respects, the 1883 Paris Convention did not accord with the earlier resolutions of the unofficial 1873 or 1878 Conferences. In particular, the government representatives at the diplomatic Conferences sidestepped the major issue of clarifying the theoretical basis of the patent system. Yet, several articles of the 1883 Convention were influenced by the work of the earlier unofficial Conferences.

This Chapter examines the work of the diplomatic Conferences of 1880 and 1883, and highlights the process of formation of those articles of the 1883 Convention which were particularly relevant to patents. It also discusses the

---

1 Translation: "Is it the case that we propose to prepare, in this first Conference, a complete international treaty concerning industrial property? Evidently not: we understand too well the difficulties which would attach to any proposal for immediate unification of the legislation of each of the contracting States." (Tirard, French Minister of Agriculture and Commerce, in an opening speech to the 1880 Paris Conference.) FRANCE, Ministére des Affaires étrangéres, *Conférence Internationale pour la protection de la propriété industrielle* (Paris 1880), 16.

2 See also Ricketson, S., *The Paris Convention for the Protection of Industrial Property* (Oxford, Oxford University Press, 2015), 50–59.

 | DOI:10.1163/9789004470125_009

similarities and differences between those articles and the Resolutions of the 1878 Paris Conference, and gives some explanation for these outcomes.

A The Paris Conference of 1880

(a) *Representation at the 1880 Conference, and the Importance of the Jagerschmidt Draft Treaty.*

As the 1880 Paris Conference was a diplomatic Conference, the delegates were restricted to those persons chosen to represent their respective governments. Consequently, unlike the 1878 Conference where 484 delegates attended, there were only 35 delegates at the 1880 Conference. The different types of people involved in the unofficial (1873 and 1878) and diplomatic (1880 and 1883) Conferences was a major reason for the gulf between the Resolutions of the 1878 Conference and the text of the 1883 Paris Convention. No persons attended both the 1873 Vienna Congress and the diplomatic Conference of 1880, and only seven persons were present at both the 1878 and 1880 Conferences.[3] This would appear to be a different situation from that which prevailed in connection with the 1884 and 1885 diplomatic Conferences which preceded the signing of the Berne Convention for the Protection of Literary and Artistic Works in 1886. In those two Conferences there were many delegates present who were members of ALAI (l'Association littéraire et artistique internationale), had participated in the earlier ALAI Berne Conference, or were persons with "a high general awareness of, and familiarity with, the issues involved in international copyright protection."[4]

As can be seen from the following list, most of the delegates to the 1880 Conference did not have any real background in industrial property law, and in fact, many were diplomats with responsibility to represent their countries in a wide range of matters. This contrasted sharply with the occupational experience of the delegates to the earlier unofficial Conferences. In such circumstances, it is unsurprising that the 1883 Paris Convention should have deviated from the objectives of the 1878 Conference.

It can be seen from the list of Conference participants at Table 1 below, 21 States sent representatives to the 1880 Paris Conference. The only notable country missing from the Conference was Germany, which did not attend because of fears that adherence to the Convention would necessitate

3 Statistics derived from studying the list of participants of the 1873, 1878 and 1880 Conferences.
4 Ricketson, S., *The Berne Convention for the Protection of Literary and Artistic Works: 1886–1986* (London, Centre for Commercial Law Studies, 1987), 58.

TABLE 1 Composition of the Delegates at the 1880 Paris Conference[a]

State Represented	Name and Position of Delegate
Argentine Confederation	John LE LONG, former Consul-General
Austria	Dr WOERZ, adviser to the Ministry of Commerce
	Count CASTELL, secretary to the Ministry of Commerce
Hungary	Dr HERICH, adviser to the Ministry of Commerce
Belgium	A. DEMEUR, member of the Chamber of Representatives, lawyer.
	E. DUJEUX, chief of the Bureau of Patents for Inventions, Ministry of the Interior
Brazil	J.C. DE VILLENEUVE, resident diplomat
United States of America	General NOYES, diplomat in Paris
	James O. PUTNAM, resident diplomat in Brussels
France	Senator J. BOZERIAN, lawyer
	Ch. JAGERSCHMIDT, diplomat
	GIRARD, Director of Commerce (Domestic) in the Ministry of Agriculture and Commerce
United Kingdom	H. READER-LACK, Director of the service of Patents, Designs and Trade Marks.
Guatemala	CRISANTO MEDINA, diplomat
Italy	INDELLI, former Deputy Magistrate
	R. TRINCHERI, Chief of the Bureau of Patents
Luxembourg	JONAS, Chargé d'affairs
Netherlands	H.C. VERNIERS van der LOEFF, Adviser of State
Portugal	Guilhermino-Augusto DE BARROS, Director-General of Posts, Telegraphs and Beacons
	Camillo-Claudino de MORAES, merchant
	Pedro d'ALCANTARA VIDOEIRA, civil servant and chief of the Department of Posts
Russia	A. de NEBOLSINE, Chief of the Industrial Section of the Department of Commerce and Manufacture, and adviser of State in St Petersburg.
Salvador	J.M. TORRES CAICEDO, diplomat

TABLE 1 Composition of the Delegates at the 1880 Paris Conference (*cont.*)

State Represented	Name and Position of Delegate
Sweden	A. LAGERHEIM, Secretary-General of the Ministry of Foreign Affairs
Norway	Professor O. BROCH, Institut de France
Switzerland	KERN, diplomat
	Jules WEIBEL, engineer, Vice-President of the Swiss Union of Commerce and Industry and President of the Swiss section of the Permanent Commission for the Protection of Industrial Property
	E. IMER-SCHNEIDER, civil engineer, former delegate of the Swiss Confederation to the industrial property Conference of 1878, Secretary of the Swiss international section.
Turkey	J. AMASSIAN-EFFENDI, Director-General of Agriculture
Uruguay	Colonel Juan-Jose DIAZ, Chargé d'Affairs
Venezuela	J. M. de ROJAS, diplomat
Secretaries having a Consultative Role	E. ORTOLAN, of the Ministry of Foreign Affairs in Paris
	A. DUMOUSTIER DE FREDILLY, Chief of the Bureau of Industry and Patents for Inventions at the Ministry for Agriculture and Commerce.
Assistant Secretaries	CHATAIN, attaché in the Management of Commercial Affairs, Ministry of Foreign Affairs
	Gaston BOZERIAN, Subordinate Director of the Ministry of Justice, civil engineer

[a] France, Ministére des Affaires étrangéres, *Conférence Internationale pour la protection de la propriété industrielle* (Paris 1880), 6–7. Note that in some cases, only surnames of the delegates are provided in the official report.

modification to the domestic German patent legislation, which had only been enacted in 1877.[5] Of the persons who attended the 1880 Conference, only the

5 In a note dated 12 July 1880, Prince Hohenlohe, German Minister of Foreign Affairs, wrote to the French Minister of Foreign Affairs, de Freycinet, stating that Germany would not

Belgian delegate (Demeur), the French delegates (J. and G. Bozérian, Ortolan, and A. Dumoustier de Frédilly), the Swiss delegate (Imer-Schneider) and the Russian delegate (de Nebolsine), had participated in the 1878 Paris Conference.

Although nearly all participants at the 1878 Conference were excluded from attending the 1880 Conference, the presence of Senator J. Bozérian as the President of both Conferences did provide some kind of link between the two meetings. Bozérian was one of the most visionary of all the French commentators on industrial property law, and, unlike most of the other delegates, was unafraid to criticise those provisions of the law of his own country which he considered unfair.[6] It should also be noted that several of the delegates to the 1880 Conference were persons of experience in industrial property law, even though they had not attended the 1873 or 1878 Conferences, and thus had limited knowledge of this important preliminary work. Trincheri of Italy, Dujeux of Belgium and Reader-Lack of the United Kingdom, all had senior positions in their respective Patent offices. Weibel, of Switzerland, was the President of the Swiss Section of the Permanent Committee formed after the 1878 Conference. Yet, apart from these persons, most of the delegates did not appear to be very familiar with the intricacies of industrial property law. This was particularly true of the delegates from the U.S.A.,[7] Hungary, Brazil, Guatemala,

attend the Paris Conference. He said: "The commission charged with the examination of the proposition of the French Government, entirely aware of the importance of that question to Germany, can not admit the necessity of the German Government participating in a conference of which the result will be without doubt to profoundly modify the legislation of very recent enactment which regulates this matter over the whole Empire." UNITED STATES OF AMERICA, Congressional Papers, *Report of the Commissioners appointed to Revise the Statutes relating to Patents, Trade and other Marks, and Trade and Commercial Names under Act of Congress approved June 4, 1898* (1900) 56th Congress, 2nd Session, Senate document 20, 211. However, at the tenth session of the 1880 Conference, Kern, of Switzerland, noted that as a result of reading the draft text of the Convention prepared at the 1880 Conference, the Government of the German Empire determined that its fears were unfounded, because the Convention did not greatly interfere with the operation of domestic legislation. FRANCE, Ministére des Affaires étrangéres, *Conférence Internationale pour la protection de la propriété industrielle* (Paris 1880), 149.

6 For example, Bozérian considered "barbarous" and "absolutely useless" the French law concerning forfeiture of patents for importation of patented articles. FRANCE, Ministére des Affaires étrangéres, *Conférence Internationale pour la protection de la propriété industrielle* (Paris 1880), 56. He also denounced the French law which rendered as unpatentable inventions prior published in a foreign country. *Ibid.* 49.

7 The U.S.A. was represented at the 1880 Conference by two diplomats, Noyes and Putnam. The decision to send diplomats to the Conference rather than persons skilled in industrial property law was later criticised in the 1900 Report of the Patent and Trademark Law Reform Commissioners. The Commissioners stated that at none of the industrial

Luxembourg, the Netherlands, Portugal, Salvador, Sweden, Norway, Turkey, Uruguay and Venezuela. Most of these delegates did not contribute greatly to the work of the 1880 Conference. Not only were they generally unskilled in industrial property law, but (apart from the U.S.A.) their countries did not have very developed industrial property legislation.

Typical of such countries was Brazil. As the former President of the Brazilian National Institute of Industrial Property, A.C. Bandeira, stated over a century later, Brazil ratified the Paris Convention in 1883 at a time when "slavery still represented an important factor in the country's economic life".[8] The country's economy was based on agriculture, and most work was done by slaves, rather than machines. Thus, while there was little need for industrial property legislation, Brazil acceded to the Paris Convention because of its "tendency to establish legal and institutional relations that are in advance of its real socio-economic conditions."[9] Brazil's upper classes also had strong cultural ties with France, and participating in the work of the 1880 Conference and ratifying the Convention would have been seen to be strengthening these ties.[10] Thus, it would not have been expected that the Brazilian delegate would have made much contribution to the work of the 1880 Conference.

In a similar way, one wonders how the delegate of the Netherlands could have made a useful contribution to the 1880 Conference when that country had abolished patent protection in 1869.[11] Although J.J. Bos[12] noted that the Dutch Government thought it "useful to have an exchange of views with other countries on several points of industrial property",[13] its delegate did not go to the Conference prepared to discuss any more than the most general principles.[14] The Portuguese delegates were clearly interested only in the prevention

---

property conferences between 1878 and 1886 were "there present on behalf of the United States any delegate qualified by the close and thorough knowledge of our patent system, which can be acquired only by experience, to properly present to the European delegates its principles and advantages." UNITED STATES OF AMERICA, Congressional Papers, *Report of the Commissioners appointed to Revise the Statutes relating to Patents, Trade and other Marks, and Trade and Commercial Names under Act of Congress approved June 4, 1898* (1900) 56th Congress, 2nd Session, Senate document 20, 11.

8 Bandeira, A.C., "Brazil's Ratification of the Paris Convention of 1883" [1984] *Industrial Property* 369, 370.

9 *Ibid.*

10 *Ibid.*

11 See Chapter Four on this point.

12 Bos was a former President of the Netherlands Patent Office.

13 Bos, J.J., "The Netherlands and the Paris Convention for the Protection of Industrial Property" [1984] *Industrial Property* 383.

14 *Ibid.*

of counterfeiting of agricultural products, particularly wine.[15] These peripheral motivations for attending the Conference continued into 1883, with the Serbian Government sending a representative to the 1883 Paris Conference and later ratifying the Convention, only because of its "policy of strengthening national sovereignty, based on the Berlin Treaty of July 1, 1878, by the conclusion of various multilateral and bilateral international conventions."[16] It was clear that Serbia entered into the Paris Convention as part of its eagerness to accede to any international treaty, without concern as to its contents.[17] At the time of acceding to the Paris Convention, Serbia had only one textile mill, one steam mill and some foundries in mines.[18] "Production monopolies" had been available in Serbia since 1873, but there was no evidence that any had been granted.[19] In such circumstances, Serbia did not have much experience of industrial property laws or practice to assist the preparatory work of the Paris Convention.

Another problem associated with the work of the 1880 Conference was the fact that many Governments seemed unsure of the aims of the meeting. Even though each had been previously supplied with a copy of the third draft Treaty prepared by the French Section, many delegates expressed surprise when Saint-Hilaire, French Minister for Foreign Affairs, stated that the object of the Conference was to fix on a small number of general principles with which all nations could fall into agreement, which would then be used to form an international Treaty.[20] When Bozérian subsequently asked the delegates to indicate whether, in principle, their governments would be agreeable to the French proposal to lay down the bases of an international Union, many responded that they had no instructions on the matter.[21] Only the delegates of Austria, Hungary, Belgium, Brazil, Italy, Portugal, Sweden, Norway and Venezuela agreed with the French proposal, but delegates of the U.S.A., Russia,

15 FRANCE, Ministére des Affaires étrangéres, *Conférence Internationale pour la protection de la propriété industrielle* (Paris 1880), 82–83. See also Mota Maia, J., "Development of Portuguese Industrial Property Legislation in the Light of Portugal's Ratification of the Paris Convention" [1984] *Industrial Property* 386, 388.

16 Bulajic, M., "Serbia, One of the Founding States of the 1883 Paris Union" [1984] *Industrial Property* 399.

17 This was a relatively common practice at the time.

18 Bulajic, M., "Serbia, One of the Founding States of the 1883 Paris Union" [1984] *Industrial Property* 399.

19 *Ibid.*

20 FRANCE, Ministére des Affaires étrangéres, *Conférence Internationale pour la protection de la propriété Industrielle* (Paris 1880), 13.

21 *Ibid.* 21–22.

the Netherlands, United Kingdom, Uruguay and Switzerland stated that they had received no such instructions.[22] In particular, one would question why the delegates of the U.S.A. made this reply, since U.S. Congressional Papers reveal that the U.S. Government had been previously fully informed by the French Government of the aims of the Conference, and had plenty of time to give the necessary instructions to its delegates.[23]

As can be seen from the above discussion, the 1880 Conference lacked delegates with the range of experience of those who had attended the 1873 and 1878 Conferences. It also began with a severe limitation in the scope of its inquiry because the French Government insisted upon narrowly defining the Programme of the Conference. However, the second of these difficulties was somewhat ameliorated when the Conference voted to reject the French Government's Programme (the third draft Treaty), and instead adopted an alternative draft (the Jagerschmidt draft) as the basis of its discussions.

The Jagerschmidt draft had been prepared by Charles Jagerschmidt of the French Ministry of Foreign Affairs, who had no apparent experience in industrial property law, but did have experience in legislative drafting. Jagerschmidt took the rather vague and general wording of the text of the third draft Treaty, and transformed it into a new draft which, after some amendment, formed the basis of the 1883 Convention.[24] In total, approximately 40% of the work of the Conference was devoted to general issues such as national treatment and priority rights, 10% was devoted to patent issues, 30% was devoted to other areas of industrial property law and 20% to administration of the Treaty. It is with the first two of these subjects that this chapter is particularly concerned.

---

22 *Ibid.*

23 For example, in a letter dated 9 January 1880, Max Outrey, of the French Legation in Washington, advised William Evarts, U.S. Secretary of State, that a draft Treaty had been prepared "to be concluded by the different adhering powers, the object of said treaty being to form of the contracting parties a 'union for the protection of industrial property', and to fix the general principles which should, by common consent, be rendered uniformly applicable to the matter." On 19 March 1880, Evarts acknowledged receipt of the Programme of the Conference (which took the form of the third draft Treaty), and stated that he understood that "it is proposed for the present to limit the international agreement in question to the making of such regulations as would not require serious modifications to the laws which are based in various countries on different principles." UNITED STATES OF AMERICA, Congressional Papers, *Report of the Commissioners appointed to Revise the Statutes relating to Patents, Trade and other Marks, and Trade and Commercial Names under Act of Congress approved June 4, 1898* (1900) 56th Congress, 2nd Session, Senate document 20, 231–232.

24 See Appendix Eight for the text of the Jagerschmidt draft Treaty.

(b) *An International Union for the Protection of Industrial Property*

(1) General Issues

(i) *"Industrial Property"*

Although this book has been mainly concerned with demonstrating how the concept of patent rights developed in domestic and international law prior to the Paris Convention, it is not possible to overlook the fact that by 1878 it had become well accepted that a patent was only one type of "industrial property" right. The 1878 Conference had made extensive use of the term "industrial property" to describe patents, trade marks, designs and models, and commercial names. This term was consistent with the 1878 Conference's Resolution that "[t]he right of inventors and industrial originators in their works or manufacturers and traders in their marks is a right of property".[25]

The delegates to the 1880 Conference also agreed that the term "industrial property" should be used to describe the rights protected by the Convention. Article 1 of the 1883 Convention states that the Convention creates a "Union" for the "Protection of Industrial Property". It seems, however, that these delegates did not have such a well-developed understanding of the nature of industrial property rights as the private delegates to the earlier Conference. Since the 1880 Conference sidestepped the larger theoretical issues tackled by the 1878 Conference, it is unclear whether the term "industrial property" was incorporated into the Convention because the delegates fully endorsed the earlier (1878) Resolutions, or whether (as is more likely), the term was used for reasons of convenience without a full understanding of its implications.

The title "Union for the Protection of Industrial Property" was proposed by Jagerschmidt in his original draft Article 1. This was accepted by the 1880 Conference with little discussion. The only references to any discussion on the matter were prompted by the statement of the Portuguese delegate, de Barros, who proposed that the Convention should have a title which summed up its aims.[26] He believed it was important that the Convention expressly recognise protection for agricultural products. Wines, in particular, were the subject of much fraudulent activity in Portugal, and he wanted stronger legal protection for these products.[27] Not all delegates agreed with the proposal to include

---

25 The Resolution adds that "The civil law does not create it; it only regulates it." General Section, Resolution 1 of the 1878 Conference. See Appendix Five.

26 FRANCE, Ministére des Affaires étrangéres, *Conférence Internationale pour la protection de la propriété Industrielle* (Paris 1880), 32.

27 *Ibid.* At a later meeting, the delegate of Portugal proposed that Article 1 include a reference to the name of the Union as follows: "The Union for the protection of industrial property and agricultural products." *Ibid.* 124. This proposal was not adopted.

protection for agricultural products in the Convention. While the Russian delegate said that the words "industrial property" would include agricultural products, the Hungarian delegate argued that they had a determined meaning, which did not include agricultural products.[28] In an attempt to seek some compromise on the matter, the Conference agreed that only the general term "industrial property" would be used in Article 1, but a more expansive definition would be included in the Final Protocol.[29] This is exactly what was done. Paragraph 1 of the Final Protocol, which was accepted at the 1880 Conference without further discussion stated that:

> The words 'industrial property' should be understood in the broadest sense; they relate not only to the products of industry in the strict sense but also to agricultural products (wines, grain, fruit, cattle etc.), and mineral products which are put into trade (mineral waters, etc.).

It was a great failing of the 1880 Conference that it endorsed the use of the term "industrial property" without making any attempt to explain why this term was used, and the nature of the "property" right protected. This was one major difference between the work of the 1878 and 1880 Conferences. The first saw this as an issue of immense importance, and the second as something to be dealt with as briefly as possible.

(ii) *The Question of an International "Union"*

Just as the term "industrial property" prompted little discussion at the 1880 Conference, hardly any attention was paid to the implications of implementing a Treaty which created an international "Union". Most of the provisions concerning the relationship between the members had been presented to the 1880 Conference in the Jagerschmidt draft, and, according to Bozérian, many of the most important features had been taken from earlier treaties such as the International Telegraph Union (1865) and the Universal Postal Union (1874).[30] The Paris Convention was the first multilateral industrial property treaty. Yet it is strange that the crucial issues of what was meant by the term "Union" and the concept of an "open" relationship between the member States were not discussed at the 1880 Conference except in the briefest fashion.

28 *Ibid.* 58.

29 *Ibid.* 59.

30 Bozerian, M.J., *La Convention Internationale du 20 Mars 1883 pour la Protection de la Propriété Industrielle* (Paris, Imprimerie C. Pariset, 1885), 27.

As far as can be ascertained from the Conference records, one of the important aims of the Convention was to include the largest possible number of States as members, and therefore, the Convention was to remain open for signature indefinitely. But this provision was adopted from the Jagerschmidt draft with no further discussion.[31] Another feature of the "open" Union was the inclusion of specific provisions for its periodic revision. Any member States could propose amendments to the Convention which would lead to its constant improvement. Again, this received no attention at the Conference. As the later French commentator, Roubier, notes, these were significant features of an "open" Union. By these mechanisms, the text of the Convention was likely to have influence on the development of laws in States not party to the Convention, and later induce them to enter into it.[32] Roubier also argues that these principles upon which the Union was founded "had sooner or later to bring about a complete equality of interests, at least an equality before the law in respect to the protection accorded on all the territory of the Union."[33]

On several occasions the 1880 Conference did acknowledge its debt to the earlier postal and telegraph Unions. However, this was only in relation to the provisions concerning the regulation of the International Bureau[34] and its funding.[35] At the 1883 Conference, the delegates acknowledged that the procedure for the exchange of ratifications was modelled upon the postal Union (among others).[36]

There is only one reference in the 1880 Conference records to the delegates' views about the "Union" they were creating. This arose in the context of discussions over the tasks of the International Bureau. According to the delegates of Norway, Portugal and Uruguay, the International Bureau was the lynchpin of the Union, as it created a common bond between States.[37] The Swiss delegate, Kern, agreed, noting that the Bureau was necessary to achieve the Convention's objective of eventual unification of industrial property laws.[38]

31 FRANCE, Ministére des Affaires étrangéres, *Conférence Internationale pour la protection de la propriété Industrielle* (Paris 1880), 145–146.

32 Roubier, P., "Le droit unioniste de la propriété Industrielle" [1951] *Journal du Droit International* 676, 705.

33 *Ibid.* 709.

34 FRANCE, Ministére des Affaires étrangéres, *Conférence Internationale pour la protection de la propriété Industrielle* (Paris 1880), 110 (Swiss delegate Kern).

35 *Ibid.*

36 FRANCE, Ministére des Affaires étrangéres, *Conférence Internationale pour la protection de la propriété Industrielle* (Paris 1883), 46.

37 FRANCE, Ministére des Affaires étrangéres, *Conférence Internationale pour la protection de la propriété Industrielle* (Paris 1880), 112–115.

38 *Ibid.* 115.

Roubier has further argued that the "Union is a legislative organisation insofar as it tries to establish a law common to its members [in the field of industrial property law] but it is also an administrative organisation to control certain rights to industrial property."[39] He adds that the power of the Union is drawn from the Paris Convention treaty which gives rise to the Union and "constitutes an obligation for all of those who participate in it."[40] Does Roubier describe accurately the meaning of the term "Union" under the 1883 Convention? Perhaps not, as he implies that the term has a significance which in reality did not exist in 1883. Although the term "Union" in the earlier postal and telegraph Conventions did have a strong territorial connotation, this was not the case with the 1883 Convention. In the earlier Unions, there was almost a codification of the regulations of the postal and telegraph services throughout the territory of the member States, but this did not occur with the 1883 Convention. Under the 1883 Convention, there was only a single Union in the limited sense that national treatment had to be accorded, but this requirement did not alter the fact that the extent of substantive legal protection for industrial property rights still varied markedly from one member State to another. There is also no evidence that the delegates considered that the "Union" would have an international legal personality independent of the separate legal existence of each contracting State. It is true that they thought of the International Bureau as a separate organ of the Union, having an administrative office, which would also promote unification of industrial property laws, but this did not mean that the Union itself had an express international legal personality.[41]

(2) General Provisions Which Formed a Cornerstone of the Union

(i) *National Treatment – Article Two of the Paris Convention*

The Jagerschmidt draft, like the three earlier drafts and the 1878 Conference Resolutions, proposed the establishment of a right of national treatment as one of the cornerstones of the Convention. Draft Article 2 was first proposed by Jagerschmidt in the following terms:

> The subjects and citizens of each of the contracting States shall enjoy reciprocally, in all the other States of the Union, in the matter of patents,

---

39 Roubier, P., "Le droit unioniste de la propriété Industrielle" [1951] *Journal du Droit International* 676, 691.

40 *Ibid.* 693.

41 See also Ricketson, S., *The Berne Convention for the protection of literary and artistic works: 1886–1986* (London, Centre for Commercial Law Studies, 1987), 146–156 for a discussion of the meaning of the term "Union" under the Berne Convention of 1886.

> industrial designs or models, trade marks, and commercial names, the advantages that their respective laws now accord or may hereafter accord to nationals. They shall have the same protection as the latter and the same legal remedy against any injury to their rights, upon the only condition that they accomplish the formalities imposed upon nationals by the domestic legislation of each State.[42]

In general, most of the delegates to the 1880 Conference accepted the general idea of national treatment, although there was a great deal of confusion about the full implications of this term.

Bozérian noted that the Union would not be established, for the moment at least, without the condition of respecting, as much as possible, the domestic legislation of each State.[43] He added that the objective of national treatment would be initially sufficient as it was necessary to cater to countries such as the Netherlands and Switzerland which did not have patent legislation.[44]

There was considerable confusion as to the meaning of the term "national treatment". Delegates from Italy and Uruguay believed that Article 2 would prevent their countries from extending rights to citizens of countries where the law in regard to industrial property matters was not in harmony with their own domestic law.[45] A Portuguese delegate, de Barros, agreed with this assessment,[46] and unsuccessfully proposed the adoption of the following amendment, which would have introduced the requirement of substantive reciprocity:

> All the contracting States shall enjoy reciprocally the advantages that their respective laws accord or shall accord to their nationals, in so far as the latter shall accomplish the formalities established by the legislation of each State.[47]

42 Translated from the original French. For the full text of the Jagerschmidt draft treaty, see Appendix Eight.

43 FRANCE, Ministére des Affaires étrangéres, *Conférence Internationale pour la protection de la propriété Industrielle* (Paris 1880), 33.

44 *Ibid.* The Swiss delegate (Kern) agreed that it was important that a State could not be forced to accord to foreigners greater rights than its own citizens enjoyed. However, he added that in Switzerland there was a growing feeling in favour of patents, and the Federal Conseil had voted unanimously to consider the matter. The federal Government had been invited to prepare a draft law. *Ibid.* 33–34.

45 *Ibid.* 33–34.

46 *Ibid.* 36.

47 *Ibid.*

Both Turkish and Austrian delegates found difficulty with the words in the Jagerschmidt draft: "upon the only condition that they accomplish the formalities imposed upon nationals by the domestic legislation of each State."[48] An Austrian delegate, Castell, noted that a Convention of 1879 concluded between Austria and France on the subject of trade marks required the French to file their trade marks in certain chambers of commerce, whereas Austrian nationals could file their trade marks at the chamber of their domicile. This would conflict with national treatment, and might need reform.[49] A Belgian delegate, Demeur, also raised the issue of national treatment concerning the formalities associated with the acquiring of protection. He noted that the law in Sweden required foreigners who wished to apply for patents to appoint a representative in Sweden.[50] However, Swedish nationals were not required to appoint such a representative. Such laws could be in conflict with the requirements of national treatment.

Bozérian's general reply to all these concerns was to state that national treatment did not prevent a country from extending rights to foreign nationals from countries not party to the Union.[51] He added that some of the concerns such as those of Demeur showed a confusion between the conditions imposed for acquiring the right, and the formalities of procedure. Bozérian stated that assimilation did not go that far.[52] However, Demeur was not satisfied with this reply, and, in a later session, reiterated his view that Article 2 should state plainly that its effect did not extend to harming the domestic rules of procedure.[53] Consequently, the Conference agreed to insert in a Final Protocol the following explanation:

> It is understood that the final provision of Article 2 of the Convention causes no harm to the legislation of each of the contracting States, in so far as it concerns the procedure in courts and the jurisdiction of those courts.[54]

Yet Swiss, Hungarian and Dutch delegates continued to assert that the word "reciprocally" in Article 2 was apt to confuse.[55] The misunderstanding could

48 *Ibid.* 36.
49 *Ibid.*
50 *Ibid.* 38.
51 *Ibid.*
52 *Ibid.*
53 *Ibid.* 124–125.
54 *Ibid.*
55 *Ibid.* 39.

result in the belief that Article 2 required not only the application of national treatment, but also the application of substantive reciprocity. The Swiss delegate, Weibel, said it might be argued that because Switzerland did not have a patent law, then Swiss nationals in other contracting States would not be able to avail themselves of foreign patent rights.[56] Eventually, the Conference agreed to remove the reference to the word "reciprocally", because of these concerns.[57]

The Hungarian delegate also wanted to add a provision to Article 2 stating that an "invention, design or model belonging to the public domain in its country of origin shall not be the object of exclusive enjoyment in another State."[58] However, Bozérian replied that this matter was best regulated by the law of each State, not an international Treaty.[59] Consequently, the final version of Article 2, which received the approval of the 1880 Conference, was as follows:

> **Article 2**
> The subjects or citizens of each of the contracting States shall, as regards patents, industrial designs, trademarks, and trade names, enjoy the advantages that their respective laws now grant or may hereafter grant to nationals. Consequently, they shall have the same protection as the latter, and the same legal remedy against any infringement of their rights, provided that they observe the formalities imposed upon nationals by the domestic legislation of each State.[60]

The adoption of the requirement of national treatment was one major instance where the 1878 and 1880 Conferences were in complete agreement. Support for this concept was undoubtedly due to the fact that national treatment had figured in previous bilateral commercial treaties, and so the delegates were

56 *Ibid.*
57 *Ibid.* 44.
58 *Ibid.*
59 *Ibid.* Other discussions concerning Article 2 related to the following minor points: (1) A Portuguese delegate had asked that there be removed from the first line of Article 2 one or other of the words "subjects" or "citizens". However, the Conference considered that both words were necessary because of the diverse Constitutions of the various nations. (2) A Portuguese delegate also proposed an amendment of draft Article 2 which would have had the effect of removing the second sentence. However, the rest of the delegates did not share this view. Nevertheless, the Conference did agree to add the words "in consequence" to make a connection between the two sentences. *Ibid.* 44.
60 *Ibid.* 162. Translated from the original French.

reasonably familiar with it.[61] The adoption of national treatment rather than substantive reciprocity was consistent with the idea that the Convention was only the first step towards international uniformity in industrial property law. National treatment still allowed States to maintain their domestic industrial property laws without significant amendment, and Union nationals could have the benefit of these laws throughout the States of the Union.

(ii) *Rights of Non-Union Nationals – Article Three of the Paris Convention*

Whether nationals of non-Union States should be able to claim the benefit of the Convention was a question which caused considerable debate at the 1880 Conference. It is clear that granting protection to all persons, without distinction of nationality, was consistent with the Resolutions of the 1878 Conference, and general principles recognising industrial property rights. If, as had been resolved in 1878, industrial property rights were inherent in the act of creation, and only regulated by legislation, then the 1880 Conference should have allowed no distinction to be made between the rights of Union nationals and foreigners.

This question first arose in discussions over the right of priority in Article 3 of the Jagerschmidt draft. Some amendments had been made to the original draft stating that "A person who has regularly filed an application for a patent. …" should be granted a right of priority. The issue then arose as to whether the original words in the draft – "A person who", should be replaced by the words "Tout ressortissant" (loosely translated as "Any national") "of one of the contracting States."[62]

Jagerschmidt, who supported the proposed amendment, stated that the right of priority should only be extended to those persons who were inhabitants of one of the contracting States.[63] This was a viewpoint which was consistent with customary principles in international treaties, but it was clearly not in conformity with the Resolutions made in 1878. It was for this reason that two delegates spoke out against the proposed amendment. The principal of these was Demeur, the Belgian delegate, who had also attended the 1878 Conference.

61 See for example, the Treaty of Commerce between the United Kingdom and Austria-Hungary of 5 December 1878, discussed in Chapter Five above.

62 FRANCE, Ministére des Affaires étrangéres, *Conférence Internationale pour la protection de la propriété Industrielle* (Paris 1880), 128.

63 *Ibid.*

First, Demeur argued that confining the operation of Article 3 effectively to subjects and citizens of contracting States would be in conflict with other Articles of the Convention such as Article 4, and parts of Articles 5 and 9.[64] This was because these latter Articles made no reference to nationality requirements. Second, he asserted that it would be unwise for the Convention to accord less protection than the patent laws of many States where protection was afforded to foreigners.[65] Third, he argued that justice required that foreigners were treated as nationals, especially when it was recognised that the rights are not created by the law, but are merely regulated by it. This was the view of the 1878 Conference, and the interest of the Union was to encourage all persons to obtain patents.[66] Fourth, in regard to trade marks, many States accorded protection to foreigners, provided that they had an establishment in that country. However, Demeur argued, Article 3 would not protect foreigners in that situation.[67]

Demeur further argued that the question for consideration should be whether according to the legislation of the country where the filing was made, a foreigner has the right to obtain a patent, design or trade mark. If he has such a right, then the right of priority should be accorded to him if his application is filed in one of the States of the Union.[68] The delegate of Salvador supported Demeur, stating that there must be an open Union, espousing principles of wide application.[69]

In general, however, the majority of the delegates did not support Demeur's proposals for a truly open Union. Jagerschmidt replied that the Convention should only concern the rights of "ressortissants" of the contracting States, and that States could decide to apply its benefits more widely if they wished, but should be under no obligation to do so.[70] The Swedish delegate, Lagerheim, agreed with Jagerschmidt and stated that, while Demeur invoked the interests of justice, it was not just to extend the benefits of the Convention to all without conditions of reciprocity.[71] However, he agreed that the use of the term "ressortissant" did result in problems, because it would not apply to foreigners domiciled in one of the States of the Union.[72]

64 *Ibid.* 129.
65 *Ibid.*
66 *Ibid.*
67 *Ibid.*
68 *Ibid.*
69 *Ibid.* 130.
70 *Ibid.*
71 *Ibid.*
72 *Ibid.*

One of the main reasons why most delegates were unprepared to support Demeur's liberal concept of an "open Union" was the fear that the Union would not gain adherents if its benefits were extended to the nationals of countries not party to it. A statement to this effect was made by Kern, a Swiss delegate.[73] However, he agreed with the Swedish delegate that Article 3 should be extended to foreigners established in one of the contracting States.[74] This proposal gained the general approval of the delegates (with the exception of the Venezuelan), and, in consequence, the Conference adopted the Swedish proposal as follows:

> Subjects or citizens of States not forming part of the Union, who are domiciled or who have industrial or commercial establishments in the territory of one of the States of the Union, are treated in the same manner as subjects or citizens of the contracting States.[75]

This provision became Article 3 of the Paris Convention. Despite the strong arguments of Demeur, it was an important instance where the 1880 Conference rejected the earlier Resolutions of the private Conference of 1878. This demonstrates the gulf between the aspirations of 1878 where the concept of natural property rights and equality for all prevailed, and the more limited, political concerns of 1880.

(iii) *The Priority Period – Article Four of the Paris Convention*

The principle of national treatment was the general foundation upon which the 1883 Convention was based, but recognition of priority periods in which to file applications for industrial property rights was probably the most tangible benefit of the 1883 Convention. Although a system of priority rights had not been recommended by the 1878 Conference, it was simply a more modern and efficient alternative to the 1878 proposals for simultaneous deposit of applications at foreign consulates.

Jagerschmidt justified priority rights by explaining that when a person filed an application for a patent, design or trade mark in one country, there was a likelihood that the resultant publicity might allow a foreigner to improperly profit from the filing, by applying for a similar patent, design or trade mark in his own country.[76] His proposal (then draft Article 3) was intended to prevent

73 *Ibid.* 131.
74 *Ibid.*
75 *Ibid.* 131.
76 *Ibid.* 47.

such activity by giving to the first person a right of priority of registration for a predetermined time in all the States of the Union.[77] Bozérian added that the draft Article was intended to overcome some of the problems of laws, (such as those in France), which rendered inventions unpatentable because of prior publicity in another country.[78] He referred particularly to the fact that inventors were usually not wealthy, and unable to afford the expense of taking out patents in many countries, particularly at the time of the initial development of the invention, when its commercial success was uncertain.[79] The Jagerschmidt proposal received a mixed response, because of a number of perceived problems with the concept of priority rights, and their practical application.

The Russian delegate, de Nebolsine, considered that there was a difficulty when two people in different countries both developed the same invention. If one had obtained the right of priority, then the other would be deprived of his rights.[80] In Russia, if two people developed the same invention, then neither would be granted a patent, provided that there was no evidence of copying. De Nebolsine seemed opposed to the right of priority being effective in other States.[81]

A Swiss delegate, Weibel, considered that priority rights were very important, but that they should be of a different duration for patents, designs and trade marks.[82] The original Jagerschmidt proposal envisaged the same priority period applying to all forms of industrial property. However, Weibel argued that, as designs and models had only transitory value, their priority periods should be shorter than for patents.[83]

The Dutch delegate considered that the Jagerschmidt draft was flawed because the right of priority should not operate to prejudice third parties who had already legitimately acquired rights. He was particularly concerned about the rights of those who had unregistered trade marks in the Netherlands, who might find that foreigners copied their mark, registered it in another country, and then claimed a right of priority in the Netherlands.[84] On the other hand, the Belgian delegate, Demeur, considered the rights of third parties were too strongly protected by the draft Article. He argued that there was a real problem

---

77 *Ibid.*
78 *Ibid.* 49–50.
79 *Ibid.*
80 *Ibid.* 47–48.
81 *Ibid.* 48.
82 *Ibid.*
83 *Ibid.*
84 *Ibid.*

that third parties could make use of the invention during the period between the filing of the application and its later registration, because during this time the Article did not make it clear that the inventor should have an exclusive right.[85] He wished it to be more clearly stated that during the period mentioned there be absolutely no lawful use of the invention by third parties, and that any such use would not result in the invention falling into the public domain.[86] However, Bozérian replied that the Article already prevented such uses by third parties.[87]

Due to lack of clarity in the draft Article concerning the rights of third parties, the Dutch delegate proposed that Article 3 include a reference to the preservation of rights legitimately acquired by third parties.[88] Jagerschmidt then re-drafted his proposal in accordance with these concerns.[89] At the same time, Demeur, of Belgium, presented an amended Article 3 which included amendments suggested by Austrian and Russian delegates. One of the major differences between the Jagerschmidt draft and the Belgian proposal was the use of the term "author" to describe the person who filed the application.[90] This term was also intended to include the author's transferees and beneficiaries etc. Also, the proposed Article was said to provide more distinctly that a third party who did an act during the period of time supervening between the filing of the application and the official granting of the right, could not affect the validity of the right, even though it might have had that effect under previous domestic law.[91]

However, the Swedish delegate objected to the use of the term "author" and the President agreed that it would be preferable to refer to "A person who has regularly effected the filing".[92] After a discussion between the delegates, the Conference adopted an Article 3 based upon the draft proposed by Demeur, together with the amendment proposed by Jagerschmidt, and also including a reference to the rights of third parties demanded by the Dutch delegate. The text of this Article was subsequently adopted as Article 4 of the 1883 Convention.[93]

85 *Ibid.* 50.
86 *Ibid.*
87 *Ibid.* 51.
88 *Ibid.* 60.
89 *Ibid.*
90 *Ibid.* 61.
91 *Ibid.*
92 *Ibid.*
93 *Ibid.* 64.

Length of the Priority Period

Although the original Jagerschmidt draft had adopted a uniform priority period for all forms of industrial property rights, the 1880 Conference early agreed that the priority period for patents should be of a longer duration than for other rights. Under the 1883 Convention, the priority period for patents was fixed at 6 months, with 3 months for designs, models and trade marks. However, at the 1880 Conference, several delegates supported longer priority periods, more in line with provisions in operation today.[94]

While noting that the priority period would be a time of uncertainty when industrial competitors would be hampered by their ignorance about whether the inventor would apply for rights in a particular country, the Swiss delegate Weibel, supported a one year priority period for patents.[95] He stated that this was realistic because of the length of the preliminary examination in countries such as the U.S.A.[96] Bozérian also favoured a one year priority period for patents, and said that the other delegates tended to exaggerate the interests of industry.[97] He said that the normal duration before putting to work a patented invention was one year, and it was not equitable to impose on the inventor the expense of applying for a patent in a foreign land if he did not know if the invention would work or be profitable.[98] Demeur, of Belgium, also considered that 6 months was too short for patents, particularly as some countries such as the U.K. permitted a right of opposition of 6 months.[99] He added that eight months was the shortest period that was acceptable to him.[100]

The majority of the delegates, however, did not support a one year priority period for patents, despite the strong evidence that this was necessary

---

94 Note that under the present, 1967 Stockholm text of the Paris Convention, Article 4(c)(1) states that the priority period is 12 months for patents and utility models, and 6 months for industrial designs and trade marks.

95 FRANCE, Ministére des Affaires étrangéres, *Conférence Internationale pour la protection de la propriété Industrielle* (Paris 1880), 52.

96 *Ibid.* He supported a 6 month period for designs, and 3 months for trade marks.

97 *Ibid.* 54.

98 *Ibid.* Bozérian added that most designs were of only fleeting importance before improvements were made which effectively stopped exploitation. Trade marks were quick and easy to obtain. Therefore, a priority period of 3 months was sufficient for both.

99 *Ibid.* 55.

100 *Ibid.* This problem has worsened since 1880, and in most cases an invention would not be profitable until several years after a patent application is filed. There are many expensive and time-consuming legal and procedural hurdles to overcome in order to gain patent protection. The process of obtaining a patent is much longer than in 1880. In Australia, for example, examination of the patent application might not occur for two years.

to overcome procedural delays in some countries.[101] The final vote of the Conference favoured six months priority for patents and three months for designs, models and trade marks.[102] It was also decided that the period be extended by one month for applicants from "overseas" [non-European] countries.[103] This result illustrates the fact that the majority of the delegates were unskilled in the practical aspects of industrial property law and procedure. Those with practical experience of patent law, such as Weibel, Demeur and Bozérian realised that a one year priority period was necessary in many countries in order for the application to pass through the many procedural stages and for the patentee to determine if the invention was valuable. The majority, who knew little of patent law or procedure, were the ones who made the final decision to restrict the priority period for patents to six months.[104]

(iv) *Temporary Protection for Inventions and Allied Rights Exhibited at International Exhibitions – Article Eleven of the Paris Convention*

The final important general provision in the 1883 Convention was Article 11, which conferred temporary protection upon patentable inventions, industrial designs and models and trade marks in respect of goods exhibited at official or officially recognised international exhibitions. As has been demonstrated in relation to the 1873 Vienna Congress, the desire of inventors to gain some form of legal protection for their exhibited inventions was one of the primary factors which prompted wider interest in international industrial property protection.[105] Thus, Article 11 was of important historical significance to the founding of the Paris Convention.

The 1880 Conference adopted Article 11 with little change from the original Jagerschmidt draft.[106] An Italian delegate, Indelli had proposed an alternative

101 The Norwegian delegate, Broch, favoured only six months for patents, and three months for other industrial property rights. The Italians agreed with Broch as to patents, and supported four months priority for designs, models and trade marks. The Swedish delegate also replied that one year was too long for patents, and that 6 months was usually sufficient for the preliminary examination. The Uruguayan delegate considered that four months priority would be sufficient for patents, with three months for designs and models, and two months for trade marks. *Ibid.* 52–55.

102 *Ibid.* 55.

103 *Ibid.* 56.

104 It is unsurprising, therefore, that the Brussels text of 1900 increased the priority period for patents to one year, with four months for designs, models and trade marks.

105 The matter had also been raised as early as the 1851 Universal Exposition in London. The U.K. Government responded by enacting special legislation providing temporary protection for inventions displayed at the Exposition. See Chapter Five for further details of this legislation.

106 It was Article 9 in the original Jagerschmidt text.

which would have extended protection only where the inventor notified the industrial bureau of an application for a patent, design or trade mark within two months following the close of the exhibition.[107] The reason for the proposal was to facilitate conformity at a basic level between the various laws of the contracting States.[108] However, this proposal was not supported by the other delegates, who preferred the more general Jagerschmidt text.[109] Indelli agreed to withdraw his amendment.

As Jagerschmidt explained, the draft Article embodied only a general principle and it was left to each State to determine the means of putting the provision into practice.[110] He noted that the Italian proposal did not refer to protection for the period before the Exhibition began, and that this was a grave oversight because it was when a machine was being set up that copiers could glean valuable information. A Swiss delegate, Lagerheim, agreed that it was necessary to extend protection to the period of installation.[111] The Conference therefore adopted the first paragraph of the Jagerschmidt draft Article without amendment, but found it necessary to remove the second paragraph relating to seizure of illicit articles. The general view appeared to be that this paragraph was not necessary, because the execution of the Article should be left to the domestic law of each State.[112] The adoption of Article 11, together with the support for national treatment, were the two major instances where the 1880 diplomatic Conference closely followed the earlier Resolutions of the unofficial Conference of 1878.[113] It can be argued that the Paris Convention was developed around these two points upon which there was a high level of consensus.

(3) Provisions Specifically Related to the Protection of Patents

Importation of Patented Articles and Compulsory Working – Article Five of the Paris Convention

The 1878 Conference voiced its severe disapproval of national patent systems, (such as the French Law of 5 July 1844), which provided for forfeiture of patents on the grounds of importation of goods of a similar nature to those covered by the patent.[114] The Jagerschmidt draft also aimed to outlaw any such provisions,

107 FRANCE, Ministére des Affaires étrangéres, *Conférence Internationale pour la protection de la propriété Industrielle* (Paris 1880), 105.

108 *Ibid.*

109 *Ibid.*

110 *Ibid.* 106.

111 *Ibid.*

112 *Ibid.* 107.

113 See General Section, Resolution 5 of the 1878 Conference.

114 Patents Section, Resolution 8 of the 1878 Conference Resolutions. See Appendix Five.

which were described by Bozérian as "barbarous" and "absolutely useless".[115] The general attitude of the delegates to the 1880 Conference was that it was reasonable that a patent should not be forfeited merely on the grounds of importing goods, but some still believed that a patentee should be subject to the obligation to work the patented invention in the country where the patent was granted.

Various delegates noted that, in their countries, importation was not of itself a ground for forfeiture of the patent. In countries such as Sweden and Belgium, importation was not prevented, but the patentee did have the obligation to exploit the patent within the country.[116] In Belgium it was necessary for the patentee to engage in domestic manufacture of considerable numbers of the objects, as exploitation meant "manufacture" and not merely "sell".[117] Weibel stated that the Swiss agreed that the mere fact of importation should not be a ground for forfeiture of patent rights. However, his country could not accept that a patentee could take a patent in one contracting State, and have complete freedom to import the manufactured article into all the other contracting States where the object was likewise patented, without having the obligation to also manufacture in those States.[118] He noted also that, unlike most of the countries surrounding Switzerland, the Swiss did not protect their industry by customs tariffs. Thus, the Jagerschmidt draft Article 4 would have had the effect of opening the Swiss borders to products manufactured by foreigners, while other countries would try to control the influx of imported products through customs duties, and Swiss products would not find such an open market in those other States.[119] He believed the result of Article 4 would be inequitable unless some requirement of compulsory working was also attached.[120] The Conference was advised that in Uruguay, the patentee had an obligation of domestic manufacture during a period of time determined by the Government,[121] and similar laws prevailed in Austria and Hungary.[122] As a result of these discussions, the Austrian delegate, Woerz, proposed that the draft be amended by adding the following proviso:

115 FRANCE, Ministére des Affaires étrangéres, *Conférence Internationale pour la protection de la propriété Industrielle* (Paris 1880), 56.
116 *Ibid.*
117 *Ibid.*
118 *Ibid.* 65.
119 *Ibid.*
120 *Ibid.*
121 *Ibid.* 68.
122 *Ibid.*

> provided that he exploits the said invention in conformity with the laws of the country into which he imports the patented articles.[123]

A number of delegates, however, spoke out against the addition of the compulsory working requirement. The Belgian delegate, Demeur, believed that the time had come for an international perspective, and that there should no longer be these types of legal frontiers.[124] He proposed that any object made in one of the contracting States be considered as made in any of the others in regard to the application of patent laws. Thus, he advocated the abolition of the obligation to exploit, which, at that time 15 to 20 countries (including Belgium) imposed.[125] Demeur considered that it was preferable for the patentee to choose for himself the best place of manufacture, and the best market. He proposed to amend Article 4 as follows:

> The holder of a patent who exploits his invention in one of the States of the Union shall not be able to be declared as having forfeited his rights in the others for failure to exploit.[126]

Delegates of Austria and Hungary agreed with this view in principle, but the Hungarian delegate feared that such a move would be seen as a threat to national industry.[127] The U.K. delegate, Reader-Lack, declared his approval of the Belgian proposal, as it reflected the state of the law in the United Kingdom.[128] The Italian delegate, Indelli, agreed that the obligation to exploit was outmoded, and that it would be preferable to permit the patentee to choose the most profitable place to manufacture, but he considered it essential to respect the various laws of the participating nations.[129] The Turkish delegate considered that the Austrian amendment would have a destructive effect, and that it was in the interests of consumers that patentees should be able to manufacture goods in the country or countries of their choice. He supported the Belgian proposal.[130] The Russian delegate also agreed that it was unjust to oblige a patentee to put to work his invention in all the countries where he had

123 *Ibid.* 64–65.
124 *Ibid.* 57.
125 *Ibid.* 66.
126 *Ibid.*
127 *Ibid.*
128 *Ibid.* 67.
129 *Ibid.*
130 *Ibid.* 68.

obtained patent rights, without being able to choose the place which was most convenient. In Russia at the time the only obligation was to provide evidence that the invention had actually been put into practice.[131] Bozérian criticised the various delegates who had insisted upon the continuance of the requirement of domestic exploitation. He asked why those who professed generous and "liberal" theories would not vote for the minimum standards proposed.[132]

While delegates of States such as Austria and Switzerland understood the advantages of the Belgian proposal, they could not accept it. A Swiss delegate, Weibel, reiterated the problem of customs regulations, and stated that the Swiss market would be dominated by French goods, while manufacturers would move their operations to larger countries such as France.[133] The delegate of Hungary stated that it was essential that the Austrian amendment be accepted, to enable States to insist upon domestic exploitation of inventions.[134]

Although the records of the 1880 Conference disclose that a majority of the delegates appeared to favour the abolition of all compulsory working requirements, the fact that a small minority still supported such provisions meant that their views would have to be recognised or else it was possible that Austria, Hungary and Switzerland would not accede to the Convention. Consequently, the 1880 Conference added a provision to draft Article 4 (later Article 5 of the 1883 Convention). It read:

> Nevertheless, the patentee shall remain under the obligation to exploit his patent, in accordance with the laws of the country into which he introduces the patented articles.[135]

This draft Article also included a slightly modified version of the Jagerschmidt draft Article 4 relating to the abolition of forfeiture for importation of patented goods.[136] These provisions became Article 5 of the 1883 Convention.[137] In

131 *Ibid.* 69.
132 *Ibid.*
133 *Ibid.* 65.
134 *Ibid.* 68.
135 *Ibid.* 69. See for further discussion of the deliberations of the 1880 Conference in relation to compulsory working of inventions: Akerman, C., *L'Obligation d'Exploiter et la Licence Obligatoire en Matiére de Brevets d'Invention* (Paris, Librairie du Recueil Sirey, 1936), 61–64; Donzel, L., "Commentaire de la Convention Internationale signée á Paris le 20 mars 1883 pour la protection de la Propriété Industrielle" (1891) *Journal des Procés en Contrefaçon* 1, 137–140.
136 *Ibid.* 163.
137 The full text of Article 5 of the 1883 Convention was as follows: "The importation by the patentee into the country where the patent has been granted of articles manufactured in

general terms, the 1880 Conference followed the 1878 Conference Resolutions in rejecting forfeiture for importation of patented goods,[138] but maintaining compulsory working requirements.[139] However, it will be recalled that the 1878 Conference supported only forfeiture of the patent in the event of non-working, and rejected compulsory licensing.[140] In contrast, the 1880 Conference did not discuss the acceptability or otherwise of compulsory licensing, and left it to the domestic legislation of each State to determine the penalty for failure to work the invention.

Conclusion

The draft text of the 1883 Convention prepared by the 1880 diplomatic Conference contained several Articles which were in accord with the Resolutions of the private Conference of 1878. These related to the requirement of national treatment, temporary protection at international exhibitions, and the abolition of forfeiture for importation of patented goods. The 1880 Conference's acceptance of forfeiture for non-working was also generally in accordance with the Resolutions of 1878. However, there were many points where the 1880 draft text differed markedly from the 1878 Resolutions. In one respect, the 1880 draft text was an improvement upon the work of 1878. This was in its acceptance of priority rights, rather than the 1878 proposal for simultaneous lodging of applications at foreign consulates. However, the 1880 Conference failed to adequately address the meaning of the term "industrial property", which contrasted markedly with the theoretical debates of the 1878 Conference. Further, under the 1880 draft text, non-Union nationals were denied rights, which was inconsistent with the resolutions of the 1878 Conference.

These differences can largely be explained by understanding that the main aim of the 1878 Conference was to ensure maximum protection for the property rights of inventors and other industrial creators. It was not concerned greatly with wider social concerns because of its paramount interest in advancing the concept of "natural" industrial property rights. In contrast, the delegates to the 1880 Conference adopted a more instrumentalist approach to the international protection of industrial property rights, and were guided by wider social,

any of the States of the Union shall not entail forfeiture of the patent. Nevertheless, the patentee shall remain under the obligation to exploit his patent, in accordance with the laws of the country into which he introduces the patented articles."

138 Patents Section, Resolution 8 of the 1878 Conference. See Appendix Five.

139 Patents Section, Resolution 10 of the 1878 Conference. See Appendix Five.

140 Patents Section, Resolution 2 of the 1878 Conference. See Appendix Five.

political and economic concerns. They were primarily interested to promote the industrial development of their own countries, and did not wish to enter into general theoretical discussions about the basis of inventors' rights. Perhaps if the delegates to the 1878 Conference had spent time discussing proposals for the practical application of their Resolutions, and the delegates to the 1880 Conference spent more time on theoretical concerns such as the meaning of "industrial property" then there would have been greater consistency in the work of the two Conferences. In this way, the 1883 Convention would have had a firmer theoretical basis, and possibly some additional substantive provisions.

B The Paris Conference of 1883 and Its Aftermath

(a) *The Work of the 1883 Conference*

Although the text of the Paris Convention of 1883 was essentially that which resulted from the work of the 1880 Conference, none of the delegates present in 1880 had their Government's authority immediately to accede to the Convention. All that was signed at the 1880 Conference was a document recording its work and stating the agreement of the delegates to submit the text of the draft Convention to their respective Governments.[141] In the period between the 1880 Conference and the subsequent meeting in March 1883, the draft text was the object of "attentive study" by most of the Governments who had sent representatives to the Conference.[142] The French Government

141 FRANCE, Ministére des Affaires étrangéres, *Conférence Internationale pour la protection de la propriété Industrielle* (Paris 1880), 147.

142 FRANCE, Ministére des Affaires étrangéres, *Conférence Internationale pour la protection de la propriété Industrielle* (Paris 1883), 15 (Statement of Challemel-Lacour, French Minister of Foreign Affairs). Note that it is Challemel-Lacour's assertion that the 1880 draft text was the object of detailed study by the Governments which had been represented at the Conference. In the case of the United Kingdom, for example, there is no evidence that such studies were carried out. U.K. Parliamentary Papers have been thoroughly searched, but there are none devoted to Paris Convention negotiations before 1886. (The Rome Revision Conference – UNITED KINGDOM, Parliamentary Papers, *Papers Relative to the Recent Conference at Rome on the subject of Industrial Property and Correspondence Relating to the Fraudulent Use of Trade Marks* (1886) vol LX, C. 4837, 413). In the case of the U.S.A., Congressional Papers provide no evidence that the U.S. Government studied the 1880 draft treaty in any detail. The papers contain merely the report from the U.S. delegate to the 1880 Conference, James Putnam, to the Secretary of State, William Evarts, dated 10 December 1880. UNITED STATES OF AMERICA, Congressional Papers, *Report of the Commissioners appointed to Revise the Statutes relating to Patents, Trade and other Marks, and Trade and Commercial Names under Act of Congress approved June 4, 1898* (1900) 56th Congress, 2nd Session, Senate document 20, 235–243.

decided that by early 1883 the Governments had been afforded sufficient time to study the draft text, and a second diplomatic Conference was convened.[143]

On 6 March 1883, delegates from 20 countries met in Paris at the invitation of the French Government to consider the draft Convention and, if possible, sign their assent to the terms already established.[144] The 20 States represented at the 1883 Conference were Argentina, Belgium, Brazil, Spain, U.S.A., France, United Kingdom, Guatemala, Italy, Luxembourg, the Netherlands, Portugal, Romania, Russia, Salvador, Serbia, Sweden and Norway,[145] Switzerland and Uruguay.[146] Missing were delegates from Austria-Hungary, Turkey and Venezuela, who had attended the 1880 Conference, but were unwilling or unable to attend the meeting in 1883. Of particular note was the absence of Austria-Hungary, which had informed the French Government that it judged the provisions of the draft Convention to be incompatible with domestic legislation, and that it would only accede to the Convention if it was re-drawn to include a requirement of reciprocity.[147] This was not a convincing reason for Austria-Hungary's objection to the draft Convention. If it thought so strongly that reciprocity should be substituted for national treatment, then the Austrian or Hungarian delegates to the 1880 Conference should have demanded this change. In fact, as was shown above, the Hungarian delegate to the 1880 Conference did not object to the concept of national treatment, and the Austrians only raised the point that there might be some difficulties in relation to formal matters associated with filing applications.[148] It was also strange that Austria-Hungary should object to national treatment, since it had previously been willing to enter into bilateral

---

143 *Ibid.*

144 *Ibid.* See also Ricketson, S., *The Paris Convention for the Protection of Industrial Property* (Oxford, Oxford University Press, 2015), 59–61. For a general discussion of the work of the 1883 Conference see also: Pieper, C., and Schmid, P., *Geschichte der internationalen Union für den Schutz des gewerblichen Eigentums sammt Konvention und Staatsverträgen* (Berlin, Deutschen Vereins für den Schutz des gewerblichen Eigentums, 1894), 28–29; De Iturralde, T., *La Union Internacional para la proteccion de la Propriedad Industrial* (Paris, 1890), 5–6; Plasseraud, Y., and Savignon, F., *Paris 1883: Genése du droit Unioniste des Brevets* (Paris, Litec, 1983), 189–192; Donzel, L., "Commentaire de la Convention Internationale signée á Paris le 20 mars 1883 pour la protection de la Propriété Industrielle" (1891) *Journal des Procés en Contrefaçon* 1, 142–144.

145 Sweden and Norway were represented by the same delegate, Broch, who had only represented Norway at the 1880 Conference.

146 FRANCE, Ministére des Affaires étrangéres, *Conférence Internationale pour la protection de la propriété Industrielle* (Paris 1883), 6–7.

147 *Ibid.* 20.

148 FRANCE, Ministére des Affaires étrangéres, *Conférence Internationale pour la protection de la propriété Industrielle* (Paris 1880), 36.

commercial treaties which specifically protected industrial property rights on this basis.[149]

It is more likely that Austria-Hungary did not attend the 1883 meeting because of concerns about the operation of the priority period under Article 4 of the Convention. There is clear evidence that Austria-Hungary thought a 6 month priority period for patents was too short in countries such as its own where all patents were subject to preliminary examination which took more than 6 months. Although Austrian and Hungarian delegates did not raise this objection at the 1880 Conference, they did so at later revision conferences. At the Brussels Conference of 1897 and 1900, the Austro-Hungarian delegate, Beck von Mannagetta, stated that his country required a 12 month priority period for patents before it could accede to the Convention.[150] After this amendment was made to Article 4 in the 1900 Brussels text of the Convention, Austria-Hungary finally acceded to it on 1 January 1909.[151]

Germany also maintained its refusal to attend the treaty negotiations, despite the message conveyed to the Swiss Government at the end of the 1880 Conference that the draft Convention posed no real threat to domestic legislation.[152] Germany did not accede to the Paris Convention until 1 May 1903.[153] On the other hand, the 1883 Conference was attended by three new delegations: Spain, Romania and Serbia.

As has been previously explained, the text signed in Paris on 20 March 1883 was essentially the same as that drafted in 1880. There was one major reason

149 See for example, the Commercial Treaty between the United Kingdom and Austria, dated 16 December 1865. UNITED KINGDOM, Parliamentary Papers, *Extracts from Treaties and Declarations now in force between Great Britain and Foreign Powers relating to Trade Marks, Designs, and Industrial Property, August 1888* (1888) vol XCVIII, C. 5554, 745.

150 BUREAU INTERNATIONAL DE L'UNION POUR LA PROTECTION DE LA PROPRIETE INDUSTRIELLE, *Conférence de Bruxelles: Décembre 1897 et Décembre 1900* (Berne 1901), 212.

151 By a note dated 30 November 1908, Austria-Hungary advised the Swiss Federal Council of its accession to the Paris Convention to be effective from 1 January 1909. At that time, Austria-Hungary acceded to the following texts: (i) The 1883 Convention, as modified by the 1900 Brussels text. (ii) The 1891 Protocol concerning the expenses of the International Bureau. (iii) The Arrangement of Madrid of 1891 concerning the International Registration of Trademarks (as amended in 1900). Source: [1908] 24 *La Propriété Industrielle* 173.

152 See the statements made by the Swiss delegate, Kern, at the end of the 1880 Conference. FRANCE, Ministére des Affaires étrangéres, *Conférence Internationale pour la protection de la propriété Industrielle* (Paris 1880), 149.

153 By a note dated 21 March 1903, the German Government advised the Swiss Federal Council of its accession to the following texts from 1 May 1903: (i) The 1883 Convention, as modified by the 1900 Brussels text. (ii) The 1891 Protocol concerning the expenses of the International Bureau. Source: [1903] 19 *La Propriété Industrielle* 37.

for this. Nine States (France, Belgium, Brazil, Guatemala, Italy, Romania,[154] Salvador, Serbia and Switzerland) attended the 1883 Conference with unrestricted authority to sign the Convention as drafted in 1880, and any changes would have needed to be referred back to the Governments for their consideration.[155] As Jagerschmidt stated, if the meeting permitted any significant alteration to the text drafted in 1880, then the modified text would have had to be re-examined by their Governments, and this would cause another undesirable delay before the Convention could be signed, and eventually come into operation.[156] Therefore, the Conference agreed not to make any important substantive amendments to the text of the Convention itself, but to permit points of clarification to be included in the Final Protocol.[157] Thus, the meeting allowed an amendment to Paragraph 4 of the Final Protocol proposed by the Spanish delegate to clarify the operation of Article 6.[158] It also allowed the delegates of the Netherlands and Switzerland to make a declaration, inscribed in the official records of the Conference, to the effect that their countries would not conform to Article 11 respecting temporary protection at exhibitions, until such time as they had adopted patent legislation.[159]

All of these measures ensured that the representatives of eleven countries were able to give their signature of assent to the terms of the Paris Convention on 20 March 1883. These countries were Belgium, Brazil, Spain, France, Guatemala, Italy, the Netherlands, Portugal, Salvador, Serbia and Switzerland.[160] Of the nine States who sent representatives to the Conference but who did not sign, there were various reasons for their refusal. Some lacked

154 But, after making this statement, the delegate of Romania did not attend the session on 20 March 1883 to sign the Convention! FRANCE, Ministére des Affaires étrangéres, *Conférence Internationale pour la protection de la propriété Industrielle* (Paris 1883), 45–46. By a note dated 26 August 1920, the Romanian Government advised the Swiss Federal Council of its accession to the following texts, to take effect from 6 October 1920: (i) The 1883 Convention, as amended. (ii) The Arrangement of Madrid of 1891 concerning the International Registration of Trademarks (as amended). Source: [1920] 36 *La Propriété Industrielle* 97.

155 *Ibid.* 23.

156 *Ibid.* 26.

157 The only amendments made to the text of the Convention were the enumeration in Article 1 of the signatory States, the removal of the words "in all the other States of the Union" in the first sentence of Article 2 of the 1880 text, and some changes to Article 14 necessitated in designating the place of the next meeting.

158 FRANCE, Ministére des Affaires étrangéres, *Conférence Internationale pour la protection de la propriété Industrielle* (Paris 1883), 32.

159 *Ibid.* 34.

160 *Ibid.* 51.

authority to sign. For example, the delegate of the United Kingdom, Reader-Lack, stated that the U.K. had no objection to the text, but he could not sign until the correct "Parliamentary procedures" had been performed.[161] By this term he was referring in an oblique way to the still unsuccessful quest to reform U.K. industrial property legislation. At the time, U.K. law had no provision for the granting of priority periods to Union nationals in accordance with Article 4 of the Convention, and no provisions permitting Union nationals to file their trade marks in accordance with Article 6.[162] The revision of the U.K. industrial property legislation in 1883 (in the form of the Patents, Designs and Trade Marks Act 1883 (U.K.))[163] meant that it was only in 1884 that the U.K. was in a position to accede to the Paris Convention.[164] Other representatives not signing because of a lack of instructions or lack of authority included the delegates of Argentina,[165] Uruguay,[166] Russia,[167] Sweden and Norway.[168]

In the cases of Luxembourg and the U.S.A., there were other, more complicated reasons why their representatives did not sign the 1883 text when it was presented to the Conference. The delegate of Luxembourg, Bastin, informed the Conference that his country could not accede to the Convention while Germany remained opposed to it.[169] He explained that the industrial property legislation of Luxembourg was modelled upon that of Germany, and, in addition, Luxembourg had a commonality of interests with Germany.[170] It was

---

161 *Ibid.* 21.

162 Note, [1885] 1 *La Propriété Industrielle* 82.

163 This Act came into force on 1 January 1884. Source: [1885] 1 *La Propriété Industrielle* 65.

164 By an instrument of accession dated 17 March 1884 and accepted by the French Government on 5 April 1884, the Government of the United Kingdom ratified the 1883 Paris Convention. The Convention came into force on 7 July 1884 for the U.K. and all of the other original signatories. Source: [1885] 1 *La Propriété Industrielle* 5.

165 FRANCE, Ministére des Affaires étrangéres, *Conférence Internationale pour la protection de la propriété Industrielle* (Paris 1883), 20. Argentina did not accede to the Paris Convention until 10 February 1967. Source: [1996] 2 *Industrial Property and Copyright* 9.

166 *Ibid.* 23. Uruguay did not accede to the Paris Convention until 18 March 1967. Source: [1996] 2 *Industrial Property and Copyright* 11.

167 *Ibid.* 22. Russia (then the U.S.S.R.) did not accede to the Paris Convention until 1 July 1965. Source: [1996] 2 *Industrial Property and Copyright* 10.

168 *Ibid.* 23. By a note dated 29 May 1885, the Minister of Foreign Affairs of Norway and Sweden informed the Swiss Federal Council of the accession of the above countries to the 1883 Paris Convention. The actual date of accession was fixed as 1 July 1885. Source [1885] 1 *La Propriété Industrielle* 62 and [1885] 1 *La Propriété Industrielle* 75.

169 *Ibid.* 22.

170 *Ibid.*

apparent that Luxembourg was not sufficiently independent of Germany to enter into the Paris Convention so long as Germany remained opposed to it.[171]

The U.S.A. had constitutional reasons for its inability to accede to the Convention in 1883. The U.S. Supreme Court had held in 1879 that the Federal Trademarks Acts of 1870 and 1876 were unconstitutional and invalid because (1) authority to legislate on the subject of trade marks was not within the Constitutional power to "promote the progress of science and the useful arts"[172] and (2) the Federal Trademarks Acts, relating as they did to all trade marks, whether interstate or intrastate, were broader than the Constitutional power to "regulate commerce with foreign nations, and among the several States, and with the Indian tribes."[173] Thus, when the U.S. representatives attended the 1880 Paris Conference, they were under instructions that the U.S. could not ensure Federal protection of foreign trade marks, and thus the U.S. could not enter into any international treaties containing provisions relating to trade marks. As a result, the U.S. delegates to the 1880 Conference succeeded in obtaining a Reservation to be included in Paragraph 4 of the Final Protocol which stated that:

> The representative of the United States, having declared that in terms of the Federal Constitution, the right to legislate in relation to trade marks is, in a certain measure, reserved to each of the States of the Union, it is understood that the provisions of the Convention shall not be applicable

171 Even though Germany acceded to the Paris Convention in 1903, Luxembourg did not do so until 30 June 1922. By a note dated 12 May 1922, the Legation of Luxembourg in Berne advised the Swiss Federal Council of Luxembourg's accession to the 1883 Convention (as revised at Brussels in 1900 and at Washington in 1911). The ratification took effect on 30 June 1922. (Source: [1922] 38 *La Propriété Industrielle* 81).

172 The Federal Patent and Copyright Acts were given Constitutional basis under Article 1, Section 8 of the U.S. Constitution: "To promote the Progress of Science and useful Arts, by securing for limited Times to Authors and Inventors the exclusive Right to their Respective Writings and Discoveries."

173 Article 1, Section 8 of the U.S. Constitution. See further: Seeley, F.A., *The International Union for the Protection of Industrial Property* (prepared under the direction of the Commissioner of Patents, Washington, 1 September 1887), 15–16; Sautter, M., *La Convention Internationale pour la Protection de la Propriété Industrielle aux états-Unis: Argumentation de M.A. Pollok, de Washington, devant le Sénat Fédéral* (Paris, 1886), 8; UNITED STATES OF AMERICA, Congressional Papers, *Report of the Commissioners appointed to Revise the Statutes relating to Patents, Trade and other Marks, and Trade and Commercial Names under Act of Congress approved June 4, 1898* (1900) 56th Congress, 2nd Session, Senate document 20, 59; Browne, W.H., "Has Congress Authority to legislate on the subject of Trade-Marks?" (1880) 14 *American Law Review* 156.

except within the limits of the constitutional powers of the contracting parties.[174]

Although the U.S.A. passed a revised Trademark Act in 1881, which related only to "the very limited class of trademarks which are used in foreign commerce or in commerce with the Indian tribes",[175] the U.S. Government still did not feel that its trade mark system was sufficient to allow it to accede to the Paris Convention in 1883. When it finally did accede to the Convention in 1887, this accession was made subject to the express Reservation included in Paragraph 4 of the Final Protocol of the 1880 draft text.[176] Even after the U.S. accession, there was continued debate as to whether it could fully give effect to its international trade mark obligations.[177] However, the constitutionality of the 1881 Act was firmly established by a series of judicial decisions between 1881 and 1900.[178]

On 6 June 1884, representatives of the eleven original signatories to the 1883 Convention met in Paris to deposit their Governments' instruments of ratification.[179] At that time, the instruments of ratification of the Convention were also received on behalf of the United Kingdom,[180]

---

174 FRANCE, Ministére des Affaires étrangéres, *Conférence Internationale pour la protection de la propriété Industrielle* (Paris 1880), 167.

175 UNITED STATES OF AMERICA, Congressional Papers, *Report of the Commissioners appointed to Revise the Statutes relating to Patents, Trade and other Marks, and Trade and Commercial Names under Act of Congress approved June 4, 1898* (1900) 56th Congress, 2nd Session, Senate document 20, 63.

176 By a note dated 18 March 1887, the U.S.A. informed the Swiss Federal Council of its accession to the 1883 Convention, which would take effect from 30 May 1887. The Reservation was expressly included in this Notice of Accession. Source: [1887] 3 *La Propriété Industrielle* 40.

177 For example, in various articles written in 1887, Louis Donzel argued that the U.S. had no valid trade mark protection for nationals of Union States, and it was inequitable that U.S. trade marks could be protected in France, but there was no reciprocal right of protection of French trade marks in the U.S.A. He claimed that the U.S. Trademark Act of 1881 was also unconstitutional and would soon be struck down by the U.S. Supreme Court. To these allegations, the International Bureau replied that Donzel was completely wrong, and that there was protection for foreign trade marks in the U.S.A. Not only was the 1881 Act constitutional, but the various U.S. States had very comprehensive trade mark laws which afforded satisfactory protection to foreign nationals *residing in the U.S.* Sources: [1887] 3 *La Propriété Industrielle* 51; [1887] 3 *La Propriété Industrielle* 68.

178 See: UNITED STATES OF AMERICA, Congressional Papers, *Report of the Commissioners appointed to Revise the Statutes relating to Patents, Trade and other Marks, and Trade and Commercial Names under Act of Congress approved June 4, 1898* (1900) 56th Congress, 2nd Session, Senate document 20, 104–105.

179 [1885] 1 *La Propriété Industrielle* 5.

180 See note 165 above.

Tunisia[181] and Ecuador.[182] These fourteen countries formed the membership of the Paris Convention which it came into force on 7 July 1884.[183]

(b) *Germany, Austria-Hungary and Russia – Reasons Why Three Important States Did Not Accede*

These three important States did not accede to the Paris Convention either in 1883 or within the following ten years. It is necessary to explain why the Governments of these States did not recognise the advantages of membership of the Paris Convention.

(1) Germany

One of the most common reasons given for Germany's failure to accede to the Convention until 1903 was the Government's fear that the obligations imposed by the Convention would necessitate reform of domestic legislation, especially the newly enacted Patent Law of 25 May 1877.[184] However, this reason is not particularly convincing because the Paris Convention did not require member

---

181 Instrument of ratification dated 20 March 1884, accepted by the French Government on 12 April 1884. Tunisia became a party to the Convention from 7 July 1884. Source [1885] 1 *La Propriété Industrielle* 5.

182 Instrument of ratification dated 21 December 1883, accepted by the French Government on 28 May 1884. Ecuador became party to the Convention from 7 July 1884. However, by a note dated 26 December 1885, the Minister of Foreign Affairs of Ecuador notified the Swiss Federal Council of Ecuador's denunciation of the 1883 Convention. The reason for the denunciation was said to be that when the Convention was submitted to the Ecuador National Congress, the Congress refused to approve the Convention because it was considered that it was of little relevance to Ecuador, considering the poor state of industrial development. [1886] 2 *La Propriété Industrielle* 24.

183 Article 18 of the 1883 Convention stipulated that the Convention would come into effect one month after the exchange of ratifications.

184 See for example, the discussion at note 153 above concerning the explanation given to the Swiss Government in 1880. See also Plasseraud, Y., and Savignon, F., *Paris 1883: Genése du droit Unioniste des Brevets* (Paris, Litec, 1983), 229. For detailed overviews of the reasons why Germany finally acceded to the Paris Convention see the following: Rauter, G., *Das Deutsche Patentgesetz und die Vorschläge des Deutschen Vereins für den Schutz des gewerblichen Eigentums* (Stuttgart, Verlag von Ferdinand Enke, 1904); Osterrieth, A., and Wassermann, M., *Der Anschluss des Deutschen Reichs an die Internationale Union für gewerblichen Rechtsschutz* 39 (Berlin, Carl Heymanns Verlag, 1902); Osterrieth, A., "Der Anschluss Deutschlands an die Internationale Union für gewerblichen Rechtsschutz" (1902) *Jahrbuch der Internationalen Vereinigung fuer Vergleichende Rechtswissenschaft und Volkswirtschaftlehre zu Berlin* 240; DEUTSCHEN VEREINS FUR DEN SCHUTZ DES GEWERBLICHEN EIGENTUMS, *Kongress für gewerblichen Rechtsschutz, Hamburg 5, 6, und 7 Mai 1902;* Kronstein, H., and Till, I., "A re-evaluation of the International Patent Convention" (1947) 12 *Law and Contemporary Problems* 765.

States to undertake any major reforms in their domestic patent legislation. In this regard, the Convention only required Germany to take active steps to afford national treatment to foreigners, to recognise the six month priority period and to grant temporary protection for inventions displayed at international exhibitions. There was certainly no attempt to regulate patentable subject matter, or harmonise procedures for obtaining patents, which clearly would have had an impact upon the operation of domestic legislation. Therefore, it was not accurate for Germany to state that the Paris Convention was incompatible with domestic patent legislation, and to use this as an excuse not to accede to it.

It has been argued by the U.S. commentators Kronstein and Till that Germany finally acceded to the Paris Convention in 1903 because of economic considerations.[185] These included the adoption of a high tariff, indirectly prohibiting importation of foreign goods, and the development of U.S. – German patent cartels.[186] Under the German patent legislation, German and foreign inventors had equal rights to obtain patents, but the effect of the tariffs was that the foreign patentee was forced either to manufacture in Germany, or abandon the German market and export only to free-trade countries.[187] In addition, beginning in the 1890s, German industries exercised monopolies over the international market in relation to the production of certain classes of goods. Most prominent was the dyestuffs cartel – a pooling of all patents taken out by the major German firms in the dyestuffs industry, which soon ensured that the entire world dyestuffs market fell under the control of German manufacturers.[188] In addition, German cartels entered into patent exchange agreements with major U.S. manufacturers, thus effectively eliminating competition in the home markets of the U.S. and German producers, and creating a powerful international force. This was particularly apparent in the area of electrical production.[189] In the late 1890s, it became clear that the Paris Convention would be of some benefit to German ambitions in connection with the development of these domestic and international cartels, as German firms increasingly sought patent protection in countries which were members of the Convention.[190]

185 Kronstein, H., and Till, I., "A re-evaluation of the International Patent Convention" (1947) 12 *Law and Contemporary Problems* 765, 775. Note that Kronstein received much of his education in Germany.

186 *Ibid.* 776–777.

187 *Ibid.*

188 *Ibid.* 778.

189 *Ibid.* 779.

190 This view is supported by contemporary sources. See, for example, [1894] 10 *La Propriété Industrielle* 66; [1896] 12 *La Propriété Industrielle* 37.

This is one major reason why Germany was prepared to accede to the Paris Convention in 1903.

Another important reason for Germany's accession in 1903 was the particular attractions of the revised text of the Convention in Brussels in 1900. The German Imperial Office of the Interior considered that the establishment of reciprocal rights regarding unfair competition was an excellent new feature, which outweighed the problems which the Germans perceived to be associated with the Convention.[191] In addition, Germany had been strongly behind the decision to increase the priority period for patents from 6 to 12 months, and it was thought that this amendment would overcome some of the difficulties in reconciling the requirements of the Convention with Germany's system of preliminary examination of patent applications.

(2) Austria-Hungary

Austria-Hungary was another country which believed that it could not accede to the 1883 Convention because of incompatibility with domestic legislation. In particular, it was thought that the Austro-Hungarian system of preliminary examination of patent applications was inconsistent with the priority requirements under Article 4.[192] However, there were additional reasons why Austria-Hungary did not accede to the Convention until 1909.

Until at least 1906, Austria-Hungary's major interest was the revision of its domestic industrial property legislation, including new laws concerning patents, trade marks, industrial designs and models and unfair competition.[193] A new Patent Law was passed on 11 January 1897, which came into operation in 1899. During this period of domestic law reform, the Parliamentary Commission

---

191 See generally: [1902] 18 *La Propriété Industrielle* 27; [1897] 13 *La Propriété Industrielle* 12.

192 See discussion of this point at the beginning of B of this chapter. For general texts on patent law reform in Austria-Hungary see: Beck von Mannagetta, P., *Das Neue Osterreichische Patentrecht auf Grund des Patent-Gesetzes vom 11 Jänner 1897* (Vienna, Alfred Hölder, 1897); Beck von Mannagetta, P., *Die Internationale Union zum Schutze des gewerblichen Eigentumes und ihre Bedeutung für Osterreichs Handel und Industrie* (Vienna, Niederösterreichischen Gewerbevereines, 1903); Bettelheim, E., *Das Recht des Erfinders in Osterreich nach dem Gesetze vom 11 Jänner 1897* (Vienna, Manz K.K. Hof-, Verlags, 1901); Goldberger, S., *Das neue Osterreichische Patent-recht* (Vienna, U. Hartleben Verlag, 1899); Kuzel, H., "Ueber Erfindungsschutz, Patentsysteme und moderne Patentgesetzgebung" in *Vorträge über Erfindungsschutz, moderne Patentgesetzgebung und Oesterreichisches Patentwesen gehalten im 'Verein Oesterreichischer Chemiker in Wien' sowie Berichte über die bezüglichen Debatten* 5–20 (Vienna, Ferdinand Brück, 1899).

193 Sources: [1892] 8 *La Propriété Industrielle* 84; [1897] 13 *La Propriété Industrielle* 24; [1899] 15 *La Propriété Industrielle* 2; [1900] 16 *La Propriété Industrielle* 163; [1901] 17 *La Propriété Industrielle* 175; [1906] 22 *La Propriété Industrielle* 82.

responsible for the task agreed that accession to the Paris Convention was a future, rather than an immediate, goal.[194] However, it is clear that the general opinion in Austria-Hungary was in favour of accession to the Convention from the late 1880s. For example, in 1889 a Permanent Commission composed of influential industrialists and inventors was established, and this affirmed the desirability of Austria-Hungary's accession to the Convention.[195] There were, however, some constitutional difficulties which hindered Austria-Hungary's accession to the Convention. Under the terms of the *Ausgleichgesetz* of 1867 which regulated the relationship between the two parts of the Empire, there were separate laws in Austria and Hungary relating to industrial property, but the two parts were to work towards a common position.[196] This had not been achieved by 1883, and in fact, it was not until October 1907 that the two parts finally agreed the terms of their relationship in respect of industrial property rights.[197] Consequently, it was only at this stage that Austria-Hungary was able to accept the obligations imposed by the Paris Convention.

(3) Russia

Although Russia, (then the U.S.S.R.) did not accede to the Paris Convention until 1965,[198] Russia's interest in international protection of industrial property rights was very strong before the 1917 Revolution. This was evidenced by the attendance of Russian delegates at the international conferences on the subject in 1878, 1880, 1883 and 1911. In principle, Russia approved of the concept of the Paris Convention, but for various practical reasons it was unable to accede to it until 1965.

As early as 1895 it was reported that Russia was eager to accede to the Paris Convention, but awaited the introduction of new patent and trade mark laws.[199] Although a new patent law came into force in July 1896,[200] and a trade mark law shortly thereafter,[201] Russia did not accede to the Convention. The main reason appeared to be Russia's liberal requirements for patentability,

194 *Ibid.*

195 [1890] 6 *La Propriété Industrielle* 67.

196 Plasseraud, Y., and Savignon, F., *Paris 1883: Genése du droit Unioniste des Brevets* (Paris, Litec, 1983), 239–240.

197 *Ibid.*

198 See generally: Levin, H., "Soviet Adherence to International Patent Convention" (1965) 1351 *The Department of State Bulletin* 758.

199 Source: [1895] 11 *La Propriété Industrielle* 76; [1896] 12 *La Propriété Industrielle* 44; [1896] 12 *La Propriété Industrielle* 58.

200 Source: [1896] 12 *La Propriété Industrielle* 96.

201 *Ibid.*

and especially the fact that an invention remained patentable even after its publication or prior patent grant elsewhere.[202] It was hoped that this provision would encourage inventors to bring their inventions to Russia,[203] but it meant that Russia could not give full effect to Article 4 of the Convention. However, Russia did incorporate some provisions of the Paris Convention into its domestic legislation. In 1901, the Russian Government passed an Ordinance in accordance with Article 11 of the Convention which granted temporary protection for patentable inventions exhibited at the International Exposition in St Petersburg.[204] In 1904 the Russian Government reported that a Patent Law Reform Commission had been established, and Russian accession to the Paris Convention was a matter of priority.[205] There were, however, no further developments in the matter until 1965, largely because of the change in government policy which followed the 1917 Revolution.

Speaking on behalf of all foreign delegates at the end of the 1883 Conference, Professor Broch, representative of Norway and Sweden, made the following statement:

> Certes, cette Convention n'est pas une panacée pour les crises industrielles et commerciales; car il n'en existe pas d'autre que le travail assidu, bien dirigé, et l'économie intelligente. Mais c'est un acte de justice conçu dans la pensée de protéger l'industrie et le commerce contre une concurrence déloyale et stérile et qui laisse le champ libre á la concurrence légitime et fertile.[206]

This view, that the 1883 Convention is an act of justice to creators of intellectual work, as well as affording protection to more general industrial and commercial interests, is essentially what the Convention still represents today. This "justice" is particularly apparent in the two major features of the 1883 Convention: national treatment and priority rights.

---

202 Plasseraud, Y., and Savignon, F., *Paris 1883: Genése du droit Unioniste des Brevets* (Paris, Litec, 1983), 244–245.

203 *Ibid.*

204 Source: [1901] 17 *La Propriété Industrielle* 147.

205 Source: [1904] 20 *La Propriété Industrielle* 44.

206 Translation: "Certainly, this Convention is not a panacea for industrial and commercial crises; because it operates only in a well and intelligently planned economy. Nevertheless, it is an act of justice, concerned to protect industry and commerce against unfair and unproductive competition and which leaves the field free for legitimate and productive competition." FRANCE, Ministére des Affaires étrangéres, *Conférence Internationale pour la protection de la propriété Industrielle* (Paris 1883), 40.

The successful negotiation of a multilateral industrial property treaty with these features was a great leap beyond the system of bilateral commercial treaties which had existed before 1883. These achievements have an even greater significance when one examines the process by which the Convention was drafted and the compromises which had to be made in order to ensure its widest acceptability. The French Government, and the diplomatic Conferences undertook this task when all they had to assist them were the examples of bilateral commercial treaties and the postal and telegraph Unions. In such circumstances, it is understandable that the 1883 Convention contained few substantive provisions and avoided theoretical issues altogether.

Despite its shortcomings, the 1883 Convention represented a great achievement in international law and diplomacy, and remains the parent of all other multilateral intellectual property treaties. These are its most important legacies.

CONCLUSION

Linking the Past, Present and Future

This book began by asking two related questions. These were: (1) In what way was the founding of the Paris Convention influenced by earlier developments at the national level? and (2) What was the role of theoretical debate in the evolution of norms of national and international industrial property protection? The previous seven chapters have argued that, at least in regard to the patent system, theoretical debate was the most significant factor prompting such evolution in the period 1790 to 1883. In the important economies of France, the United Kingdom, and Prussia/Germany, patent law reform did not occur in this period without such extensive debate. From the 1850s, some commentators even questioned whether or not the patent system should be retained at all. So long as the theoretical justification for the patent system remained uncertain, there could be no international consensus on the legal protection of inventors' rights.

The last three chapters of the book conclude that there was a clear link between the resolution of the theoretical debates at the national level in the 1870s, and the beginning of a movement in favour of international protection of patent rights. Previous scholarship on the founding of the Paris Convention has usually referred only to the work of the diplomatic Conferences of 1880 and 1883,[1] and has rarely mentioned in any detail the occurrence of the earlier unofficial Conferences in Vienna in 1873 and in Paris in 1878.[2] Yet these chapters show that the earlier unofficial Conferences formed the crucial intermediate link between developments in the purely domestic arena, and the later diplomatic Conferences which led to the signing of the Convention.

There are two reasons why the work of the unofficial 1873 and 1878 Conferences was so pivotal to the founding of the Paris Convention. First, they highlighted the importance of legal recognition of inventors' property rights, and evidenced a strong determination on the part of the delegates to ensure that these rights were respected and protected throughout the world. Thus,

1 See, for example WORLD INTELLECTUAL PROPERTY ORGANIZATION, *1883 Paris Convention Centenary* (Geneva, W.I.P.O., 1983).

2 See, for example, Penrose, E., *The Economics of the International Patent System* (Baltimore, John Hopkins Press, 1951). An exception to this is Ricketson, S., *The Paris Convention for the Protection of Industrial Property* (Oxford, Oxford University Press, 2015) which contains discussion of the work of the 1873 and 1878 Conferences.

 DOI:10.1163/9789004470125_010

the 1873 Vienna Congress began its work with a Resolution stating that the protection of inventions should be guaranteed by the laws of all "civilised"[3] nations. The 1878 Paris Conference went even further, declaring that inventors and other industrial creators had a natural right of property in their industrial creations which had to be protected by all nations. Without this acceptance of the value of patents and other forms of industrial property by opinion leaders and those who were most directly affected by the operation of the patent laws, there would have been no basis for moving forward to the next stage of forming an international Convention on the subject.

The second, and more concrete, contribution of the unofficial Conferences is to be seen in their support for uniform patent legislation. While the protection of inventors' property rights was the most important object sought by both unofficial Conferences, there needed to be agreement as to the means by which this goal could be achieved. Both Conferences supported uniform patent legislation as the way to do this, although their work in this area fell far short of the ideal because neither specified how the goal of uniformity could be attained. However, their work did prompt the French and other Governments to consider seriously the feasibility of the introduction of a multilateral industrial property Convention. This was the case even though the unofficial Conferences and the Governments had different motivations for supporting international arrangements respecting patent rights. The unofficial Conferences were primarily interested in protecting property rights of inventors and were less concerned about wider social and economic aspects of the patent system. The Governments also believed that industrial property rights should be protected, but focused more particularly upon general economic questions, such as the use of the patent system to break down international trade barriers. Thus, for example, the 1878 Conference spent a great deal of time discussing the question of "natural" property rights of inventors, whereas the diplomatic Conferences sidestepped this issue and instead examined at length proposals for inclusion in the Treaty of articles which would ensure that patented inventions were more readily available throughout the Union territory.[4] However, despite these differences, the fact remains that the unofficial Conferences were the first international meetings to focus attention upon the

---

3 Pieper, C., *Der Erfinderschutz und die Reform der Patentgesetze. Amtlicher Bericht über den Internationalen Patent-Congress zur Erörterung der Frage des Patentschutzes. Mit einer Einleitung von Dr. C.W. Siemens F.R.S.* (Dresden, Commission der Schulbuchhandlung, 1873), 259 (First Resolution).

4 See, for example, Article 5 of the 1883 Convention.

need for international patent protection, and the Governments responded to this concern.

At the same time, it must be accepted that the 1883 Convention avoided a number of important issues raised at the unofficial Conferences. Again, this was largely because the diplomatic Conferences had different priorities from their unofficial predecessors, and were concerned to ensure that the provisions of the Convention would be practical and widely acceptable at the international level. These differences are well illustrated in the fact that the term "industrial property" was only loosely defined in the 1883 Convention,[5] and the diplomatic Conferences ignored the question of whether "industrial property" was concerned with a "natural" property right inherent in the intellectual creator, or whether it was solely a right existing by virtue of operation of civil law. As the book sets out, these issues were a central preoccupation in the work of the unofficial 1873 and 1878 Conferences, just as they had been central to patent law reform debates since de Boufflers introduced the French Patent Law of 7 January 1791. As the discussion of the work of the 1878 Conference shows, acceptance of the notion of natural property rights in invention shaped the Conference's Resolutions concerning such matters as the right of foreigners to be treated as nationals, compulsory licensing, forfeiture of patents for non-working, and the types of inventions which should be patentable. It is possible that if the diplomatic Conferences had followed the same path of initially examining the theoretical basis of industrial property rights, and then moving on to more practical issues, the 1883 Convention might have contained several additional substantive provisions. Avoidance of theoretical issues might also be one reason for the slow rate of amendment of the Paris Convention in the successive revisions after 1883.

Despite its failure to confront important theoretical issues, the 1883 Paris Convention contained a number of substantive provisions which were a remarkable advance in international law at the time. Its main achievements – the requirement of national treatment, priority rights and the concept of an "open Union" with possibility of revision and extension of membership – were innovative features in 1883, and this Convention was to serve as a model for later international agreements in the area of industrial property law such as the Madrid Agreement Concerning the International Registration of Marks 1891, the Madrid Agreement for the Repression of False or Deceptive Indications of Source on Goods 1891, the Hague Agreement Concerning the International

5 See paragraph 1 of the Final Protocol of the 1883 Convention. The latest, 1967 Stockholm text, of the Paris Convention defines "industrial property" in Articles 1(2) and 1(3).

Deposit of Industrial Designs 1925, the International Convention for the Protection of New Varieties of Plants 1961, the Patent Cooperation Treaty 1970, the Budapest Treaty on the International Recognition of the Deposit of Microorganisms for the Purposes of Patent Procedure 1977, the Trademark Law Treaty 1994, and the Patent Law Treaty 2000. These Special Agreements were contemplated by Article 15 of the 1883 Convention, which stated that:

> It is understood that the High Contracting Parties reserve the right to make separately between themselves special arrangements for the protection of industrial property, in so far as these arrangements do not contravene the provisions of the present Convention.

Although many of these Agreements came into existence after failed attempts to include the relevant subjects in the text of the Paris Convention,[6] they were reliant upon the model of the Paris Convention for substantive provisions such as the requirements of national treatment, membership was often only open to Paris Union States, and the International Bureau was usually employed as the administrative organ of the Agreements.

Although this book has not examined national or international industrial property reforms after the founding of the Paris Convention in 1883, it is relevant to note that it has only been within the last thirty years that governments have moved towards fulfilling more of the goals of the unofficial Conferences of 1873 and 1878. Between 1883 and 1967 the Paris Convention underwent several revisions,[7] but little was added which had substantial impact upon international legal protection of patent rights. The membership of the Paris Convention has increased from 14 States in July 1884 to 177 in March 2021,[8] and this is the main way in which its international significance has grown.

The 1883 Paris Convention was founded as part of a movement to break down the international legal barriers which hindered the free circulation of patented inventions. Before 1883, it was often difficult for patentees to secure

---

6 See for example, the difficult negotiations concerning the two Madrid Agreements of 1891. BUREAU INTERNATIONAL DE L' UNION POUR LA PROTECTION DE LA PROPRIETE INDUSTRIELLE, *Procés-Verbaux de la Conférence de Madrid de 1890 de l'Union pour la protection de la Propriéte Industrielle suivis des Actes signés en 1891 et ratifiés en 1892* (Berne 1892). UNITED KINGDOM, Parliamentary Papers, *Industrial Property and Merchandise Marks: Further Papers and Correspondence relative to the Recent Conference at Madrid on the Subject of Industrial Property and Merchandise Marks* (1891) vol LXXVII, C. 6417, 507.

7 At Brussels in 1900, at Washington in 1911, at The Hague in 1925, at London in 1934, at Lisbon in 1958 and at Stockholm in 1967.

8 Source: WIPO Lex Database of members of the Paris Convention at 17 March 2021.

legal protection for their inventions in foreign countries, and they also had to contend with working requirements and threats of forfeiture. The founding of the Paris Convention overcame many of these problems, and thus promoted international trade in inventions and patented goods. Further significant protection was not achieved by the Paris Convention but by the 1994 *Agreement on Trade-Related Aspects of Intellectual Property Rights* (T.R.I.P.S.). That Agreement represents a similar concern to ensure adequate patent protection, and promote international trade. As stated by Joseph Straus, the rationale of T.R.I.P.S. is to:

> ensure and permit access to markets ... for products embodying intellectual property [and] ... by providing effective patent protection TRIPS will also contribute to an increase in technology transfer, in the amount of direct investments and to an overall advance in the achievements of national economies in a large number of threshold and developing countries.[9]

It should be noted, however, that while T.R.I.P.S. and the Paris Convention may have some common goals, there is a contrast in the way in which these are achieved. It was essential to the 1878 Paris Conference Resolutions that international industrial property protection should be the subject of "special conventions, independent of commercial treaties",[10] because commercial treaties were often repudiated by one of the parties at short notice, and industrial property rights were consequently lost. It was thought that a treaty devoted exclusively to industrial property rights would have a greater chance of endurance, and, indeed, this was correct, since the Paris Convention is still in operation today. However, T.R.I.P.S. challenges the traditional view that industrial property protection should be separate from commercial treaties. It is possible that the slow rate of reform of the Paris Convention was due in a large measure to the fact that its subject matter was isolated from more general commercial concerns.

---

9 Straus, J., "Implications of the TRIPS Agreement in the Field of Patent Law" in Beier, F.-K. and Schricker, G., (eds) *From GATT to TRIPS – The Agreement on Trade-Related Aspects of Intellectual Property Rights* (Munich, Max Planck Institute, 1996) 160, 215.

10 FRANCE, Ministére de L' agriculture et du Commerce, *Comptes rendus Sténographiques publiés sous les auspices du Comité Central des Congrés et Conférences et la direction de M. CH THIRION, Secrétaire du Comité, avec le concours des Bureaux des Congrés et des auteurs de Conférences: Congrés International de la Propriété Industrielle tenu á Paris du 5 au 17 Septembre 1878* (Paris 1879), General Section, Resolution 3.

T.R.I.P.S., which is essentially a trade treaty, and part of the *Final Act embodying the results of the Uruguay Round of Multilateral Trade Negotiations*,[11] has achieved substantive reforms which have proved impossible within the context of the Paris Convention. T.R.I.P.S. offers for the first time substantive international legal protection for inventors in relation to such matters as the duration of patent rights,[12] and types of patentable subject-matter which must be protected.[13] These were issues of importance to the 1873 and 1878 unofficial Conferences, but were not included in the 1883 Convention. The linking of industrial property protection and trade means that States with limited industrial property protection prior to 1994 were in a difficult position if they wanted the trade benefits of the T.R.I.P.S. Agreement. Such States were forced to adopt the T.R.I.P.S. standards or face trade sanctions under the W.T.O. Agreement.[14] As Ricketson states, the Paris Convention assumed more contemporary relevance though the requirements of Article 2.1 of the T.R.I.P.S Agreement requiring WTO members to comply with Articles 1 to 12 and 19 of the Paris Convention, even if not party to that Convention.[15] By this means, T.R.I.P.S. is providing the substantive legal protection sought by the 1873 and 1878 Conferences, but which proved impossible to achieve under the Paris Convention.

The Paris Convention of 1883 was never intended to be the final word on international protection of industrial property rights; it was only a point of commencement. The Paris Convention was the first step in breaking down the international legal barriers which hindered the free circulation of inventions. As Jean-François Bozérian told the 1880 Paris Conference, their work would amount to only "la preface d'un livre qui va s'ouvrir et qui ne sera peut-être fermé que dans de longues années."[16] This book has shown that since the 1870s, there has been general agreement on the identification of goals or standards of international patent protection. It has been disagreement over the method of implementation of these goals which has given rise to most difficulties.

11 The final Act was signed by the representatives of 108 countries at Marrakesh on 15 April 1994. Fraser C., "The Final Act of the Uruguay Round, the World Trade Organization, Its Framework and Purpose" [1995] 8 *European Intellectual Property Review* 395.

12 See Article 33, T.R.I.P.S.

13 See Article 27.1, T.R.I.P.S.

14 *The Agreement establishing the World Trade Organization* – also part of the *Final Act embodying the results of the Uruguay Round of Multilateral Trade Negotiations* 1994.

15 Ricketson, S., *The Paris Convention for the Protection of Industrial Property* (Oxford, Oxford University Press, 2015), liii.

16 Translation: "the preface of a book which once opened would not be closed again except after a long time." FRANCE, Ministére des Affaires étrangéres, *Conférence Internationale pour la protection de la propriété Industrielle* (Paris 1880), 20.

Expanding T.R.I.P.S. or establishing new international agreements which are distinct from, but operate parallel to, the Paris Convention, are possible solutions with much future promise.[17]

17 For a detailed discussion of various future options for both T.R.I.P.S. and the Paris Convention see Ricketson, S., *The Paris Convention for the Protection of Industrial Property* (Oxford, Oxford University Press, 2015), Chapter 15 – The Paris Convention and the Future.

POSTSCRIPT

The Patent System and Current International Concerns

In his 2015 commentary upon the Paris Convention, Sam Ricketson notes that a current issue of debate concerning the role of industrial property in modern society revolves around human rights.[1] In particular, the revision Conferences of the Paris Convention after 1883 have often provided a forum in which "differences between countries at different stages of development have come to the fore."[2] He adds that the most notable flashpoint has been in relation to compulsory licences for patents, where there has been sharply diverging views of the developed and developing blocs of nations. Interest groups, scholars and some governments have argued for greater access to material protected by industrial property rights, on the basis that there are fundamental human rights to health, education, food and an adequate standard of living,[3] and in some instances, industrial property rights interfere with access to these basic human rights. Of particular concern is what Ricketson describes as the struggle over pharmaceutical patents and public health considerations.[4] He adds that "[p]ainful crisis points arise where the issue becomes one of whether one set of rights (those of industrial property owners) should pre-empt those of an equally compelling human rights claim (for example the right to health and medicine)."[5]

As Ricketson also notes, exceptions exist in many national and regional laws which recognise the co-existence of competing claims of industrial property rights holders and society at large.[6] One such example long employed is compulsory licensing of industrial property rights (particularly patents) in the public interest.

However, although less developed nations have a point that industrial property laws may not currently offer them or their citizens the same economic benefits as developed nations, nevertheless this is taking a very short-term view. It assumes that such less developed nations will remain in their present state of

1 Ricketson, S., *The Paris Convention for the Protection of Industrial Property* (Oxford, Oxford University Press, 2015), 786–792.
2 *Ibid.* 786.
3 *Ibid.*
4 *Ibid.* 791.
5 *Ibid.* 791–792.
6 *Ibid.* 792.

 | DOI:10.1163/9789004470125_011

economic development. It does not take into account the natural course of development as expounded by economic philosophers such as Adam Smith, who emphasised the cumulative and self-propelling nature of the development process.[7] However, it is necessary for the governments of such less developed nations to understand that they have a key role to play in accelerating the process of economic development in their economies, and that they must provide strong laws to allow their economies to grow and flourish.

Since the Paris Convention was signed in 1883, there have been examples of countries which have progressed from economically underdeveloped to superpowers. No better example of this is the case of China. China introduced a patent law in 1985, even though it was a communist country, and in 1985 was largely still an agrarian economy. Even though such circumstances would have suggested that China would have rejected the notion of a patent system, its decision to embrace patents as part of its plan for economic expansion is worth examining in further detail, particularly as an example to less developed countries hoping to learn from China's experience.

China – Patents and Economic Development

On 1 April 1985, the modern Patent Law of China came into force.[8] The law has been subsequently amended three times, most recently in 2008. As of 2019, there were 2,670,784 patents in force in China. In that year alone, 1,243,568 Chinese residents made applications for patents in China, together with 157,093 non-residents, and 84,279 applications were made from abroad.[9] By way of comparison, in 2019, there were 3,131,427 patents in force in the U.S.A. In that year, 285,113 U.S. residents made applications for patents in the U.S.A.,

7 Smith, A., *An Inquiry into the Nature and Causes of the Wealth of Nations* (Edinburgh 1814) (first published in 1776).

8 The Patent Law of China was adopted at the 4th Meeting of the Standing Committee of the Sixth National People's Congress on 12 March 1984, however, it did not go into force until 1 April 1985. The law was subsequently amended for the first time in accordance with the Decision of the Standing Committee of the Seventh National People's Congress on Amending the Patent Law of the People's Republic of China at its 27th Meeting on 4 September 1992, amended for the second time in accordance with the Decision of the Standing Committee of the Ninth National People's Congress on Amending the Patent Law of the People's Republic of China adopted at its 17th Meeting on 25 August 2000, and amended for the third time in accordance with the Decision of the Standing Committee of the Eleventh National People's Congress on Amending the Patent Law of the People's Republic of China at its 6th Meeting on 27 December 2008.

9 Source: WIPO Statistical Country Profiles: China.

together with 336,340 non-residents, and 236,032 applications were made from abroad.[10] The fact that the number of patents in force in China is approaching the number of patents in force in the U.S.A. is an extraordinary achievement, considering the Chinese patent system has only been in operation for 35 years. These remarkable statistics relating to the use of the patent system in China, also coincide with the great economic boom in China over that same period.

(i) *Patents in China prior to 1949*

Prior to the adoption of the modern Chinese patent law in 1984, there had been no patent system in China since 1949, when the Communist Party came to power. However, earlier Governments in China prior to 1949 had recognised that patents could have economic benefits.

As early as June 1927 there was established in China a mechanism by which foreigners who had obtained patent protection in their country of origin could make provisional application for a patent in China, even though no Chinese patent system was in existence.[11] Initially the privilege of provisional filing was only accorded to "qualified persons from contracting States",[12] namely, nationals or persons having an establishment in a state which had entered into treaty obligations with China providing for the protection of patent rights. However, by a Declaration of the Minister of Industry in September 1927 revising the provisional registration procedure, it was provided in Art 1 that: "any citizen capable of contracting who possesses a patent granted by his government or by another government or where he has acquired the same by virtue of inheritance or cession, in regard to an invention, a discovery or a new industrial method may, during the validity of the patent, and awaiting the promulgation of a special patent law in China, request from the Minister a provisional registration."[13]

When a limited patent registration system was introduced into China in 1932 only Chinese nationals were permitted to obtain protection for their inventions, but both foreigners and Chinese could oppose the grant within six months of registration, with the result that the Chinese patentee would be

10 Source: WIPO Statistical Country Profiles: U.S.A.

11 See also the longer article upon which this chapter is based: Duncan, L., and Wang, Y., "Reflections on the Changing Face of the Chinese Patent System" (1994) 5 *Australian Intellectual Property Journal* 165.

12 Declaration of the Minister of Agriculture and Commerce Concerning Applications for Patents filed by Foreigners of 12 June 1927 (1927) 43 *La Propriété Industrielle* 18.

13 Declaration of the Minister of Industry concerning Revision of the Procedure relating to Provisional Registration of Patents by Foreigners dated 2 September 1927 (1928) 44 *La Propriété Industrielle* 238.

granted non-exclusive rights. The registration system established in 1932 was clearly only intended to be a transitional arrangement as China moved towards a more comprehensive system of patent protection.[14] However, this period was one of severe political upheaval in China, as Japan had invaded Manchuria in September 1931, and was to commence its invasion of China's eastern ports and cities in July 1937. As a result of this upheaval, the Chinese government was delayed in carrying out its expressed intention of introducing more comprehensive patents and unfair competition legislation. Despite the pressing problems of national defence, the Chinese government's commitment to protection of industrial property rights was demonstrated by the enactment of the Law of 29 May 1944 concerning Patents, Utility Models and Designs. The Law was intended to replace the legislation of 1932 which had extended patent protection only to Chinese nationals, and reflected the Chinese government's desire to be seen as actively promoting industrial property protection, despite the practical considerations associated with the wartime hostilities which made the implementation of the new Law impossible until 1949. The Law of 1944, together with the accompanying Regulations of 26 September 1947 did not enter into force until 1 January 1949, and only enjoyed a brief period of operation before the People's Republic was proclaimed on 1 October 1949.[15] However, whilst the practical effect of the earlier patent system was limited, the provisions contained in the Law as finally enacted in 1949 demonstrated a deep commitment to the notion of the patent system, and a recognition of the fact that the grant of patents to foreign applicants could be used as a means of encouraging foreign investment in China.

(ii) *Protection for Inventors in China between 1949 and 1984*

After the People's Republic was founded in 1949, the Chinese government had to reassess the whole concept of patent rights, and industrial property rights generally. At the level of socialist philosophy, the patent system, with its grant of private monopoly rights, was contrary to the ideals of the People's Republic.[16] However, the Chinese government faced a dilemma as to how to achieve its stated objective to "[e]ncourage and reward scientific discoveries

14 Duncan, L., and Wang, Y., "Reflections on the Changing Face of the Chinese Patent System" (1994) 5 *Australian Intellectual Property Journal* 165, 167.

15 *Ibid.* 168.

16 *Ibid.* Huang Kunyi notes that even in 1984 when the patent system was re-introduced in China, there remained those who considered that the patent system was contrary to socialist philosophy and had no place in China: Huang K., "The Birth of the First Patent Law in the People's Republic of China" (1984) 23 *Industrial Property* 152, 152–153.

and inventions, and popularize scientific knowledge".[17] It was initially decided that the building of "New China" would be best achieved by adopting a patent system suitably modified for socialist acceptance and influenced by the Soviet system.[18] Thus, under the Provisional Regulations of 11 August 1950 concerning Patents and Inventor's Certificates, the Chinese government established a dual system of protection for inventions. In accordance with Art 2 of the Provisional Regulations, any resident of the People's Republic, having made an invention individually or in a group, could submit the invention for examination to the relevant central organ. The inventor could request either an inventor's certificate or a patent, although certain types of important inventions such as those relating to defence, pharmaceutical and agricultural products and inventions made by an employee of a state enterprise or in fulfilment of a contract with a state enterprise, were eligible only for the inventor's certificate. The inventor's certificate was not an exclusive right, granting the inventor only the rights to receive state recompense, medal and/or honorary title. The inventor was also permitted to apply to the Central Organ for the right to be allowed to name the invention. On the other hand, the patent right was an exclusive right to exploit the invention, including the right to grant licences and take action against infringers. Although the Provisional Regulations of 11 August 1950 nominally appeared as the People's Republic's confirmation of the validity of the concept of a patent system, in practice the boundaries of the system were extremely narrow. Many important categories of invention, such as pharmaceutical and agricultural products were automatically excluded from patent protection. Even where the invention was eligible for protection, there was no set duration for a patent or inventor's certificate, which would be granted for between three and 15 years, according to the discretion of the Central Organ. The Chinese government also wished to operate a closed patent system, with the result that it was an offence to publish the invention in a foreign country without permission of the Central Organ. This effectively prevented Chinese patentees from applying for patents in any other country.[19]

The Chinese government policy also did not support the granting of rights to foreigners. Consequently, only those foreigners resident in China were

17 Art 43 of the Common Program approved at the Chinese People's Political Consultative Conference; quoted in Wu, H., "The Encouragement, Rewards for the Protection of Inventions and Creations in China" (1985) 24 *Industrial Property* 73.

18 Kansky, J., "Nouvelle réglementation de la protection des inventions dans la République populaire chinoise" (1954) 70 *La Propriété Industrielle* 1.

19 See further: Duncan, L., and Wang, Y., "Reflections on the Changing Face of the Chinese Patent System" (1994) 5 *Australian Intellectual Property Journal* 165, 170.

permitted to apply for rights under the Provisional Regulations. As a result of the severe limitations imposed upon the operation of the Chinese patent system, only six inventor's certificates and four patents were granted between 1950 and 1963.[20] The Chinese government soon terminated its experimental patent system, the main reason being that "in the early period of New China, industry and agriculture were just being revived and the development of the national economy relied mainly on the introduction of foreign technology".[21] In this situation, socialist philosophy still hostile to the concept of a patent system was supported by practical considerations in evaluating the limited national benefit which would result from granting patent rights to foreign applicants. The Provisional Regulations of 11 August 1950 were abolished in 1963 and replaced by the Regulations of Rewards for Inventions of 3 November 1963. These Regulations established a national reward system for Chinese inventors, based on a limited inventor's certificate concept, but were of little practical effect, since between 1963 and 1984 less than 1000 rewards were granted.[22]

(iii) *The Basis of the Patent Law of 1984*

Chinese socialist philosophies and the practice of Chinese industries in imitating, rather than innovating were the two main factors which delayed the introduction of a patent system until 1984. However, from the 1970s these factors were modified. In regard to socialist philosophy, in the late 1970s the Chinese government introduced an "open door" policy which, in relation to science and technology, involved the realisation that "no country can achieve a rapid development in its economic construction if it attempts to develop its technology in isolation and to keep itself from international contacts".[23] The "open door" policy was also seen as a precondition to the achievement of the goal of "socialist modernization". In the Constitution of the People's Republic of China adopted by the Fifth Session of the National People's Congress on 4 December 1982, the Preamble expressly stipulated that the "basic task of the nation in the years to come is to concentrate its effort on socialist modernization". In regard to the economy, "socialist modernization" would be achieved through modernisation of industry, agriculture, national defence, science and technology, and success measured by the achievement of targets in relation to the gross annual value of industrial and agricultural production.[24]

---

20 Liu, G., "Review of the Chinese Patent System and Future Prospects" [1987] EIPR 198.

21 Wu, H., *Op cit.* 73.

22 *Ibid.*

23 *Ibid.* 74.

24 Ren, J., "The Patent Law of the People's Republic of China and Economic and Technological Exchange with Foreign Countries" (1985) 24 *Industrial Property* 114.

Although the Chinese economy is a planned, rather than a market economy, the Chinese have realised that production and exchange of commodities exist even in a socialist system, and that modernisation must be achieved through an acceleration in such commodity production. Thus, certain features of the market economy, such as the patent system, are no longer viewed as fundamentally at variance with the socialist concept. In essence, modern China sees the patent system as a tool in the construction of a new economy; a tool which can be used to promote expansion of economic and technological exchanges and co-operation with other countries.[25] It is also Chinese government policy to encourage the independent economic identity of each enterprise, to the extent that each enterprise is responsible for its own profit and loss.[26] Chinese enterprises are strongly encouraged by the state to achieve innovations in their area of expertise, and to develop products which are internationally competitive.[27] Unlike in the 1950s and 1960s, the Chinese government is no longer content to see its manufacturing base relying almost exclusively on the introduction of foreign technology. Thus, with these changes in government policy, it is logical to see why the Chinese now embrace the patent system at both the national and international level.

On 19 March 1985, China acceded to the Paris Convention, and then on 1 January 1994 it acceded to the Patent Co-operation Treaty. Subsequently, on 11 December 2001, China joined the World Trade Organization and became party to the T.R.I.P.S. Agreement.[28] As the modern Chinese patent system moves into the fourth decade of its existence, it is appropriate to reflect upon China's rapid achievement of an international standard of patent protection within a State where socialist policies remain dominant. It is apparent that even dating from pre-revolutionary China, official Chinese attitudes to the patent system have been shaped by the perceived close association between the patent system and economic policies. The last 35 years have seen the former Chinese policy of "socialist modernisation" giving way to newer theories and practices of the "socialist market economy". Along with this change has come greater acceptance and utilisation of patents within the Chinese economy, with concomitant benefits to both Chinese and foreign patentees, and remarkable growth and prosperity in China.

---

25 *Ibid.* 115.

26 *Ibid.*

27 MA, L., "PCT and China" in *Symposium on the Patent Cooperation Treaty (PCT) and China – Beijing, September 13–14, 1993*, 3.

28 Source: World Trade Organization: Member List; WIPO Lex Database.

The example of China shows that the patent system is not inherently unsuitable for developing countries, and indeed, can be used to attract technological investment to a developing country, and thus spur economic progress. Granted, there are situations where there may be strong competing claims of industrial property rights holders versus society at large. Recently, this has arisen, for example, in relation to access to pharmaceutical products at reasonable prices. However, there are remedies available to ameliorate such problems. One remedy long employed is compulsory licensing of industrial property rights (particularly patents) in the public interest. Other options include specific "Crown use" provisions in patent legislation, allowing the State to exploit or authorise the exploitation of the patent for the benefit of the public. Recently, the World Trade Organization issued an Information Note, *The TRIPS Agreement and COVID-19*, dated 15 October 2020, confirming the wide range of options available to member States to improve access to vital medicines to tackle the COVID-19 crisis. Such options include:

(1) Sharing relevant intellectual property and clinical trial data to facilitate cooperation in research and development;
(2) Licensing intellectual property rights, possibly free of charge, for use by third parties in commercial applications for specific purposes;
(3) Pooling technologies amongst intellectual property rights owners and mutual licensing, subject to royalty payments;
(4) Imposition by Government of compulsory licensing of intellectual property rights;
(5) Government Use provisions.

In the case of pharmaceuticals, the W.T.O. has also referred to the potential utility of the Special Compulsory Licensing System first introduced in 2003 by means of a waiver decision and now permanently incorporated in Article 31*bis* of the amended T.R.I.P.S. Agreement. The Special Compulsory Licensing System has been conceived to facilitate access to affordable medicines for countries that rely on import of medicines to deal with a public health problem. For this purpose, it removes the condition in Article 31(f) that a compulsory licence be predominantly used for the supply of the domestic market. The trade-related compulsory licence under the Special Compulsory Licensing System is specifically designed to enable export to countries that are especially dependent on imports for medicines. It ensures a legal pathway for a country to permit the manufacturing of patented medicines under compulsory licence exclusively for export to countries with insufficient or no local manufacturing capacities in the pharmaceutical sector.

There is no doubt that considerable work is being done at the international level to ensure that industrial property rights co-exist successfully with basic human rights, even during a time of international health crisis.

APPENDIX 1

A Note on the Meaning of the Terms "Socialist" and "Communist" in the 1840s and 1850s

The terms "socialist" and "communist" in the 1840s and 1850s did not have the same meaning as they do today. The meaning of such terms can be understood by reading Karl Marx and Friedrich Engels, *Manifesto of the Communist Party* (1848).

Marx and Engels state that in 1847, socialism was a middle-class movement, with communism a working-class movement. In Europe, socialism was respectable, but communism was not. The immediate aim of the communists was the formation of the proletariat into a class, the overthrow of the bourgeois supremacy, and the conquest of political power by the proletariat. Communism did not seek to abolish property generally, only bourgeois, private property. Marx and Engels stated that "[w]e communists have been reproached with the desire of abolishing the right of personally acquiring property as the fruit of man's own labour, which property is alleged to be the groundwork of all personal freedom, activity and independence." They further argued that wage labour did not create any property for the labourer, only capital, which exploits wage labour. The concept of free trade, as supported by economists in the 1840s and 1850s was also not part of communist philosophy, as it was a system suited to bourgeois means of production.

The socialists to which economic philosophers such as de Molinari referred would most probably have been conservative, or bourgeois socialists. Marx and Engels note that these were members of the bourgeoisie, who were desirous of redressing social grievances, in order to secure the continued existence of bourgeois society. Persons falling into this group included "economists, philanthropists, humanitarians, improvers of the condition of the working class, organisers of charity, members of societies for the prevention of cruelty to animals, temperance fanatics, hole-and-corner reformers of every imaginable kind." The socialist bourgeois sought the maintenance of the existing state of society without the revolutionary elements, such as the proletariat.

Other classes of socialists included petty-bourgeois socialists, or people who, like Simonde de Sismondi, sided with the proletariat against the bourgeoisie. These socialists sought to redress "the misery of the proletariat, the anarchy in production, the crying inequalities in the distribution of wealth" and aimed to restore "the old property relations and the old society".

Reproduced in FEUER, L., (ed), *Marx and Engels: Basic Writings* (New York, Fontana, 1969), 43–82.

 | DOI:10.1163/9789004470125_012

APPENDIX 2

Questions Asked of Witnesses before the 1862–64 U.K. Select Committee on Patents and List of Individuals and Organisations Who Made Written Submissions

(A) Questions asked of Witnesses before the 1862–1864 U.K. Select Committee on Patents

The following is a list of the topics upon which witnesses before the 1862–1864 U.K. Select Committee on Patents were asked to give their opinions:

(1) The cost of obtaining letters patent.
(2) Whether there should be a preliminary examination before grant of the patent.
(3) If there should be such an examination, the way in which it should be conducted.
(4) Whether public inconvenience was being caused by the multiplicity of patents.
(5) Whether patents should be refused if they were of a trifling or frivolous nature.
(6) Whether there should be greater facilities for repeal of invalid patents.
(7) Whether there should be any change in the tribunal appointed to try cases concerning patent infringement.
(8) Whether a system of compulsory licenses should be introduced.
(9) Whether patents should be granted to importers of foreign inventions.
(10) Whether patents should be granted to foreigners residing abroad, or their nominees.
(11) Whether the law relating to prolongations and confirmations should be amended.
(12) Whether the law relating to disclaimers and memoranda of alterations should be amended.

Source: UNITED KINGDOM, Parliamentary Papers, *Report of the Commissioners appointed to Inquire into the Working of the Law relating to Letters Patent for Inventions* (1864) 3419, vol XXIX, 321, 178.

(B) List of Individuals and Organisations Who Made Written Submissions to the 1862–1864 U.K. Select Committee on Patents

Individuals, Companies

(1) Sir John Romilly, M.R.
(2) Lord Chelmsford

 | DOI:10.1163/9789004470125_013

(3) Sir Roundell Palmer
(4) E.J. Hughes, Patent Agent, Manchester
(5) Evan Leigh, Engineer, Manchester
(6) Peter J. Linsey, Patent Agent, Manchester
(7) James Holden
(8) W. Ecroyd and Sons
(9) G.H. Leather
(10) M. Henry, London
(11) John Potter, civil engineer, Manchester
(12) John Crossley and Sons
(13) William Tasker, Patent Agent, Halifax
(14) Macfie and Sons, Liverpool
(15) James Fletcher, Manchester
(16) J. Spence, Liverpool
(17) John Fairrie, sugar refiner
(18) James Thomson, Professor of Civil Engineering, Queens College, Belfast
(19) William Hancock, Secretary to the English and Irish Courts of Law and Chancery Commission
(20) James Richardson and Co, Merchants, Glasgow
(21) Ebenezer Henry, Manufacturer, Glasgow
(22) John Finlay, Glasgow
(23) John Ronald, Merchant, Glasgow
(24) A.M. Pattison, Agent for the Bridgewater Trust, Glasgow
(25) Messrs Mitchell and Whytlaw, Manufacturers, Glasgow
(26) Walter Macfarlane and Co, Iron Founders, Glasgow
(27) W.J. Macquorn Rankine, Glasgow
(28) Edmund Hunt, Glasgow
(29) Thomas Wingate and Co, Glasgow
(30) E. A. Cowper
(31) Harrison Blair, Manchester
(32) George Jabet

Organisations

(1) Leeds Chamber of Commerce
(2) Chamber of Commerce, Huddersfield
(3) Chamber of Commerce, Nottingham
(4) Chamber of Commerce, Bradford
(5) Halifax Chamber of Commerce
(6) Liverpool Chamber of Commerce
(7) Bristol Chamber of Commerce

(8) Inventors' Institute
(9) Chamber of Commerce, Wolverhampton
(10) Chamber of Commerce, Glasgow
(11) Institute of Engineers in Scotland
(12) Philosophical Society of Glasgow
(13) Memorial of 99 Engineers, Manufacturers, Chemists, Members of Parliament and Scientific Men
(14) The Manchester Patent Law Reform Association
(15) Birmingham Chamber of Commerce
(16) Sugar Refiners of Liverpool

Source: UNITED KINGDOM, Parliamentary Papers, *Report of the Commissioners appointed to Inquire into the Working of the Law relating to Letters Patent for Inventions* (1864) 3419, vol XXIX, 321, 178–221.

APPENDIX 3

Select List of Bilateral Commercial Treaties Containing Provisions Relating to Industrial Property before the Paris Convention

United Kingdom – Commercial Treaties

(1) Treaty with Austria of 16 December 1865 and Treaty with Austria-Hungary of 5 December 1876 (trade marks and designs)
(2) Treaty with Belgium of 23 July 1862 (trade marks and designs)
(3) Treaty with Colombia of 16 February 1866 (trade marks and designs)
(4) Treaties with France of 23 January 1860 and 28 February 1882 (trade marks and patterns)
(5) Treaty with Italy of 6 August 1863 (trade marks and designs) and Treaty with Italy of 15 June 1883 (trade marks, designs and patents)
(6) Treaty with Russia of 12 January 1859 (trade marks only) and Declaration respecting trade names of 11 July 1871
(7) Treaty with the Zollverein of 30 May 1865, which was later applied to the German Empire from 14 April 1875 (trade marks and patterns)
(8) Declaration with Denmark of 28 November 1879 (trade marks and designs)
(9) Treaty with Ecuador of 18 October 1880 (trade marks and designs)
(10) Treaty with Montenegro of 21 January 1882 (trade marks and designs)
(11) Treaty with Portugal of 6 January 1880 (trade marks and designs)
(12) Treaty with Romania of 5 April 1880 (trade marks and designs)
(13) Treaty with Serbia of 7 February 1880 and Declaration of 4 July 1881 (trade marks and designs)
(14) Declaration with Spain of 14 December 1875 (trade marks and designs)
(15) Declaration with Switzerland of 6 November 1880 (trade marks only)
(16) Declaration with U.S.A. of 24 October 1877 (trade marks only)

Sources: UNITED KINGDOM, Parliamentary Papers, *Extracts from Treaties and Declarations now in force between Great Britain and Foreign Powers relating to Trade Marks, Designs, and Industrial Property, August 1888* (1888) vol XCVIII, C. 5554, 745.

UNITED KINGDOM, Parliamentary Papers, *Reports relative to legislation in Foreign Countries on the Subject of Trade Marks* (1872) C. 596, vol LIV, 585.

UNITED KINGDOM, Parliamentary Papers, *Treaty Stipulations between Great Britain and Foreign Powers on Trade Marks* (1872) C. 633, vol LIV, 673.

 | DOI:10.1163/9789004470125_014

UNITED KINGDOM, Parliamentary Papers, *Reports Relative to Legislation in Foreign Countries on the Subject of Trade Marks. Part One – European Countries* (1878–9) C. 2284 vol LXXIII, 469.

UNITED KINGDOM, Parliamentary Papers, *Reports Relative to Legislation in Foreign Countries on the Subject of Trade Marks. Part Two – Non European Countries* (1878–9) C. 2420 vol LXXIII, 613.

France – Commercial Treaties

(1) Treaties with Italy of 1869 and 3 November 1881 (patents, trade marks)
(2) Treaty with Prussia and the Zollverein of 2 August 1862 (patents, trade marks, designs and models)
(3) Treaty with Spain of 30 June 1876 (patents, trade marks)
(4) Treaties with U.S.A. of 10 April 1869 (patents) and 16 April 1869 (trade marks)
(5) Treaties with the United Kingdom of 23 January 1860 (trade marks and patterns), 28 February 1865 (trade marks, designs and commercial names), and 28 February 1882 (patents and trade marks)
(6) Treaty with Austria of 7 November 1881 (patents, trade marks)

Source: *Ibid.* and PELLETIER, M. and VIDAL-NAQUET, E., *La Convention d'Union pour la Protection de la Propriété Industrielle du 20 mars 1883 et les Conférences de Revision Postérieures* (Paris, L. Larose, 1902), 4–5; PLAISANT, M., *Traité de Droit Conventionnel International concernant la Propriété Industrielle* (Paris, Sirey, 1949), 12–13.

U.S.A. – Commercial Treaties

(1) Treaties with Russia of 6 December 1832 and 21 January 1868 (trade marks only)
(2) Treaty with Belgium of 17 July 1858 and 20 December 1868 (trade marks only)
(3) Treaty with France of 16 April 1869 (trade marks only)
(4) Treaty with United Kingdom of 24 October 1877 (trade marks only)

Source: UNITED KINGDOM, Parliamentary Papers, *Reports relative to legislation in Foreign Countries on the Subject of Trade Marks* (1872) C. 596, vol LIV, 585.

UNITED KINGDOM, Parliamentary Papers, *Treaty Stipulations between Great Britain and Foreign Powers on Trade Marks* (1872) C. 633, vol LIV, 673.

Spain – Commercial Treaties

(1) Treaty with Belgium of 12 February 1870 (trade marks and designs)
(2) Treaty with Italy of 22 February 1870 (trade marks and designs)

(3) Treaty with Austria-Hungary of 21 March 1870 (trade marks and designs)
(4) Declaration with United Kingdom of 14 December 1875 (trade marks and designs)
Source: *Ibid.*

APPENDIX 4

Composition of the Preparatory Committee of the 1873 Vienna Congress

The Preparatory Committee was composed of the following members:

Dr André, (lawyer in Osnabrück, Germany, founding member of *Deutsche Patentschutz-Verein*)

Dr Bauer, (Professor at the Polytechnic at Vienna, member of the Commission for the Vienna Exposition)

W.P. Blake, (U.S. delegate of the Centennial Commission)

Brachelli (of the Statistical Department of the Ministry of Commerce in Vienna, also a member of the Commission for the Vienna Exposition)

W. Ritter von Engerth, (President of the Austrian *Ingenieure Vereins*)

Hermann Grothe (Engineer in Berlin, Editor of the *Polytechnischen Zeitung*)

Prof. Hartig, (Member of the Patent Commission of Saxony)

G. Haseltine, (Patent agent in London)

Hamilton Hill, (Associate Commissioner for Massachusetts)

Jannasch, (Professor of the Academie Proskau, Germany)

Jenny, (Professor at the Polytechnic at Vienna, member of the Commission for the Vienna Exposition)

Friedrich Kaupe, (Engineer in St Petersburg, Russia)

Klostermann, (Professor in Bonn, author of the standard work on patent law)

Eugen Langen, (of Cologne, President of the *Vereins Deutscher Ingenieure*)

Josef Neuwirth, (Bookseller in Vienna, a member of the Commission for the Vienna Exposition)

Carl Pieper, (of Dresden, founding member of the *Deutsche Patentschutz-Verein*)

M. Ratkowsky, (Academic in Vienna, author of works on Austrian patent law)

G. Reuleaux, (Director of the *Gewerbe-Academie* in Berlin)

Franz Rosas, (of the Finance Ministry of Vienna)

Rosenthal, (of Cologne, lawyer, member of the *Vereins Deutscher Ingenieure*)

Schwarz, (Professor of chemical technology in Graz)

Werner Siemens, (Engineer in Berlin, founding member of the *Deutsche Patentschutz-Verein*)

William Siemens, (of London, President of the Institute of Mechanical Engineers)

J.M. Thacher, (Assistant Commissioner of Patents in Washington)

Thomas Webster, (Q.C. of London)

F.L. Weinmann, (of London, member of the U.K. Commission of the International Exposition)

 | DOI:10.1163/9789004470125_015

Source: PIEPER, C., *Der Erfinderschutz und die Reform der Patentgesetze. Amtlicher Bericht über den Internationalen Patent-Congress zur Erörterung der Frage des Patentschutzes. Mit einer Einleitung von Dr. C.W. Siemens F.R.S.* (Dresden, Commission der Schulbuchhandlung, 1873), 4–5.

APPENDIX 5

Resolutions of the 1878 Paris Conference

Some of the more important Resolutions included the following:

The right of inventors and industrial originators in their works or manufacturers and traders in their marks is a right of property. The civil law does not create it; it only regulates it. (General Section, Resolution 1)

Foreigners must be treated as nationals. (General Section, Resolution 2)

Stipulations of reciprocal guarantee of industrial property rights should be the object of special conventions, independent of commercial treaties … (General Section, Resolution 3)

It is desirable that applications for patents, trade marks, designs and models may be simultaneously effected at the office of a competent local authority as well as at the consulates of the various foreign nations. (General Section, Resolution 12)

Apart from financial and credit schemes and plans, and inventions contrary to public order and morality, all industrial inventions should be patentable. Patents should be accorded to inventions of chemical, food, and pharmaceutical products. (Patents Section, Resolution 1)

Patents must assure, during their period of validity, to inventors or to their third party successors, the exclusive right to exploit the invention and not simply a right to remuneration paid by third party exploiters. (Patents Section, Resolution 2)

The patent should be granted to any applicant, at his risk and peril. However, it is useful if the applicant receive a preliminary and secret opinion, relating to the question of novelty, so that he may, at his choice, maintain, modify or abandon his application. (Patents Section, Resolution 4)

Importation by the patentee into the country where the patent has been granted, of goods made overseas, should not be forbidden by law. (Patents Section, Resolution 8)

It is acceptable to allow forfeiture for non-working. Such forfeiture must be pronounced by a competent judicial authority. (Patents Section, Resolution 10)

Rights resulting from patent applications or filings effected in different countries for the same object are independent of each other, and not to be treated as one, as is the case currently in many countries. (Patents Section, Resolution 11)

The protection accorded by law to authors of designs and models must be subject to the condition of prior filing. (Designs Section, Resolution 4.) (Note that designs and models were considered a right of property under Resolution 3.)

A trade mark should not be claimed unless it has been filed. (Trade Marks Section, Resolution 1)

Any trade mark filed in one country must be equally admitted, as is, to filing in all the assenting countries. (Trade Marks Section, Resolution 2)

 | DOI:10.1163/9789004470125_016

Any filing made in one of the contracting countries is to be given a priority right in all the other countries … (Trade Marks Section, Resolution 3)

The filing of a trade mark is simply declarative of a property right. (Trade Marks Section, Resolution 7)

The commercial name constitutes a property right of man, which must be protected without distinction of nationality or obligation of filing. (Commercial Names Section)

The Congress institutes an international permanent Committee, charged with assuring, within the limitations of possibility, the realisation of the propositions adopted by the Congress … (Section on the Permanent Committee, Resolution 1)

One of the aims of the permanent Committee created by this private initiative is to obtain from one of the Governments a meeting of an official international Conference to determine the bases of uniform legislation. (Section on the Permanent Committee, Resolution 3.) (In Resolution 4 the Congress decided to ask the French Minister of Commerce if France would take the lead in this matter.)

Source: FRANCE, Ministére de L' agriculture et du Commerce, *Comptes rendus Sténographiques publiés sous les auspices du Comité Central des Congrés et Conférences et la direction de M. CH THIRION, Secrétaire du Comité, avec le concours des Bureaux des Congrés et des auteurs de Conférences: Congrés International de la Propriété Industrielle tenu á Paris du 5 au 17 Septembre 1878* (Paris 1879), 427–435.

(Translated from the original French text).

APPENDIX 6

Permanent Committee – 1878 Paris Conference

The following are extracts from the Second Draft text prepared by the Permanent Committee established by the 1878 Paris Conference.

General Section

A *General Provisions Which Are Appropriate to Be Inserted in a Union Treaty.*

Article 1

In regard to patents, designs and industrial models, trade marks, and commercial names, the citizens of each of the contracting States shall enjoy the same rights as nationals in all the States of the Union.

Article 3

Provisional protection should be accorded to patentable inventions, designs and industrial models, and also to trade marks which are presented at official or officially recognised international expositions.

B *General Recommendations to the Governments*

Recommendation 1

It is desirable that in regard to those countries which do not have sufficient laws concerning industrial property, diplomatic action should be taken to ensure that these governments take effective measures to assure to inventors and industrial artists protection for their works, and to traders and manufacturers protection of their marks.

Recommendation 2

It is desirable that stipulations of reciprocal guarantee of industrial property should be the object of special conventions and independent of commercial treaties.

 | DOI:10.1163/9789004470125_017

Patents Section

A General Provisions Which Are Appropriate to Be Inserted in a Union Treaty

Article 1

Any application for a patent, regularly filed in any one of the contracting States, is to be accorded a priority of registration in all the other States during a period of …

Article 2

The rights pertaining to a patent filed in the contracting countries must be independent of each other and not dependent in any way.

B General Recommendations to the Governments

Recommendation 1

The importation into the country in which the patent has been granted, by the patentee, of objects manufactured in one of the contracting countries, shall not be a cause of forfeiture (of the patent).

Source: FRANCE, Ministére de L' agriculture et du Commerce, *Comptes rendus Sténographiques publiés sous les auspices du Comité Central des Congrés et Conférences et la direction de M. CH THIRION, Secrétaire du Comité, avec le concours des Bureaux des Congrés et des auteurs de Conférences: Congrés International de la Propriété Industrielle tenu á Paris du 5 au 17 Septembre 1878* (Paris 1879), 721–732. (Translated from the original French).

APPENDIX 7

Third Draft Treaty – Text

The following is the complete text of the Third Draft prepared by the Permanent Committee established by the 1878 Paris Conference.

General Questions

1. The adhering governments have agreed to form a Union for the protection of industrial property.
2. The subjects of each one of the States of the Union shall enjoy in all the other States the same rights as the natives thereof, in the matter of patents of inventions, of designs and industrial models, of trade marks, and any commercial use of firm names.
3. A special service of industrial property shall be established in each country; a central depot of patents of invention, of designs and industrial models, of trade marks and commercial names shall be annexed thereto, and be accessible to the public. A periodical official journal shall be published for the service of industrial property. Measures shall be likewise taken for the publication of an international journal common to all the States of the Union.
4. Temporary protection shall be given to patentable inventions, designs, and industrial models, as well as the marks of trade and commerce which shall be represented in international exhibitions either official or officially recognised.

Patents of Invention

5. The act of filing an application for a patent regularly performed in one of the States of the Union shall carry with it the priority of registration in all the other States during a period of ____.
6. The introduction by [the patentee] in the countries where the patent has been issued of articles fabricated in any one of the States of the Union shall not involve its annulment.

 | DOI:10.1163/9789004470125_018

Designs and Industrial Models

7. Designs or models deposited in any one of the States of the Union shall be guaranteed in all the other States, and the ownership shall be considered as legitimately acquired by those who make usage of it conformably to the legislation of the country of origin.
8. A deposit regularly made in one of the States of the Union shall carry with it the priority of registration in the other States during the term of _____.

Marks of Trade and of Commerce

9. Trade marks entered in one of the States of the Union shall be guaranteed in all the other States, and property shall be considered as legitimately acquired by those who make usage of it conformably to the legislation of the country of origin.
10. Any registration regularly made in one of the States of the Union shall carry with it the priority of registration in the other States during the term of _____.
11. All foreign products illicitly or unlawfully bearing the trade mark of a manufacturer or of a merchant doing business in the country of importation, or any indication of being (*sic*) [origin] produced in the said country, shall be denied entry, be excluded from transit and public storage, and liable to be seized in any place whatever.

Commercial Firm Names

12. The commercial name of a firm constitutes a property which should be protected without distinction of nationality and without obligation of registry.

Source: UNITED STATES OF AMERICA, Congressional Papers, *Report of the Commissioners appointed to Revise the Statutes relating to Patents, Trade and other Marks, and Trade and Commercial Names under Act of Congress approved June 4, 1898* (1900) 56th Congress, 2nd Session, Senate document 20, 234.

APPENDIX 8

Jagerschmidt Draft Treaty – Text

The text of the Jagerschmidt draft Treaty of 1880 was as follows:

Article 1

Austria-Hungary, Belgium, Brazil, the United States of America, France, the United Kingdom of Great Britain and Ireland, Italy, Luxembourg, the Netherlands, Portugal, Russia, the United Kingdoms of Sweden and Norway, Switzerland, Turkey, Uruguay and Venezuela are constituted the States of a Union for the Protection of Industrial Property.

Article 2

The subjects and citizens of each of the contracting States shall enjoy reciprocally, in all the other States of the Union, in the matter of patents, industrial designs or models, trade marks, and commercial names, the advantages that their respective laws now accord or may hereafter accord to nationals. They shall have the same protection as the latter and the same legal remedy against any injury to their rights, upon the only condition that they accomplish the formalities imposed upon nationals by the domestic legislation of each State.

Article 3

Every deposit of an application for a patent, design or model, or trade mark, correctly executed in one or other of the contracting States, shall constitute for the applicant a right of priority of registration in all the other States of the Union during a period of ____ commencing from the date of the lodgement.

Article 4

The owner of a patent shall have the option to import, in the countries where his patent shall have been delivered, articles manufactured in one or other of the contracting countries, without the importation being a cause of forfeiture of the patent.

 | DOI:10.1163/9789004470125_019

Article 5

Ownership of rights in designs, models and trade marks shall be considered, throughout the States of the Union, as lawfully acquired by those who exercise those rights, conforming to the legislation of the country of origin, on the said question of designs, models and trade marks.

Article 6

Any products which illegally bear either a mark of a manufacturer or of a trader established in one of the countries of the Union, or an indication of provenance of said country, shall be prohibited entry into all the other contracting States, excluded from transit and storage, and should be the object of consistent seizure, if there are grounds for an action in law.

Article 7

The deposit of a mark whether of manufacture or commerce, shall be admitted, in all the States of the Union, at the risk and peril of the depositor, whatever may be the nature of the product bearing the mark.

Article 8

The ownership of rights in a commercial name shall be guaranteed in all the States of the Union, without distinction as to nationality, and without obligation of deposit, whether or not it is part of a trade mark.

Article 9

The high contracting parties undertake to accord temporary protection to patentable inventions, designs, models and also to trade marks, in respect of goods which figure in official or officially recognised, international exhibitions. Objects which are arguably forged may be seized in the precincts of the exhibition.

Article 10

Each of the high contracting parties undertakes to establish a special service for industrial property, and a central office for the communication to the public of patents, designs, models and trade marks.

Article 11

An international organ, placed under the high authority of the Administration of the Swiss Confederation, shall be charged under the title of Bureau International de la Propriété Industrielle, to meet, to coordinate and publish information of every nature relevant to patents, designs, models and trade marks. The expenses of this institution shall be supported by all the Governments of the contracting States. The International Bureau shall write in the ____ language with the assistance of documents which shall be placed at its disposal by the said Governments, a journal of industrial property.

Article 12

The present Convention shall be submitted to periodic revisions with a view to introducing amendments of a nature to improve the system of the Union of the contracting States. To this effect, Conferences shall be held successively in the capitals of each of the contracting States between the delegates of the said States. The next meeting will be held in ____ at ____.

Article 13

The high contracting parties reserve respectively the right to make separately, between themselves, special arrangements for the protection of industrial property, in so far as these arrangements do not contravene the provisions of the present Convention.

Article 14

States which are not parties to the present Convention shall be permitted to adhere to it at their request. This adherence shall be notified by diplomatic channels to the contracting State where the last conference was held, and by this State to all the others.

This shall presuppose full adherence to all the clauses and admission to all the advantages stipulated by the present Convention.

Article 15

The present Convention shall come into force, reckoning from ____ and shall remain in force for an indefinite time, until the expiration of one year from the day of the denunciation. The denunciation shall affect only the State which has made it, the Convention remaining in force for the rest of the contracting parties.

Article 16

The present Convention shall be ratified, and the ratifications exchanged in Paris as soon as this is able to be done.

Source: FRANCE, Ministére des Affaires étrangéres, *Conférence Internationale pour la protection de la propriété Industrielle* (Paris 1880), 26–29. Translated from the original French.

Bibliography

Commentaries and Monographs

Akerman, C., *L'Obligation d'Exploiter et la Licence Obligatoire en Matiére de Brevets d'Invention* (Paris, Librairie du Recueil Sirey, 1936).

Alexander-Katz, R., *Bemerkungen zu dem Entwurf eines Patentgesetzes* (Berlin, Carl Heymann's Verlag, 1877).

Andre, W., *Der revidirte Entwurf eines Patentgesetzes für das deutsche Reich* (Chemnitz, S.C.F. Bidenhabn, 1876).

Babbage, C., *The Exposition of 1851; or, Views of the Industry, the Science, and the Government of England* (London, John Murray, 1851).

Beck Von Mannagetta, P., *Das Neue Osterreichische Patentrecht auf Grund des Patent-Gesetzes vom 11 Jänner 1897* (Wien, Alfred Hölder, 1897).

Beck Von Mannagetta, P., *Die Internationale Union zum Schutze des gewerblichen Eigentumes und ihre Bedeutung für Osterreichs Handel und Industrie* (Vienna, Niederösterreichischen Gewerbevereines, 1903).

Bentham, J., *A Manual of Political Economy* (London, 1795), in *The Works of Jeremy Bentham, vol VII,* (Edinburgh, John Bowring, 1898).

Bentham, J., *The Rationale of Reward* (London, John and HL Hunt, 1825).

Bettelheim, E., *Das Recht des Erfinders in Osterreich nach dem Gesetze vom 11 Jänner 1897* (Vienna, Manz K.K. Hof-, Verlags, 1901).

Bitzer, F., *Vorschläge für ein Deutsches Patentgesetz, beantragt durch die von der hohen deutschen Bundesversammlung durch Beschluss vom 24 Juli 1862 einberfene Commission von Fachmännern, met Erläuterungen und einer Ausführung über die principielle Rechtfertigung des Patentschutzes* (Stuttgart, August Schaber, 1864).

Blanc, E., *L'inventeur Breveté, Code des Inventions et des Perfectionnements* (Paris, Librairie Générale de Jurisprudence de Cosse, 1852).

Bodenhausen, G., *Guide to the Application of the Paris Convention for the Protection of Industrial Property* (Geneva, BIRPI, 1968).

Boehm, K., and Silberston, A., *The British Patent System: 1. Administration* (Cambridge, Cambridge University Press, 1967).

Bojanowski, *Ueber die Entwickelung des Deutschen Patentwesens in der zeit von 1877 bis 1889* (Leipzig, Verlag von Arthur Felix, 1890).

Bottomley, S., *The British Patent System during the Industrial Revolution 1700 to 1852* (Cambridge, Cambridge University Press, 2014).

Bozerian, M.J. *La Convention Internationale du 20 Mars 1883 pour la Protection de la Propriété Industrielle* (Paris, Imprimerie C. Pariset, 1885).

Bouvier, H., *Essais sur la Recherche de Principes Géneraux Applicables aux unions internationales pour la protection de la propriété Industrielle* (Paris, Imprimerie Moquet, 1889).

Brinton, C., *A Decade of Revolution 1789–1799* (New York, Harper & Brothers, 1934).

Cameron, R., (ed), *Essays in French Economic History* (Homewood, Richard D. Irwin, 1970).

Chitty, J., *Treatise on the Law of Commerce, Manufactures and Contracts* (London, 15th ed, Sweet and Maxwell, 1909, first published 1820).

Cobban, A., *A History of Modern France, vol 1, Old Regime and Revolution 1715–1799* (Oxford, Oxford University Press, 1957).

Constant, C., *Union Internationale: Protection de la Propriété Industrielle: Texte Annoté de la Convention de Paris du 20 Mars 1883 Modifiée et Complétée par les Conférences de Rome, de Madrid et de Bruxelles* (Paris, A. Pedone, 1901).

Cornish, W., et al, *The Oxford History of the Laws of England Volume XI: 1820–1914 English Legal System* (Oxford, Oxford University Press, 2010).

Coke, E., *Institutes of the Laws of England* (1628–44) 3d part, c.85.

De Iturralde, T., *La Union Internacional para la proteccion de la Propriedad Industrial* (Paris, 1890).

De Sismondi, S., *Nouveaux principes d'économie politique ou de la richesse dans ses rapport avec la population* (Paris, Delaunay, 1827).

Donzel, L., *M. Eugéne Pouillet au Congrés International pour la protection de la Propriété Industrielle tenu á Londres, les 1er, 2 et 3 Juin 1898* (Paris, Imprimerie Jean Gainche, 1898).

Donzel, L., *Rapport adressé sur sa demand a Monsieur le Ministre des Affaires étrangéres sur la Législation internationale de la Propriété Industrielle au point de vue de la Conférence internationale qui aura lieu á Madrid le 1er avril 1890* (Paris, Marchel et Billard, 1890).

Drahos, P., *A Philosophy of Intellectual Property* (Aldershot, Dartmouth Publishing, 1996).

Dutton, H.I., *The Patent System and inventive activity during the industrial revolution 1750–1852* (Manchester, Manchester University Press, 1984).

Einem Wiener Rechtsanwalte, *Zur Patent-Reform in Oesterreich: Vier Artikel der Wiener Allgemeinen Zeitung* (Wien, Alfred Hölder, 1881).

Finer, S.E., (ed) *Five Constitutions* (Bungay, Penguin, 1979).

Gareis, C., *Ueber das Erfinderrecht von Beamten, Angestellten und Arbeitern* (Berlin, Carl Heymann's Verlag, 1879).

Goldberger, S., *Das neue Osterreichische Patent-recht* (Vienna, U. Hartleben Verlag, 1899).

Goldenberg, A., *Ueber das Projectirte Patentgesetz für das Deutsche Reich; November 1876* (Strassburg, G. Fischbach, 1876).

Gomme, A.A., *Patents of Invention: Origin and Growth of the Patent System in Britain* (London, Longmans Green and Co, 1946).

Grothe, H., *Der Internationale Patent-Congress in Wien (4–9 August 1873)* (Berlin, Julius Springer, 1873).

Heggen, A., *Erfindungsschutz und Industrialisierung in Preussen 1793–1877* (Göttingen, Vandenhoeck und Ruprecht, 1975).

Henretta, James, *The Evolution of American Society, 1700–1815* (Lexington, D.C. Heath and Co, 1973).

Jobard, J.-B., A.-M., *Nouvelle économie sociale ou monautopole industriel, artistique, commercial et littéraire* (Paris, Mathias, Bruxelles, chez l'auteur, 1844).

Knoblauch, H., *Das Patentgesetz für das Deutsche Reich vom 25 Mai 1877* (Berlin, Eugen Grosser, 1880).

Kuzel, H., "Ueber Erfindungsschutz, Patentsysteme und moderne Patentgesetzgebung" in *Vorträge über Erfindungsschutz, moderne Patentgesetzgebung und Oesterreichisches Patentwesen gehalten im 'Verein Oesterreichischer Chemiker in Wien' sowie Berichte über die bezüglichen Debatten* 5–20 (Vienna, Ferdinand Brück, 1899).

Ladas, S., *Patents, Trademarks and Related Rights; National and International Protection* (Cambridge, Harvard University Press, 1975).

Landgraf, J., *Das deutsche Reichsgesetz betreffend den Schutz von Erfindungspatenten* (Stuttgart, Julius Maier, 1877).

Lefebvre, G., *La Révolution Française* (Paris, Presses Universitaires de France, 1951).

Lenz, O., *Entwurf eines Patentgesetzes vom Reichskenzleramt veröffentlicht* (Berlin, Julius Springer, 1877).

Liebesny, F., (ed) *Mainly on Patents* (London, Butterworths, 1972).

Locke, J., *Two Treatises on Civil Government* (London, Awnsham Churchill, 1690).

Macfie, R.A., *The Patent Question Under Free Trade* (London, Longmans, Green, Reader and Dyer, 1863).

Macfie, R.A., (ed), *Recent Discussions on the Abolition of Patents for Inventions in the United Kingdom, France, Germany, and the Netherlands: evidence, speeches and papers in its favour* (London, Longmans and Co, 1869).

Macleod, C., *Inventing the Industrial Revolution: The English Patent System, 1600–1800* (Cambridge, Cambridge University Press, 1988).

Madelin, L., *The French Revolution* (London, Heinemann, 1925).

Martin, K., *French Liberal Thought in the Eighteenth Century* (London, Turnstile Press, 1954).

Mignet, F.A.M., *History of the French Revolution* (London, J.M. Dent and Sons, 1915).

Milhaud, L., *Des Brevets d'invention dans les Rapports Internationaux* (Paris, Larose et Forcel, 1892).

Morillot, A., *De la Protection accordée aux Oeuvres d'art, aux Photographies, aux Dessins et Modéles Industriels et aux Brevets d'Invention dans l'Empire d'Allemagne* (Paris, Cotillon et Cie, 1878).

Osterrieth, A., and Axter, A., *Die Internationale Ubereinkunft zum Schutze des gewerblichen Eigentums vom 20 märz 1883 (Pariser Konvention) nebst den übrigen Verträgen des Deutschen Reichs über den gewerblichen Rechtsschutz* (Berlin, Carl Heymann's Verlag, 1903).

Pataille, J., and Huguet, A., *Code International de la Propriété Industrielle Artistique et Littéraire contenant les legislations Française et étrangéres et les Traités Internationaux en Matiére de Brevets d'invention, Littérature, Théatre, Musique, Beaux-Arts Dessins, Modéles, Noms et Marques de Fabrique et Concurrence Commerciale* (Paris, Marescq, 1865).

Pelletier, M., and Vidal-Naquet, E., *La Convention d'Union pour la Protection de la Propriété Industrielle du 20 mars 1883 et les Conférences de Revision Postérieures* (Paris, L. Larose, 1902).

Penrose, E., *The Economics of the International Patent System* (Baltimore, John Hopkins Press, 1951).

Phillips, J., *Charles Dickens and the "Poor Man's Tale of a Patent"* (Oxford, ESC Publishing, 1984).

Philippson, F., *Die Reform der Patent-gesetzgebung, beartbeitet im Auftragedes handels- und Gewerbe-Vereins für Rheinland und Westphalen* (Düsseldorf, Schaubsche Buchhandlung, 1890).

Pieper, C., *Der Erfinderschutz und die Reform der Patentgesetze. Amtlicher Bericht über den Internationalen Patent-Congress zur Erörterung der Frage des Patentschutzes. Mit einer Einleitung von Dr. C.W. Siemens F.R.S.* (Dresden, Commission der Schulbuchhandlung, 1873).

Pieper, C., and Schmid, P., *Geschichte der internationalen Union für den Schutz des gewerblichen Eigentums sammt Konvention und Staatsverträgen* (Berlin, Deutschen Vereins für den Schutz des gewerblichen Eigentums, 1894).

Pieper, C., *Zur Reform des Patentgesetzes und des Gebrauchs-Musterschutzes* (Berlin, Polytechnische Buchhandlung, 1890).

Pieper, C., *Sind die Industrie-Schutzgesetze verbessert? – nach dem stenographischen Bericht und den Protocollen der Conferenz für den Schutz des gewerblichen Eigentums* (Berlin, Puttkammer und Mühlbrecht, 1891).

Plaisant, M., *Traité de Droit Conventionnel International concernant la Propriété Industrielle* (Paris, Sirey, 1949).

Plaisant, M., and Fernand-Jacq, *Les Brevets d'Invention en Droit International* (Paris, Recueil Sirey, 1931).

Plant, Sir A., *Selected Economic Essays and Addresses* (London, Routledge and Kegan Paul, 1974).

Plasseraud, Y., and Savignon, F., *L'etat et L'invention: Histoire des Brevets* (Paris, La Documentation Française, 1986).

Plasseraud, Y., and Savignon, F., *Paris 1883: Genése du droit Unioniste des Brevets* (Paris, Litec, 1983).

Rauter, G., *Das Deutsche Patentgesetz und die Vorschläge des Deutschen Vereins für den Schutz des gewerblichen Eigentums* (Stuttgart, Verlag von Ferdinand Enke, 1904).

Regnault, T., *De la Législation et de la Jurisprudence concernant les Brevets d'Invention, de Perfectionnement et d'Importation* 135 (Paris, Antoine Bavoux, 1825).

Ricketson, S., *The Paris Convention for the Protection of Industrial Property* (Oxford, Oxford University Press, 2015).

Ricketson, S., *The Berne Convention for the protection of literary and artistic works: 1886–1986* (London, Centre for Commercial Law Studies, 1987).

Schumpeter, J., *Capitalism, Socialism and Democracy* (New York, Harper & Brothers, 1942).

Smith, A., *An Inquiry into the Nature and Causes of the Wealth of Nations* (Edinburgh 1814) vol III, (first published in 1776).

Sieber, E., *Kurze Bemerkungen zum Entwurf eines deutschen Patentgesetzes* (Berlin, Dümmlers Verlagsbuchhandlung, 1877).

Soboul, A., *The French Revolution 1787–1799* (Oxford, Oxford University Press, 1976).

Stewart, J.H., (ed) *A Documentary Survey of the French Revolution* (New York, The Macmillan Company, 1951).

Taylor, C.T., and Silberston, Z.A., *The Economic Impact of the Patent System: A Study of the British Experience* (Cambridge, Cambridge University Press, 1973).

Vidal-Naquet, E., *Des Marques de Fabrique et de Commerce et du Nom Commercial en droit International* (Paris, L. Larose, 1898).

Vidal-Naquet, E., *La Convention d'Union pour la Protection de la Propriété Industrielle du 20 mars 1883 et les Conférences de Revision Postérieures* (Paris, L. Larose, 1902).

Von Kleinschrod, C. TH., *Die Internationale Patentgesetzgebung nach ihren Prinzipien nebst Vorschlägen für ein Künftiges Gemeines Deutsches Patentrecht* (Erlangen, Verlag von Ferdinand Enke, 1855).

Von Rosas, F.E., *Das Industrielle Eigenthum (Privilegien-, Marken- und Musterschutz). Bericht uber die Verhandlungen des Internationalen Congresses zu Paris 1878* (Wien, Verlag der Handels-und Gewerbekammer, 1878).

Wood, H., *A History of the Royal Society of Arts* (London, John Murray, 1913).

Journal Articles and Papers

Adams, J., and Averley, G., "The Patent Specification: The Role of Liardet v Johnson" (1986) 7 *Journal of Legal History* 156.

Alexander-Katz, R., "Die Entstehung der Union und ihre Grundzüge" in Alexander-Katz, R., Lau, R., Osterrieth, A., and Wassermann, M., *Der Anschluss des Deutschen*

Reichs an die Internationale Union für gewerblichen Rechtsschutz 39 (Berlin, Carl Heymann's Verlag, 1902).

Bandeira, A.C., "Brazil's Ratification of the Paris Convention of 1883" (1984) *Industrial Property* 371.

Batzel, V.M., "Legal Monopoly in Liberal England: The Patent Controversy in the Mid-Nineteenth Century" (1980) 22 *Business History* 189.

Benard, T.N., "Les Inventions: sont-elles une propriété?" (1868) XI (3rd Series) *Journal des économistes* 47.

Bohmert, V., "Die Erfindungspatente, nach volkswirthschaftlichen Grundsätzen und industriellen Erfanrungen; mit besondrer Rüchsicht auf England und die Schweiz" (1869) *Vierteljahrschrift für Volkswirthschaft und Culturgeschichte* 28.

Bos, J.J., "The Netherlands and the Paris Convention for the Protection of Industrial Property" (1984) *Industrial Property* 383.

Boros, R., "Italy and the Establishment of the Paris Union for the Protection of Industrial Property" (1984) *Industrial Property* 379.

Browne, W.H., "Has Congress Authority to legislate on the subject of Trade-Marks?" (1880) 14 *American Law Review* 156.

Bulajic, M., "Serbia, One of the Founding States of the 1883 Paris Union" [1984] *Industrial Property* 399.

Capuccio, M., "Le Convenzioni Internazionali per La Tutela della Proprietá Industriale" (1903) 3 *Rivista Tecnica* 1.

Chevalier, M., 'Les Brevets d'Invention contraires a la Liberté du Travail' (1878) *Journal des économistes* 169.

Combaldieu, J.C., "The Ratification of the Paris Convention by France and the Reactions Thereto" [1984] *Industrial Property* 374.

"Commercial relations of England and France: Review of recent works by Chevalier, Amé and Faucher" (1860) 111 *The Edinburgh Review* 277.

Cooke, C.E.B., "Patent Law Amendment" (1876–7) 2 *The Law Magazine and Review* (4th Series) 209.

Davis, I.J.G., and Harrison, J., "Prelude to the United Kingdom's Accession to the Paris Convention, March 17, 1884", (1984) *Industrial Property* 395.

De Molinari, G., 'De la Propriété des Inventions' (1855) *Journal des économistes* 410.

De Molinari, G., 'La Propriété des Inventions' (1856) *Journal des économistes* 133.

Dietzel, H., "The German Tariff Controversy" (1903) 17 *The Quarterly Journal of Economics* 365.

Donzel, L., "Commentaire de la Convention Internationale signée á Paris le 20 mars 1883 pour la protection de la Propriété Industrielle" (1891) *Journal des Procés en Contrefaçon* 1.

Drouets, C., "La Convention d'Union de la Propriété Industrielle: L'oeuvre de la Conférence de Revision de Londres de 1934" (1935) 134 *Bulletin de la Société d'Encouragement pour L'Industrie Nationale* 376.

Duncan, L., and Wang, Y., "Reflections on the Changing Face of the Chinese Patent System" (1994) 5 *Australian Intellectual Property Journal* 165.

Field, D., "On an International Code" (1874) 3 *The Law Magazine and Review* (New Series) 251.

Fraser C., "The Final Act of the Uruguay Round, the World Trade Organization, Its Framework and Purpose" [1995] 8 *European Intellectual Property Review* 395.

"Free Trade in England", *New York Times*, 16 December 1891, at 4.

Frey-Godet, B. "*Comparaison du texte de la Convention et de la législation britannique correspondante"* (1898) *Annuaire de l'association Internationale pour la Protection de la Propriété Industrielle* 151.

Garnier, J., 'Les Vingt Questions de M. Jobard sur la Concurrence suivies de vingt Réponses par M. Joseph Garnier' (1855) *Journal des économistes* 247.

Ginsburg, J., "A Tale of Two Copyrights: Literary Property in Revolutionary France and America" (1990) 64 *Tulane Law Review* 991.

Hawes, W., "On the Economical Effects of the Patent Laws" (1863–4) 16 *The Law Magazine and Law Review* 61.

Hawes, W., "Patent Law Amendment" (1863–4) 16 *The Law Magazine and Law Review* 355.

Huang K., "The Birth of the First Patent Law in the People's Republic of China" (1984) 23 *Industrial Property* 152.

Huet, A., "Aperçu Historique de la Législation sur les Brevets d'Invention dans les Pays-Bas" (1888) 4 *La Propriété Industrielle* 86.

Hulme, E.W., "On the History of Patent Law in the Seventeenth and Eighteenth Centuries" (1902) 18 *Law Quarterly Review* 280.

Jacobsohn, N., *Patentfrage und Krisis* (Berlin, Puttkammer und Mühlbrecht, 1876).

Jobard, J-B., A-M., 'Defense du Monautopole' (1854) 4 *Journal des économistes* 442.

Jobard, J-B., A-M., 'La Concurrence et Le Monautopole – Nouvelle Lettre de M. Jobard, en réponse a des Observations de M. Joseph Garnier' (1855) *Journal des économistes* 100.

Jobard, J-B., A-M., 'La Concurrence et Le Monautopole – Nouvelle Lettre de M. Jobard, et réponse de M. Joseph Garnier' (1855) *Journal des économistes* 138.

Kansky, J., "Nouvelle réglementation de la protection des inventions dans la République populaire chinoise" (1954) 70 *La Propriété Industrielle* 1.

Klostermann, R., "Zur Reform der Patentgesetzgebung" in *Die Patentgrage: Sechs Breisschriften über Reform der Patent-gesetzgebung. Prämiirt durch den Verein deutscher Ingenieure* (Köln, Verlag von Eduard Heinrich Maher, 1876).

Kronstein, H., and Till, I., "A re-evaluation of the International Patent Convention" (1947) 12 *Law and Contemporary Problems* 765.

"L'avant-Projet de Loi Hollandais sur les Brevets d'Invention (1893) 9 *La Propriété Industrielle* 130.

Lascelles, J., "Our Patent Laws: Their Origin and Policy, with suggestions for their Amendment" (1870–1) 30 *The Law Magazine and Review* 1.

"Le Congrés International de la Propriété Industrielle tenu á Paris en Septembre 1878" (1878) *Journal des économistes* (4th Series) 87.

Le Hardy De Beaulieu, C., 'Discussion sur la Propriété des Inventions' (1862) XXXIV (2nd Series) *Journal des économistes* 72.

Le Hardy De Beaulieu, C., "Les Progrés Techniques et économiques dans les Houilléres et les Brevets d'Invention" (1866) *Journal des économistes* 238.

Le Hardy De Beaulieu, C., "La Propriété des Inventions est une Propriété comme une autre" (1868) XII (3rd Series) *Journal des économistes* 251.

Letort, C., "Une Législation Internationale sur les Brevets d'invention" *L'économiste Français,* 29 September 1877.

Levin, H., "Soviet Adherence to International Patent Convention" (1965) 1351 *The Department of State Bulletin* 758.

Liu, G., "Review of the Chinese Patent System and Future Prospects" [1987] EIPR 198.

"Lord Brougham" (1868) 25 *The Law Magazine and Law Review* 177.

Ma, L., "PCT and China" in *Symposium on the Patent Cooperation Treaty (PCT) and China – Beijing*, September 13–14, 1993.

Machlup, F., and Penrose, E., "The Patent Controversy in the Nineteenth Century" (1950) X *The Journal of Economic History* 1.

Marx, K., "The Class Struggles in France 1848 to 1850" in Feuer, L., (ed) *Marx and Engels: Basic Writings* (New York, Fontana, 1959).

Mota Maia, J., "Development of Portuguese Industrial Property Legislation in the Light of Portugal's Ratification of the Paris Convention" (1984) *Industrial Property* 386.

Note, "On Reform in the Law of Patents" (1870) 28 *The Law Magazine and Review* 83.

Note, "De l' indépendance réciproque des Brevets d'aprés l'Article 4*bis* de la Convention d' Union Revisée" (1903) 19 *La Propriété Industrielle* 97.

Passy, F., 'Lettre á M. Michel Chevalier sur deux articles parus dans le Journal des Débats touchant cette question' (1854) *Journal des économistes* 258.

Passy, F., 'Question de la Propriété des Inventions' (1855) *Journal des* économistes 262.

Picard, E., "Suppression des Brevets d'Invention" (1871) 3 *Revue de Droit International et de Législation Comparée* 391.

Prince-Smith, J., "Ueber Patente für Erfindungen" (1863) *Vierteljahrschrift für Volkswirthschaft und Culturgeschichte* 150.

"Property and Patents" (1871) 5 *The Irish Law Times and Solicitors' Journal* 169.

Ren, J., "The Patent Law of the People's Republic of China and Economic and Technological Exchange with Foreign Countries" (1985) 24 *Industrial Property* 114.

Rentzsch, H., "Geistiges Eigenthum" in *Handwörterbuch der Volkswirtschaft* (Leipzig 1866).

"Reports of Cases argued and decided in the High Court of Chancery. By F. Vesey, junior." (1823) 38 *The Edinburgh Review* 281.

Rivier, A., "Note sur la Question des Brevets d'Invention en Suisse" (1869) 1 *Revue de droit International et de Législation Comparée* 617.

Rodriguez, G., "De la Propriété des Inventions" (1862) XXXIV (2nd Series) *Journal des économistes* 79.

Rogers, J.E.T., "On the Rationale and Working of the Patent Laws" (1863) 26 *Journal of the Statistical Society of London* 121.

Rolin-Jaequemyns, G., "De Quelques Manifestations Récentes de l'Opinion Publique en Europe au Sujet des Brevets d'Invention" (1869) 1 *Revue de droit International et de Législation Comparée* 600.

Roubier, P., "Le droit unioniste de la propriété Industrielle" (1951) *Journal du Droit International* 676 (Part One); 1040 (Part two).

Rose, J.A., "The principles and Policy of a Law of Patents" (1867) 11 *The Solicitors' Journal and Reporter* 159 at 160 (Part One), 178 (Part Two).

Savignon, F., "The French Revolution and Patents" (1989) *Industrial Property* 391.

Seely, F., "L'opinion d'un Américain sur la protection internationale de la propriété industrielle" (1893) 9 *La Propriété Industrielle* 88; "A Centenary of Patents" New York Times, 22 March 1891.

Smith, C., 'A Century of Patent Law' (1891) 5 *The Quarterly Journal of Economics* 44.

Straus, J., "Implications of the TRIPS Agreement in the Field of Patent Law" in Beier, F.-K. and Schricker, G., (eds) *From GATT to TRIPS – The Agreement on Trade-Related Aspects of Intellectual Property Rights* (Munich, Max Planck Institute, 1996).

Thaller, E., "Dépendance ou indépendance de Brevets pris pour une même invention dans divers états" (1908) *Revue de droit international privé* 5.

"The Brussels Conference for the Reform and Codification of the Law of Nations" (1873) 2 *The Law Magazine and Review* (New Series) 1094.

"The Fallacy of Protection", *The Economist,* 16 September 1843 at 34.

"The Patent Laws" (1830) 3 *The Law Magazine* 282.

"The Patent Law" (1862–3) 14 *The Law Magazine and Law Review* 94.

"The Policy of Patents" 17 (1864) *Law Magazine and Law Review* 315.

"The Progress of Mechanical Invention: Review of the Patent Journal and the Mechanics Magazine" (1849) 84 *The Edinburgh Review* 47.

Webb, S., "Tariffs, Cartels, Technology, and Growth in the German Steel Industry, 1879 to 1914" (1980) 40 *Journal of Economic History* 309.

Webster, T., "Reform and Codification of the Law of Nations" (1874) 3 *The Law Magazine and Law Review* (New Series) 1016.

Wilson, R., "On the Report of the Patent Law Commissioners" (1865) 19 *The Law Magazine and Law Review* 139.
Wright, B., "The Economics of Invention Incentives: Patents, Prizes, and Research Contracts" (1983) 73 *American Economic Review* 691.
Wu, H., "The Encouragement, Rewards for the Protection of Inventions and Creations in China" (1985) 24 *Industrial Property* 73.
Zeller, G., "Industry in France before Colbert" in Cameron, R., (ed), *Essays in French Economic History* (Homewood, Richard D. Irwin, 1970).

Newspapers

L'économiste Français (Paris).
The Times (London).
The Economist (London).
The New York Times (New York).

Official Papers and Reports

BUREAU INTERNATIONAL DE L'UNION POUR LA PROTECTION DE LA PROPRIETE INDUSTRIELLE, "Bulletin de la Propriété Industrielle" (1885) 1 *La Propriété Industrielle* 25.
BUREAU INTERNATIONAL DE L'UNION POUR LA PROTECTION DE LA PROPRIETE INDUSTRIELLE, *Conférence de Bruxelles: Decémbre 1897 et Décembre 1900* (Berne 1901).
BUREAU INTERNATIONAL DE L'DE LA PROPRIETE INDUSTRIELLE, "l'Article 4 de la Convention" (1886) 2 *La Propriété Industrielle* 17.
BUREAU INTERNATIONAL DE L'UNION POUR LA PROTECTION DE LA PROPRIETE INDUSTRIELLE, "l'Article 5 de la Convention" (1886) 2 *La Propriété Industrielle* 1.
BUREAU INTERNATIONAL DE L' UNION POUR LA PROTECTION DE LA PROPRIETE INDUSTRIELLE, "La Solidarité des Brevets" (1893) 9 *La Propriété Industrielle* 107.
BUREAU INTERNATIONAL DE L' UNION POUR LA PROTECTION DE LA PROPRIETE INDUSTRIELLE, *Procés-Verbaux de la Conférence de Madrid de 1890 de l'Union pour la protection de la Propriéte Industrielle suivis des Actes signés en 1891 et ratifiés en 1892* (Berne 1892).
COMITE CENTRAL DES CHAMBRES SYNDICALES, *Protection Internationale de la Propriété Industrielle: Rapport presenté au nom de la Commission, par M. Crinon* (Paris, 1897).

DEUTSCHEN PATENTAMT, *Hundert Jahre Patentamt: Festschrift Herausgegeben vom Deutschen Patentamt* (Munich, Carl Heymanns Verlag, 1977).

FRANCE, CONSEIL GENERAL DE LA DORDOGNE, *Rapport sur la Convention du 20 mars 1883 relative a L'Union de la propriété industrielle présenté au nom de la Commission des Objects divers* (1888).

FRANCE, Ministére de L'agriculture et du Commerce, *Comptes rendus Sténographiques publiés sous les auspices du Comité Central des Congrés et Conférences et la direction de M. CH THIRION, Secrétaire du Comité, avec le concours des Bureaux des Congrés et des auteurs de Conférences: Congrés International de la Propriété Industrielle tenu á Paris du 5 au 17 Septembre 1878* (Paris 1879).

FRANCE, Ministére des Affaires étrangéres, *Conférence Internationale pour la protection de la propriété Industrielle* (Paris 1880).

FRANCE, Ministére des Affaires étrangéres, *Conférence Internationale pour la protection de la propriété Industrielle* (Paris 1883).

FRANCE, Chambre des Députés, *Rapport fait au nom de la Commission chargée d'examiner le project de Loi portant approbation des arrangements signés, les 14 et 15 avril 1891, entre divers états faisant partie de l'Union internationale pour la protection de la propriété industrielle* (1892).

UNITED KINGDOM, Parliamentary Papers, *Report from the Select Committee on the Law Relative to Patents for Inventions* (1829) 332, vol III, 415.

UNITED KINGDOM, Parliamentary Papers, *Report and Minutes of Evidence taken before the Select Committee of the House of Lords appointed to consider of The Bill, intituled, "An Act further to amend the Law touching Letters Patent for Invention" and also of The Bill intituled "An Act for the further amendment of the Law touching Letters Patent for Invention" and to report thereon to the House: Session 1851* (1851) 486 vol XVIII, 233.

UNITED KINGDOM, Parliamentary Papers, *Report of the Commissioners appointed to Inquire into the Working of the Law Relating to Letters Patent for Inventions* (1864) 3419, vol XXIX, 321.

UNITED KINGDOM, Parliamentary Papers, *Return of any Public Official Documents received at the Foreign Office, exhibiting Reasons why Count Von Bismarck and the Government of Prussia, and Mr Fock, the Minister of the Interior of the Netherlands, and the Dutch Government, have recommended, and the Chambers of the latter Country have resolved on, the Abolition of Patents for Invention* (1870) 41, vol LXI, 527.

UNITED KINGDOM, Parliamentary Papers, *Report from the Select Committee on Letters Patent; together with the Proceedings of the Committee, Minutes of Evidence, Appendix and Index* (1871) 368, vol X, 603.

UNITED KINGDOM, Parliamentary Papers, *Report from the Select Committee on Letters Patent; together with the Proceedings of the Committee, Minutes of Evidence, Appendix and Index* (1872) 193, vol XI, 395.

UNITED KINGDOM, Parliamentary Papers, *Reports by H.M. Secs of Embassy and Legation respecting Law and Practice in Foreign Countries with regard to Inventions* (1873) C. 741, vol LXVI, 483.

UNITED KINGDOM, Parliamentary Papers, *Vienna Universal Exhibition, 1873; Report on the International Patent Congress by Thomas Webster, M.A., F.R.S., one of Her Majesty's Counsel* (March 1874).

UNITED KINGDOM, Parliamentary Papers, *Correspondence respecting International Arrangements for Assimilation in Law and Practice in regard to Letters Patent of Inventions* (1874) C. 999, vol LIV, 211.

UNITED KINGDOM, Parliamentary Papers, *Report of Her Majesty's Commissioners for the Paris Universal Exhibition of 1878* (1878) vol 1, (C 2588) XXXII, 1.

UNITED KINGDOM, Parliamentary Papers, *Extracts from Treaties and Declarations now in force between Great Britain and Foreign Powers relating to Trade Marks, Designs, and Industrial Property, August 1888* (1888) vol XCVIII, C. 5554, 745.

UNITED KINGDOM, Parliamentary Papers, *Papers Relative to the Recent Conference at Rome on the subject of Industrial Property and Correspondence Relating to the Fraudulent Use of Trade Marks* (1886) vol LX, C. 4837, 413.

UNITED KINGDOM, Parliamentary Papers, *Industrial Property and Merchandise Marks: Further Papers and Correspondence relative to the Recent Conference at Madrid on the Subject of Industrial Property and Merchandise Marks* (1891) vol LXXVII, C. 6417, 507.

UNITED STATES OF AMERICA, Congressional Papers, *Papers Relating to the Foreign Relations of the United States – Message and Foreign Relations 1872*, 42nd Congress, 3rd Session, H. Ex Docs VI, part 1 at 46.

UNITED STATES OF AMERICA, Congressional Papers, *Arguments before the Committee on Patents of the Senate and House of Representatives, in support of, and suggesting amendments to, the Bills, (S. No. 300 and H.R. 1612) to amend the Statutes in relation to Patents, and for other purposes* (1878) 45th Congress, 2nd Session, Senate 1788, Misc Docs 50.

UNITED STATES OF AMERICA, Congressional Papers, *Paris Universal Exposition of 1878* (1878) 46th Congress, 3rd Session, H. Ex Docs vol 20, No 42, Pt 1.

UNITED STATES OF AMERICA, Congressional Papers, *Report of the Commissioners appointed to Revise the Statutes relating to Patents, Trade and other Marks, and Trade and Commercial Names under Act of Congress approved June 4, 1898* (1900) 56th Congress, 2nd Session, Senate document 20 at 225.

WORLD INTELLECTUAL PROPERTY ORGANIZATION, *1883 Paris Convention Centenary* (Geneva, W.I.P.O., 1983).

Other Reports

ASSOCIATION INTERNATIONALE POUR LE PROGRES DES SCIENCES SOCIALES, *Annales de L'Association International pour le progrés des sciences sociales: Premiére Session (Bruxelles 1863)* (Paris, Guillaumin et Cie, 1863).

Blaine, R., "On International Copyright Property in Works of Literature and the fine Arts" (1859) *Transactions of the National Association for the Promotion of Social Science* 272.

Cahen, A., and Lyon-Caen, L., "De la Convention conclue á Paris entre divers états le 20 Mars 1883 pour la protection de la propriété industrielle et des Modifications urgentes á apporter á la loi du 5 Juillet 1844" *Report presented to the Association des Inventeurs et Artistes Industriels* (Paris, 1885).

DEUTSCHEN VEREINS FUR DEN SCHUTZ DES GEWERBLICHEN EIGENTUMS, *Kongress für gewerblichen Rechtsschutz, Hamburg 5, 6, und 7 Mai 1902.*

Dircks, H., "On the Policy of a Patent Law" noted in (1869) *Transactions of the National Association for the Promotion of Social Science* 185.

Macfie, R.A., 'The Law of Patents for Inventions' (1858) *Transactions of the National Association for the Promotion of Social Science* 147.

Macfie, R.A., "Long Restrictions on the Use of Inventions, and Obligation to make heavy Payments to Patentees, incompatible with free and fair trade" (1865) *Transactions of the National Association for the Promotion of Social Science* 260.

Macfie, R.A., "Some of the Objections to Patents for Inventions" (1869) *Transactions of the National Association for the Promotion of Social Science* 177.

Newton, A.V., "On our System of Patent Law Adjudication, with Suggestions for Removing the Evils arising therefrom" (1868) *Transactions of the National Association for the Promotion of Social Science* 249.

'Report of the Special Committee on the Patent Laws' (1861) *Transactions of the National Association for the Promotion of Social Science* 229.

Sautter, M., *La Convention Internationale pour la Protection de la Propriété Industrielle aux états-Unis: Argumentation de M. A. Pollok, de Washington, devant le Sénat Fédéral* (Paris, 1886).

Seeley, F.A., *The International Union for the Protection of Industrial Property* (prepared under the direction of the Commissioner of Patents, Washington, 1 September 1887).

SOCIETE D'ECONOMIE POLITIQUE, "Réunion du 5 Juin 1869" (1869) *Journal des économistes* 446.

Spence, W., "Patents as Channels of Industry" (1868) *Transactions of the National Association for the Promotion of Social Science* 256.

"The National Association for the Promotion of Social Science" (1858) 4 *The Law Magazine and Law Review* 145.

"The National Association for the Promotion of Social Science; Congress at Liverpool, October 15, 1858" (1858–9) 6 *The Law Magazine and Law Review* 117.

Webster, T., "On the Protection of Property in Intellectual Labour as embodied in Inventions, Books, Designs and Pictures, by the Amendment of the Laws of Patent-right and Copyright" (1859) *Transactions of the National Association for the Promotion of Social Science* 237.

Index

www.ingramcontent.com/pod-product-compliance
Ingram Content Group UK Ltd.
Pitfield, Milton Keynes, MK11 3LW, UK
UKHW041844031026
15587UKWH00003B/1001

9 789004 469761